KU-166-521

# 1000 great quilting stitch patterns

Luise Roberts

COLLINS & BROWN

First published in Great Britain in 2004 by
Collins & Brown Limited
The Chrysalis Building
Bramley Road
London W10 6SP

An imprint of **Chrysalis** Books Group plc



British Library Cataloguing-in-Publication Data:
A catalogue record for this book is available from the British Library.

ISBN: 1-84340-091-X

Artwork by Luise Roberts
Designed by Luise Roberts and Roland Codd
Photography by Matthew Dickens

Reproduction by Classicscan, Singapore
Printed and bound by Times Offset, Malaysia

1 3 5 7 9 10 8 6 4 2

# Contents

# Introduction

Quilting is the stitching together of three layers: a top layer of pieced-together fabrics, a middle layer of batting and a fabric lining underneath. Historically, quilting has been a woman's domain. Quiltmakers made quilts with practical purposes in mind. In an era when nothing was wasted, they recycled scraps of cloth or worn clothing into useful quilts. Drawing inspiration from family life and the environment, women used their imaginations and fine sewing skills to design quilts that ultimately raised their techniques to an art form. To symbolize unity, for example, they quilted scrolled ropes of entwined knots around quilt borders. Young girls fashioned quilts for their "hope chests," weaving dreams into their motifs. Gathered around table-sized quilting frames, whole communities of women worked on quilting projects while sharing laughter and stories.

This volume is a tribute to the legacy of women's decorative art. It's a treasury of traditional quilting designs and other folk art designs. Quilters share ideas. Browse through these many designs for inspiration and then follow your own imagination. Your project doesn't have to be large. It can simply be a quilt for a baby's cradle or a pair of slippers. Go ahead. Feel free to use your sewing machine or quilt by hand. Express your feelings in your quilts. Just let your creativity soar—and your quilts will become future heirlooms. One thing is certain. Artfully joining three layers of fabric and batting together adds warmth to the inner spirit as well as the outer body.

*Quilt dating from c.1875–1900, designed in a geometric, single Irish chain pattern.*

# Creating quilting designs

## Quilt styles

One of the most effective ways to find an ideal quilting design is to look at finished quilts and decide what you like about their quilting designs. Visit local, regional, or national quilt shows and take a small notebook along to make sketches. Write down your impressions of various quilts and notes about why you like them. Another good option is to visit a library or bookstore and browse through books that feature antique quilts. Analyze the quilting designs in traditional quilts, and make notes about why you think they work well together. Use the knowledge you've gained to select your own quilting designs. Read through the following examples of quilts with distinctive quilting styles to see if they might be good sources of quilting designs for your own quilts.

### PATCHWORK QUILTS

Blocks containing several pieced fabrics form a regularly repeating pattern. Individual blocks are often highlighted with quilting motifs in the center or outlined with a simple quilting motif. Alternately, quilting stitches can ignore the block pattern completely and overlay the entire patchwork block with their own overall design.

### AMISH QUILTS

Simplicity is the hallmark of this quilt style. The angular shapes of large geometric blocks of plain-colored fabrics contrast with large flowing quilting lines of feather stitches and entwined cable designs.

### ALBUM QUILTS

Popular during the American Civil War, album quilts feature blocks with heavily appliquéd images and fine embroidery. Quilting stitches in geometric patterns can echo or disregard the contours of the images.

### WHOLECLOTH QUILTS

The top layer is a single piece of fabric. Quilting designs tend to be elaborate. A large central motif, usually incorporating themes from nature, is often surrounded by smaller motifs that repeat the theme.

### HAWAIIAN QUILTS

Simple appliquéd designs, resembling snowflakes, display the full potential of echo quilting. The quilting designs repeat until they reach the outline of an individual block or of an entire quilt.

### NORTH OF ENGLAND STRIPED QUILTS

Fabric strips in bold colors are quilted with bands of feather stitches and flowing knot designs. The emphasis is on the contrast between the bold hard stripes of the fabrics and the softly flowing lines of the quilting designs.

### WELSH QUILTS

Blocks of monochromatic fabric pieces are joined to form the top layer. Starting in the center, quilting stitches radiate to the border in their own geometric or flowing designs, disregarding the seams of the joined blocks.

## Types of quilting designs

You may want to incorporate one or more of the following basic quilt pattern styles in your own designs.

### MOTIFS

Motifs are individual designs that follow a theme. Often, a dominant motif is located in the center of the quilt and is repeated at regular intervals. The main design can also be combined with other patterns to form a group motif.

**FILLER PATTERNs**
Geometric grids, waving lines, or elaborate repeat patterns are commonly used to fill in blank spaces in quilt tops. Their design usually function as background areas.

**BORDERS**
Border designs repeat to form one continuous design around all sides of the quilt. They may or may not incorporate turning designs at the corners.

**CORNERS**
Corner designs may be isolated motifs or simply be a part of the overall border design. Simple patterns that form a small square are common in narrow borders. Deeper borders call for more elaborate designs.

*Quilt dating from c.1930. Shades of green contrast with warm color tones, making these colors appear more luminous. The simple circular design emphasizes the straight lines of the motif.*

## Choosing materials for a quilt

It is wise to take into consideration the amount of time you'll have to create your quilt and decide whether you would like to hand quilt it, use your sewing machine, or both.

**FABRIC**
Choose cotton for an easy-to-sew quilt. Cotton is very practical. Avoid fabrics that stretch, or heavy fabrics with loosely-woven textures. Those features will detract from your quilting designs. Dark colors absorb light. If you select them for a quilt, the depths of quilting furrows will not show up well. Silk is the queen of fabrics for quilting. Be sure to choose a type of silk that has a firm weave.

**BATTING**
In days gone by, quilts needed to be densely quilted, due to the characteristics of traditional batting. Today, thanks to modern milling methods, heavy quilting is no longer necessary. Take care, however, to follow the batting manufacturer's handling instructions. Special purpose battings, dedicated for either hand or machine quilting, are available. So are general purpose battings for use in both hand and machine quilting. Check the manufacturer's wash and care instructions to see whether any batting you intend to use will be easy to launder. Aim to stitch evenly over the entire surface of your quilt, so the batting will lie flat when the quilt is finished.

## Color

Consider the following factors when choosing the thread to your quilting designs.

### Thread color

Choosing the proper threads for your quilt entails more than simply choosing matching or contrasting colors. Light impacts color, and quilted furrows create shadows. A "safe" approach is to select a thread color that is slightly darker than the color of the quilt top. It will appear to blend into the quilt top. If the quilt top features several colors, choose a thread color that falls midway in the color range of all the fabrics.

If you feel more adventurous, try some of the choices shown here.

**CONTRASTING COLOR**

Choose a contrasting color, similar in value to the quilt top color, to create impact. Use a pale blue, for example, to stitch on a pale yellow quilt top. The color of the quilt top will appear more intense.

**LIGHT OR SHINY THREADS**

Use a light-colored or shiny quilting thread to create a patchy, irregular look. Take slightly larger stitches by hand to emphasize this effect. If you machine quilt using these threads, the quilting furrows will appear flattened and will draw attention away from the design contours. The stitching line will then seem to float on top of the quilt surface.

**EMBROIDERY FLOSS**

Embroidery floss is available in a myriad of colors. Test your selection carefully on a fabric sample to make sure the floss is strong and durable enough to use for quilting.

### Special effects

Explore the effects of the techniques listed below to highlight certain areas of your quilt.

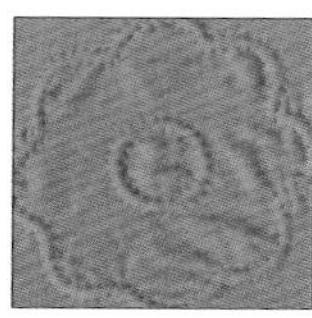

**CORDING**

Stitch two parallel lines close together in a curved design. Turn to the back of the design.Thread a cord through the space between the lines.

**TRAPUNTO**

This technique is similar to cording. Stuff large areas of the design with padding.

### Fabric factors

Choose plain, light-colored fabric if you plan to use elaborate quilting patterns.

Since dark, low-sheen fabrics and heavily patterned fabrics absorb light, the lofting effect (the springiness and density of the batting) of any quilting design will be minimized. Increasing the distance between lines of stitching on dark fabrics may help. If you choose busy prints, try stitching in the ditch of the seams. When using single-colored dark fabrics, stitch quilting designs in a light color. As a general rule, the darker the fabric, the simpler the quilting designs should be.

## Arranging quilt designs

It is helpful to photocopy your quilting designs at the full size and then trace them onto transparent sheets. Use these sheets to arrange the design elements on your actual quilt top.

Next, select a focal design point. That may be a motif in the center of the quilt or lighter areas inside blocks. Experiment with your design arrangement to determine how the patterns suit the quilt top. Designs that run over block seams will unify your quilt; curved lines contrast well with straight-line designs.

Work your way outward from the center, analyzing how each quilting design relates to the overall area of the quilt. As you align and link various elements of your designs, check for balanced symmetry. Choose similar patterns to echo a main central motif or to fill in background areas. Try not to use too many different patterns, as this may make your quilt look disjointed. Continue until you reach the borders of your quilt. Finally, decide what type of border your quilt needs. Does it need a strong framing outline? Or would a design that contrasts with the main motif highlight that area better? Stand back and view your quilting design choices from a distance and ask yourself these questions:

- Do all the design elements blend well, without any overpowering ones?
- Should you scale down your original design to a simpler one?

# Transferring quilting designs onto fabric

It's best to use templates or stencils when you transfer designs. Templates are cut along the solid outline of a design. Any internal design elements are filled in later by hand. Stencils are also shaped according to a design but have internal cutouts that allow for details inside the main design outline. It's important to position both templates and stencils accurately on a quilt top. As you construct your template or stencil, mark key design-alignment points on it. This will help you space all design repeats evenly and keep motifs level. Good points to mark as key design-alignment points are places where two lines intersect or where center lines are located.

## Single-use stencils

Tracing-paper stencils are quick and easy to make and useful for transferring motifs that appear only once in a quilting project. They also work well for transferring more complex designs that may be difficult to transfer accurately by other methods.

### Equipment

You will need:

- Tracing paper (or tissue paper)
- Permanent marking pen
- Soft cloth or blotter
- Basting thread
- Needle

(1) Cut a piece of tracing paper slightly larger than the pattern to be copied. Place the paper over the design and carefully trace it. Blot the ink to make sure no ink remains on the surface of the paper.

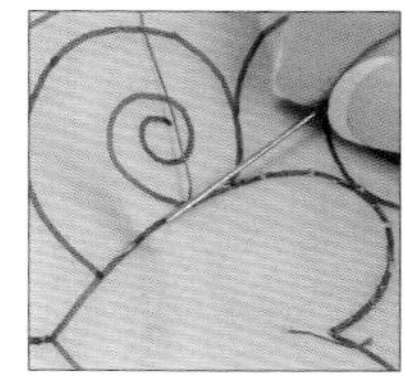

(2) Carefully position the traced design on your quilt top. Use a contrasting thread to sew basting stitches along the design outlines. Take small stitches to trace the pattern accurately. Continue until all design lines have been stitched. For a machine-quilted design, pin the paper in place on the fabric to be quilted and stitch over the design lines.

(3) Start from the outside and work your way in, gently removing the paper. Ease it carefully away from the stitches. Try not to pull on the stitches too much.

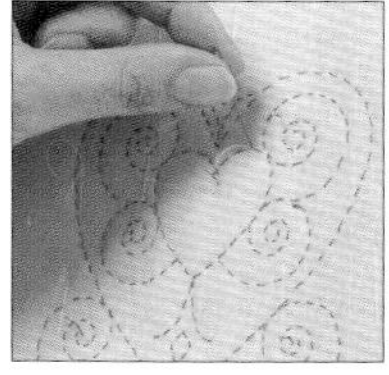

(4) Follow the basted outline as you hand or machine quilt. Remove the basting thread when you complete the design.

## *Perforated-paper stencils*

This is an excellent way to transfer marks onto a quilt top.

**Equipment**

You will need:

- Tracing paper
- A pen
- A sewing machine
- A hand-sewing needle (preferably a long one)
- Pins (preferably long ones)
- Chalk or cornstarch
- Cotton balls

(1) Trace the design on a sheet of white paper, carefully marking any alignment points.

(2) Set the stitch length on your sewing machine to the largest number. Remove the presser foot. Using an old machine needle, make holes in the paper by "stitching" along the traced design. Continue until all design lines have been pierced. Carefully lift the paper to check if all the holes were cut through cleanly. Remove any bits of paper left in the holes with a needle.

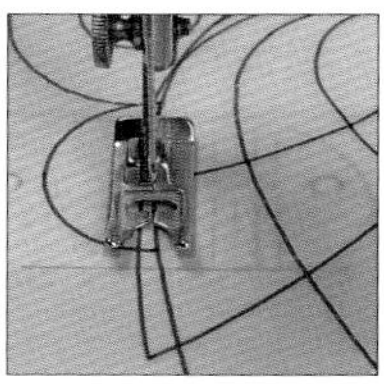

(3) Pin the stencil to the quilt top and use a cotton ball to force the chalk (or cornstarch) through the holes.

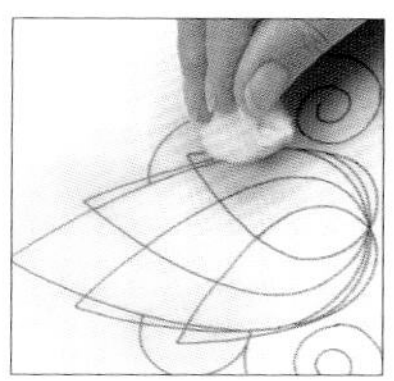

(4) Remove the stencil, taking care not to disturb the chalk markings. They are not durable. Go over the lines with a chalk marker or a pencil if desired.

**ADVANTAGES**

- This method is quick and easy.
- It calls for a minimal investment for equipment.

**DISADVANTAGES**

- Marked designs do not last long so you have to stitch the designs right away.

**HELPFUL HINTS**

- ❑ Use a dressmaker's wheel as an alternative to piercing the template with a sewing machine needle.
- ❑ To try a variation on this technique, draw the quilt design on a piece of tulle with a fine-line permanent marker. Pin the tulle with the design on it to the fabric and mark the design with a pencil. Tracing designs a number of times may obscure it.

## *Making plastic stencils*

Stencils transfer intricate designs very well. Remember to test whatever fabric marker you intend to use beforehand on small fabric scraps.

### Equipment

You will need:

- Stencil plastic
- Photocopy of the quilt design
- Pencil
- Sharp knife or double-bladed cutter
- Cutting mat
- Water-soluble marker
- Clean, dry cloth or blotter

(1) Trace the quilting design on the stencil plastic carefully. Check to see whether you need to mark any additional lines within the outline. The blank areas between these lines will need to be stabilized to keep the stencil from distorting. To do this, allow for "bridges" or "ladders" (see 2) to make connections between cut design lines.

(2) Each line of the design will require two cuts made parallel to each other, about 1/8 inch (3 mm) apart. If you use a double-bladed cutter, keep one blade in constant contact with the pattern line and let the second simply follow that. Take care near "bridges" and "ladders." If you use a single-bladed knife instead, make cuts along the pattern line. Then make duplicate cuts 1/8 inch (3 mm) away. The smaller the distance between two cuts, the more stable the stencil will be. The opening should be wide enough to accommodate a water-soluble marker or other marker. If the pattern is for a corded design, make sure the distance you leave between two cuts is equal to the width of your cording, adding a bit extra to allow for easing the cording into the design.

**HELPFUL HINTS**

Use clear, self-sticking film (available in art supply stores) instead of stencil plastic. It will be easier to cut. If your design is intricate, the film may tear or stretch. Test it beforehand on a scrap of the quilt fabric, to make sure it will not rough up the fibers of the quilt fabric nor leave a sticky residue.

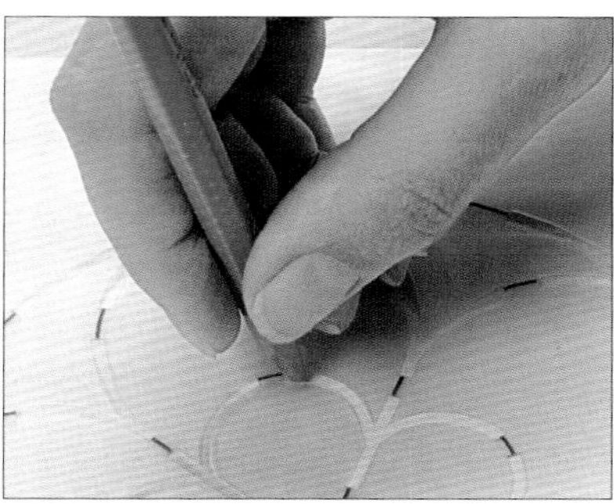

(3) Position the stencil on the quilt top and transfer the design with a water-soluble marker. Hand or machine quilt the design, as you prefer.

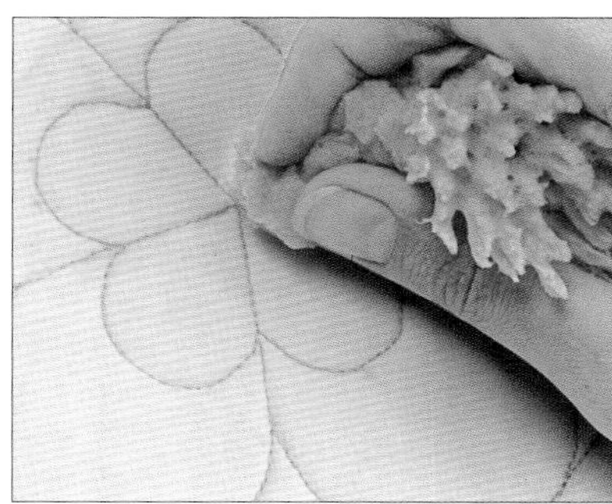

(4) To remove any marks, wash the quilt or use a damp sponge to wet the lines. Then blot with cloth or blotter.

**ADVANTAGES**

- Plastic stencils are very durable.
- They work well for designs with interior lines.

**DISADVANTAGES**

- You need to be proficient in handling a double-bladed cutter or a very sharp single-bladed knife.

**HELPFUL HINTS**

- ❑ Don't confuse stencil plastic with acetate, which is thinner.
- ❑ Use extreme caution when handling very sharp cutting instruments.
- ❑ Cut your designs on a rotary cutting mat.
- ❑ Allow plenty of room to work. To prevent accidents, don't work close to the edge of the work surface in case your knife accidentally slips from your grip.
- ❑ Change cutting blades frequently.
- ❑ Be careful to draw cutting blade(s) only toward you as you work. To go around outlines, rotate the design as necessary instead.
- ❑ Keep the hand that maneuvers the design either behind, or to one side, of the cutting blade(s) and away from the sweeping motion of your cut.
- ❑ Take your time.

## Marking tools

Many types of markers are available. Whatever kind you choose, it's important to find out if the markings can be easily removed from the quilt top. Test the marker on a scrap piece of your quilt fabric. Experiment with the following marking tools to determine which one(s) you like best.

Blue chalk dust

Cinnamon

### ❶ MASKING TAPE

A low-tack masking tape (not to be confused with sticky tapes) is ideal for marking straight lines and alignment points. Check to be sure it does not pull threads or change the surface texture of your fabric. Avoid tapes that leave a sticky residue.

### ❷ BASTING THREAD

You can use any thread in a contrasting color to outline shapes, but basting thread is spun more finely, which makes it easier to break and remove. Secure ends with knots on the right side of the fabric to make it easier to remove the thread.

¼ inch Masking tape

Soluble basting thread

Ordinary basting thread

**3 CHALK DUST, CORNSTARCH, BAKING SODA, POWDERED CINNAMON**

To transfer markings with one of these powdery substances, put it into a little bag, traditionally called a "pounce." Alternately, dip a cotton ball into the transfer medium you are using. Make a stencil that has holes to mark design lines and place it over your quilt fabric. "Pounce" color through the holes. The marks you make will be temporary. You will need to go over them with another, more durable marker. (Use chalk to mark pale fabrics.) Be sure to test all markers to make sure they can be removed easily.

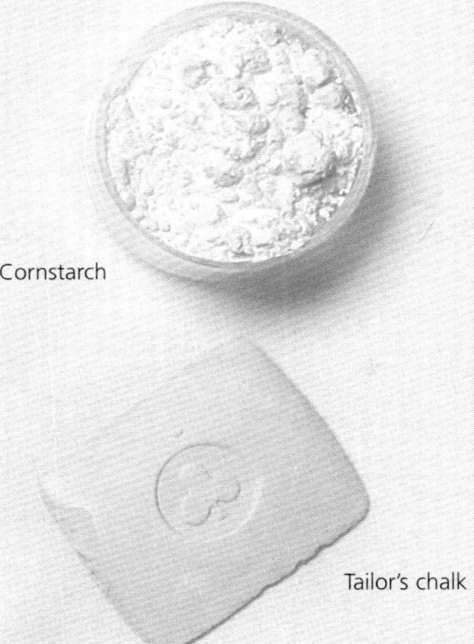

Cornstarch

Tailor's chalk

Chalk wheel

Chalk pencil

**4 CHALK WHEEL**

This tool is useful for marking straight lines and alignment points on a quilt top. Since chalk marks do not last very long, this method is not recommended for transferring complex designs.

**5 TAILOR'S CHALK**

Tailor's chalk is a waxlike substance formed into a straight blunt tool. It's useful for tracing lines and boldly shaped designs. It's difficult, however, to maneuver around complex designs. Since it leaves a wide line, you may have trouble using it to sew accurate, uniform, quilting lines.

**6 CHALK PENCIL**

This tool is easier to use than a piece of tailor's chalk. You can easily mark a stable line with it, which you can easily remove later. It has a disadvantage—a tendency to smudge when rubbed, which will make it difficult to accurately place stitches.

Tracing wheel (use on fabric)

Tracing wheel (use with dressmakers carrison)

Hera

**7 TRACING WHEEL**
Tracing wheels are equipped with either fine metal blades or teeth to transfer markings. Use one by itself to leave indentations directly in the fabric. To use with a template or stencil, simply apply pressure to the tracing wheel as you roll it along the lines of the design. Tracing wheels are very helpful for marking straight lines.

**8 HERA**
This traditional Japanese tool is ideal for scoring straight lines and simple designs. Since it does not use any pigments, there's no need to remove markings later.

**9 LEAD PENCIL**
Lead pencils are readily available, but you may find it difficult to remove marks they leave. Use a 2H hard-lead mechanical pencil for marking fine lines.

**10 QUILTER'S SILVER/SOAPSTONE PENCIL**
This type of pencil is ideal for marking dark fabrics. Markings brush away easily after you quilt. Stitch the designs immediately after you mark them.

**11 WATERCOLOR PENCIL**
Available in a wide variety of colors, watercolor pencils are useful for marking designs that are easy to see on multi-colored fabrics. Test the marks they leave carefully, however, because the color may spread. Water-soluble, markings may not wash out easily. Avoid rubbing the fabric vigorously to remove watercolor markings, since this may propel color pigments further into the fabric.

Propelling lead pencil

Fabric pencil eraser

Silver quilter's pencil

Air-soluble Pen

Water-soluble pen

Heat-soluble pen

Watercolor pencils

**⓬ DISAPPEARING INK PEN**

These pens leave a pinkish-purple chemical line that gradually fades away. The speed of this fading depends on environmental conditions. One theory suggests that chemicals in the ink may cause the fabric to rot. Launder your quilt thoroughly after you finish it to remove any invisible chemicals that may remain on the surface of the fabric.

**⓭ WATER-SOLUBLE PEN**

These pens leave a pale blue line that can be easily removed with cold water. They are ideal for marking light-colored fabrics. Launder marked fabrics carefully to remove any chemical residue. Hot, or even lukewarm, water will set brown stain marks in the fabric. Use a new pen to start your quilt project or have a replacement handy in case the original one runs dry.

**⓮ HEAT-SOLUBLE PEN**

This type of pen is ideal for marking very light-colored fabrics. The lines will disappear with the heat of an iron. It will be necessary to launder your quilt carefully after you finish it.

**⓯ TRANSFER PENCIL**

These pencils are available in a range of colors. They are useful for color-coding a complex pattern. The transfer technique requires several steps. Use a transfer pencil to draw the design on a piece of paper. Then, using a hot iron, transfer the outlines of the drawing to the reverse of your quilt (or to an interfacing). Then stitch the quilting design with that side facing up.

Transfer pen and paper

# Quilt assembly

The best time to create the quilt sandwich of quilt top, batting, and backing is a matter of personal preference. In some cases, transferring marks onto the quilting fabric is better done before the quilt layers are assembled; those methods that use pen and pencil markers and would benefit from a firm work surface. In general, markers that leave a transient mark, such as chalk dust, or rely on pressure and a soft surface, such as the hera, are better employed just before stitching.

## Batting

Battings have different characteristics that will affect the finished quilt. Batting manufacturers suggest how to use their product to the best advantage. They usually rate the loft, that is, the spring and density of the batting; list preferred techniques, optimum stitching lengths, and maximum distance between stitching lines; and suggest ways to treat their battings to prevent them from "bearding," or poking through the quilt surface. General descriptions for use and care of various battings are listed below.

### POLYESTER

Inexpensive and readily available in white and charcoal, polyester batting comes in various sizes, ranging from crib sizes, to sizes large enough for all beds. Polyester does not drape well. Stitching quilt designs too densely on polyester reduces its draping characteristics even more. Thicker battings call for machine stitching. Manufacturers treat batting surfaces so the fibers will be less likely to "beard." Polyester fibers offer only slight resistance to the needle.

### COTTON

Cotton battings are warmer than polyester ones and hold their shape or loft better. They are slightly more difficult to hand quilt, however. To prevent some cotton battings from becoming lumpy, they need to be stitched quite densely. Conversely, cotton batting is ideal for stitching quilt designs that follow a meander pattern. Cotton drapes better and is more stable than polyester.

### WOOL

Wool is warmer and softer than cotton, but it is more expensive. It does not require dense stitching and is easy to hand stitch. Tufts of wool bearding through the top quilt layer may be a problem.

### SILK

Silk batting is surprisingly warm. It's soft, easy to hand quilt and drapes well. It is very expensive. Often chosen for clothing, silk batting requires careful laundering.

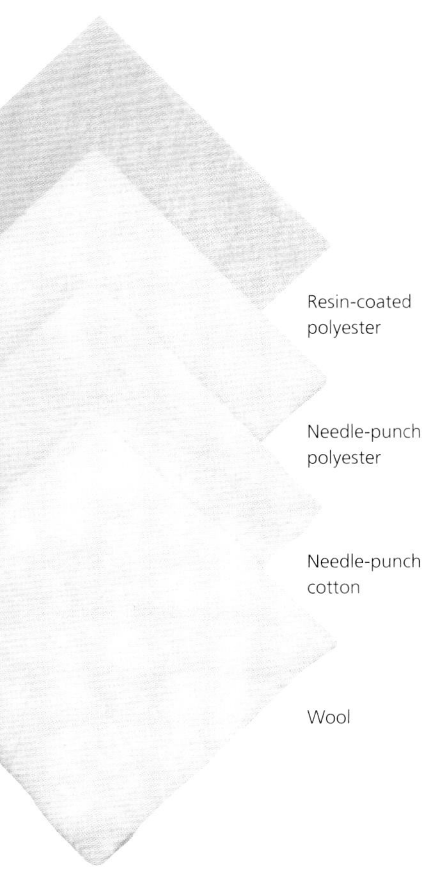


*Manufacturers commonly treat battings to prevent bearding. Thermobonding is often used with polyester. Glazing, or coating polyester batting with resin, is also common, but this can cause allergic reactions, so it may not be suitable for your quilt project. Needle punching locks batting fibers together and this type is easy to hand stitch.*

## Backing

Choose a backing fabric that is similar to your quilt top in weight and weave. For a large quilt, you may need to seam lengths together in the center, or sew two seams, each placed one-third of the way across the back. Choice of fabric is a matter of personal preference. Prints camouflage quilting stitches on the back while plain fabrics highlight them.

## Layering the quilt

Cut the backing fabric and the batting about 3 inches (7.6 cm) wider all around than the quilt top. Iron the backing and the top. Place the backing, wrong side up on a large, flat surface. Secure it with tape. Fold the batting in half, and then in half one more time. With the folded edges facing the bottom right side of the backing, position the folded lining at the top left corner of the backing. Unfold the batting, It should be perfectly centered over the backing. Fold and position the quilt top on the batting in the same manner. Then, starting in the center, pin the three layers together with straight pins, smoothing the fabric as you work your way to the edges.

Starting in the middle of the quilt, baste all the layers together, stitching straight lines parallel to the quilt borders. Take stitches about 1 inch (2.5 cm) long and space the basting lines about 3 inches (7.6 cm) apart. If you plan to machine quilt, you can use safety pins to secure the layers. An alternate method is to use a basting gun that inserts plastic tacks into the layers to secure them. Test the tacks first to make sure they do not leave permanent marks or holes in the fabric.

# The quilting process

The true beauty of quilting is revealed by even and precise stitches that flow gracefully over the quilt surface. This does not mean that hand quilting is better than machine quilting or that the smaller the stitch, the better the quilting. Good quilting techniques ensure that no visual jolts distract the eye from taking in the entire quilt.

Decide whether you want to hand quilt, use a sewing machine, or both. Machine quilting goes quickly, is durable, and the stitch length is consistently even. Hand quilting takes more time, but your project will be portable. Hand quilting provides tactile pleasure and offers opportunities for socializing with other quilters.

## Hand quilting

Spaces between all stitches should equal the length of the stitches. It is possible to quilt your project by hand, without a frame or a hoop, but if the quilt is large, it may be awkward to handle. Using a frame or hoop prevents puckering and you'll be able to spot mistakes more easily. Start stitching in the center and work your way outward. If you use a frame, start at one end, work your way down and roll the quilt around the frame as you get near the other end.

## *How to hand quilt*

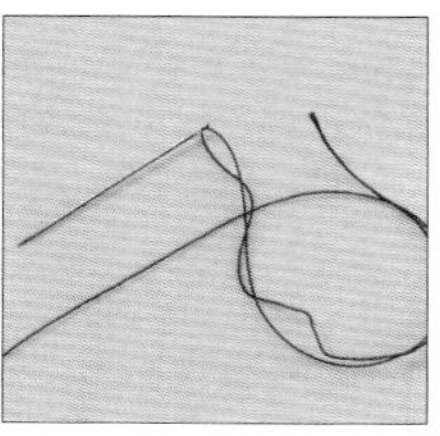

(1) Cut a length of thread about 20 inches (50 cm) long and thread it through a "between" or a quilter's needle. The thread will have to pass through several layers of fabric, so it's a good idea to strengthen it by passing it over some beeswax. Remove any excess wax.

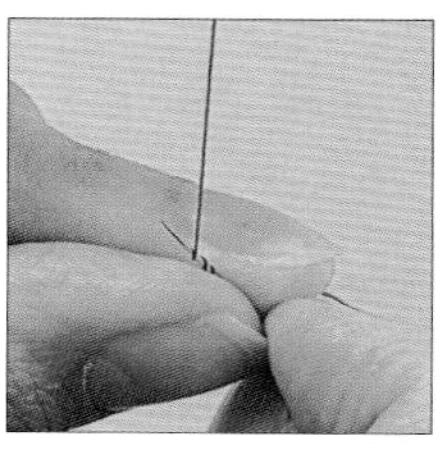

(2) Make a quilter's knot at the end of the thread. Wrap the last inch (2.5 cm) of thread twice around the needle. Then pull the needle through the loop you just made.

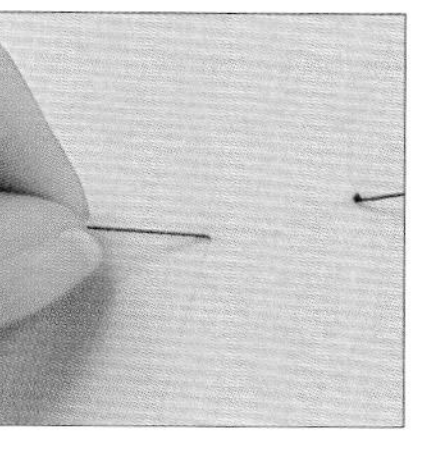

(3) Working from the top, about an inch (2.5 cm) away from the starting point, slide the needle in between the quilt layers and let it emerge at the position for the first stitch. Pull the knot through the quilt top so that it will be lodged in the batting. Make a tiny back stitch to secure the knot.

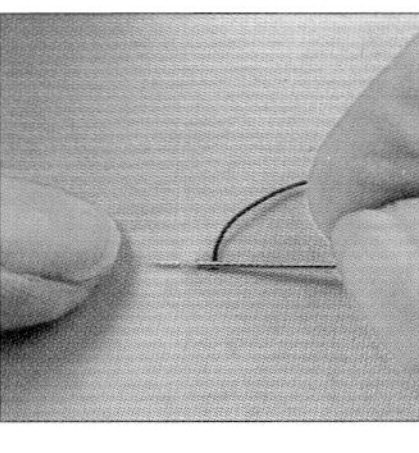

④ Start by inserting the needle through the layers, about 1⁄16 inch (1 mm) from the starting point. Let the tip of the needle just pierce slightly through the backing. Using the middle finger of your sewing hand, pivot the needle so that the eye of the needle is flat against the quilt top and the needle tip comes up through the layers again about 1⁄16 inch (1 mm) from where it went down. Use your other hand to manipulate the fabric, pushing up from under the frame to flatten the batting.

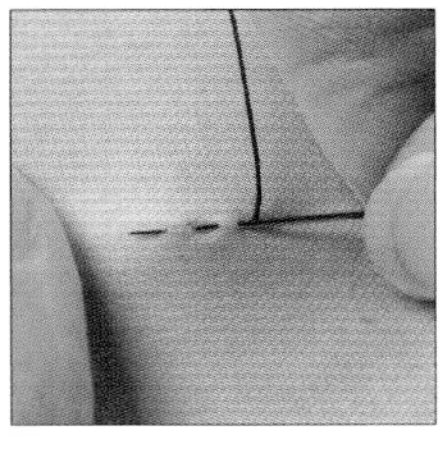

⑤ Repeat this pivotal, rocking motion until you have three stitches on the needle. Then, with the needle pointing up and pressing down with the thumb of your sewing hand, push the needle through and then pull the thread firmly through all the layers.

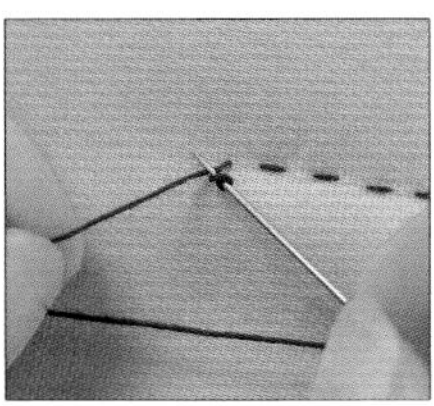

⑥ Finish off thread ends by wrapping the thread twice around the needle and then stitch through only the top and batting layers. Point the needle up and pull the thread through until the knot is lodged in the batting level. Cut the thread.

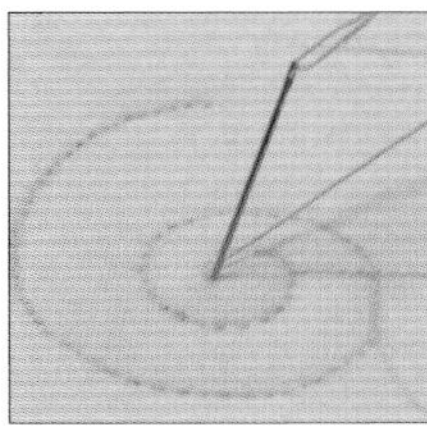

**Stitching tight corners**

When stitching complex areas of a design, either work one stitch at a time, or take stitches by stabbing the needle up and down through the layers. Try to maintain the same even stitches and uniform tension throughout the quilt.

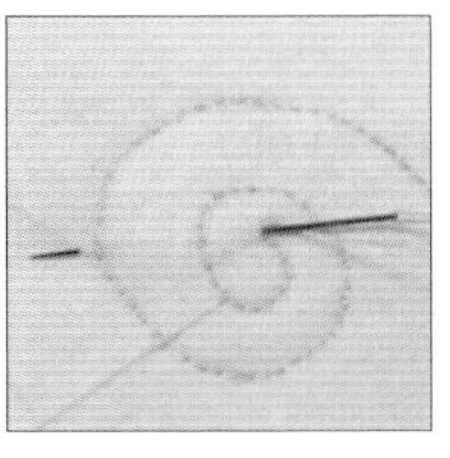

**Traveling**

"Traveling" is the quilters' term for sliding the needle through the batting in order to emerge once again at the start of a new stitching line. This technique gives you the opportunity to quilt any design without having to stop to cut the thread before starting again elsewhere.

**Stitch quality**

Learning to do fine hand quilting may take a bit of practice. If you stitch as neatly and evenly as you can, if you secure your knots inside the batting, and if your stitching does not detract from the overall quilt design, that's all that is required. If the back of your quilt doesn't seem to be as neat as it might be, feel confident that your skill will improve as you gain more experience. Try not to rip out too many stitches. This will affect the quilt surface and make the thread look frayed.

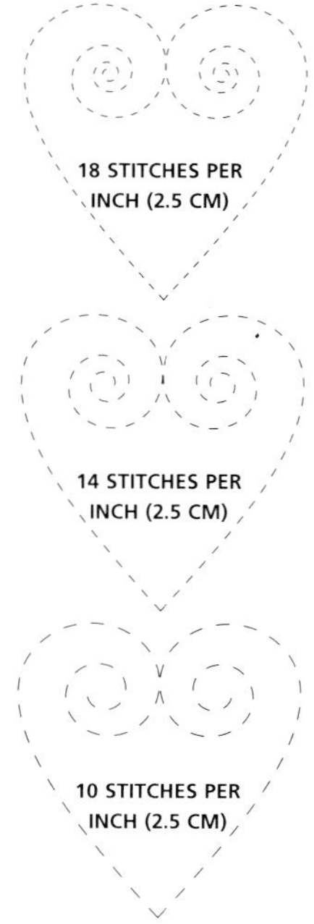


**Stitch length**

Judges often use stitch length as the criteria for good quality quilting. Records of antique quilts document that they were often sewn with 22 stitches per inch. In former times, however, women used wool blankets as batting. These tended to be a lot thinner than modern quilt battings.

In the hand quilting method (see page 21), the tip of the needle just pierces through the layers before being pivoted back through the layers. The distance the needle is allowed to protrude before being pivoted and reinserted is approximately a stitch length of ⅛ inch (1 mm). Stitches of this length will roughly equal a total of 14 stitches per inch (2.5 cm). Enjoy learning to hand quilt and watch your stitches as you gain experience.

## Machine quilting

Quilting by machine does not require a special sewing machine, although various accessories will make the technique easier. As with hand quilting, try to make all the stitches even in length and maintain a uniform tension. Increasing the number of stitches per inch will increase the level of detail you can accomplish.

**HELPFUL HINTS**

Where two lines of a pattern intersect, try to plan your stitches so that the needle comes out through the backing at that point. This is better than having a double thickness of thread on the top layer.

**Tension**

A wide variety of specialty threads are available, and tension for each type has to be specifically balanced. To ensure even stitching, adjust the thread tension on a trial sample of the combined top, batting, and backing. The stitches should look identical on both sides. Neither the top thread nor the backing thread should be too raised up on the reverse side. If you want to use the top thread as a design element, use a slightly looser tension for the top thread. This will make the stitching more prominent. When you use decorative thread on top, use it from the spool. Wind the bobbin with another thread.

## *How to machine quilt straight lines*

① Feed dogs should stay engaged; feed the fabric under the needle. You can make this easier by using a "walking foot" on the machine. Insert a size 14 needle and pull out a 5 inch (12 cm) tail on both the bobbin and the top thread. Position the needle above the starting point of the first stitch. Lower the walking foot, then insert the needle into the fabric. Make a series of tiny stitches, or a single back tack stitch, to secure the thread.

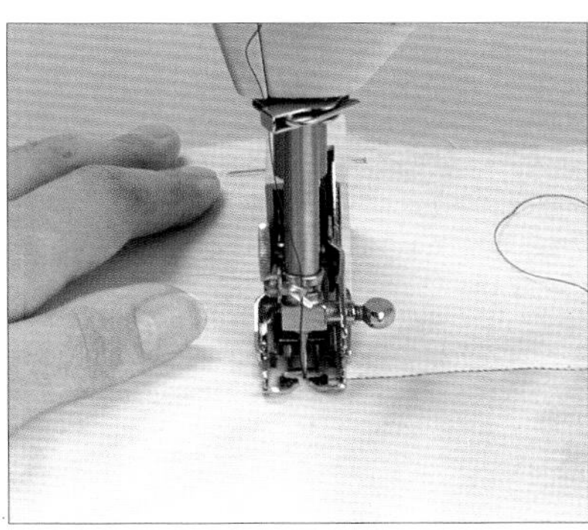

② Set the stitch length to about 14 stitches per inch. Stitch to the end of the design line.

③ You can end with a series of small stitches or a back tack stitch. For a neater finish, lift the needle and leave a 5-inch (12 cm) tail when you cut the threads.

(4) To finish off the loose ends, draw each thread through the needle, wrap it twice around the needle, and stitch through to the bottom layer. Bring the needle up again, pull the knot through to the batting layer and cut the thread.

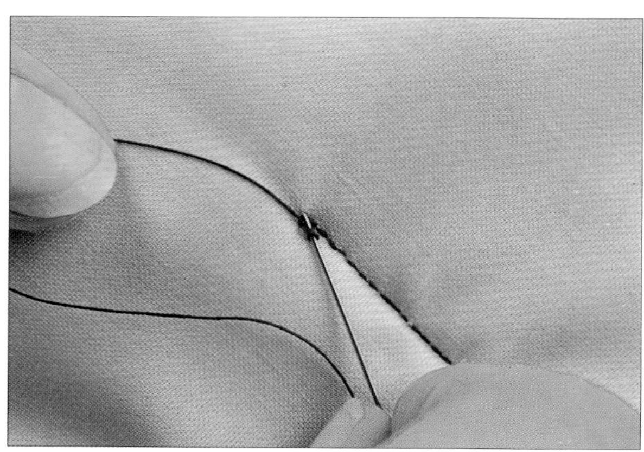

## *How to free-motion machine quilt*

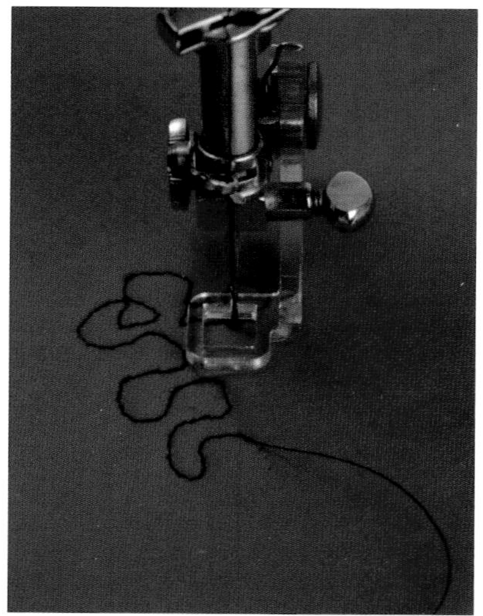

Lower the feed dogs, attach a darning foot. With the feed dogs disengaged, you can move the fabric freely in any direction under the needle. Use your hands to hold the layers as you move the quilt under the needle. You control the stitch length by moving the fabric between each drop of the needle. Free-motion patterns usually follow specific rules: no straight lines in designs; lines never intersect; curved lines do not mix with straight lines. Whatever design you choose, remember to keep the stitch density even over the entire quilt top. Too many stitches/lines will stiffen the quilt.

**HELPFUL HINT**

If a decorative thread keeps breaking or snagging, try loading it into the bobbin. It will pass through fewer tension wheels before being stitched.

# Finishing the quilt

Once you complete the quilting, you will need to enclose the raw edges of the quilt with a binding. Use binding strips of the same weight as the quilt fabric. You can use a contrasting color or fabric from the quilt top.

## Binding

Decide how wide you wish to make the finished binding. Cut strips of fabric twice the width of the intended binding, plus twice the seam allowance. Cut the ends of the strips at a 45 degree angle and join them to form one long length, right sides together. Fold the binding in half lengthwise with wrong sides together. Pin the binding to the quilt top, right sides together, and stitch, mitering the corner seams. Fold the unstitched edge over to the back of the quilt and slip stitch it in place.

A quick method for finishing a quilt (not quite as strong as applying a separate binding) is to trim the batting back by about 1 inch (2.5 cm). Next, fold the backing over the batting only (and not the top) and then pin it in place. Turn the quilt top under by about 1 inch (2.5 cm). Now the backing and the quilt top fabric face each other. Stitch these together, or, for a stronger edge finish, use a sewing machine to stitch 1/8 inch (6 mm) in from the edge of the border and then stitch (6 mm) in again from the previous stitching line.

### USEFUL SEWING MACHINE FEATURES

If you plan to buy a sewing machine specifically for machine quilting, look for these features:

- ❑ The ability to lower the feed dogs, crucial for free-motion stitching.
- ❑ A darning foot attachment to facilitate free-motion stitching.
- ❑ A walking foot to help move the quilt top at the same speed as the backing. This helps to prevent puckering.
- ❑ A transparent appliqué foot to make it easier to see the stitching line.
- ❑ Adjustable seam guides to ensure even distances between rows of stitching.
- ❑ A built-in selection of embroidery stitches for embellishing quilting designs.
- ❑ The ability to do a mock running stitch that resembles hand-quilted stitches
- ❑ Blanket stitch or buttonhole capability.
- ❑ A pedal to lift the presser foot to help maneuver around design corners.
- ❑ A good-size surface between the needle and the control panel for handling large quilts.
- ❑ An extension arm on the sewing machine to make maneuvering easier.

# How to use this book

This book is divided into two main sections: traditional designs and regional designs that have been adapted for quilting. Within the traditional section, the designs have been grouped by overall shape and by the number of sides the shape has. For instance, this section starts with triangles, followed by squares, polygons, circles, stars, hearts, pictorial motifs and then border and filler patterns. In the second section, the patterns have been divided by the regions of the world that inspired them and the section includes some useful motifs and typefaces.

To make selecting quilt designs easier, each pattern is accompanied by a range of symbols that are designed to suggest the technical and creative possibilities of the design. These symbols are explained in the pages that follow.

398 PATTERNS ADAPTED FOR QUILTING • CELTIC DESIGNS

720
(1in (2.5cm)) to 5in (12.7cm) 500%
(1in (2.5cm)) to 9in (22.9cm) 900%

721
(1in (2.5cm)) to 6in (15.25cm) 600%
(1in (2.5cm)) to 8in (20.3cm) 800%

Design number

Hand quilting recommended

**NOTE:** The designs in this book are for your personal use only and should not be resold.

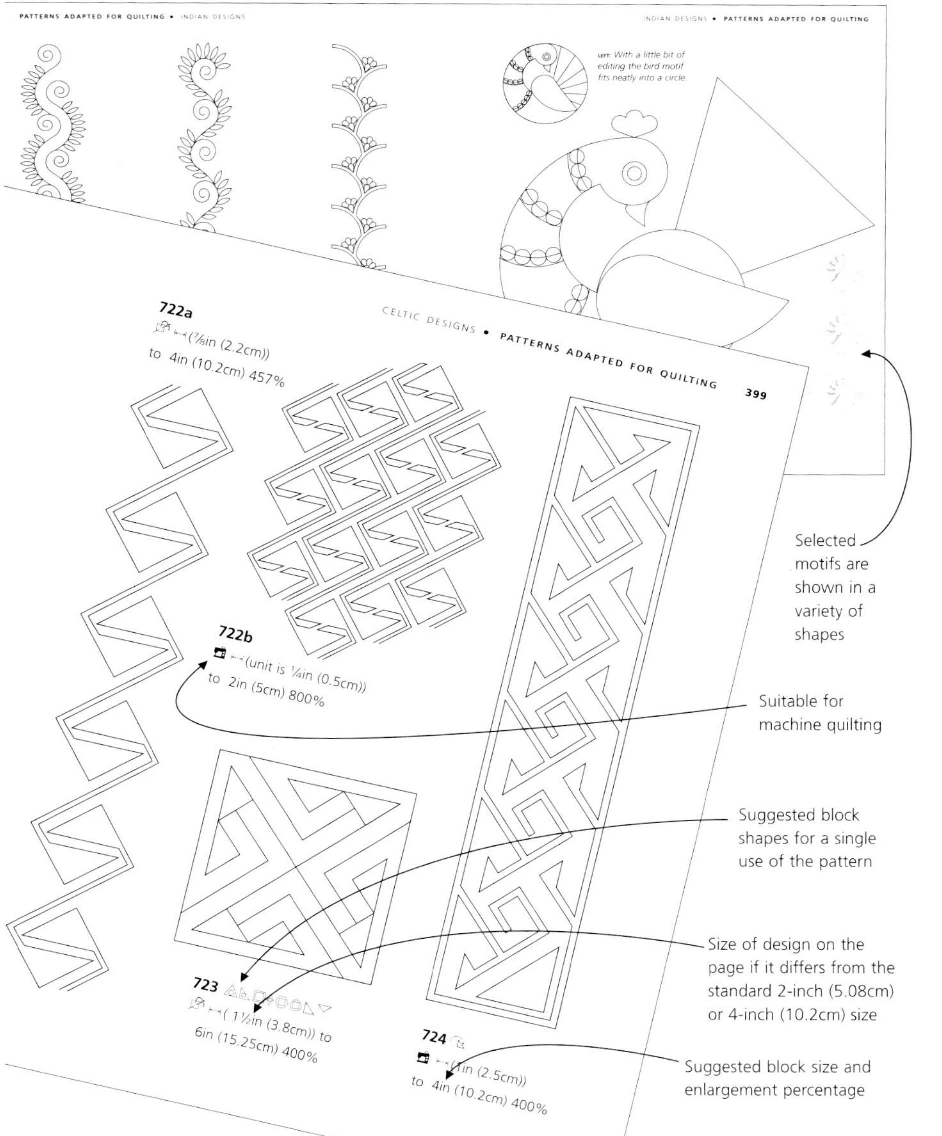
PATTERNS ADAPTED FOR QUILTING • INDIAN DESIGNS
INDIAN DESIGNS • PATTERNS ADAPTED FOR QUILTING
LEFT: With a little bit of editing the bird motif fits neatly into a circle.
CELTIC DESIGNS • PATTERNS ADAPTED FOR QUILTING 399
722a
(⅞in (2.2cm)) to 4in (10.2cm) 457%
722b
(unit is ¼in (0.5cm)) to 2in (5cm) 800%
723
( 1½in (3.8cm)) to 6in (15.25cm) 400%
724
(1in (2.5cm)) to 4in (10.2cm) 400%
Selected motifs are shown in a variety of shapes
Suitable for machine quilting
Suggested block shapes for a single use of the pattern
Size of design on the page if it differs from the standard 2-inch (5.08cm) or 4-inch (10.2cm) size
Suggested block size and enlargement percentage

## Single motif symbols

Below is a description of the overall shape of each design type and how the design might look when contained within another shape.

### TRIANGLES

Two main triangle shapes are featured: the equilateral triangle and the right triangle. The equilateral triangle has three sides of equal length and internal angles of 60 degrees. The right triangle has two sides of equal length perpendicular to each other, a 90 degree angle and two other internal angles of 45 degrees.

**The equilateral triangle** When used as a single motif only, it looks good inside a circle,

in another equilateral triangle or a right triangle. To work well in a square or hexagon, it needs to be reduced and repeated.

**The right angle triangle** When used as a single motif, it looks good in a variety of shapes,

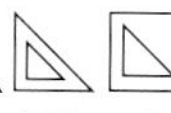

but only accompanied by other motifs when used in diamonds, hexagons and circles.

### SQUARES

The square is a four-sided shape in which all the sides and angles are equal. Due to this

inherent symmetry, squares work well inside most shapes. However, by reducing a square, you can always add another motif along with it. Don't forget to analyze the motifs at an angle of 45 degrees for on-point quilts. This is the angle at which the motifs will most often be seen.

### DIAMONDS

A diamond is properly defined as a shape with

equal opposite angles and four equal sides. It is often two equilateral triangles base to base. Diamonds work well in most shapes, especially when used with other motifs.

### POLYGONS

A polygon is a regular, multi-sided shape. The

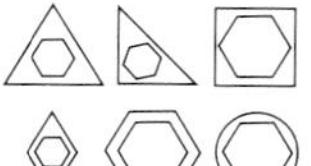

category includes pentagons (five-sided shapes) and hexagons (six-sided) shapes and others as well. Similar to squares and, due to their symmetry, polygons look good in most shapes. The more sides they have the more they possess the properties of the infinite-sided polygon, the circle.

### CIRCLES

A circle is an infinite-sided polygon and is

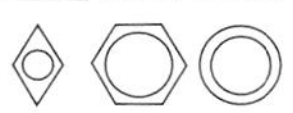

symmetrical in an infinite number of directions. Depending upon the pattern, almost any motif or shape will look good with a circle in it, and circles can be easily combined with other motifs.

### STARS

A star is made up of triangles rotated around a central point. The number of triangles and their length can vary a great deal and so can the way they look in other shapes. However, the more points a star has, the more likely it will work well in most shapes.

The variety of types and styles means that no attempt has been made to show how other shapes will look bound by a star. The central area of a star is always a circle or, if the inner points are joined together with a straight line, a polygon. In order to find a design that will look good bound by a star, concentrate on circular patterns and polygons with the same number of sides or elements as the star has points. To find patterns to place within the points of a star, look at designs suitable for triangles, enlarging them on the photocopier if necessary (see page 37).

### HEARTS

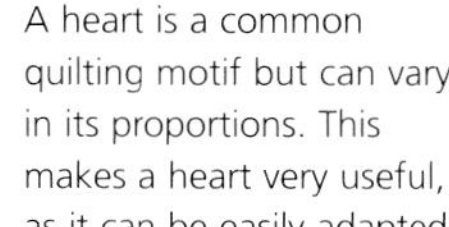

A heart is a common quilting motif but can vary in its proportions. This makes a heart very useful, as it can be easily adapted to a shape that surrounds it and will still be recognizable as a heart. Some shapes, however, do suit a heart shape better than others. In some cases, second filler motifs will be required. It is difficult to generalize about what designs will suit a heart shape because the proportions of the heart can vary so much. To use a heart in a quilt, pay particular attention to circular and diamond shapes and adapt them to fit.

### PICTORIAL MOTIFS

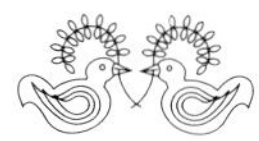

To get an quick idea of how a design will look, try reducing the design and placing it in different shapes. Try to reflect it (see page 30), or rotate it (see page 30)or repeat it to see how it may look as a border design.

## Symbols for using sections of a pattern

The sections of some patterns are suitable for other shapes. To avoid repeating similar patterns, the following symbols are used:

**This section of the diamond design can also be used in an equilateral triangle shape.**

**This section of the polygon design can also be used in an equilateral triangle shape.**

**This section of the circle design can also be used in an equilateral triangle shape.**

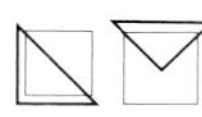
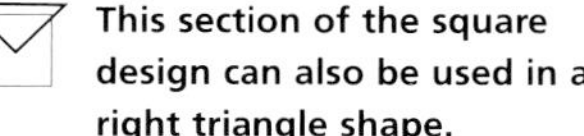

**This section of the square design can also be used in a right triangle shape.**

**This section of the circle design can also be used in a right triangle shape.**

## Orientation symbols

Many popular patterns have a useful symmetry to them. The left and right, top and bottom halves may be a mirror shape of each other, or a reflection. They may also be made up of a single element that is rotated around a fixed point. These are useful characteristics to note, as following the lines of a design's symmetry is often a very successful device when combining a design with other motifs.

However, not only may a design itself have lines of symmetry, but symmetry can be created by duplicating a pattern and using it in successive rotations or reflections.

### REFLECTION

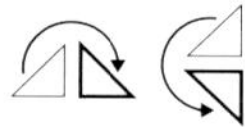

Some patterns may already have a reflected symmetry, so reflecting them in the same way again makes no difference to their appearance. The circular design shown above is an example.

To reflect a pattern, simply make a template as usual, but use it with the pattern face down on the fabric. To see what a design would look like before cutting a template, photocopy it to size, hold the copy up to a mirror and the motif will appear reflected. To have a permanent record of the design, use a pen to trace the reflected image on the reverse side of the photocopy. Then combine both images on one piece of paper.

### ROTATION

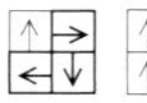
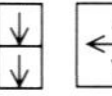

An image can be rotated around any point, either within its boundaries or outside, but it is usually an extreme point on the outer edge. To rotate an image, divide 360 degrees by the number of repeat rotations and mark the resulting number of degrees around a fixed point using a protractor.

If you don't have a protractor, use the following method:

① Enlarge the radiating grid opposite by 400%. Decide how many times you would like to rotate the image and mark the degree intervals on the photocopy. If you will rotate the image 3, 4, 5, 6, 8, 12, or 16 times, then each repeat is represented by a black circle with the number of repeats at each of its rotation positions. Tape a piece of tracing paper to the top edge of the photocopy.

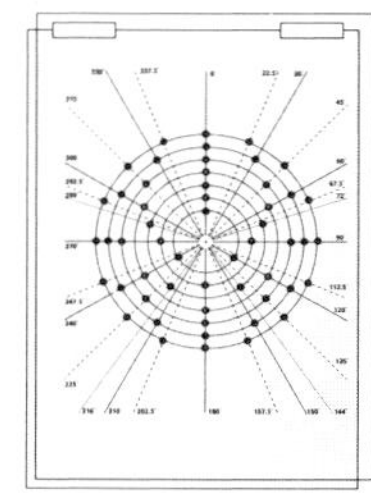

② Cut out the motif and position it under the tracing paper with the fixed rotation point at the center point of the grid and the top aligning with zero degrees. Mark the motif on the tracing paper.

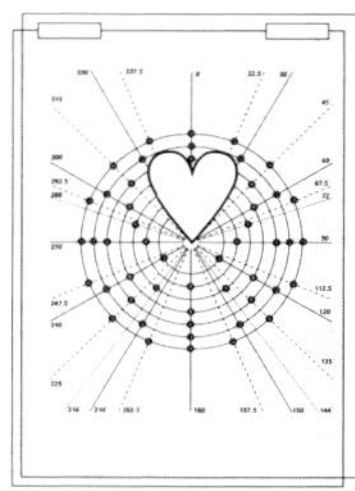

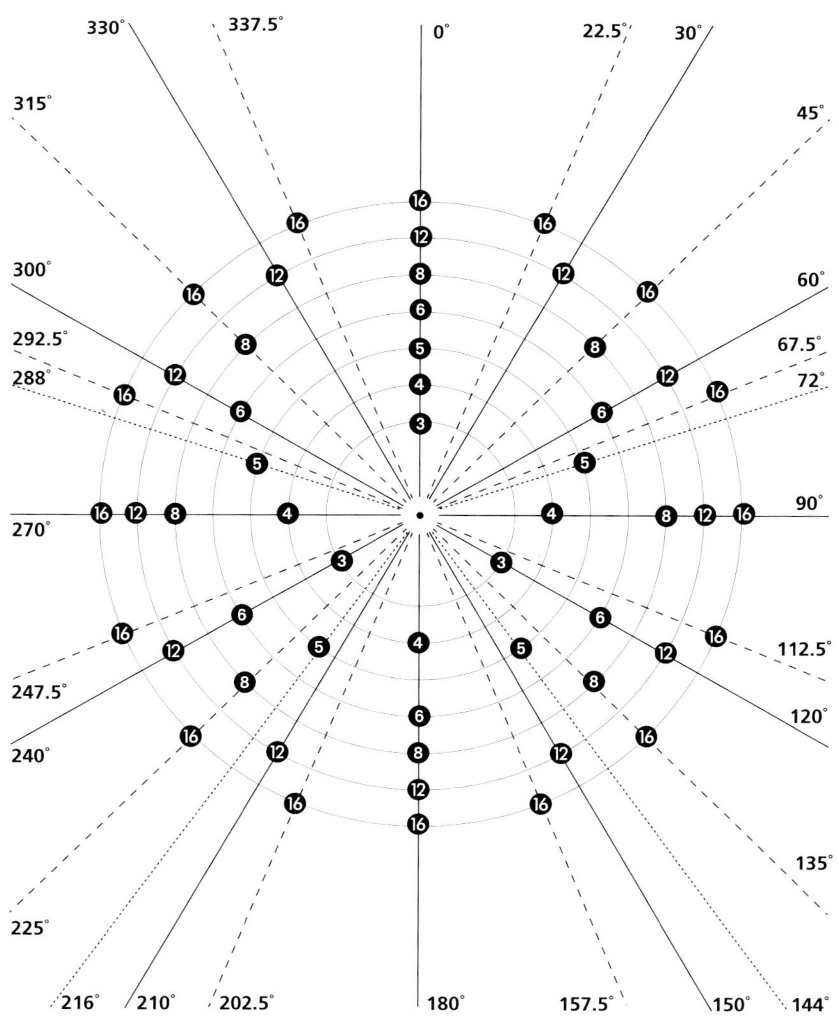

0°
22.5°
30°
45°
60°
67.5°
72°
90°
112.5°
120°
135°
144°
150°
157.5°
180°
202.5°
210°
216°
225°
240°
247.5°
270°
288°
292.5°
300°
315°
330°
337.5°

③ Move the motif around so that the fixed rotation point is still at the center point of the grid but the top now aligns with the next marked point or appropriate number of repeats printed on the grid.

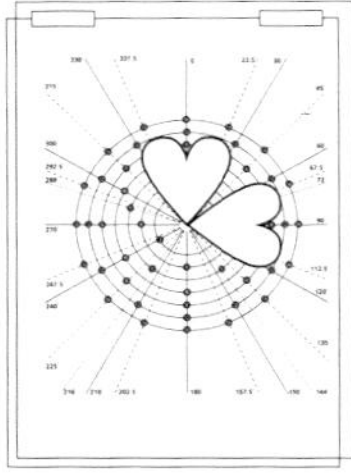

④ Continue until all of the rotated image points have been drawn.

For speed, make multiple copies of the motif and then glue them to a photocopy of the radiating grid (see page 31) in the appropriate positions. Use white correction fluid to obliterate any unwanted lines. Photocopy the new pattern to create a clean image from which to make a template.

To calculate the maximum width the motif can be for a given rotation or the straight line distance between two points on the same circle circumference, see page 503.

## Other symbols

The symbols below indicate quilting techniques, characteristics, and enlargement percentages for designs.

### SUITABLE FOR HAND QUILTING

All designs in this book can be hand quilted, but this symbol denotes designs that are better done by hand than by machine. The design has either several lines that do not link up with others, or complex lines and sharp curves that would be difficult to execute by machine at the suggested sizes.

### SUITABLE FOR MACHINE QUILTING

These designs are made up of long, continuous lines that makes them more suitable for machine quilting.

### SUGGESTED ENLARGEMENTS

These symbols indicate the greater dimension of the design and whether it is a vertical or horizontal measurement. In most cases, this measurement is either 2 inches (5.08 cm) or 4 inches (10.2 cm). Whenever this is not the case, the actual measurement is given in brackets after the symbol. The symbol and measurement, if one is given, is then followed by a suggested block size and the percentage enlargement required for that block. None of the percentages takes into account any spacing or turning allowances for the design.

Refer to page 504 for a table of enlargement percentages.

# How to use the patterns

The designs in this book are just the starting point of a creative quilting adventure. How the designs are combined, manipulated and varied can completely change the look and feel of a design. In fact, the selection and adaptation of the designs for your own needs is one of the most challenging and enjoyable aspects of quilting design.

Rotating and reflecting a pattern has already been discussed as a way of altering the look and feel of a design. There are more ways of looking at the motifs in this book to ensure the perfect quilting designs for every project.

## Double outlines

A simple, single line design can be emphasized by stitching a second line about 1/8 inch (3 mm) from the first. Depending on the size and scale of the design, this measurement can vary. It is often better to stitch two outlines close together in order to emphasize the shape. Whether a shape is outlined once or twice, it is usually easier to put the additional lines outside the first, so it doesn't interfere with any internal lines. Stitching an outline outside the design, however, will make the motif look larger. Make this decision at the beginning and cut a smaller stencil taking the outlines into consideration.

There are no rules. To be on the safe side, look at the design and decide what will look best. Try it first on a piece of scrap fabric from the quilt.

*The original design is very uniform, but it has a lot of room for customizing.*

*Outlining the whole pattern lifts it from the shape of the right triangle.*

*Too much outlining can have the opposite effect. Echo quilting may be better (see page 34).*

*Outlining selective elements of patterns is like drawing on paper and using a thicker pen to highlight certain areas.*

## Using repeat or filler designs

Repeat designs are useful for filling in small areas within a motif and for filling large background areas. Choose a design that is in scale with the area to be stitched; for smaller areas, a simple crosshatch pattern or a random stipple effect. Be bold with large areas. Filler patterns can shift the emphasis of an overall design. To be on the safe side, stitch the design on a scrap of fabric from your project, then check to see if you achieved the effect you want.

Stitching that is close together recedes slightly, giving emphasis to areas around it that have less dense stitching and therefore a slightly higher profile to catch the light.

### GEOMETRIC FILLER DESIGNS

You can find these on pages 310 to 395. Some patterns with square, rectangles, triangles and circles work well within a pieced motif. Others are only suitable for large background areas. When filling in small areas, use a hera to mark the design before you stitch it.

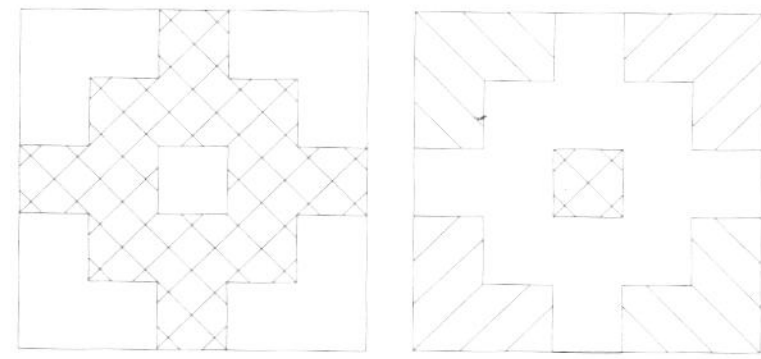

*Each of these geometric filler designs gives a different emphasis to the simple step diamond pattern.*

### RANDOM FILLER DESIGNS

Stippling is the most common random filler design for hand quilting and is a series of small stitches placed at random angles and distribution that as a whole appears uniform. Meander stitching is the machine quilting version of stippling but is more suitable for large areas.

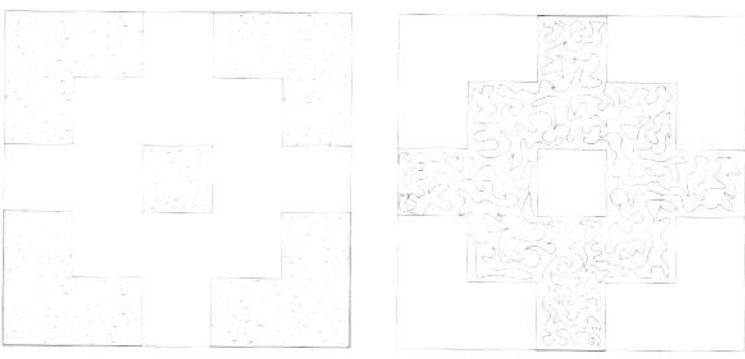

*The stippling on the left is quick and easy to sew. The meander stitching on the right is best worked by machine. Lines of stitching should never cross each other.*

### ECHO STITCHING

This features concentric lines of stitching that are an equal distance apart, following the contours of the shape to be filled. Use a quilter's quarter or 1/8-inch (3 mm) wheel to mark the lines.

*Echo stitching emphasizes the shape of areas not stitched, so it is particularly useful for quilts with appliquéd motifs.*

## Creating design variations

Several of the more complex designs in this book can be used to create interesting variations. Some will only work well on a large scale, or can be interpreted in many of your own creative ways. In some cases, elements have been repeated to provide a choice of size or number. Look closely at the design and keep a bottle of white correction fluid handy as you lay out photocopies.

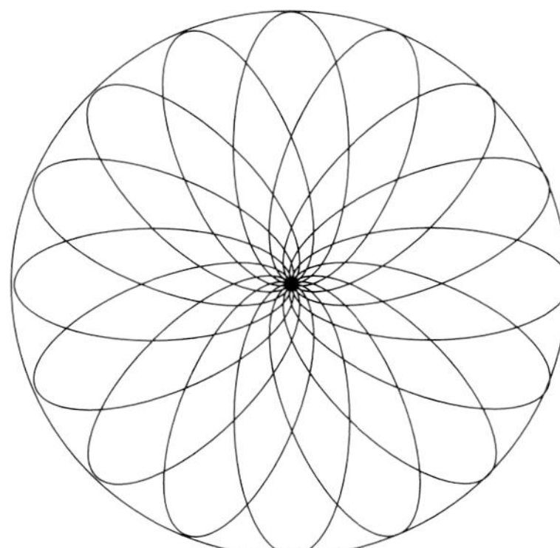

*The designs at right are all based on the pattern shown above.*

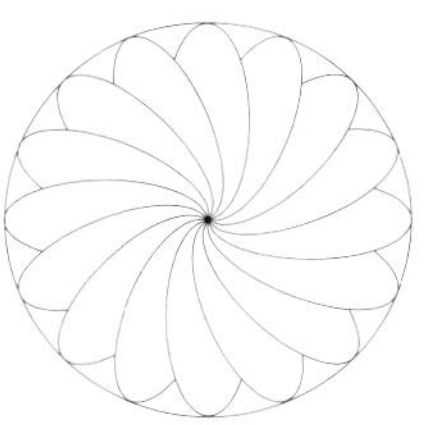

Each oval is represented as a solid shape radiating around a central point.

Every second oval appears in front of those adjacent to it. "Petals" have been added, aligned within points that were already part of the pattern. Concentric circles fill in the center.

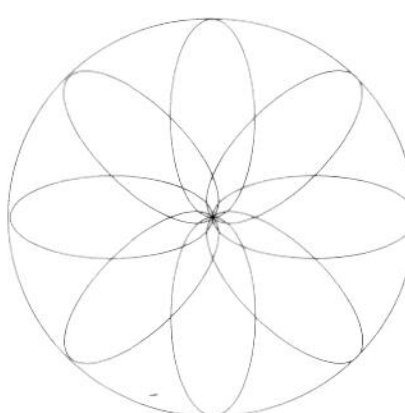

Every second oval has been deleted, but the overlapping lines of those that remain are still visible.

Every second oval has been deleted. Lines were added to the center of each oval, and a circle was added to fill in the center. As the pattern has a symmetry of eight elements, it lends itself to an octagonal shape.

## Changing the shape of designs

The choice of shapes available from the designs in this book can be increased even more when a photocopier is used to its full creative potential. Most elliptical and rectangular designs are variations of a circle and a square. These shapes can vary so much that this book may never contain the perfect shape required, but a bit of imagination and photocopying can supply the rest.

### CHANGING A SQUARE TO A RECTANGLE

The process is the same as that described for an ellipse. In quilting, the standard rectangle shape is usually twice the length in one direction than the other.

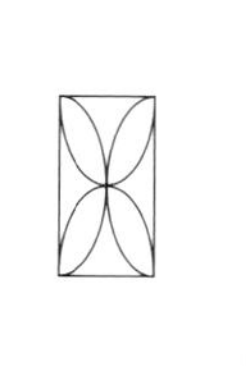

### CHANGING A CIRCLE TO AN ELLIPSE

① Measure the maximum width and height of the oval required. Use the following formula:
**size required ÷ actual size = percentage**

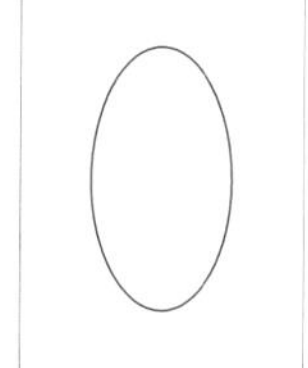

Calculate separate enlargement percentages for each dimension using the design you wish to manipulate for the actual size measurements.

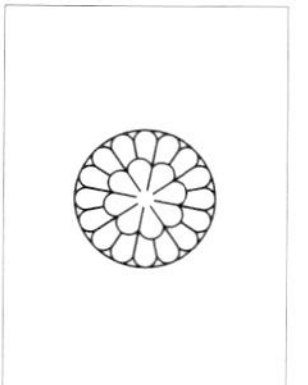

② Photocopy the pattern with different percentage values for the width and height. Most photocopying machines show the width as X and the height as Y.

### CHANGING A SQUARE TO A DIAMOND

① Use the following formula to change a square to a diamond:
**size required**
**÷ actual size**
**= percentage**
Photocopy a square motif so that the diagonal measurement matches that of the width of the required diamond shape. Then, using either a quilter's ruler or by folding corner A to edge B bisecting C, mark a 45 degree angle across the bottom left of the photocopy and cut off the corner.

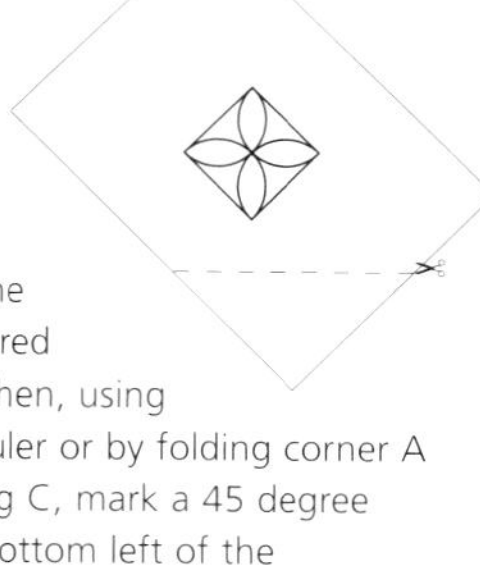

② Place the cut edge against the edge of the photocopier glass and enlarge the photocopy of the motif, this time matching the height of the diamond shape.

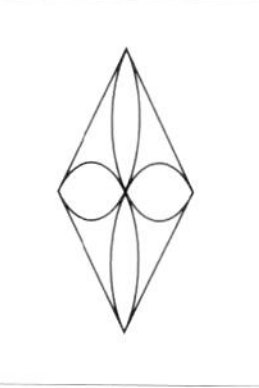

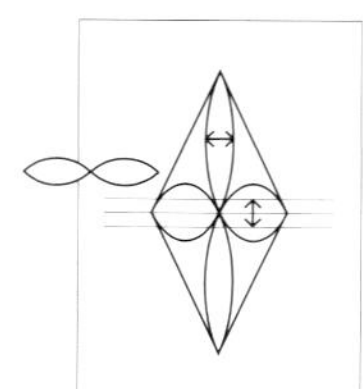

③ The enlargement distorts the regular shape of the original design. To remedy this, cut out the relevant area from the photocopy in step ①.

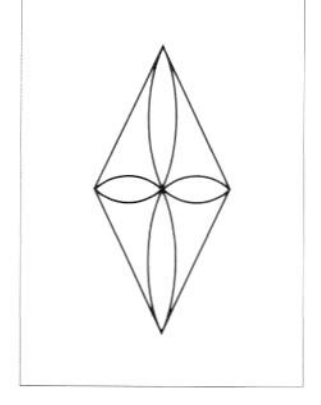

④ Glue the cut-out shapes on the second photocopy and using white correction fluid, remove any lines that are not needed. Photocopy the final montage to achieve a clean image to make your design.

## CHANGING A SQUARE TO MAKE AN EQUILATERAL TRIANGLE OR KITE SHAPE

The method just described can also be used to create a design for an equilateral triangle.

### For an equilateral triangle

Read through the instructions for changing a square to a diamond (left). However, at step ①, match the distance across the base and at step ②, match the height of the triangle. Then on the resulting photocopy, remove any lines you don't need to create a clean image to make your design. Use this for hexagonal shapes, made up of six equilateral triangles.

### For a kite shape variation

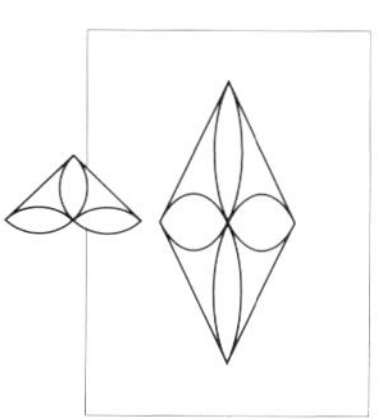

Start with steps ① and ② of changing a square to a diamond (left) but then at step ③, cut out a larger area from the first photocopy.

④ Glue the cut-out shape on the second photocopy and remove any lines you do not need. Photocopy the final montage to achieve a clean image to make the design.

## CHANGING THE SCALE OF PATTERNS

Once you understand the technique of changing geometric shapes, you can adapt this technique to change other images.

This original bird motif has been altered by enlarging the tail with different height and width percentages and by changing its position. The head was drawn slightly larger and the legs moved farther apart.

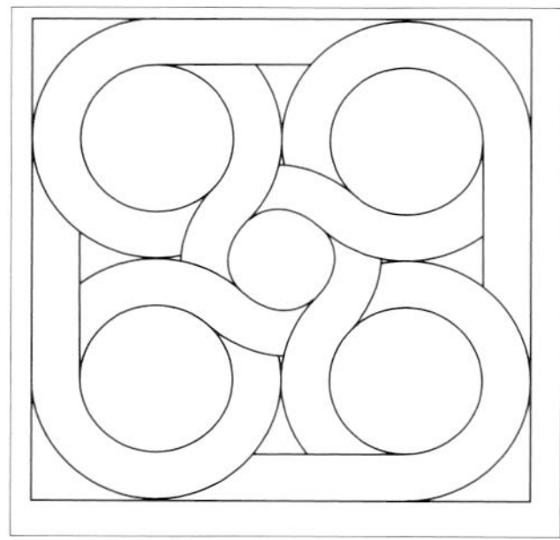

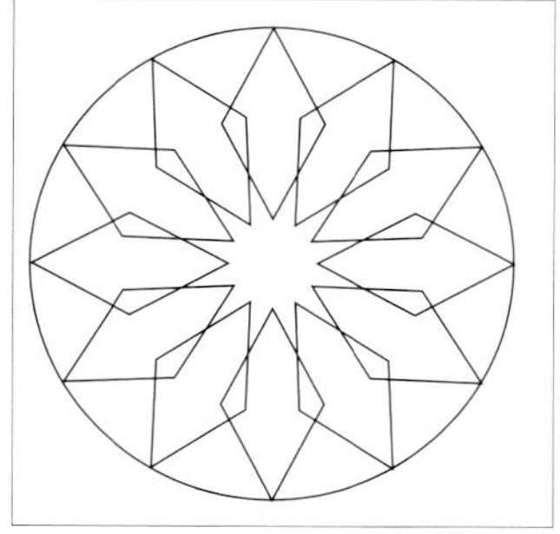

# Traditional quilting patterns

*You'll find a wonderful range of traditional designs in this section. Remember that all the designs can be enlarged to any of the sizes in the table on pages 504–506. The sizes beneath each design are given as suggestions only and to show the range of enlargements that can be used.*

# Equilateral Triangles

All shapes except the circle can be divided into triangles; however, this chapter concentrates on two types of triangles, the equilateral triangle and the right angle triangle. These two form the basis of many patchwork designs but you can also use the ideas that follow to fill any other type of triangle.

## Equilateral triangle

This is a useful triangle as six make up a hexagon and it tessellates into a pyramid quilt. In addition it can be subdivided into four further equilateral triangles (see number 1), two equilateral triangles and a diamond (see number 2), three kites or three darts (see number 21).

Six equilateral triangles rotated by 60 degrees around one point makes a hexagon so for further ideas on how to quilt this triangle look at the hexagons in the polygon chapter (see page100) or look at any pattern with a repeat symmetry of six and use one section.

1

6in (15.25cm) 300%

8in (20.3cm) 400%

2

5in (12.7cm) 250%

12in (30.5cm) 600%

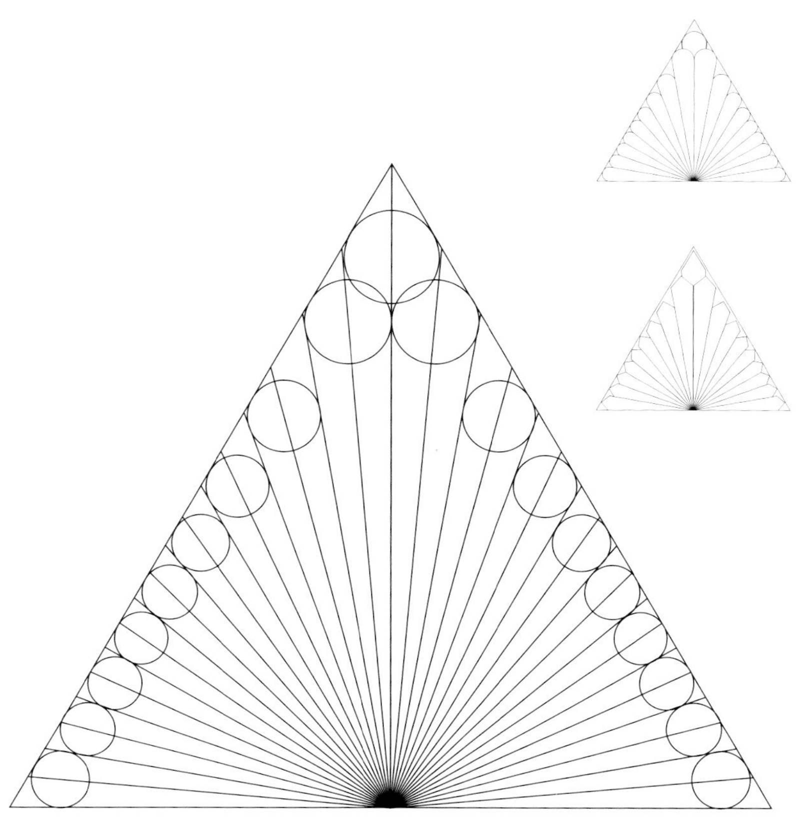

**3**

8in (20.3cm) 200%

12in (30.5cm) 300%

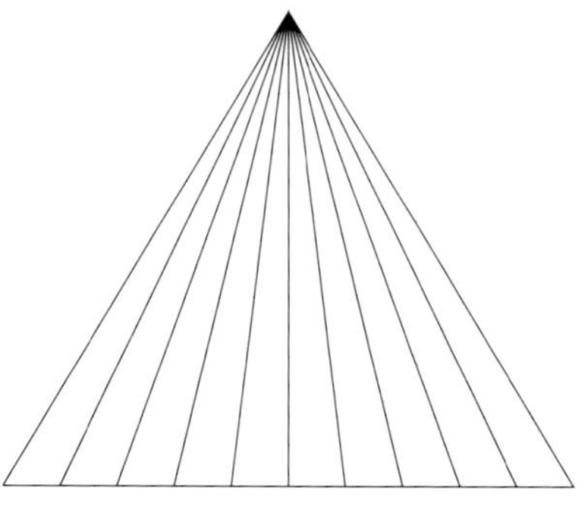

**4** 

4in (10.16cm) 200%

8in (20.3cm) 400%

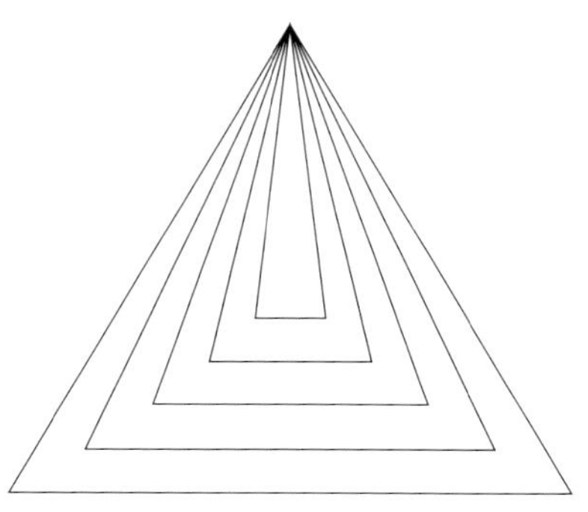

**5**

4in (10.2cm) 200%

8in (20.3cm) 400%

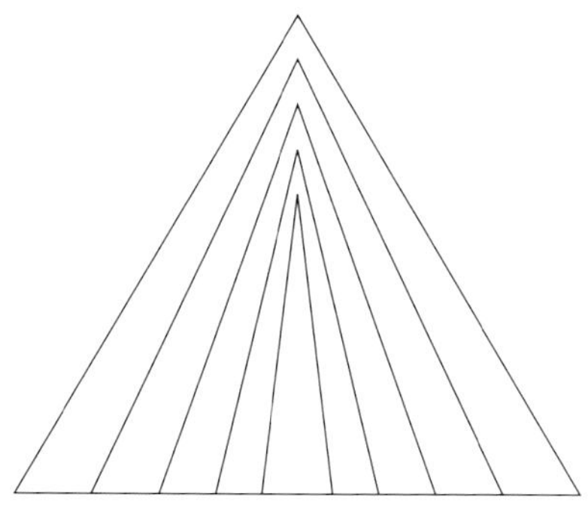

**6**

6in (15.25cm) 300%

8in (20.3cm) 400%

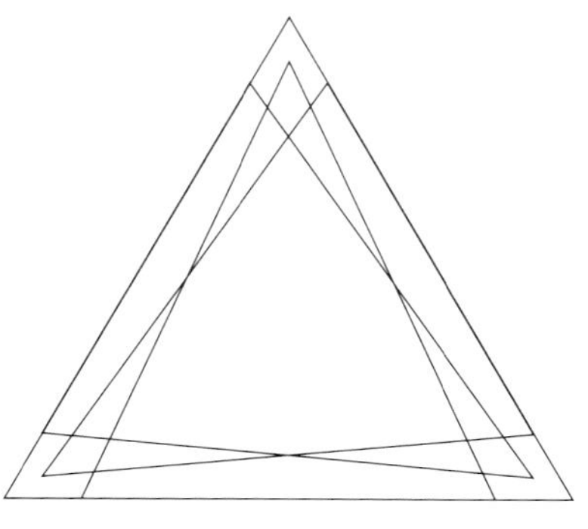

**7**

6in (15.25cm) 300%

8in (20.3cm) 400%

ALL PATTERNS ARE STANDARD 2IN (5CM) OR 4IN (10.2CM) UNLESS OTHERWISE STATED

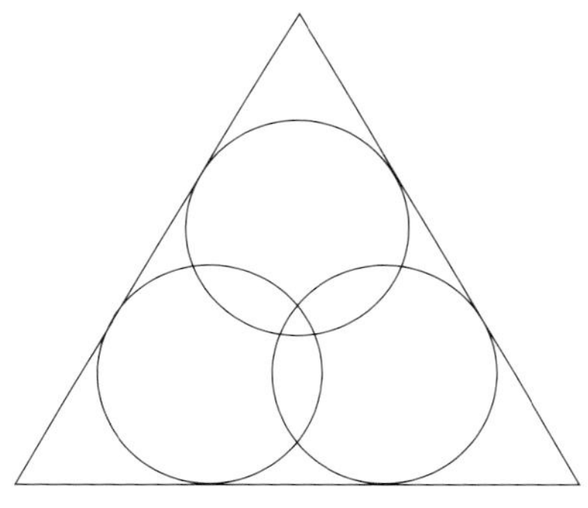

**8**

6in (15.25cm) 300%

8in (20.3cm) 400%

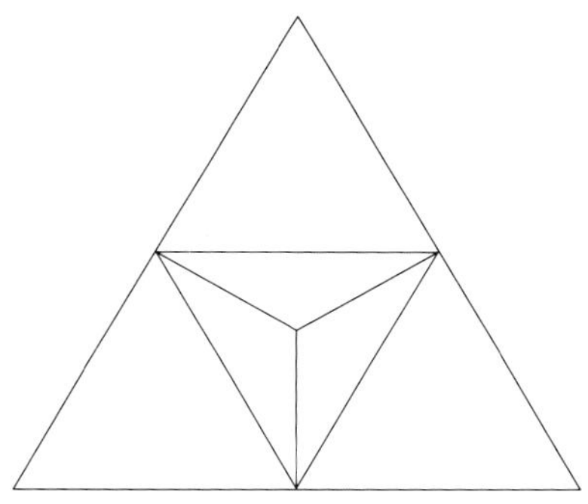

**9**

6in (15.25cm) 300%

8in (20.3cm) 400%

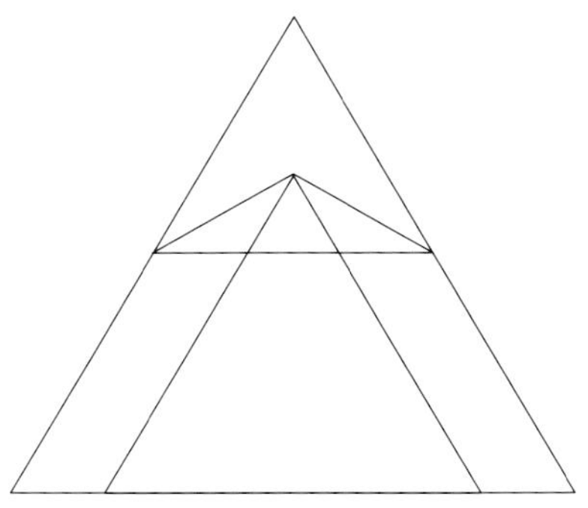

**10**

4in (10.2cm) 250%

10in (25.4cm) 500%

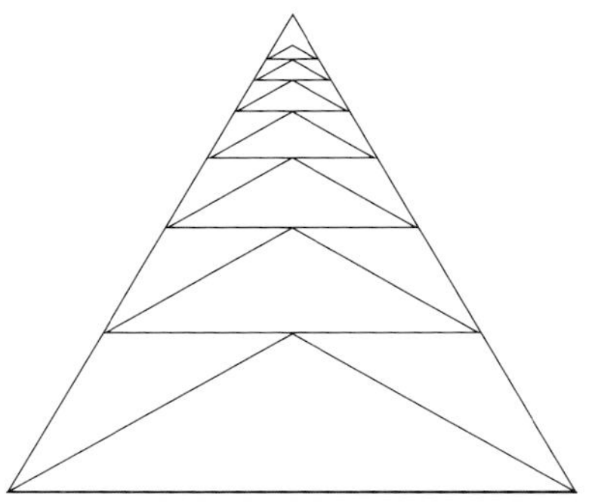

**11**

5in (12.7cm) 250%

8in (20.3cm) 400%

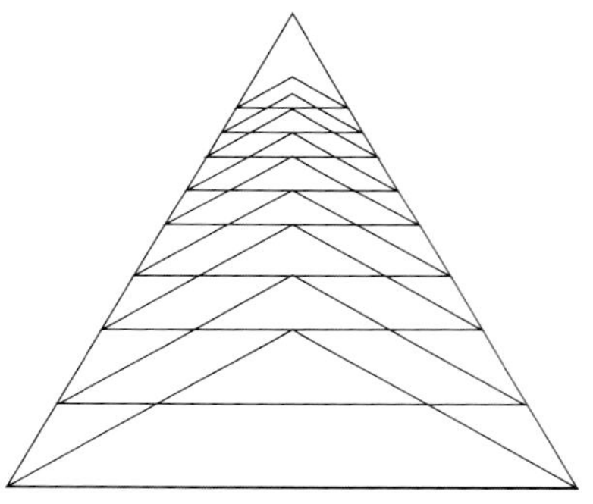

**12**

⟼ 6in (15.25cm) 300%

⟼ 8in (20.3cm) 400%

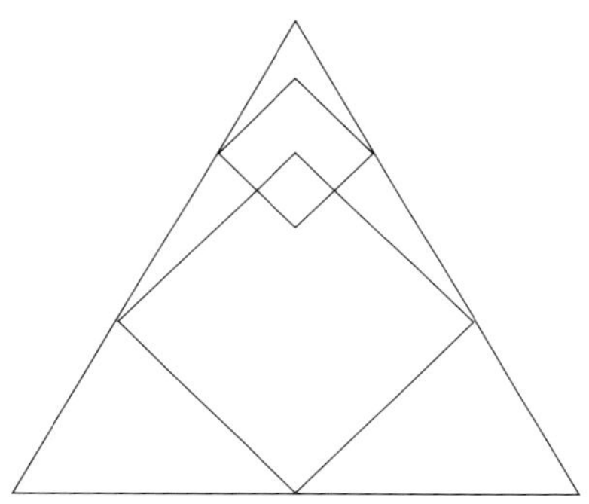

**13**

⟼ 5in (12.7cm) 250%

⟼ 8in (20.3cm) 400%

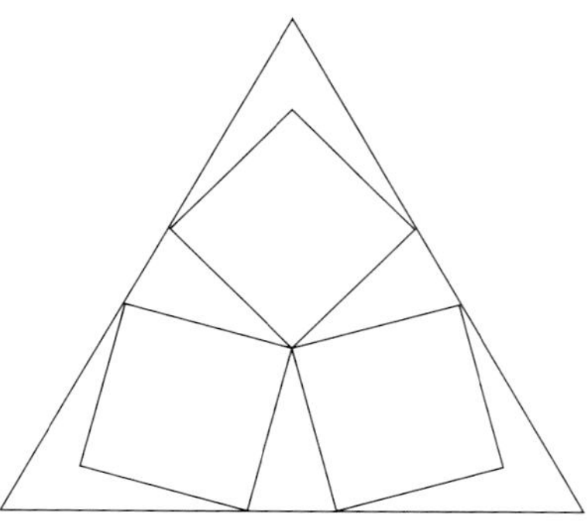

**14**

⟼ 4in (10.3cm) 200%

⟼ 8in (20.3cm) 400%

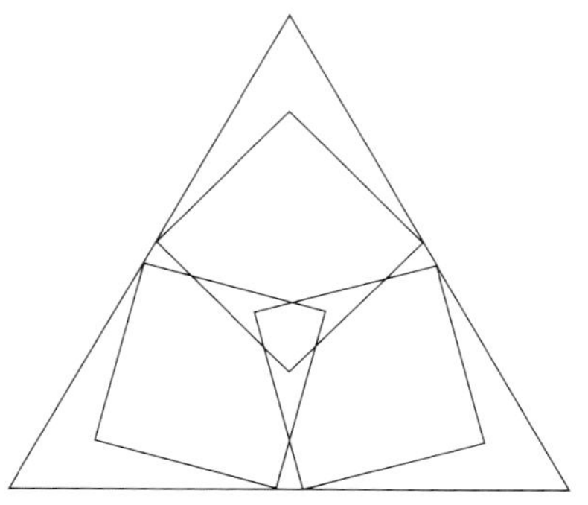

**15**

⟼ 6in (15.25cm) 300%

⟼ 8in (20.3cm) 400%

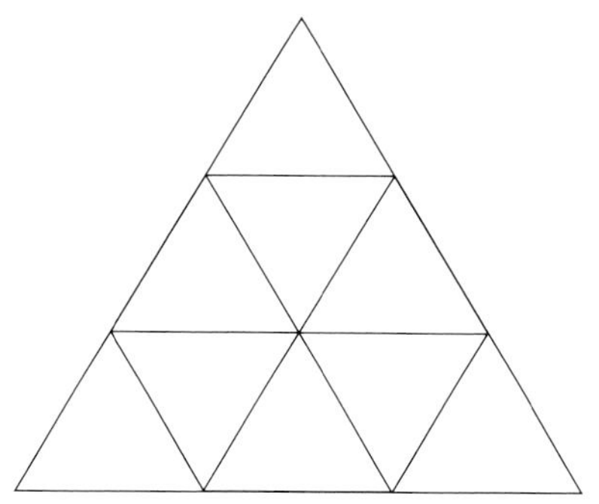

**16** 

⟷ 6in (15.25cm) 300%

⟷ 8in (20.3cm) 400%

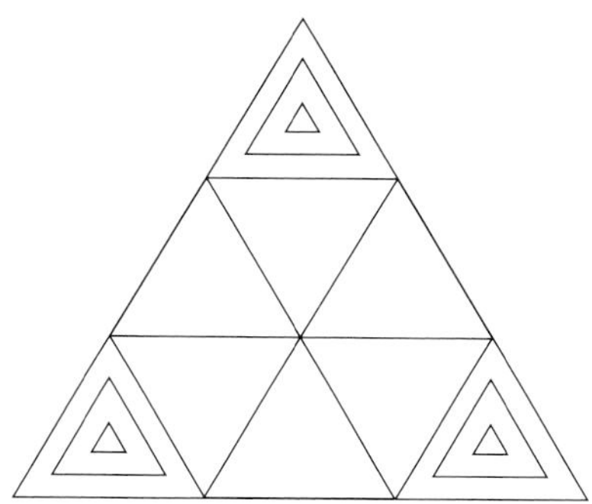

**17**

⟷ 6in (15.25cm) 300%

⟷ 8in (20.3cm) 400%

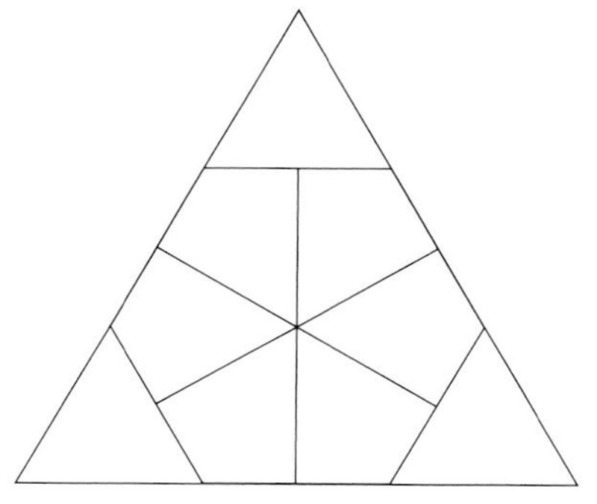

**18**

⟷ 4in (10.2cm) 200%

⟷ 8in (20.3cm) 400%

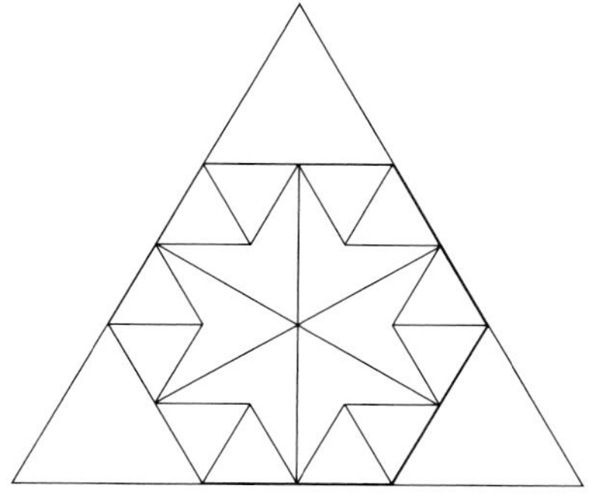

**19**

⟷ 8in (20.3cm) 400%

⟷ 12in (30.5cm) 600%

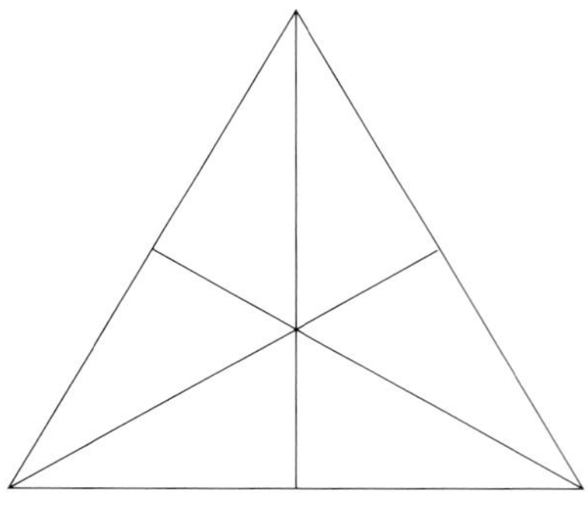

**20**

⟼ 6in (15.25cm) 300%

⟼ 8in (20.3cm) 400%

**21a**

⟼ 6in (15.25cm) 300%

⟼ 8in (20.3cm) 400%

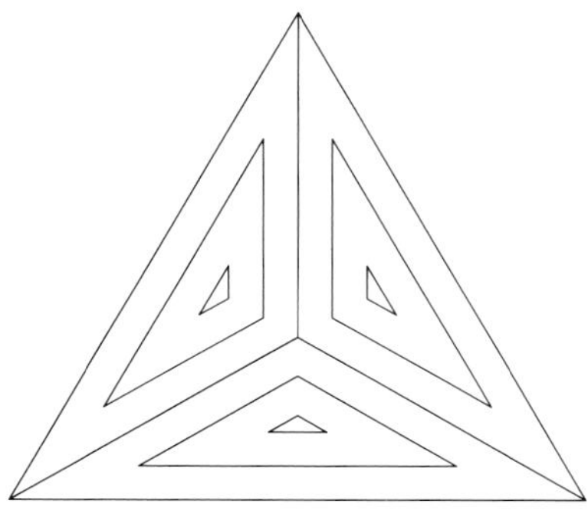

**21b**

⟼ 4in (10.2cm) 200%

⟼ 8in (20.3cm) 400%

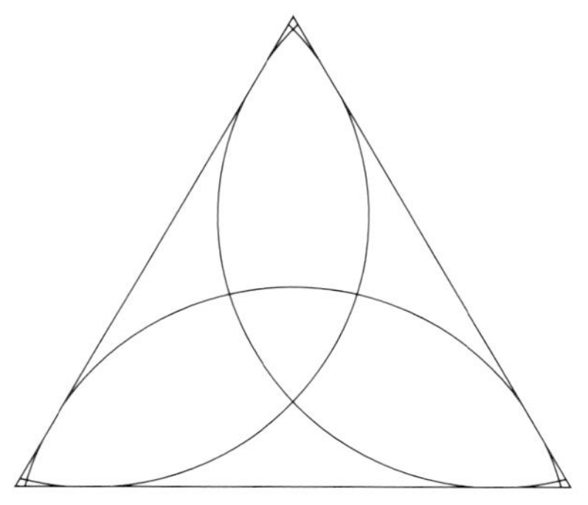

**22a**

⟼ 4in (10.2cm) 400%

⟼ 5in (12.7cm) 250%

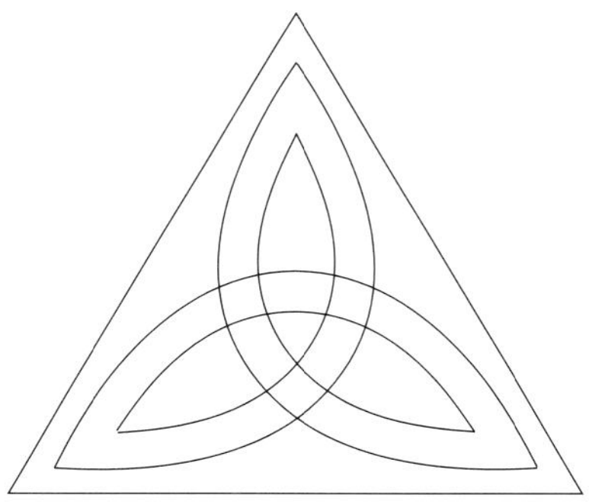

**22b**

⟼ 4in (10.2cm) 200%

⟼ 5in (12.7cm) 250%

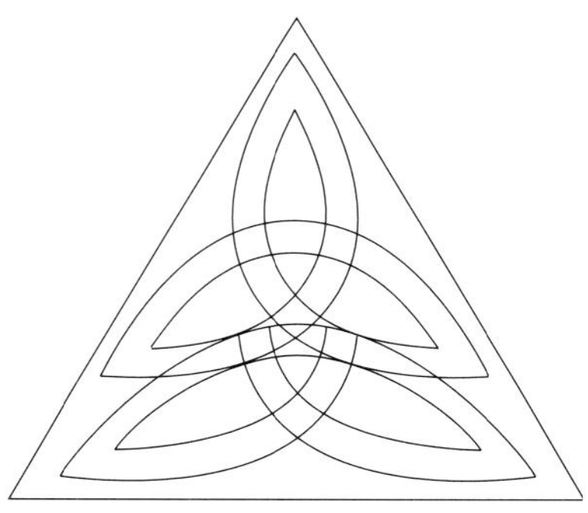

**23**

⟼ 6in (15.25cm) 300%

⟼ 8in (20.3cm) 400%

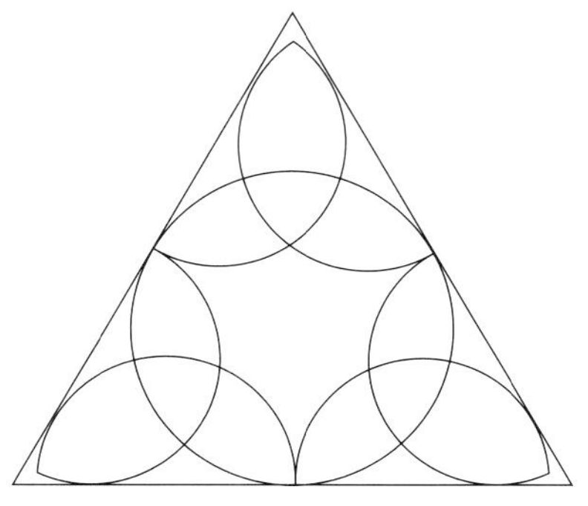

**24a**

⟼ 4in (10.2cm) 400%

⟼ 5in (12.7cm) 250%

**24b**

⟼ 6in (15.25cm) 300%

⟼ 8in (20.3cm) 400%

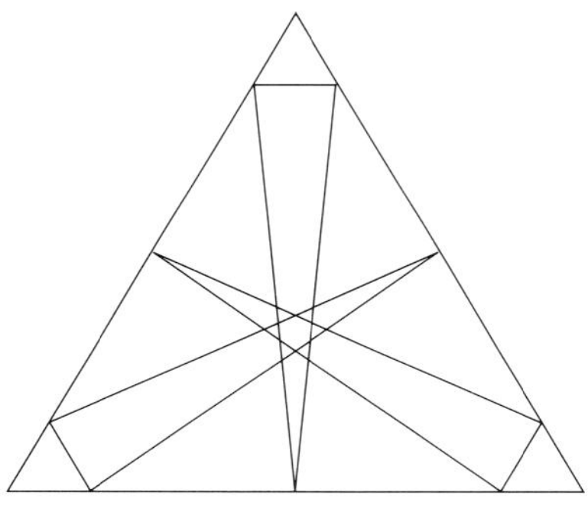

**25**

⟷ 6in (15.25cm) 300%

⟷ 8in (20.3cm) 400%

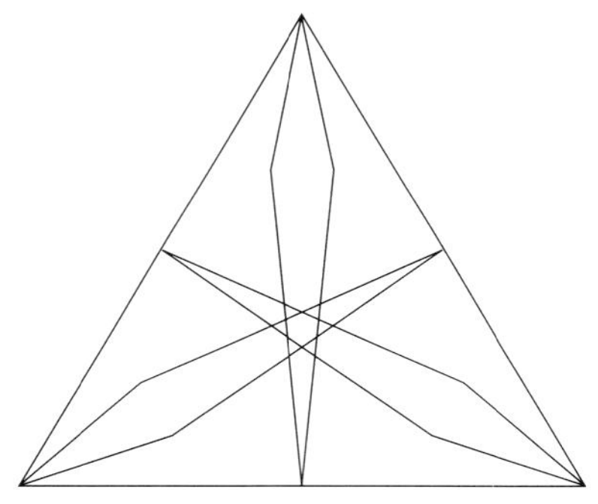

**26**

⟷ 4in (10.2cm) 200%

⟷ 8in (20.3cm) 400%

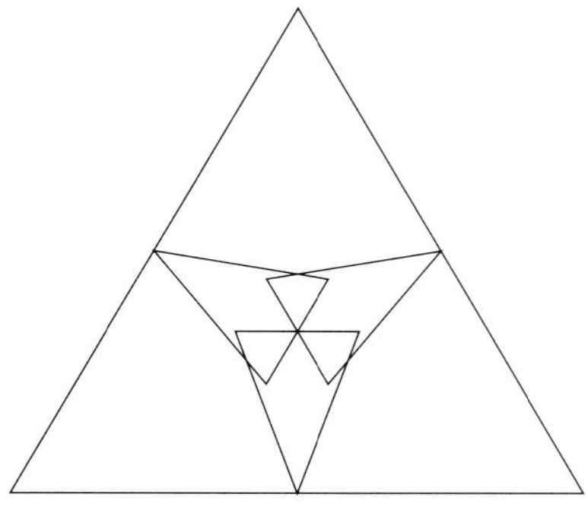

**27**

⟷ 6in (15.25cm) 300%

⟷ 8in (20.3cm) 400%

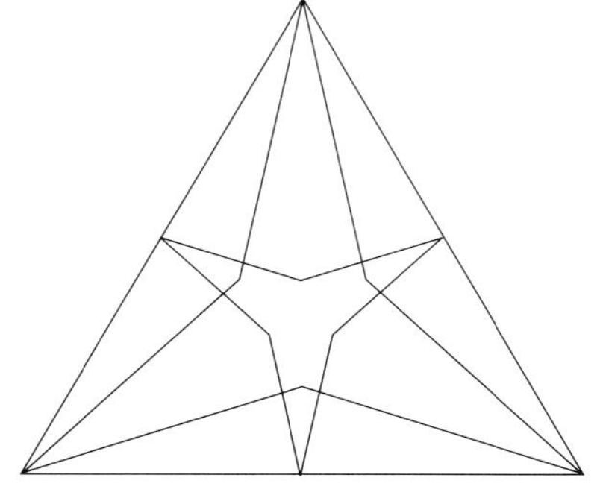

**28**

⟷ 4in (10.2cm) 200%

⟷ 5in (12.7cm) 250%

ALL PATTERNS ARE STANDARD 2IN (5CM) OR 4IN (10.2CM) UNLESS OTHERWISE STATED

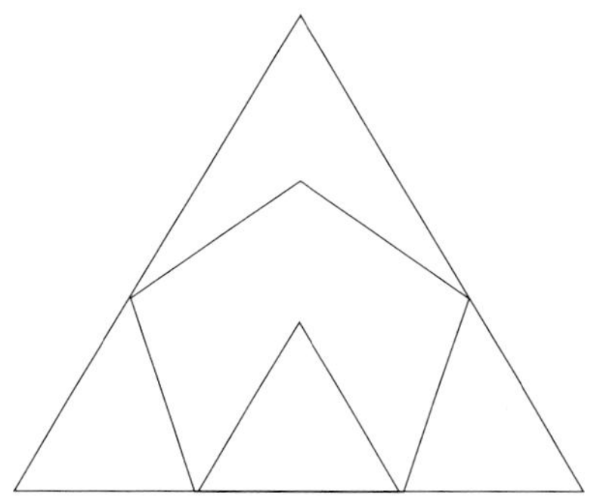

**29** 

⟼ 4in (10.2cm) 200%

⟼ 5in (12.7cm) 250%

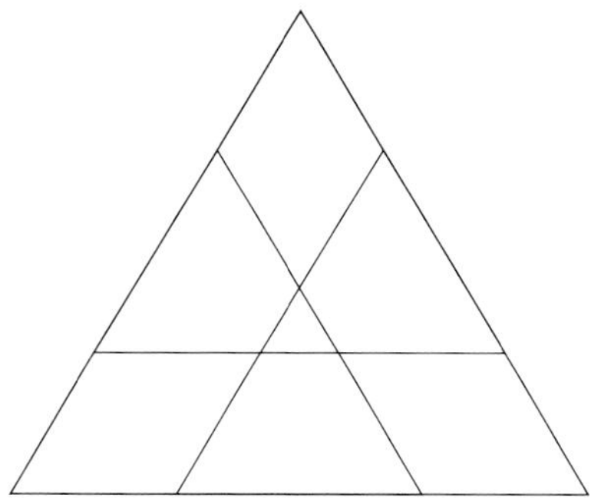

**30**

⟼ 4in (10.2cm) 200%

⟼ 5in (12.7cm) 250%

**31**

⟼ 6in (15.25cm) 300%

⟼ 8in (20.3cm) 400%

**32**

⟼ 8in (20.3cm) 400%

⟼ 12in (30.5cm) 600%

## Right-angle triangle

This triangle is formed by dividing a square diagonally. These triangles occur around the edges and corners of on-point quilts. For more ideas on how to quilt a right-angle triangle, look at the square and circle designs that can be split diagonally.

A right-angle triangle is not a dart, but using a photocopier some of the designs could be adapted for a dart shape. Measure the height and width of the two shapes separately and, using the formula on page 504, calculate the two enlargments; one for each dimension.

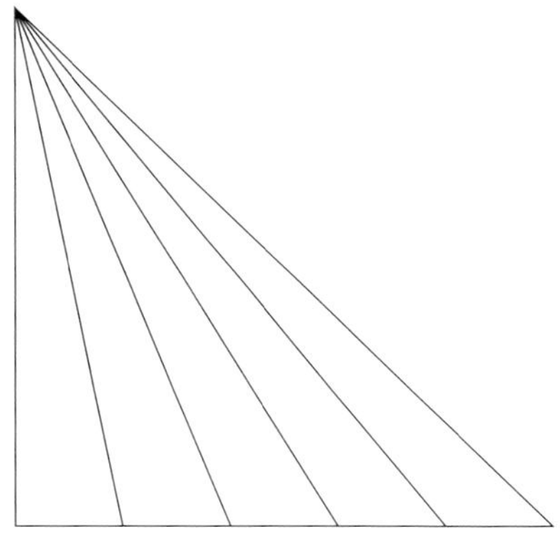

**33**

4in (10.2cm) 200%

5in (12.7cm) 250%

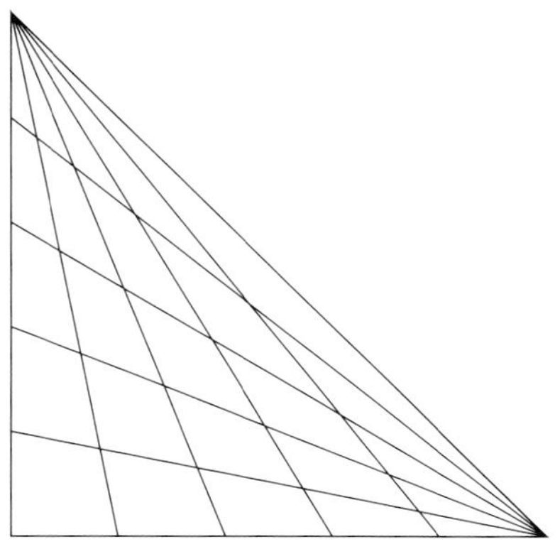

**34**

6in (15.25cm) 300%

8in (20.3cm) 400%

**35** 

⟷ 6in (15.25cm) 300%

⟷ 8in (20.3cm) 400%

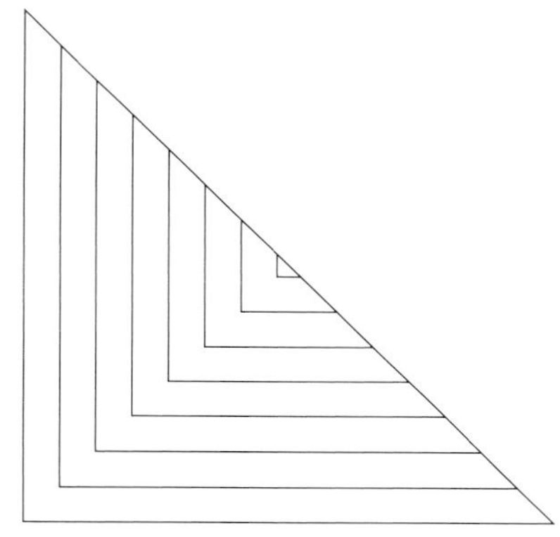

**36**

⟷ 4in (10.2cm) 200%

⟷ 5in (12.7cm) 250%

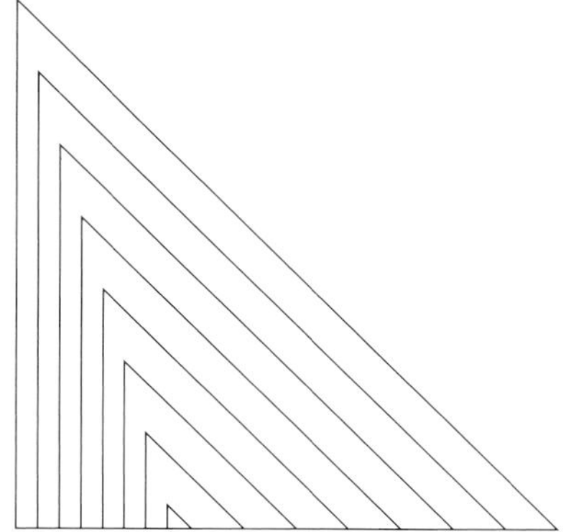

**37**

⟷ 6in (15.25cm) 300%

⟷ 8in (20.3cm) 400%

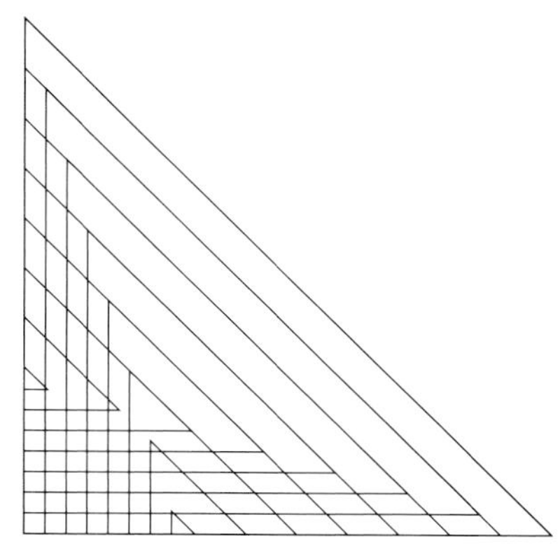

**38**

⟷ 8in (20.3cm) 400%

⟷ 12in (30.5cm) 600%

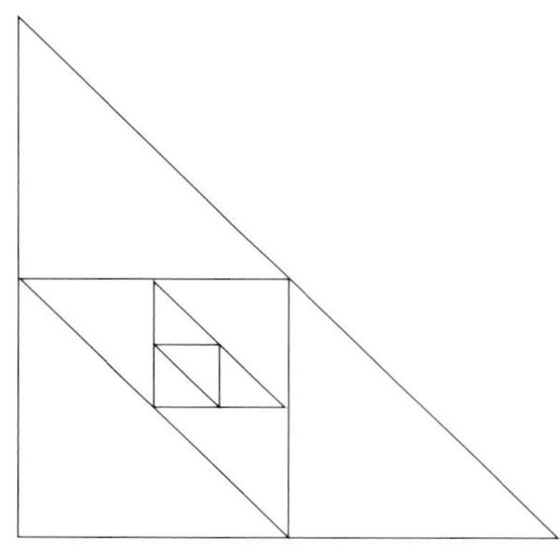

**39**

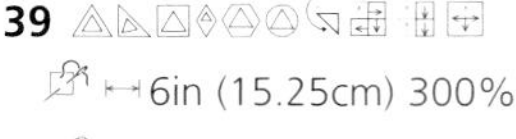

6in (15.25cm) 300%

8in (20.3cm) 400%

**40**

4in (10.2cm) 200%

6in (15.25cm) 300%

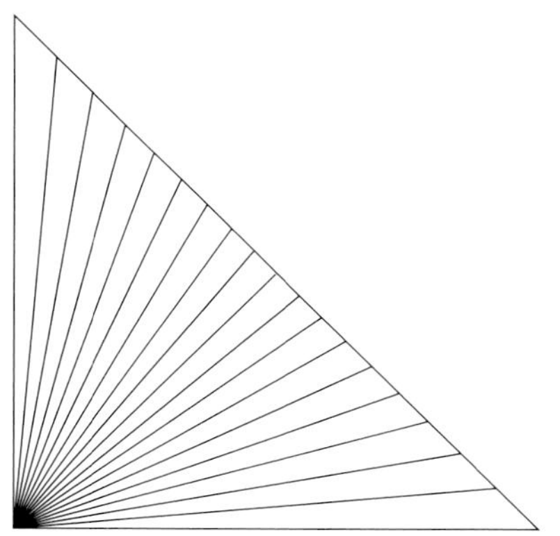

**41**

6in (15.25cm) 300%

8in (20.3cm) 400%

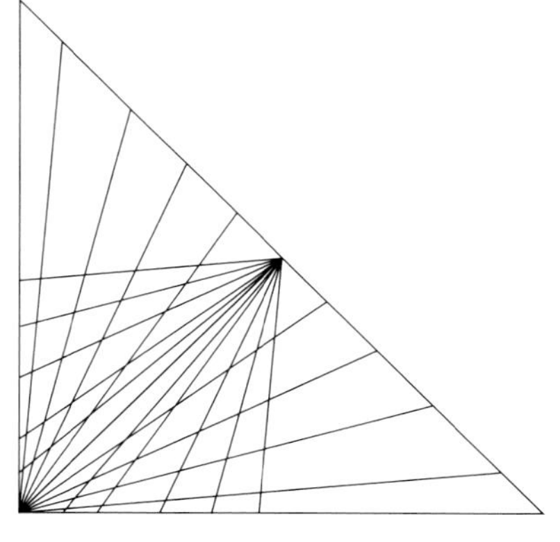

**42**

8in (20.3cm) 400%

12in (30.5cm) 600%

ALL PATTERNS ARE STANDARD 2IN (5CM) OR 4IN (10.2CM) UNLESS OTHERWISE STATED

**43** 

⟼ 6in (15.25cm) 300%

⟼ 8in (20.3cm) 400%

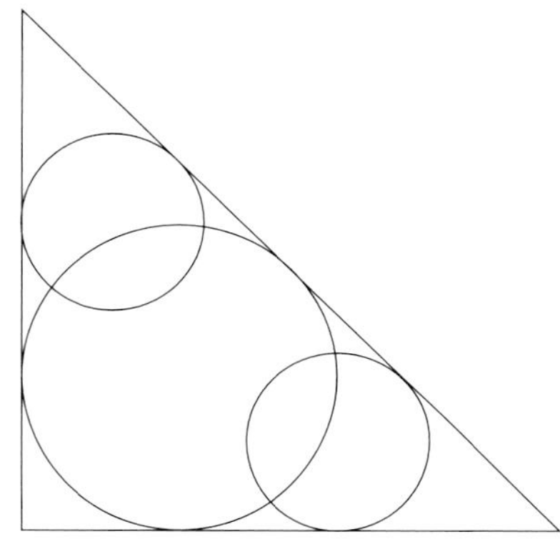

**44**

⟼ 4in (10.2cm) 200%

⟼ 8in (20.3cm) 400%

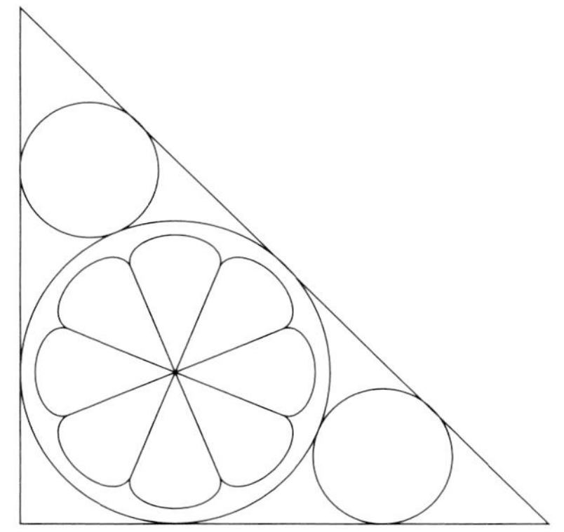

**45**

⟼ 6in (15.25cm) 300%

⟼ 8in (20.3cm) 400%

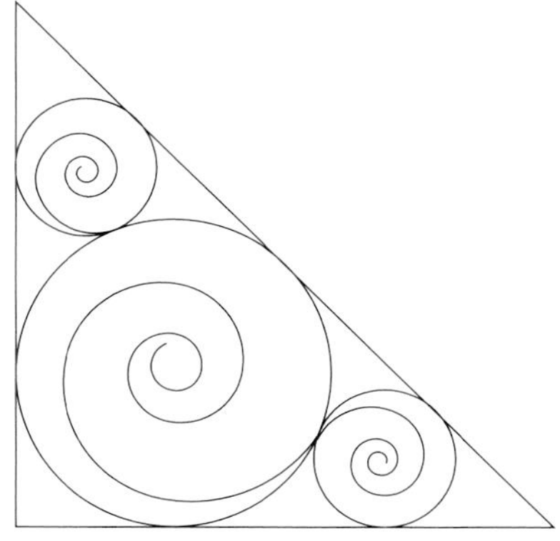

**46**

⟼ 6in (15.25cm) 300%

⟼ 8in (20.3cm) 400%

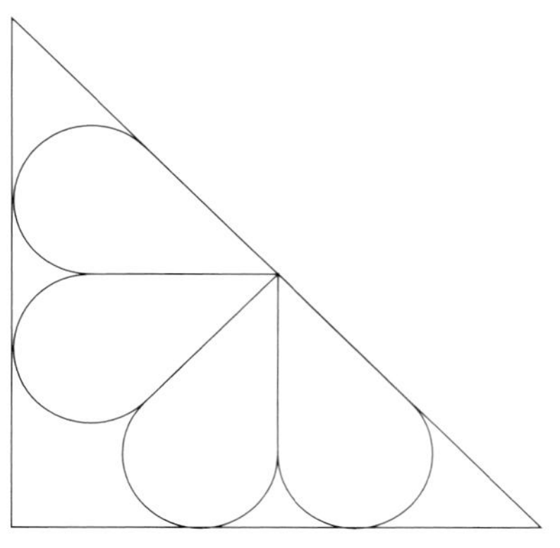

**47** 

⟼ 4in (10.2cm) 200%

⟼ 8in (20.3cm) 400%

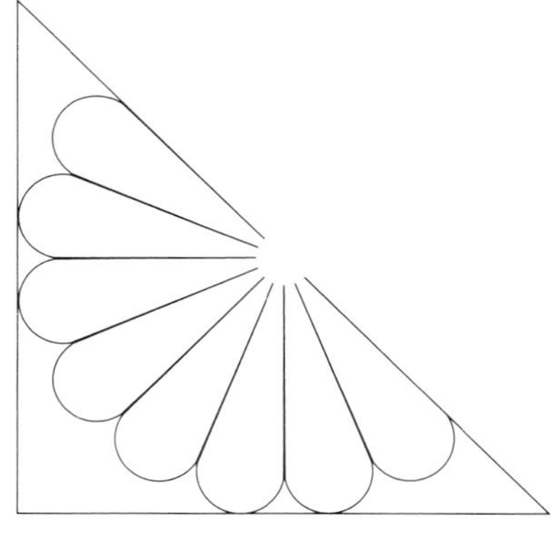

**48**

⟼ 6in (15.25cm) 300%

⟼ 8in (20.3cm) 400%

**49**

⟼ 6in (15.25cm) 300%

⟼ 8in (20.3cm) 400%

**50**

⟼ 8in (20.3cm) 400%

⟼ 12in (30.5cm) 600%

ALL PATTERNS ARE STANDARD 2IN (5CM) OR 4IN (10.2CM) UNLESS OTHERWISE STATED

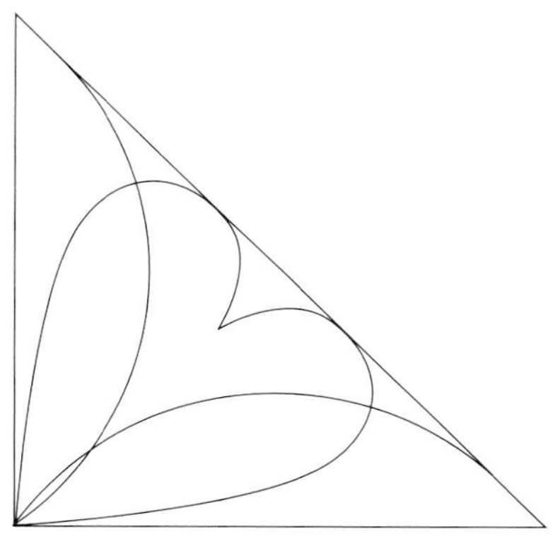

**51** 

4in (10.2cm) 200%

8in (20.3cm) 400%

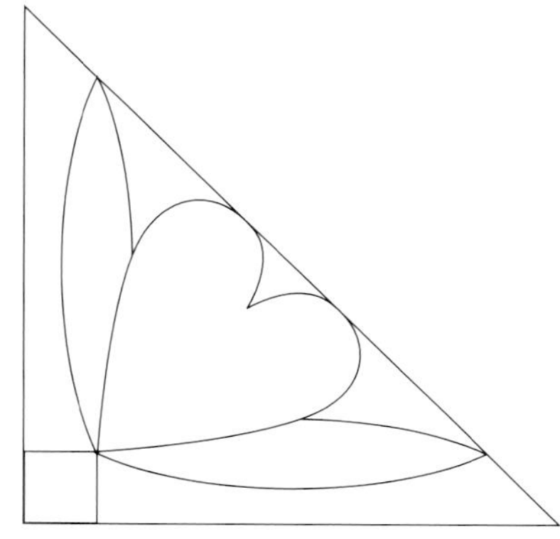

**52**

6in (15.25cm) 300%

12in (30.5cm) 600%

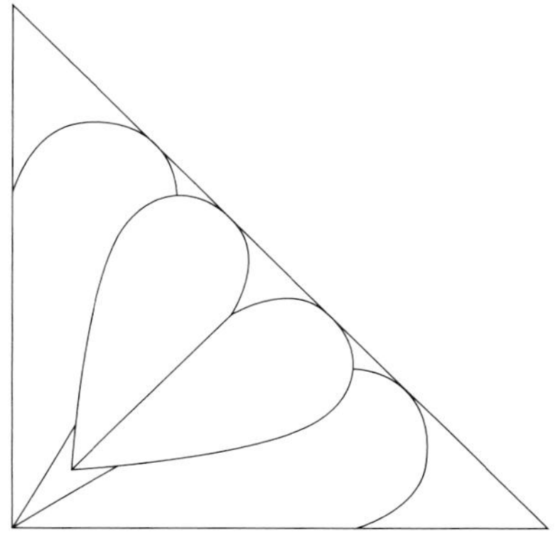

**53**

6in (15.25cm) 300%

8in (20.3cm) 400%

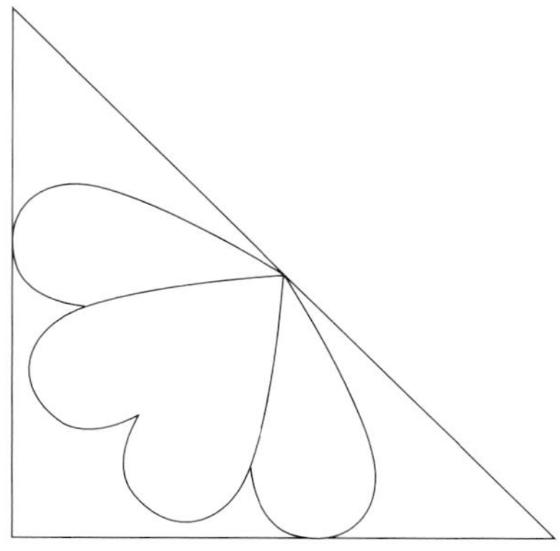

**54**

4in (10.2cm) 200%

8in (20.3cm) 400%

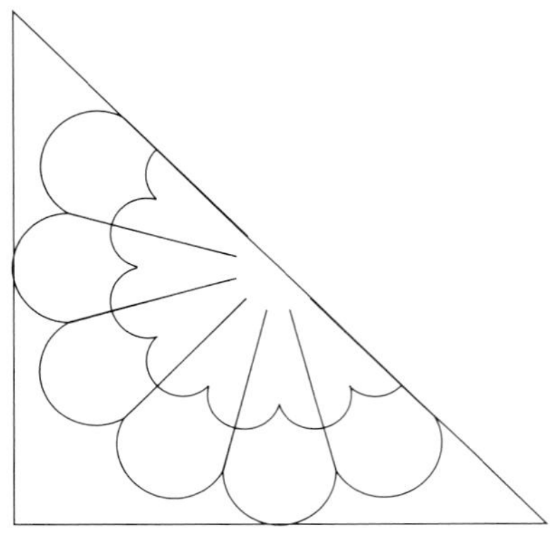

**55**

⟼ 6in (15.25cm) 300%

⟼ 8in (20.3cm) 400%

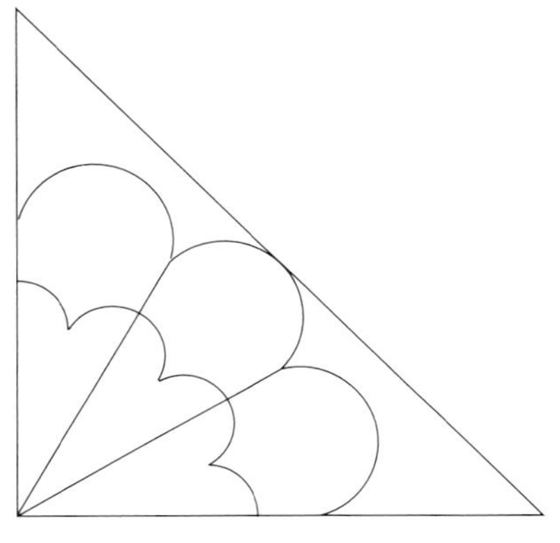

**56**

⟼ 4in (10.2cm) 200%

⟼ 5in (12.7cm) 250%

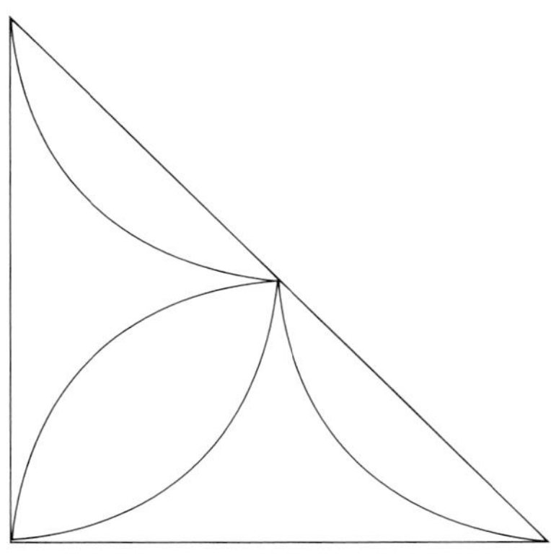

**57**

⟼ 5in (12.7cm) 250%

⟼ 8in (20.3cm) 400%

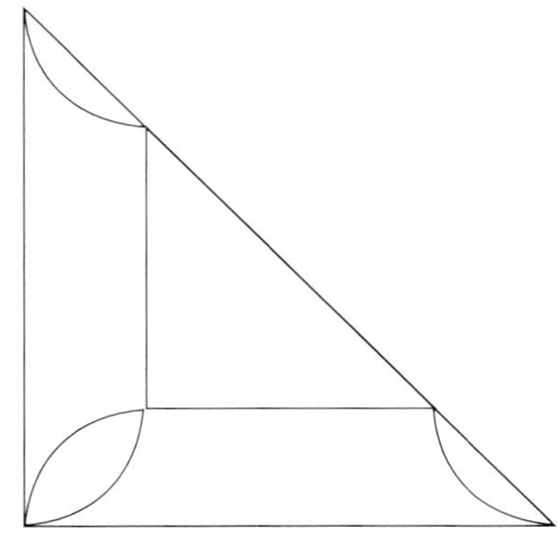

**58**

⟼ 6in (15.25cm) 300%

⟼ 8in (20.3cm) 400%

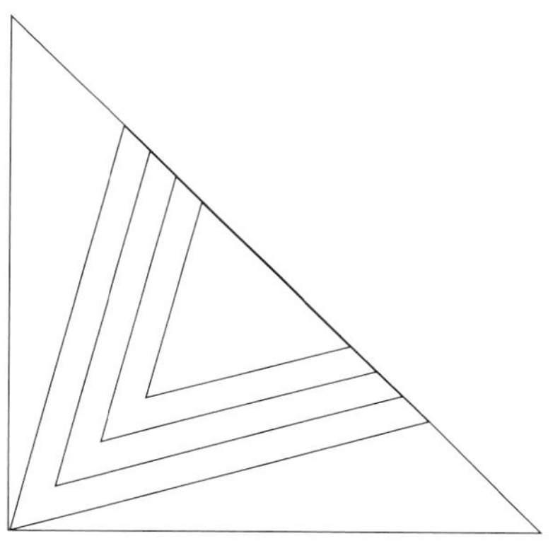

**59** 

⊢⊣ 4in (10.2cm) 200%

⊢⊣ 6in (15.25cm) 300%

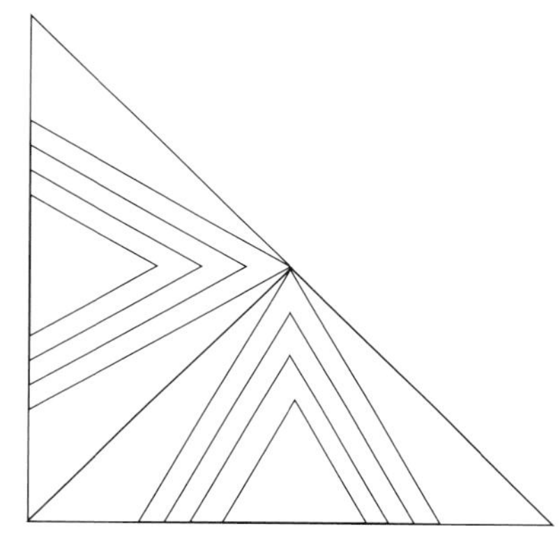

**60**

⊢⊣ 6in (15.25cm) 300%

⊢⊣ 8in (20.3cm) 400%

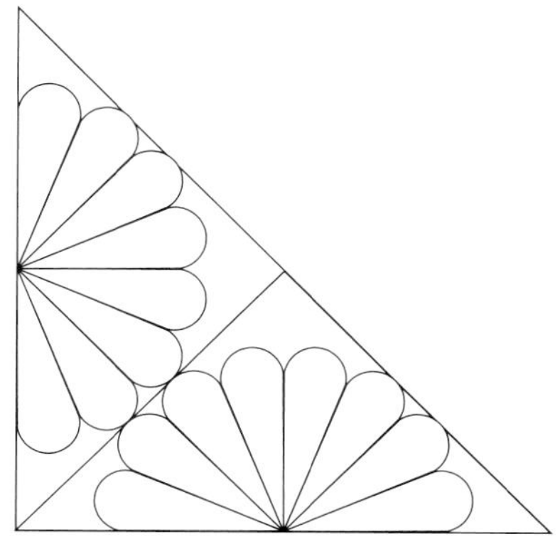

**61**

⊢⊣ 15in (38.1cm) 750%

⊢⊣ 18in (45.7cm) 900%

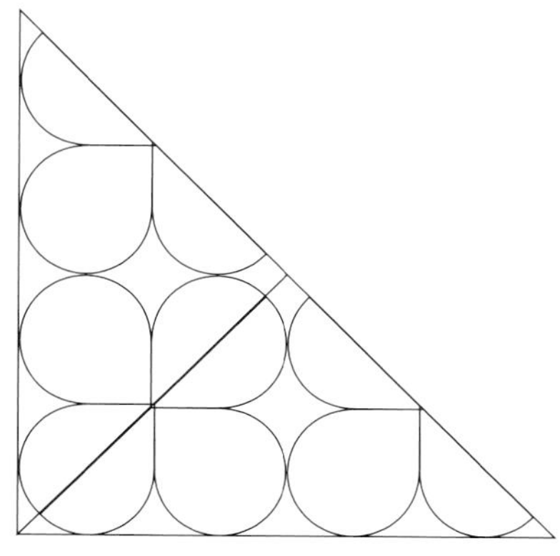

**62**

⊢⊣ 8in (20.3cm) 400%

⊢⊣ 12in (30.5cm) 600%

# Squares

The square is a common patchwork block shape and can be a versatile frame or structure for a quilting design. However, it isn't always a good idea to confine the quilting design within a single block; quilting irrespective of the block shapes can add a unity, and flowing lines an interesting contrast.

For more ideas for quilting designs, take a look through the chapter of circle designs (see page 116)—the combination of the straight- sided square and the curves of a circular design are a classic combination.

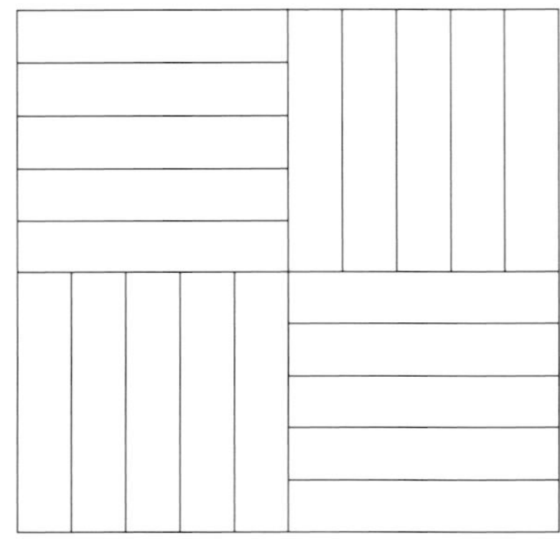

**63**

↔ 4in (10.2cm) 200%

↔ 5in (12.7cm) 250%

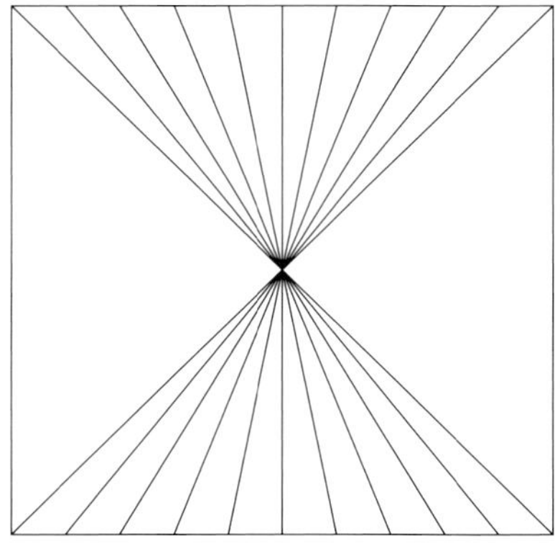

**64**

↔ 4in (10.2cm) 200%

↔ 6in (15.25cm) 300%

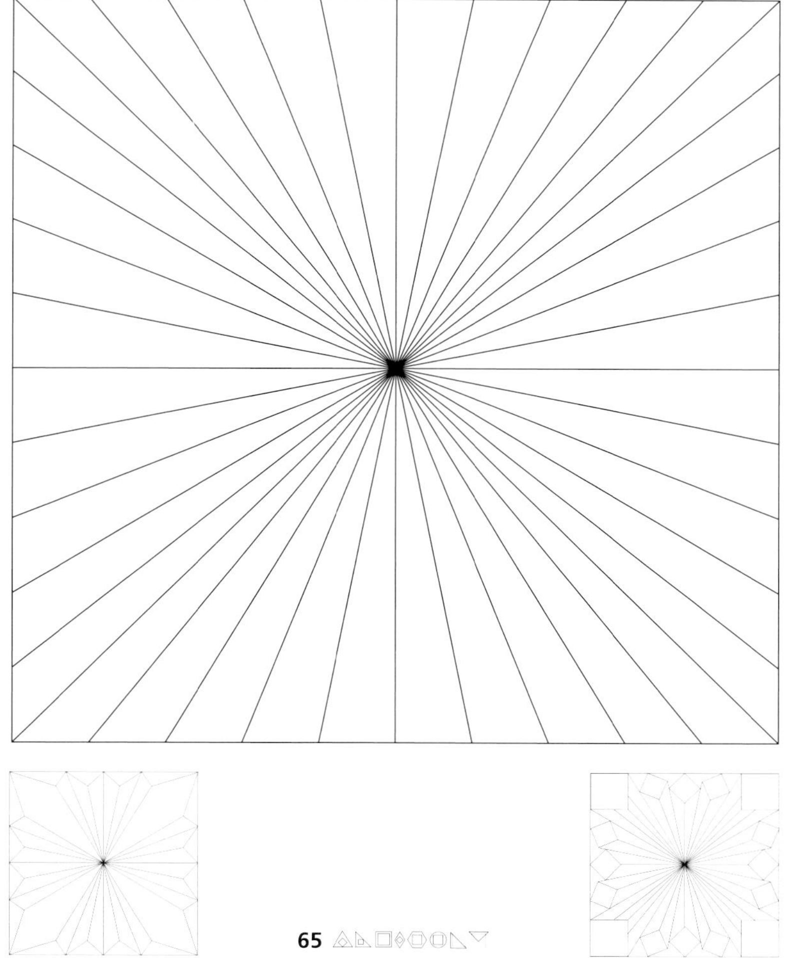

65

8in (20.3cm) 200%

12in (30.5cm) 300%

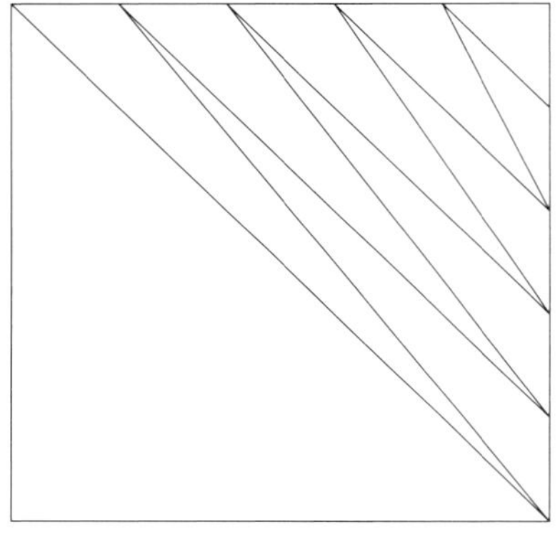

**66a**

↔ 4in (10.2cm) 200%

↔ 5in (12.7cm) 250%

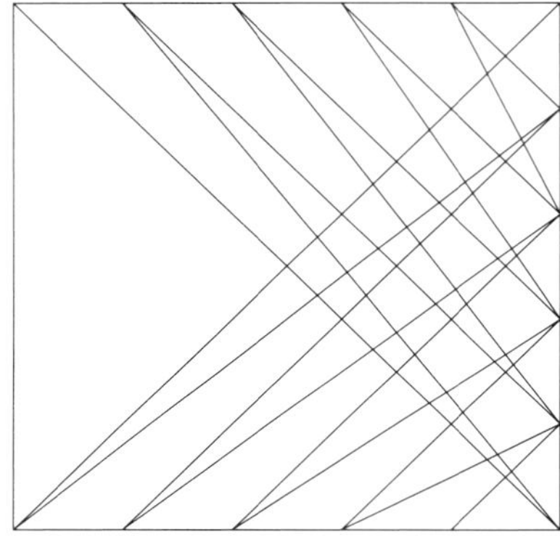

**66b**

↔ 6in (15.25cm) 300%

↔ 8in (20.3cm) 400%

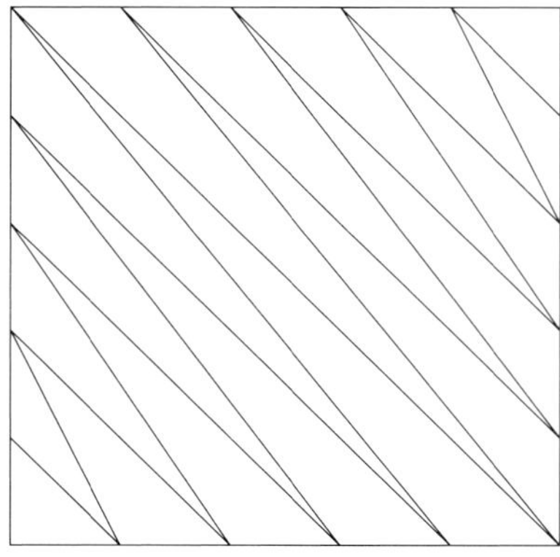

**66c**

↔ 6in (15.25cm) 300%

↔ 8in (20.3cm) 400%

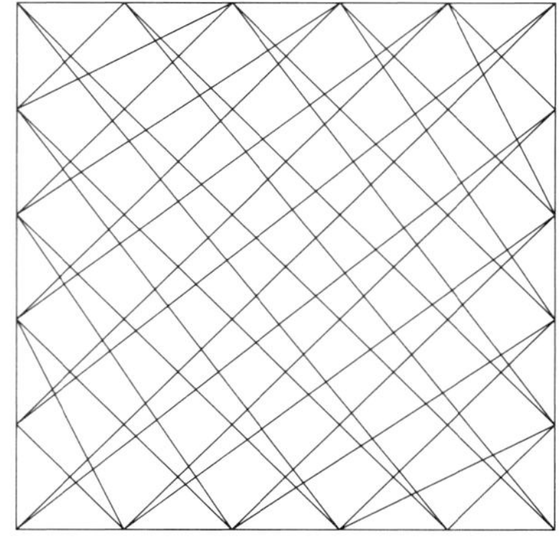

**66d**

↔ 10in (25.4cm) 500%

↔ 12in (30.5cm) 600%

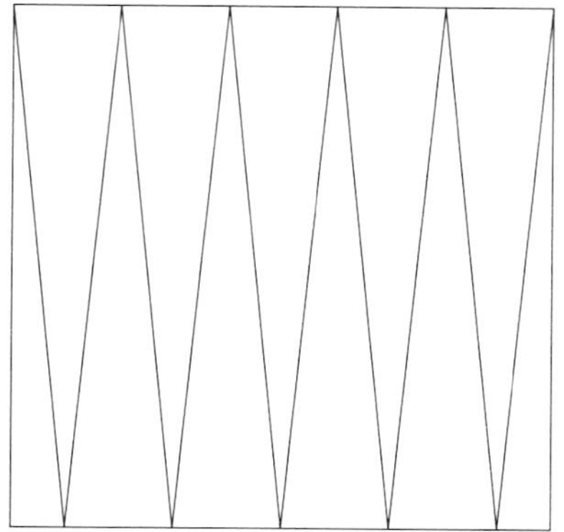

**67a**

⟼ 4in (10.2cm) 200%

⟼ 5in (12.7cm) 250%

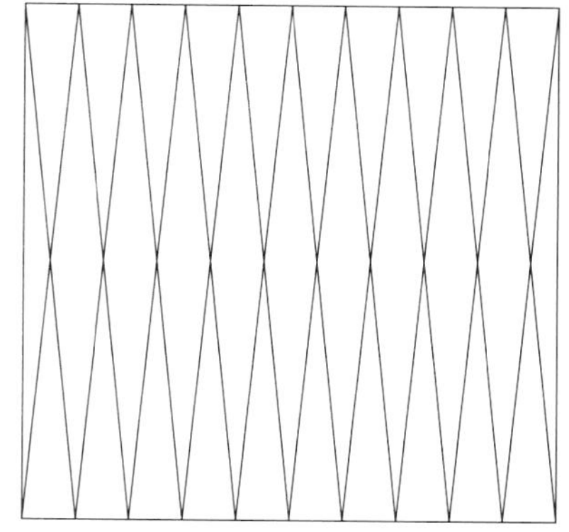

**67b**

⟼ 6in (15.25cm) 300%

⟼ 8in (20.3cm) 400%

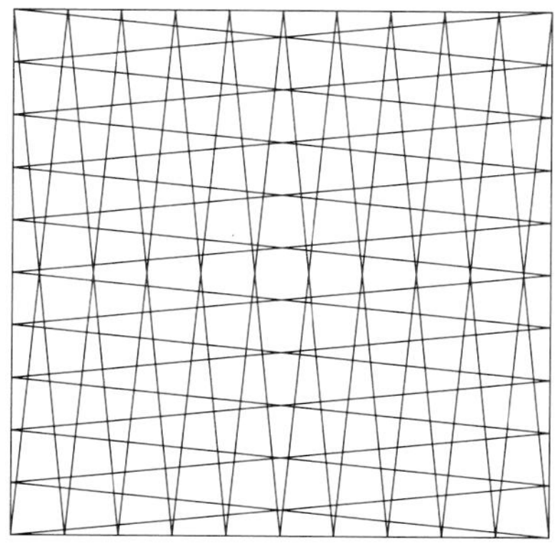

**67c**

⟼ 6in (15.25cm) 300%

⟼ 8in (20.3cm) 400%

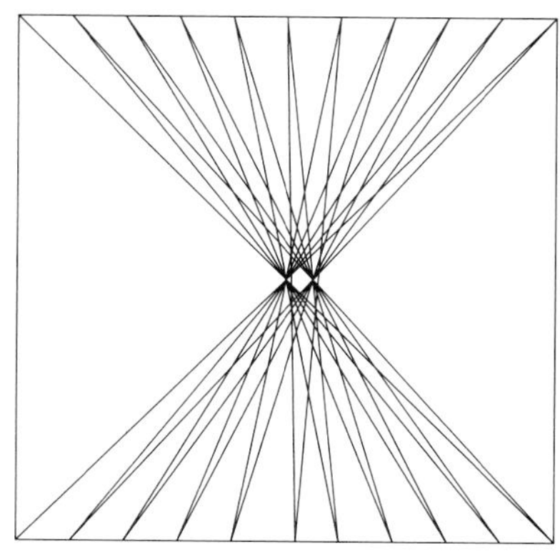

**68**

⟼ 10in (25.4cm) 500%

⟼ 12in (30.5cm) 600%

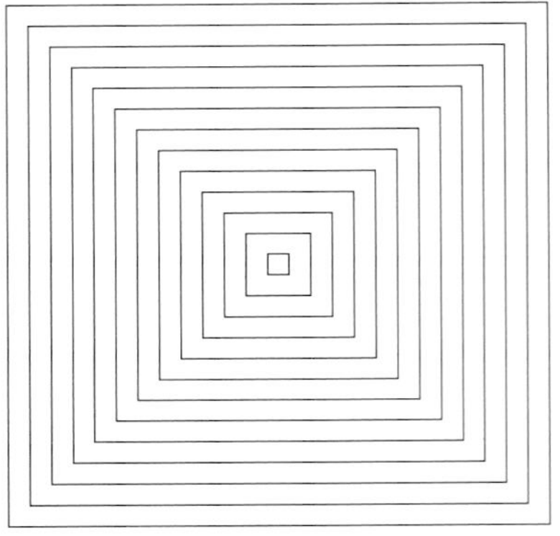

**69a** 

⟼ 4in (10.2cm) 200%

⟼ 5in (12.7cm) 250%

**69b**

⟼ 6in (15.25cm) 300%

⟼ 8in (20.3cm) 400%

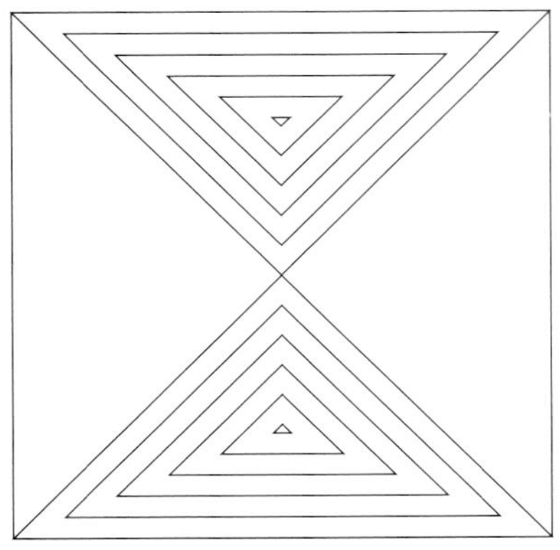

**70a**

⟼ 6in (15.25cm) 300%

⟼ 8in (20.3cm) 400%

**70b**

⟼ 8in (20.3cm) 400%

⟼ 10in (25.4cm) 500%

**71**

⟷ 8in (20.3cm) 400%

⟷ 10in (25.4cm) 500%

**72**

⟷ 6in (15.25cm) 300%

⟷ 8in (20.3cm) 400%

**73**

⟷ 8in (20.3cm) 400%

⟷ 10in (25.4cm) 500%

**74**

⟷ 12in (30.5cm) 600%

⟷ 15in (38.1cm) 750%

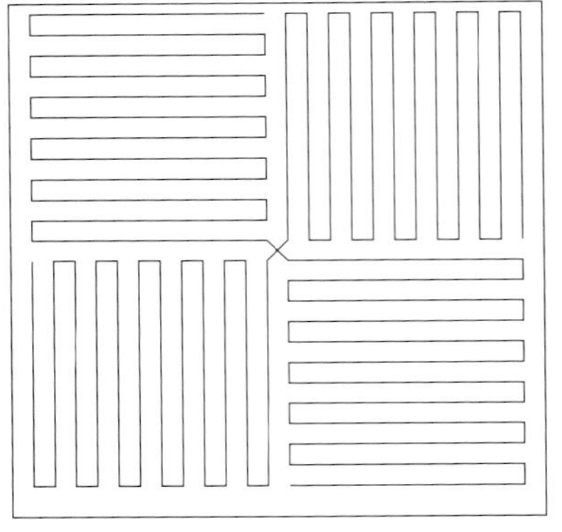

**75**

6in (15.25cm) 300%

8in (20.3cm) 400%

**76**

6in (15.25cm) 300%

8in (20.3cm) 400%

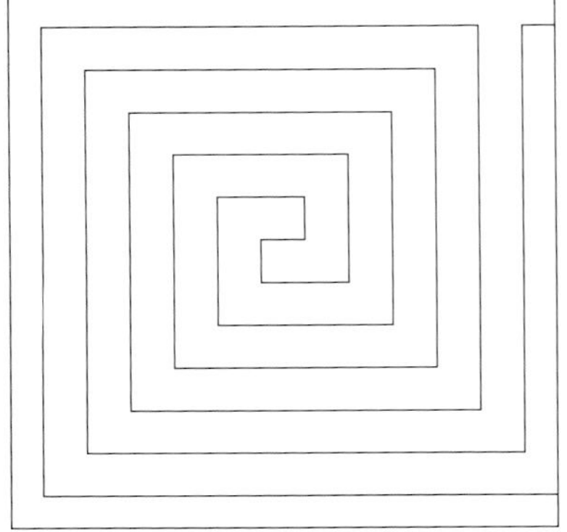

**77a**

4in (10.2cm) 200%

5in (12.7cm) 250%

**77b**

10in (25.4cm) 500%

12in (30.5cm) 600%

ALL PATTERNS ARE STANDARD 2IN (5CM) OR 4IN (10.2CM) UNLESS OTHERWISE STATED

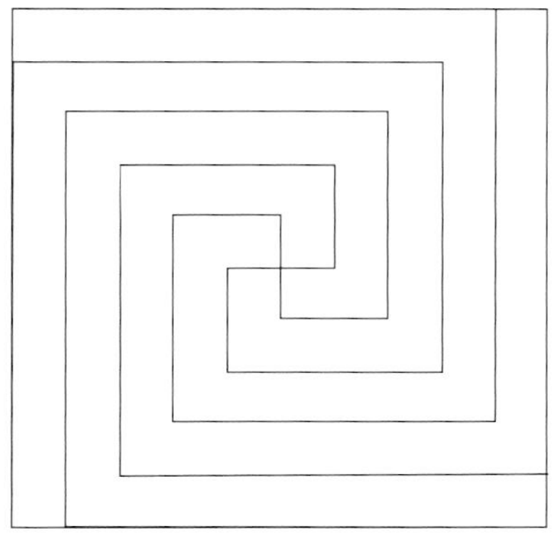

**78a**

6in (15.25cm) 300%

8in (20.3cm) 400%

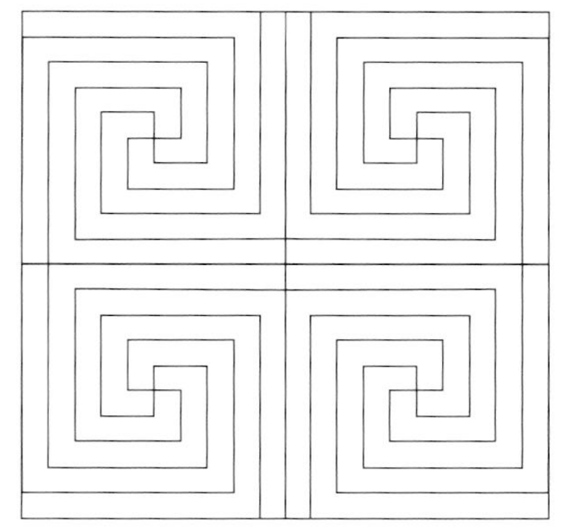

**78b**

12in (30.5cm) 600%

15in (38.1cm) 750%

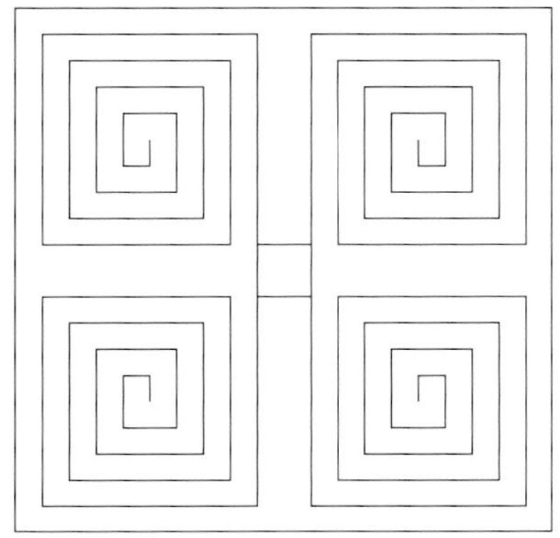

**79**

8in (20.3cm) 400%

10in (25.4cm) 500%

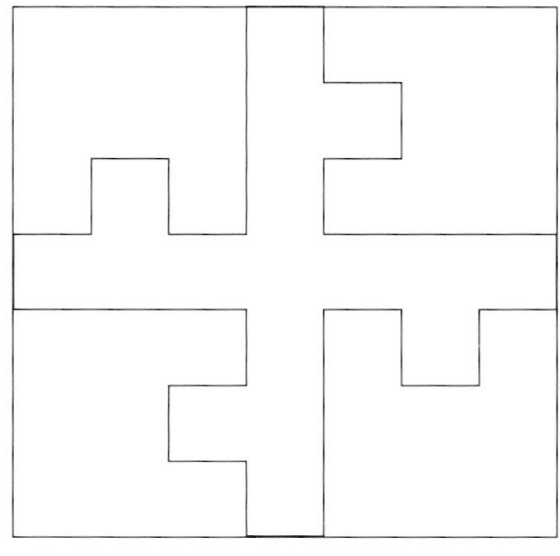

**80**

4in (10.2cm) 200%

5in (12.7cm) 250%

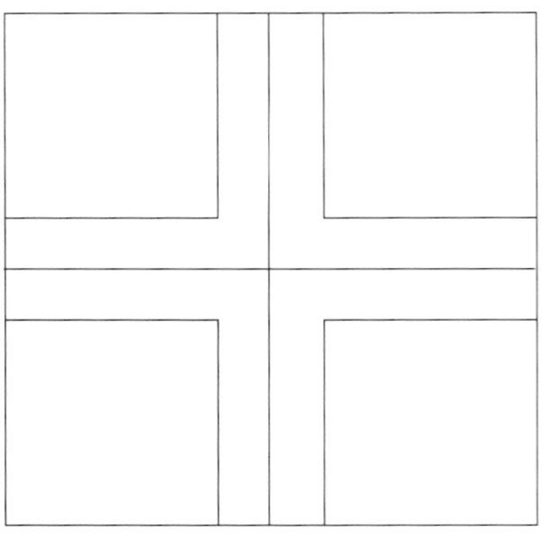

**81** 

5in (12.7cm) 250%

6in (15.25cm) 300%

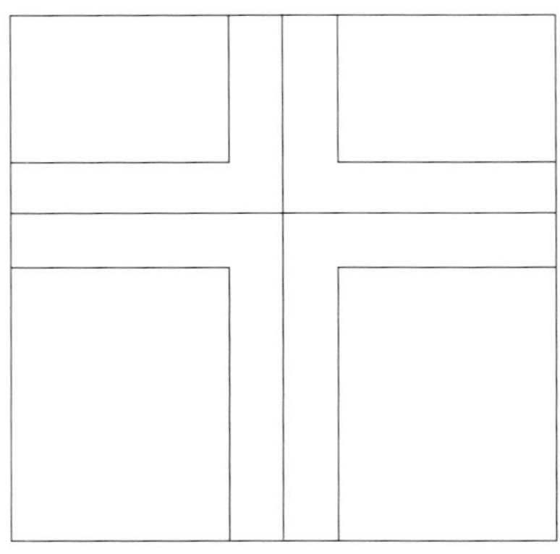

**82**

5in (12.7cm) 250%

6in (15.25cm) 300%

**83**

6in (15.25cm) 300%

8in (20.3cm) 400%

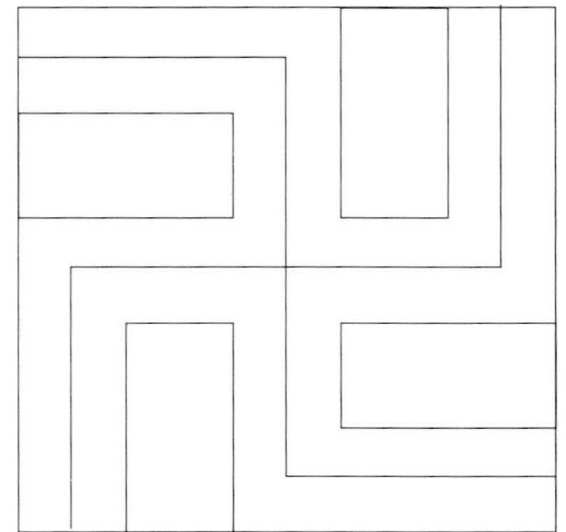

**84**

5in (12.7cm) 250%

6in (15.25cm) 300%

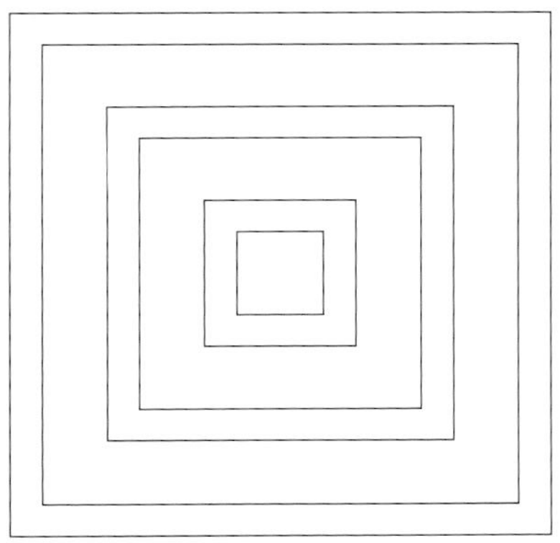

**85a**

⟷ 4in (10.2cm) 200%

⟷ 5in (12.7cm) 250%

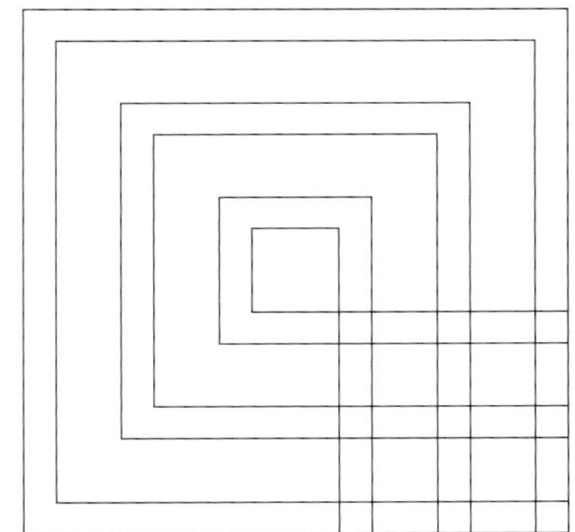

**85b**

⟷ 6in (15.25cm) 300%

⟷ 8in (20.3cm) 400%

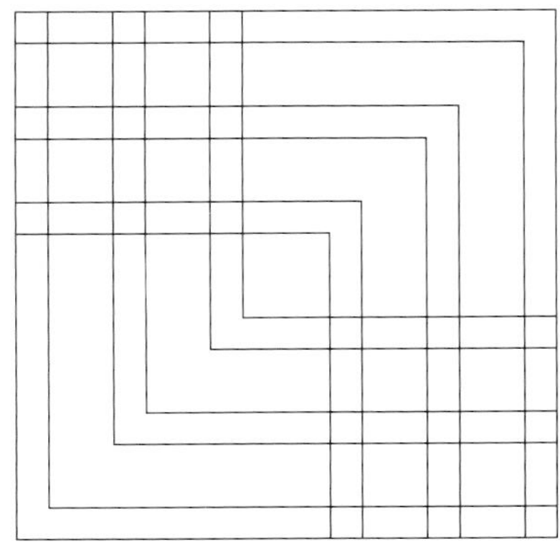

**85c**

⟷ 8in (20.3cm) 400%

⟷ 10in (25.4cm) 500%

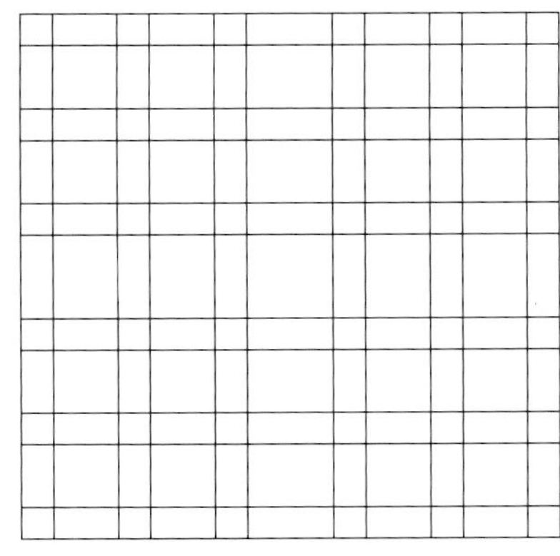

**85d**

⟷ 8in (20.3cm) 400%

⟷ 10in (25.4cm) 500%

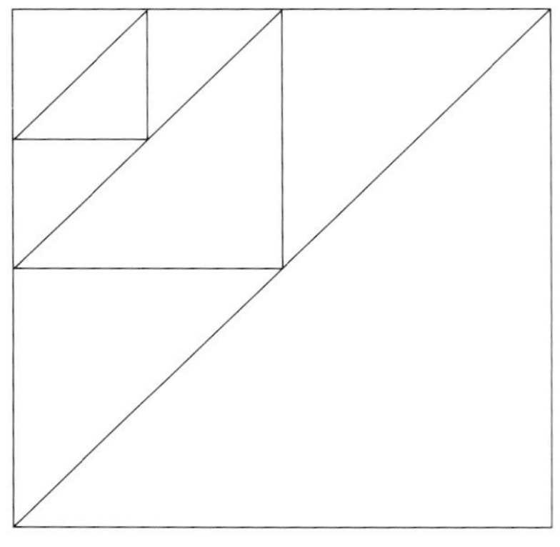

**86** 

⟼ 4in (10.2cm) 200%

⟼ 5in (12.7cm) 250%

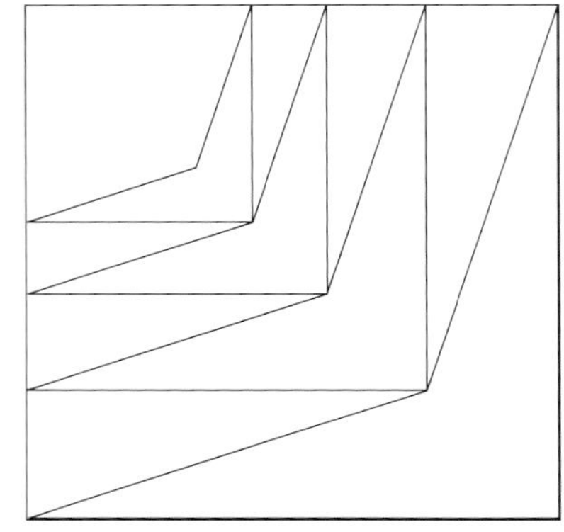

**87**

⟼ 6in (15.25cm) 300%

⟼ 8in (20.3cm) 400%

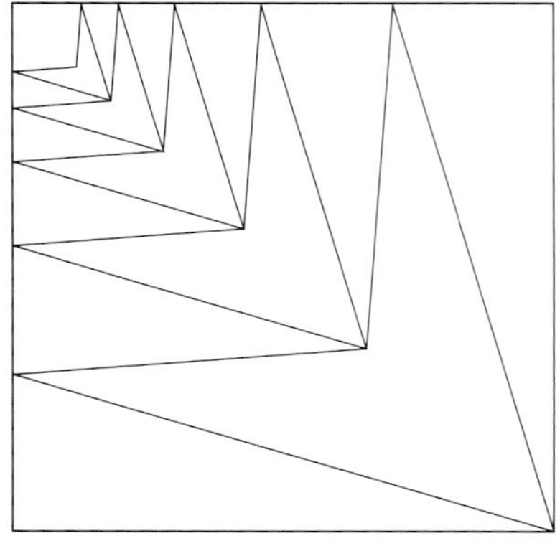

**88a**

⟼ 6in (15.25cm) 300%

⟼ 8in (20.3cm) 400%

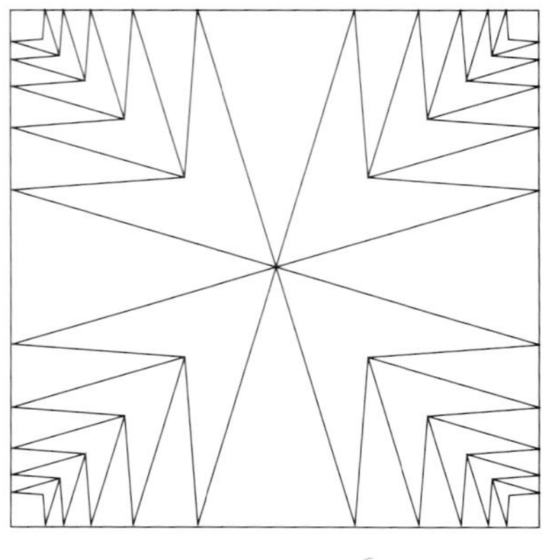

**88b**

⟼ 10in (25.4cm) 500%

⟼ 12in (30.5cm) 600%

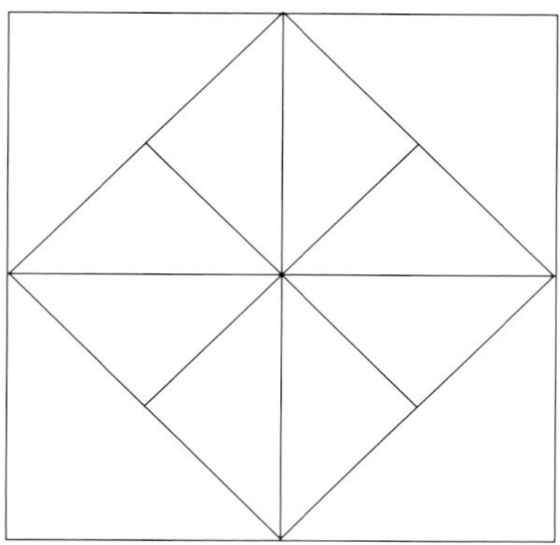

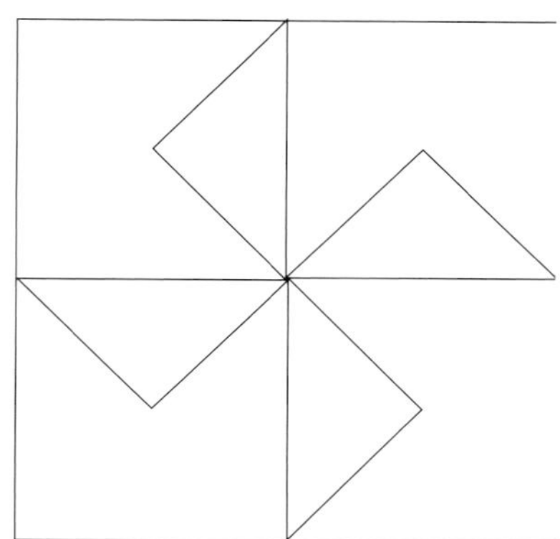

**89a**

↦ 4in (10.2cm) 200%

↦ 5in (12.7cm) 250%

**89b**

↦ 6in (15.25cm) 300%

↦ 8in (20.3cm) 400%

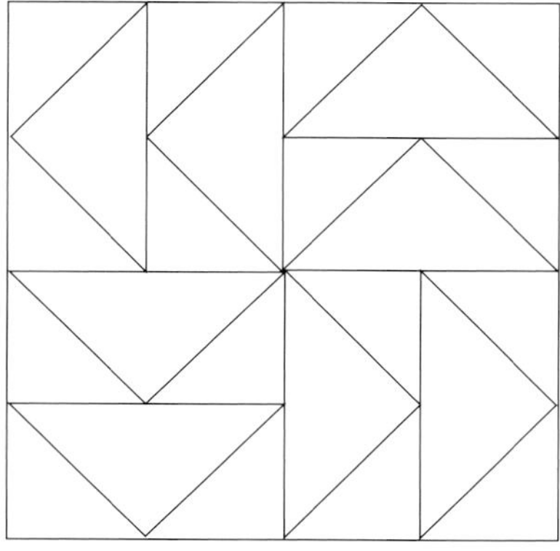

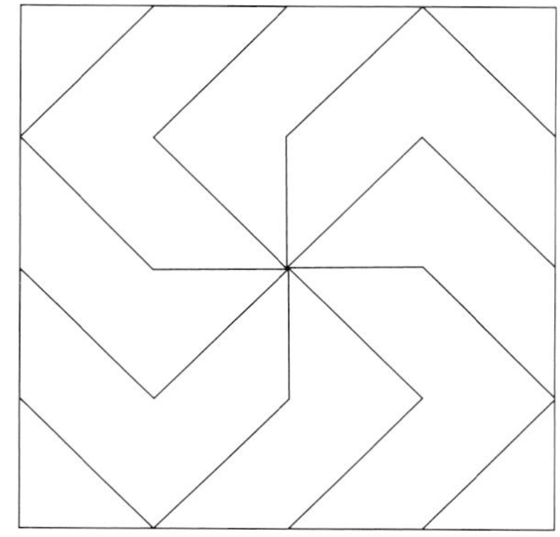

**90**

↦ 10in (25.4cm) 500%

↦ 12in (30.5cm) 600%

**91**

↦ 10in (25.4cm) 500%

↦ 12in (30.5cm) 600%

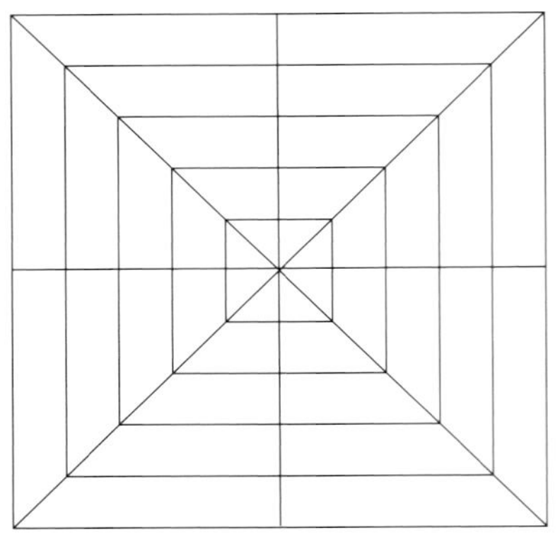

**92a** 

4in (10.2cm) 200%

5in (12.7cm) 250%

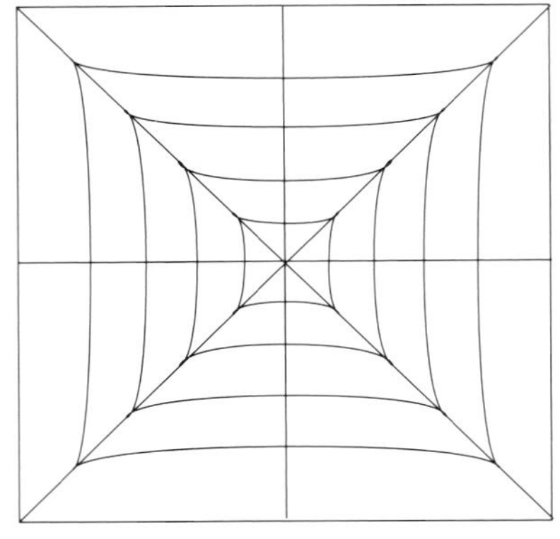

**92b**

6in (15.25cm) 300%

8in (20.3cm) 400%

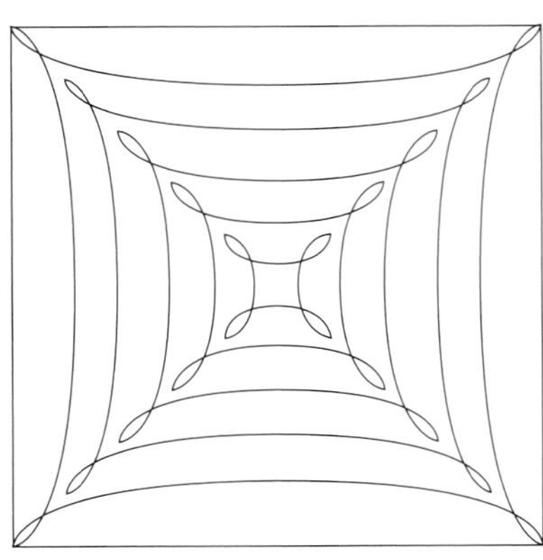

**93**

8in (20.3cm) 400%

10in (25.4cm) 500%

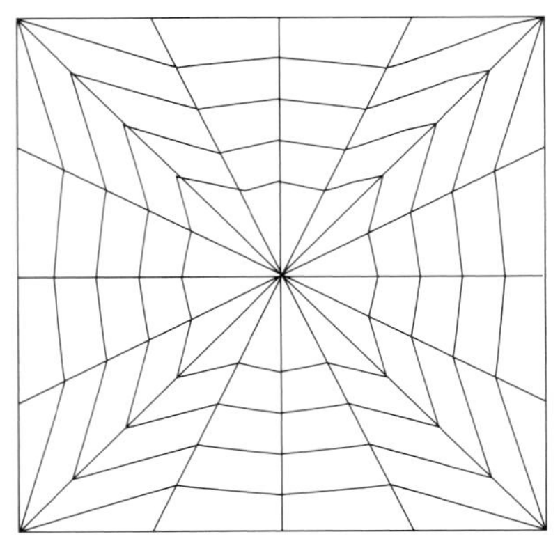

**94**

8in (20.3cm) 400%

10in (25.4cm) 500%

ALL PATTERNS ARE STANDARD 2IN (5CM) OR 4IN (10.2CM) UNLESS OTHERWISE STATED

**95**

4in (10.2cm) 200%

5in (12.7cm) 250%

**96**

6in (15.25cm) 300%

8in (20.3cm) 400%

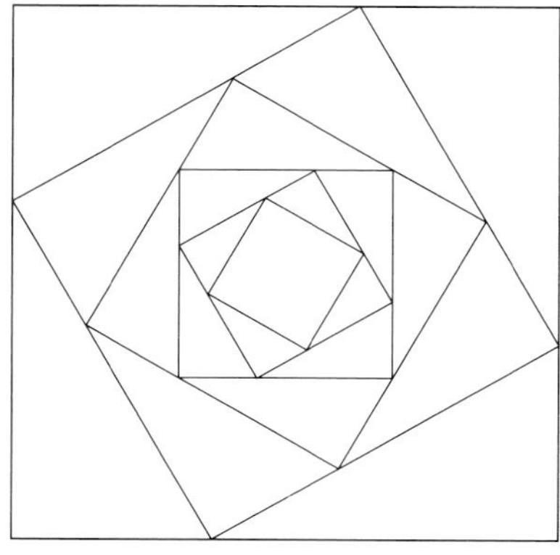

**97**

4in (10.2cm) 200%

5in (12.7cm) 250%

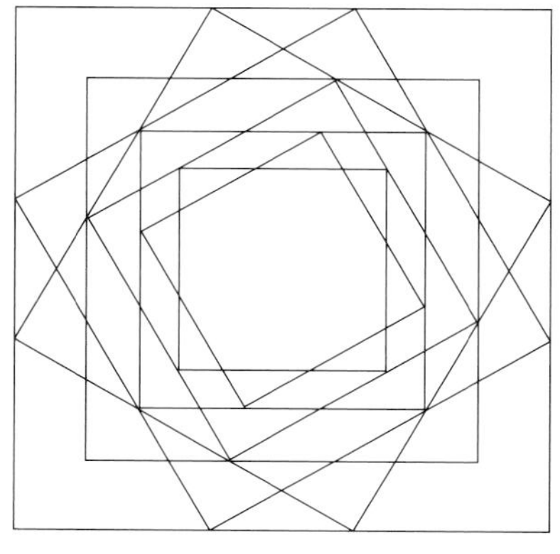

**98**

8in (20.3cm) 400%

10in (25.4cm) 500%

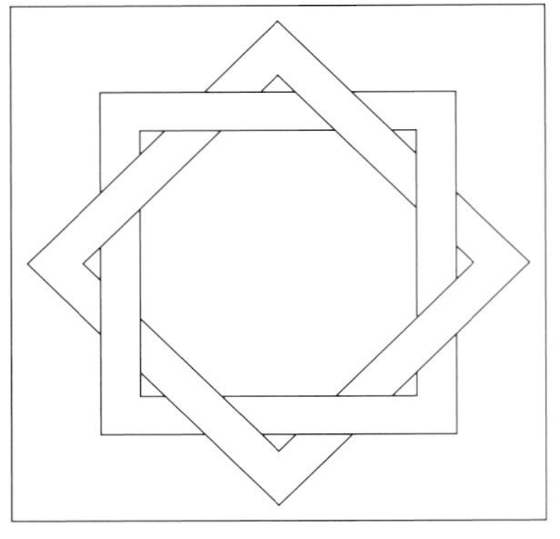

**99a**

6in (15.25cm) 300%

8in (20.3cm) 400%

**99b**

8in (20.3cm) 400%

10in (25.4cm) 500%

**99c**

10in (25.4cm) 500%

12in (30.5cm) 600%

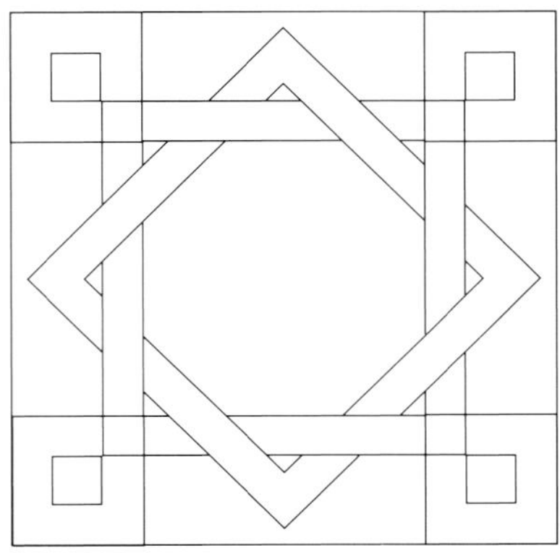

**100**

8in (20.3cm) 400%

10in (25.4cm) 500%

ALL PATTERNS ARE STANDARD 2IN (5CM) OR 4IN (10.2CM) UNLESS OTHERWISE STATED

**101**

8in (20.3cm) 400%

12in (30.5cm) 600%

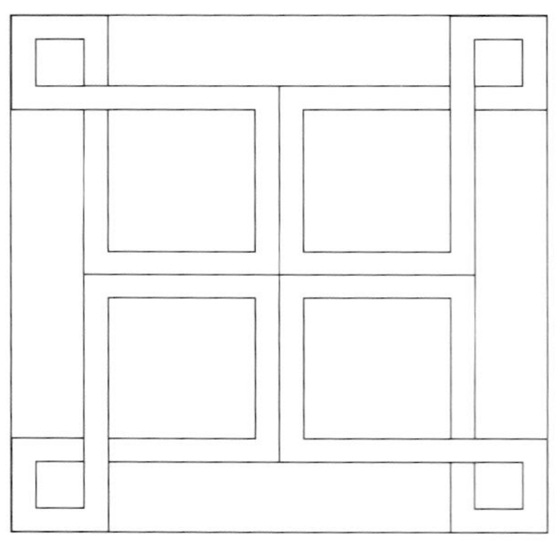

**102**

4in (10.2cm) 200%

5in (12.7cm) 250%

**103**

6in (15.25cm) 300%

8in (20.3cm) 400%

**104**

8in (20.3cm) 400%

10in (25.4cm) 500%

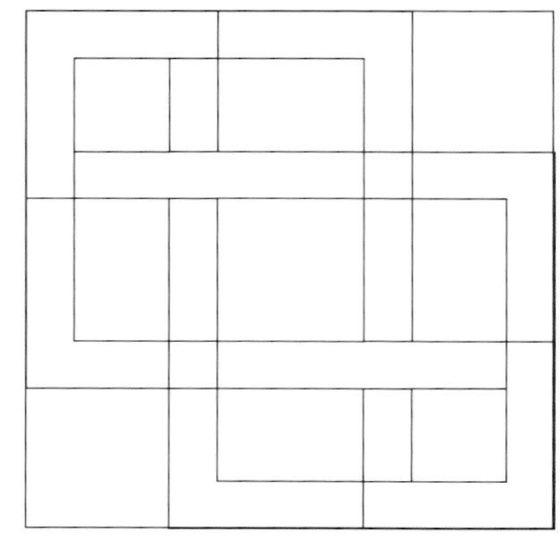

**105**

4in (10.2cm) 200%

5in (12.7cm) 250%

ALL PATTERNS ARE STANDARD 2IN (5CM) OR 4IN (10.2CM) UNLESS OTHERWISE STATED

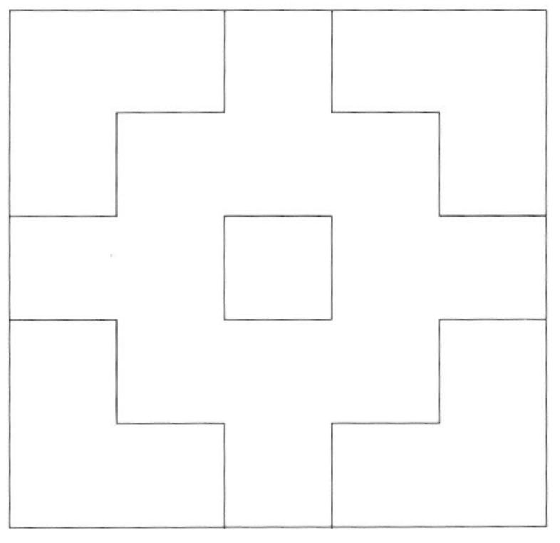

**106a**

⟼ 4in (10.2cm) 200%

⟼ 5in (12.7cm) 250%

**106b**

⟼ 6in (15.25cm) 300%

⟼ 8in (20.3cm) 400%

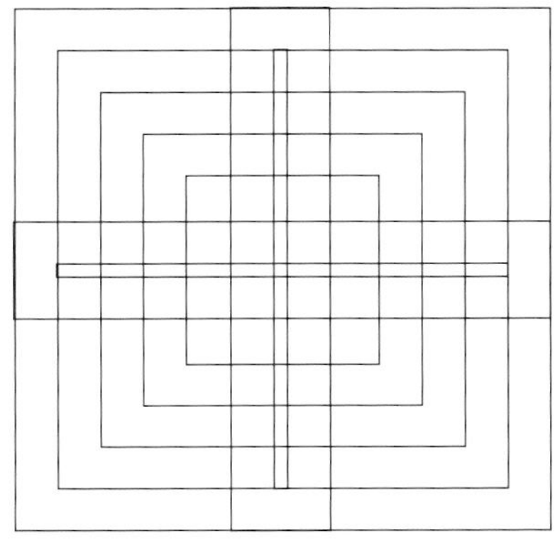

**107a**

⟼ 4in (10.2cm) 200%

⟼ 5in (12.7cm) 250%

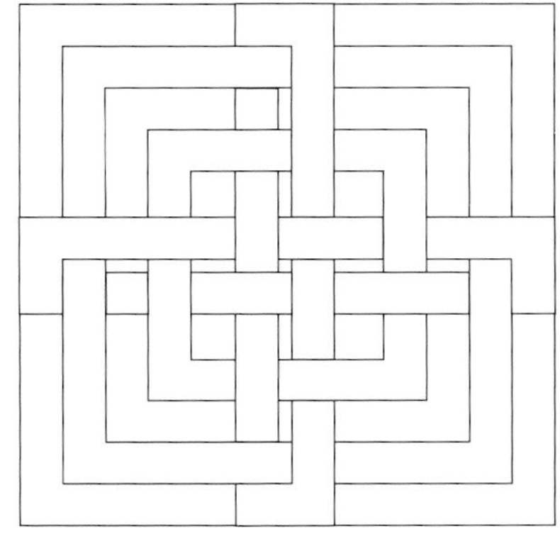

**107b**

⟼ 6in (15.25cm) 300%

⟼ 8in (20.3cm) 400%

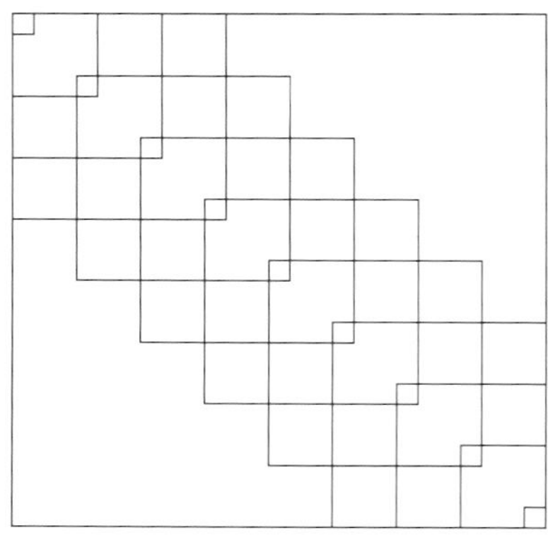

**108a** 

⟷ 6in (15.25cm) 300%

⟷ 8in (20.3cm) 400%

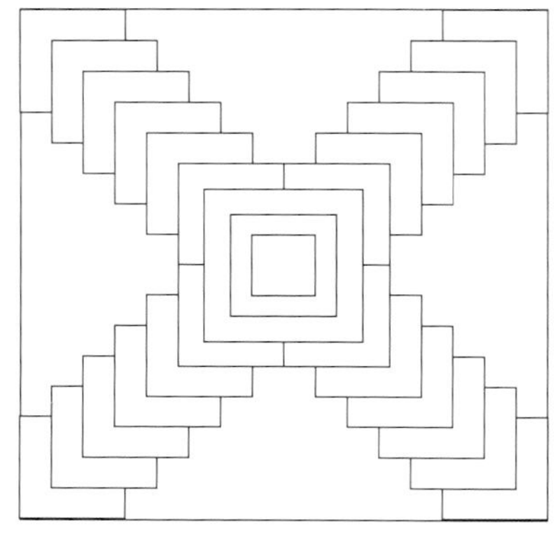

**108b**

⟷ 15in (38.1cm) 750%

⟷ 18in (45.7cm) 900%

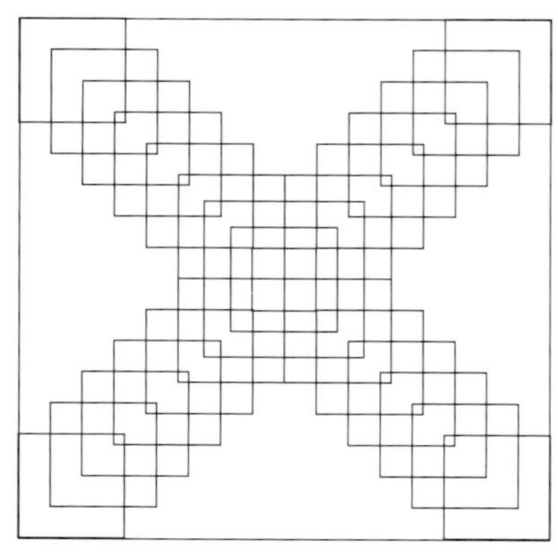

**108c**

⟷ 15in (38.1cm) 750%

⟷ 18in (45.7cm) 900%

**108d**

⟷ 15in (38.1cm) 750%

⟷ 18in (45.7cm) 900%

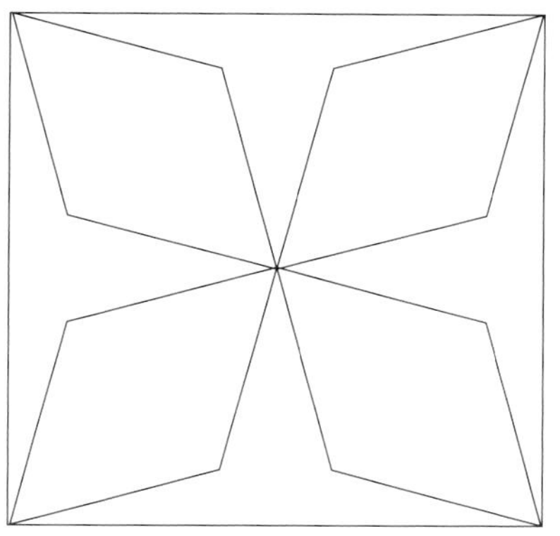

**109a** 

↦ 4in (10.2cm) 200%

↦ 5in (12.7cm) 250%

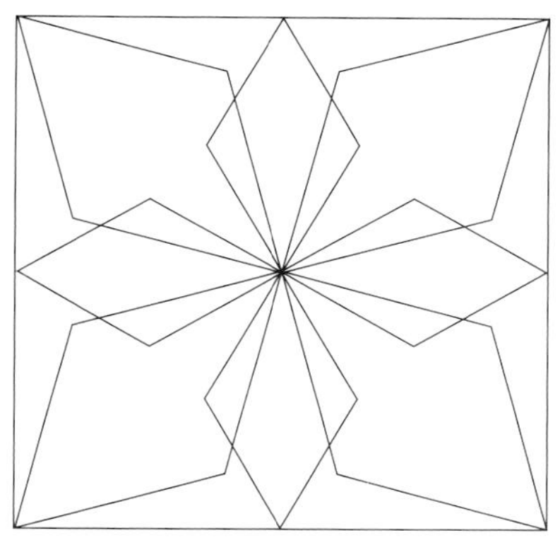

**109b**

↦ 6in (15.25cm) 300%

↦ 8in (20.3cm) 400%

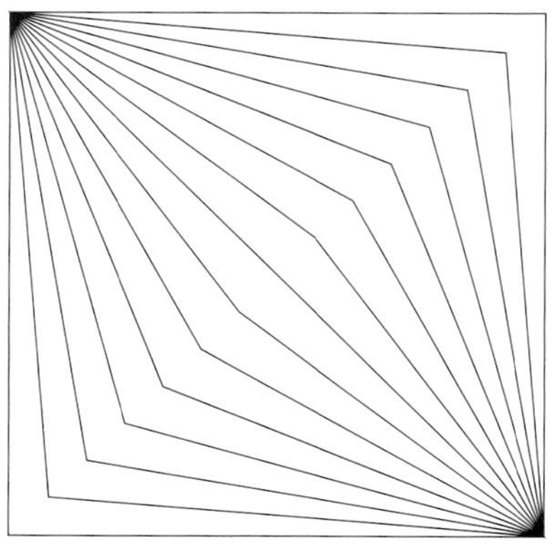

**110a**

↦ 6in (15.25cm) 300%

↦ 8in (20.3cm) 400%

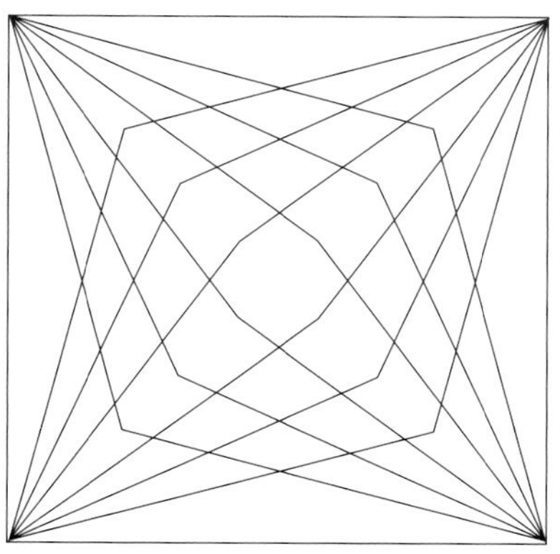

**110b**

↦ 8in (20.3cm) 400%

↦ 10in (25.4cm) 500%

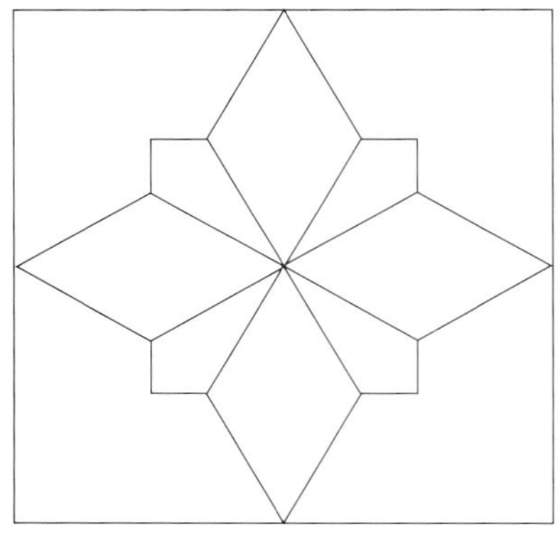

**111**

⟼ 4in (10.2cm) 200%

⟼ 5in (12.7cm) 250%

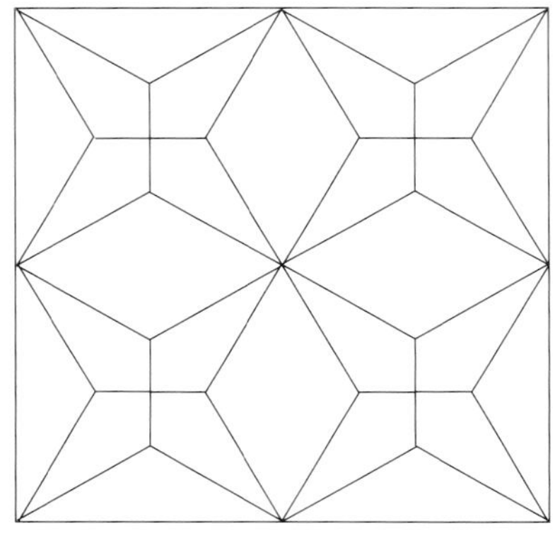

**112**

⟼ 6in (15.25cm) 300%

⟼ 8in (20.3cm) 400%

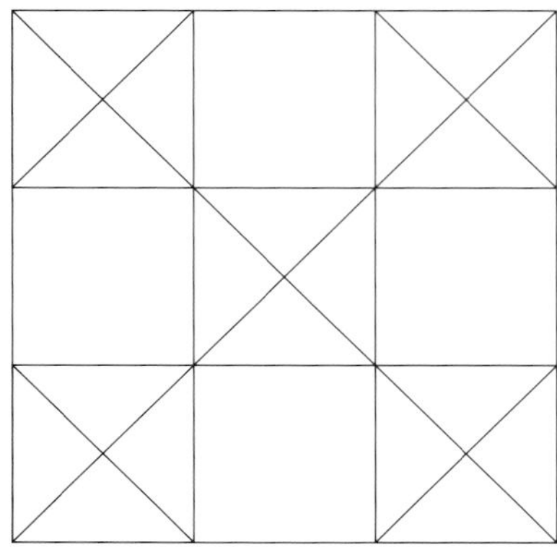

**113**

⟼ 6in (15.25cm) 300%

⟼ 8in (20.3cm) 400%

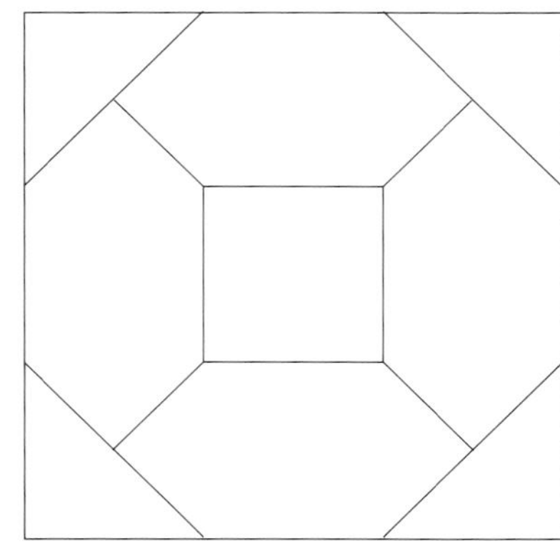

**114**

⟼ 4in (10.2cm) 200%

⟼ 5in (12.7cm) 250%

ALL PATTERNS ARE STANDARD 2IN (5CM) OR 4IN (10.2CM) UNLESS OTHERWISE STATED

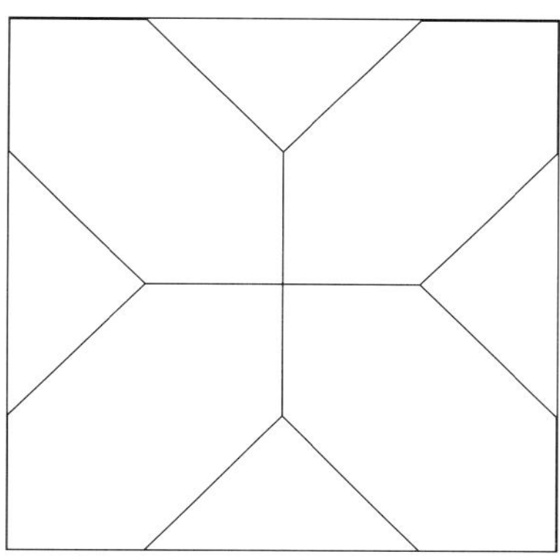

**115**

⟷4in (10.2cm) 200%

⟷5in (12.7cm) 250%

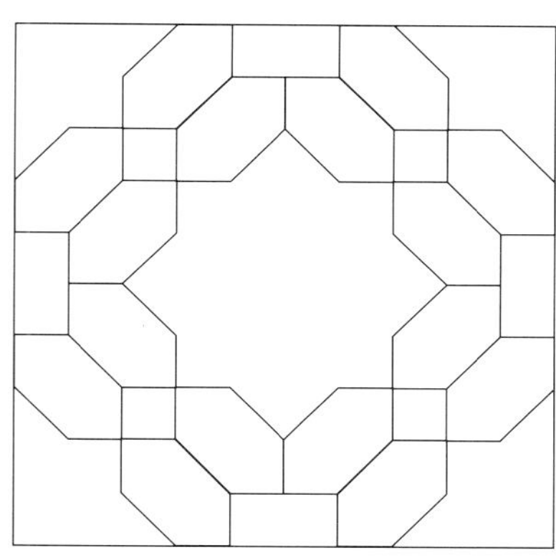

**116**

⟷8in (20.3cm) 400%

⟷10in (25.4cm) 500%

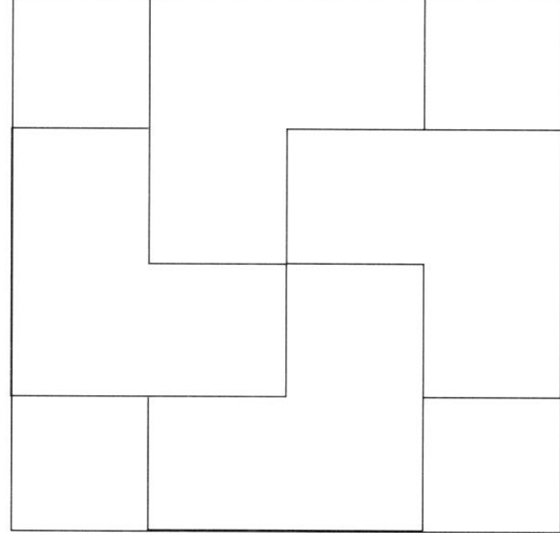

**117a**

⟷4in (10.2cm) 200%

⟷5in (12.7cm) 250%

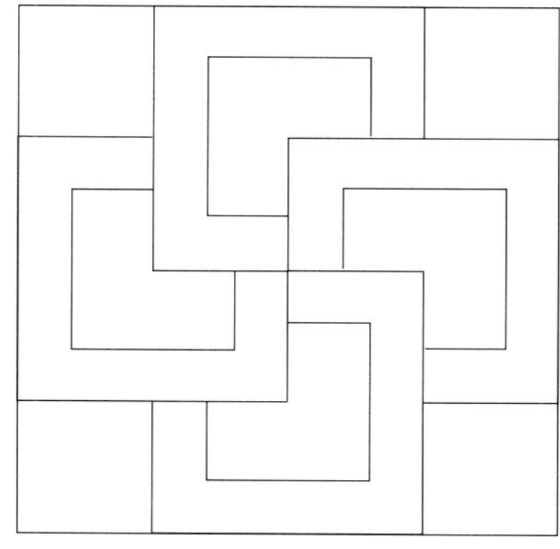

**117b**

⟷6in (15.25cm) 300%

⟷8in (20.3cm) 400%

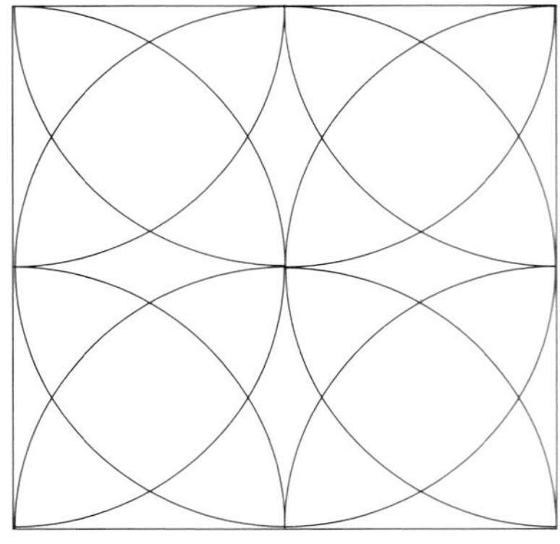

**118a**

↦ 6in (15.25cm) 300%

↦ 8in (20.3cm) 400%

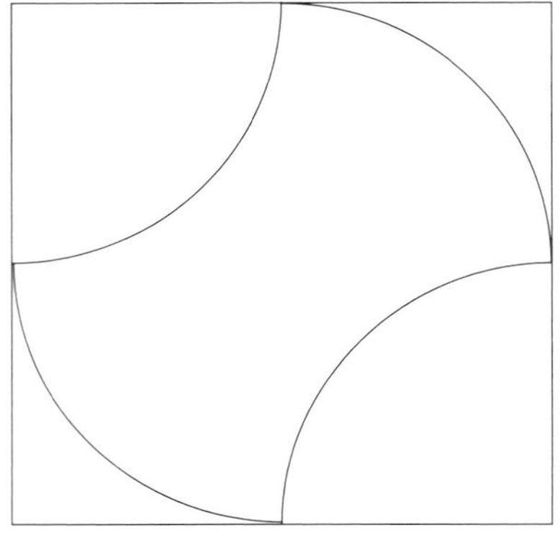

**118b**

↦ 4in (10.2cm) 200%

↦ 5in (12.7cm) 250%

**118c**

↦ 6in (15.25cm) 300%

↦ 8in (20.3cm) 400%

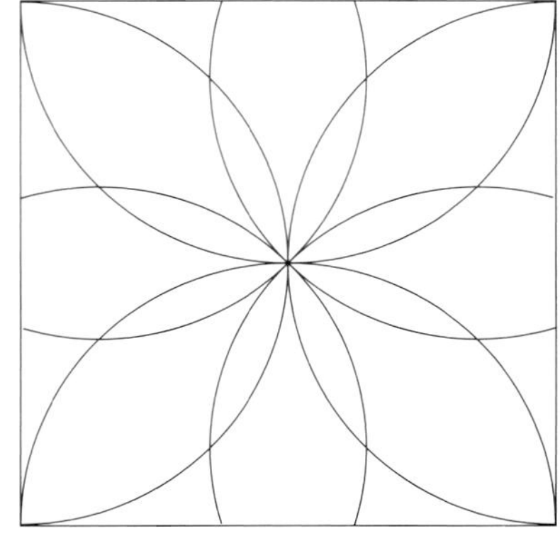

**118d**

↦ 8in (20.3cm) 400%

↦ 10in (25.4cm) 500%

ALL PATTERNS ARE STANDARD 2IN (5CM) OR 4IN (10.2CM) UNLESS OTHERWISE STATED

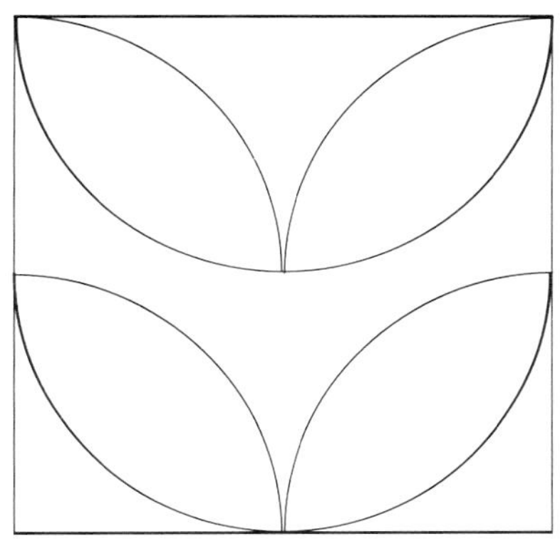

**118e**

4in (10.2cm) 200%

5in (12.7cm) 250%

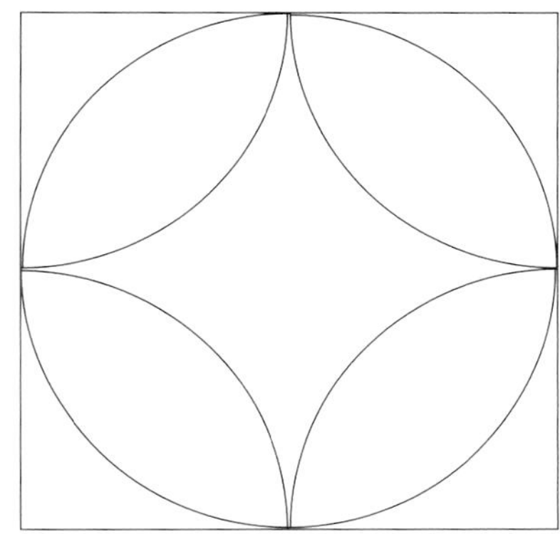

**118f**

4in (10.2cm) 200%

5in (12.7cm) 250%

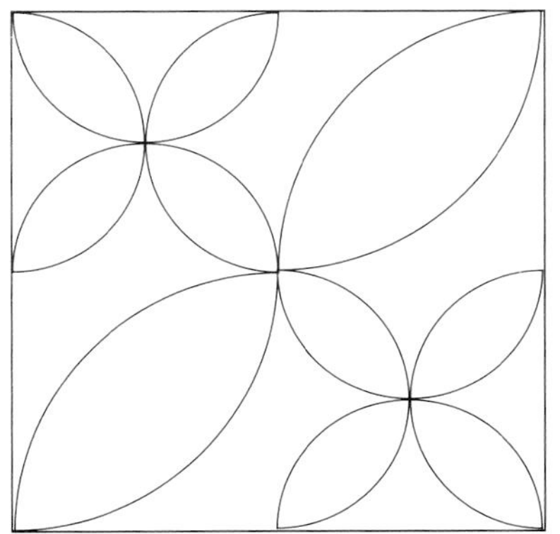

**119**

6in (15.25cm) 300%

8in (20.3cm) 400%

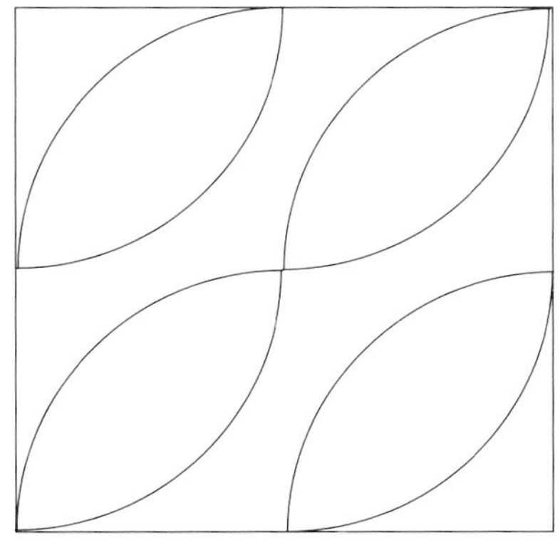

**120**

4in (10.2cm) 200%

5in (12.7cm) 250%

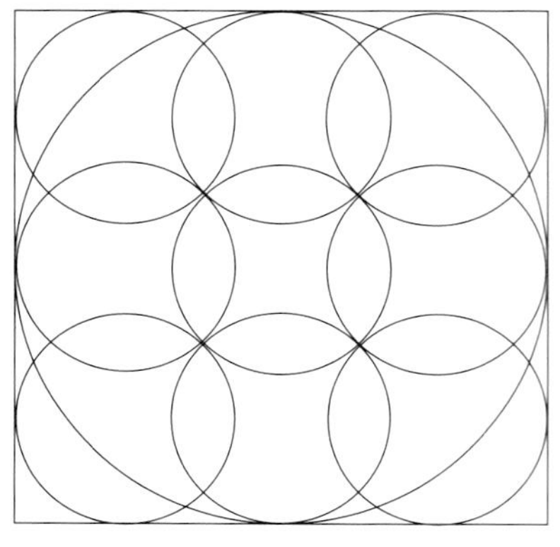

**121**

⟼ 6in (15.25cm) 300%

⟼ 8in (20.3cm) 400%

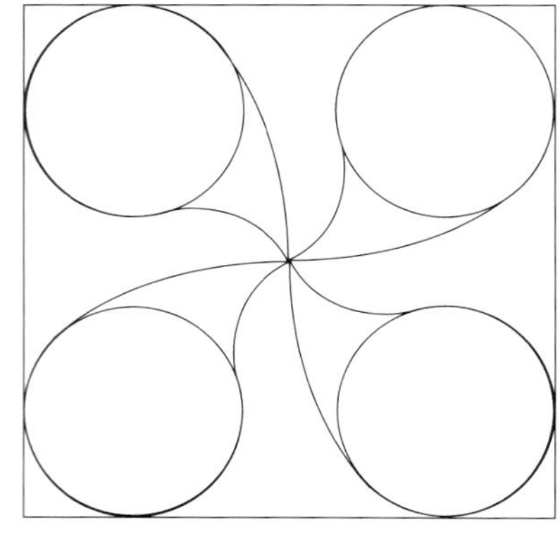

**122**

⟼ 6in (15.25cm) 300%

⟼ 8in (20.3cm) 400%

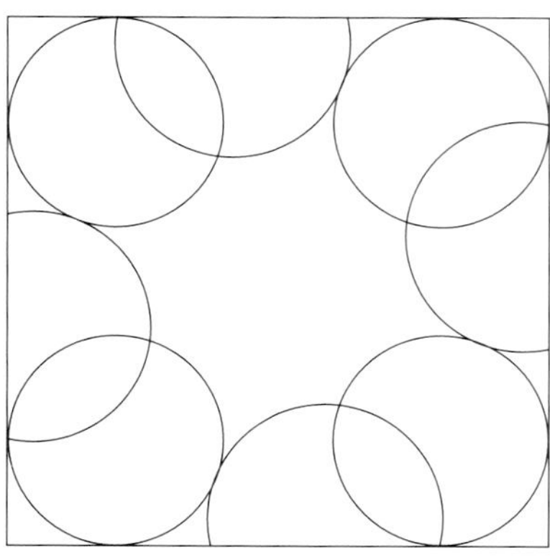

**123a**

⟼ 6in (15.25cm) 300%

⟼ 8in (20.3cm) 400%

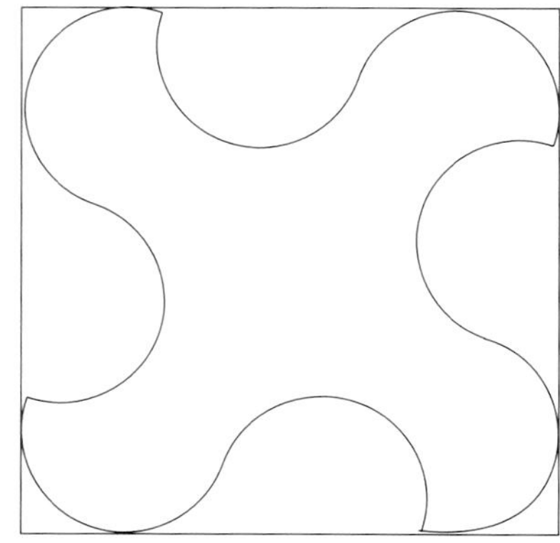

**123b**

⟼ 4in (10.2cm) 200%

⟼ 5in (12.7cm) 250%

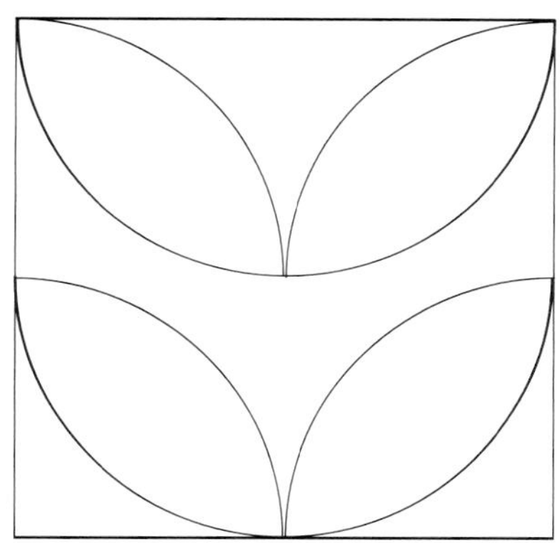

**124**

6in (15.25cm) 300%

8in (20.3cm) 400%

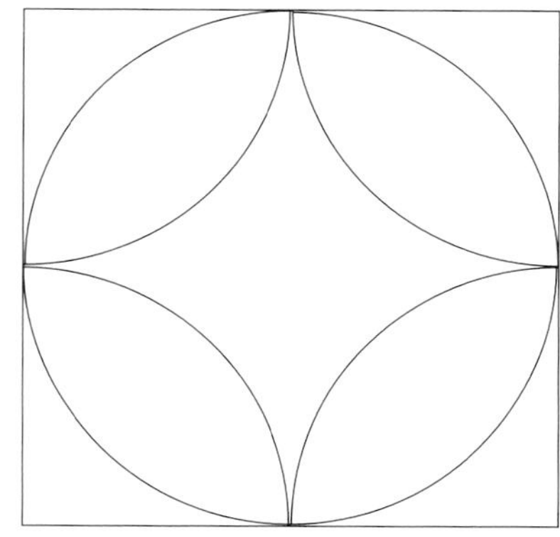

**125**

6in (15.25cm) 300%

8in (20.3cm) 400%

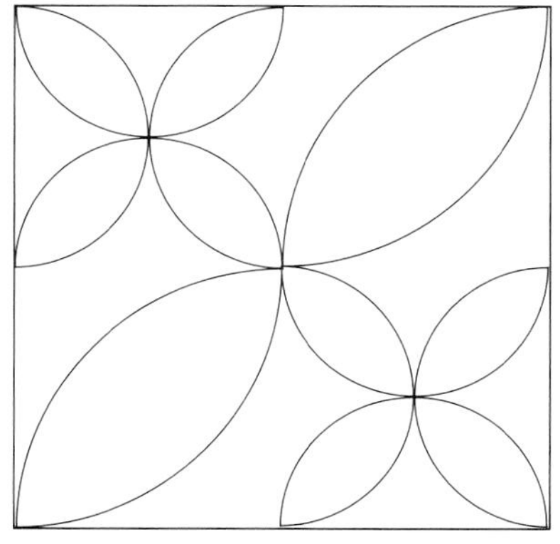

**126**

10in (25.4cm) 500%

12in (30.5cm) 600%

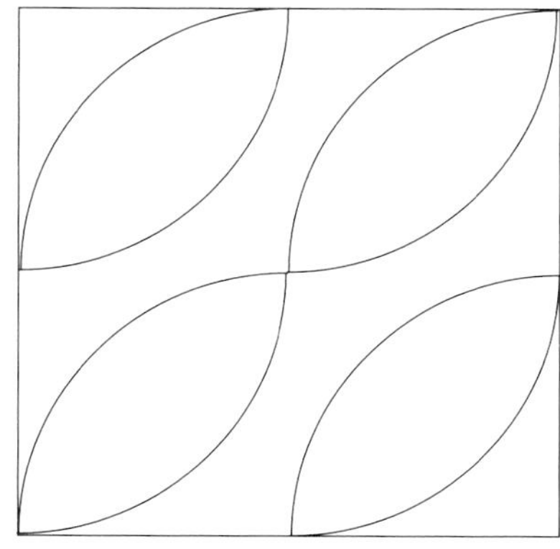

**127**

6in (15.25cm) 300%

8in (20.3cm) 400%

**128**

↦ 4in (10.2cm) 200%

↦ 5in (12.7cm) 250%

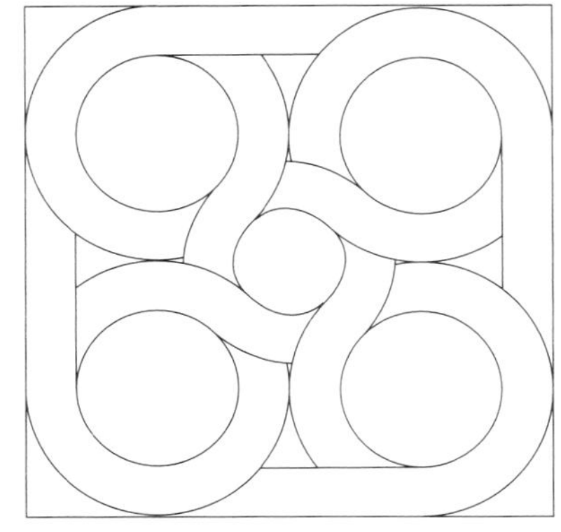

**129**

↦ 6in (15.25cm) 300%

↦ 8in (20.3cm) 400%

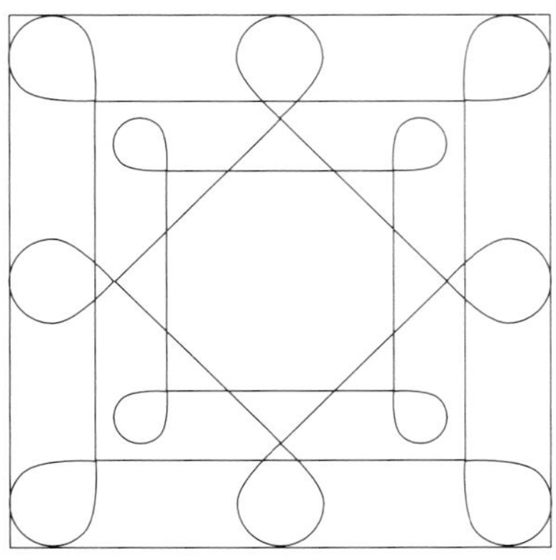

**130**

↦ 6in (15.25cm) 300%

↦ 8in (20.3cm) 400%

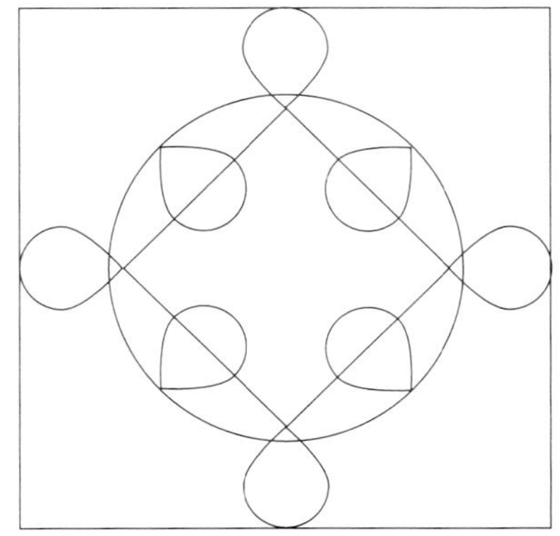

**131**

↦ 6in (15.25cm) 300%

↦ 8in (20.3cm) 400%

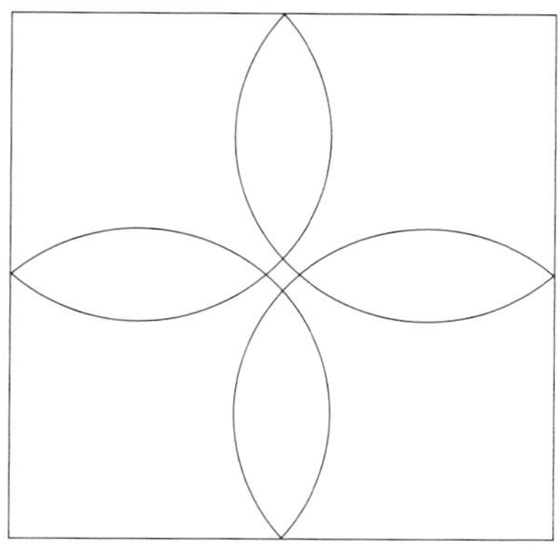

**132**

⟷ 4in (10.2cm) 200%

⟷ 5in (12.7cm) 250%

**133a**

⟷ 6in (15.25cm) 300%

⟷ 8in (20.3cm) 400%

**133b**

⟷ 10in (25.4cm) 500%

⟷ 12in (30.5cm) 600%

**133c**

⟷ 6in (15.25cm) 300%

⟷ 8in (20.3cm) 400%

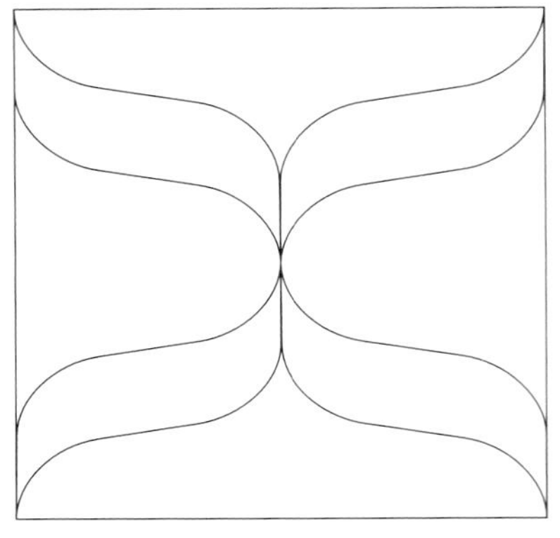

**134a**

⟷ 4in (10.2cm) 200%

⟷ 5in (12.7cm) 250%

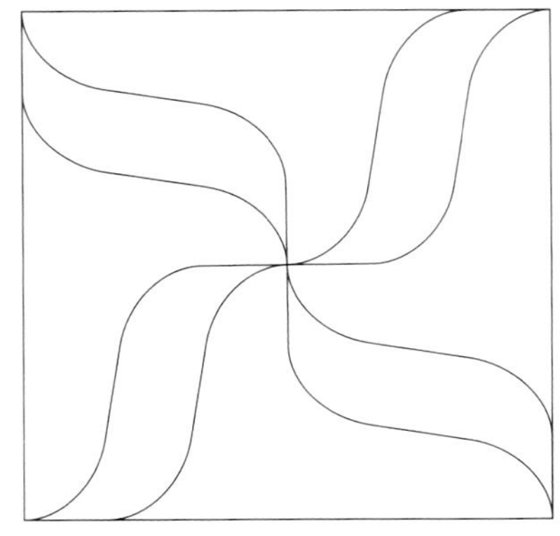

**134b**

⟷ 6in (15.25cm) 300%

⟷ 8in (20.3cm) 400%

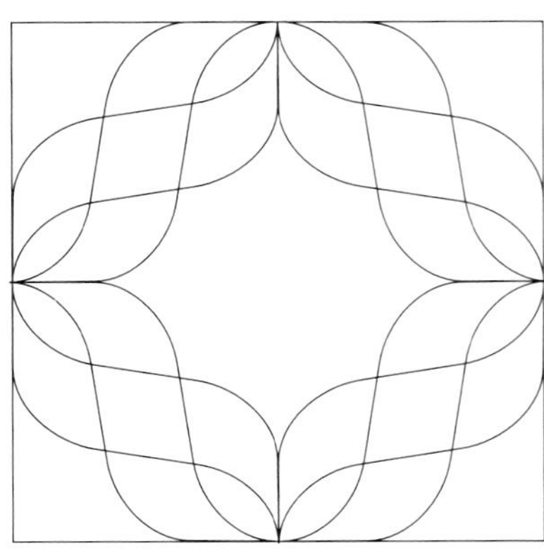

**134c**

⟷ 8in (20.3cm) 400%

⟷ 10in (25.4cm) 500%

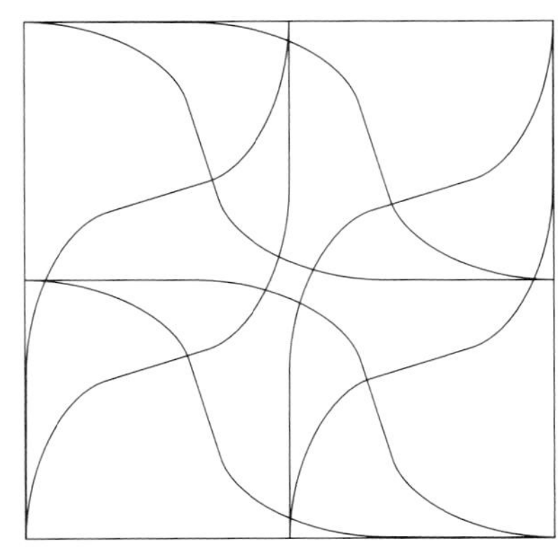

**134d**

⟷ 6in (15.25cm) 300%

⟷ 8in (20.3cm) 400%

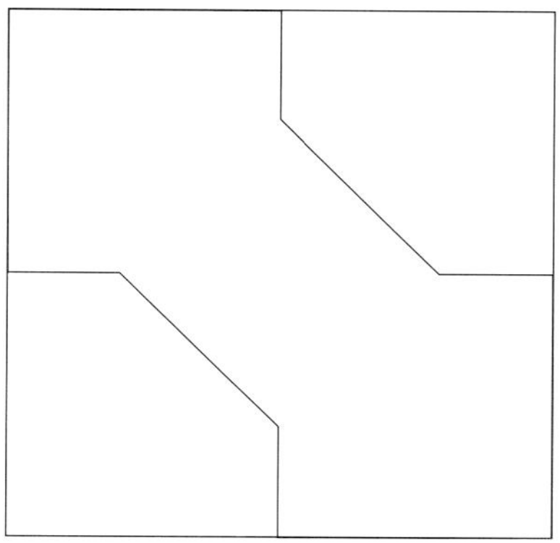

**135a**

↦ 4in (10.2cm) 200%

↦ 5in (12.7cm) 250%

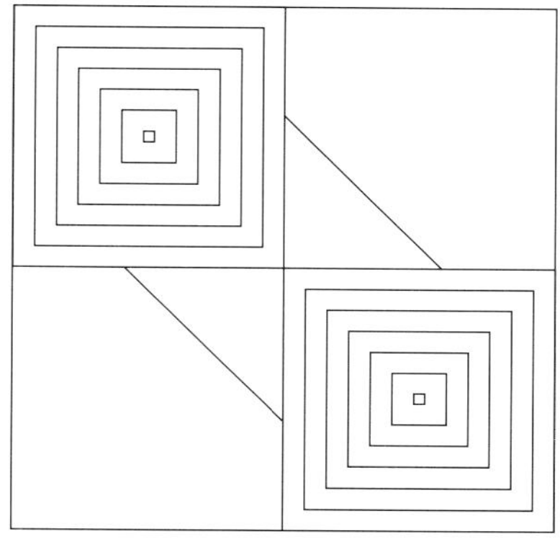

**135b**

↦ 6in (15.25cm) 300%

↦ 8in (20.3cm) 400%

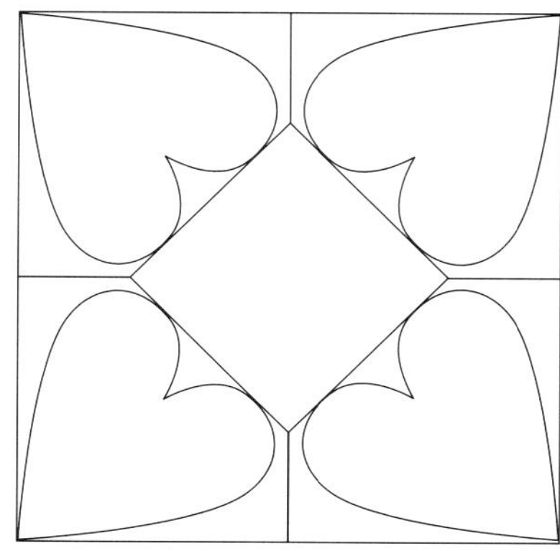

**135c**

↦ 4in (10.2cm) 200%

↦ 5in (12.7cm) 250%

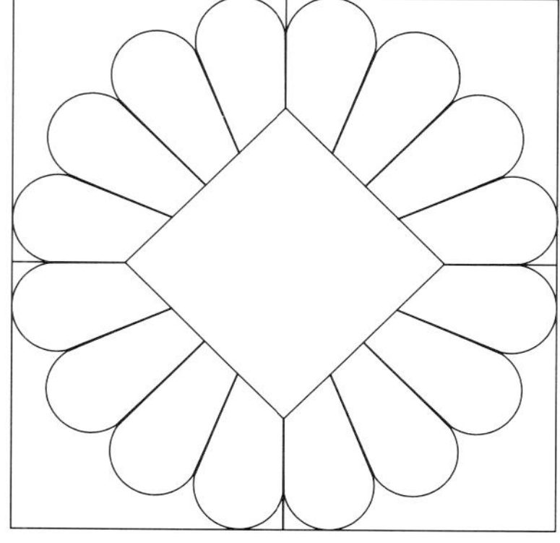

**135d**

↦ 6in (15.25cm) 300%

↦ 8in (20.3cm) 400%

# Diamonds and kites

Diamonds and kites can be used as single designs within other shapes or as a repeat pattern. The diamond in particular is often found in patchwork quilting designs.

## Diamonds

Diamonds are made up of two equilateral triangles base to base. For more ideas for quilting designs look at equilateral triangles (pages 40–49). Because equilateral triangles rotated around a center point create a polygon, look also at the hexagon designs (pages 105–109). To adapt a square design to a diamond shape, see page 37.

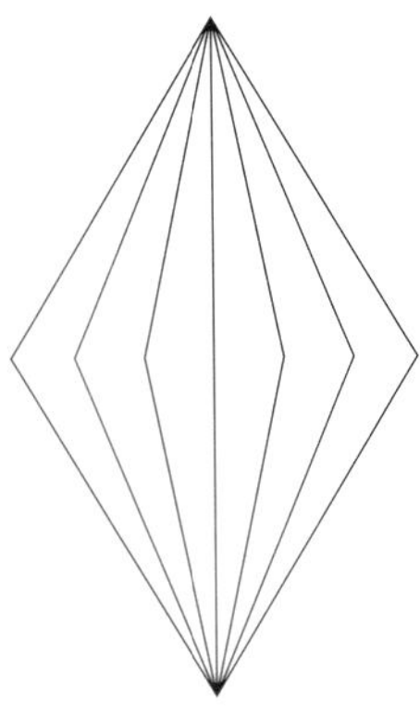

**136**

4in (10.2cm) 200%

6in (15.25cm) 300%

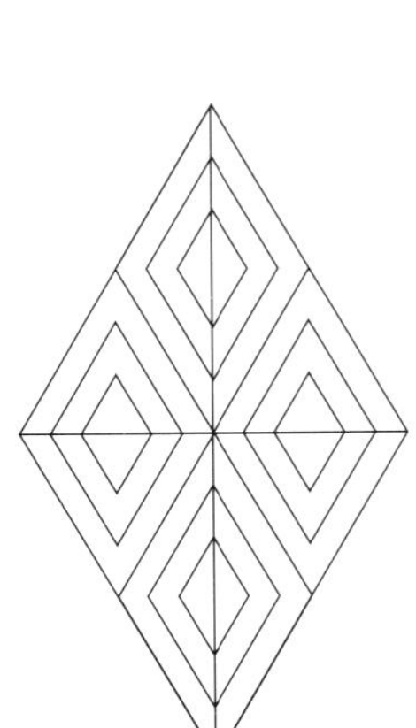

**137a**

8in (20.3cm) 400%

12in (30.5cm) 600%

**137b**

6in (15.25cm) 300%

8in (20.3cm) 400%

**138a**

6in (15.25cm) 300%

8in (20.3cm) 400%

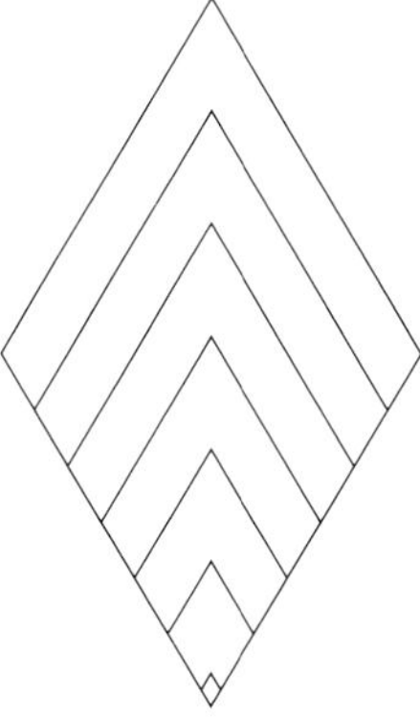

**138b**

6in (15.25cm) 300%

8in (20.3cm) 400%

**139**

6in (15.25cm) 300%

8in (20.3cm) 400%

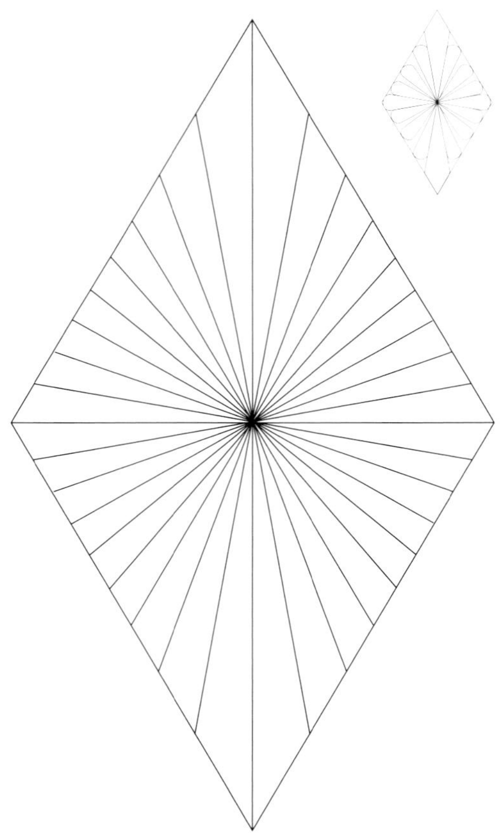

**140**

⟷ (2½in (6.4cm)) to 6in (15.25cm) 240%

⟷ (2½in (6.4cm)) to 8in (20.3cm) 320%

**141**

(2½in (6.4cm)) to 6in (15.25cm) 240%

(2½in (6.4cm)) to 10in (25.4cm) 400%

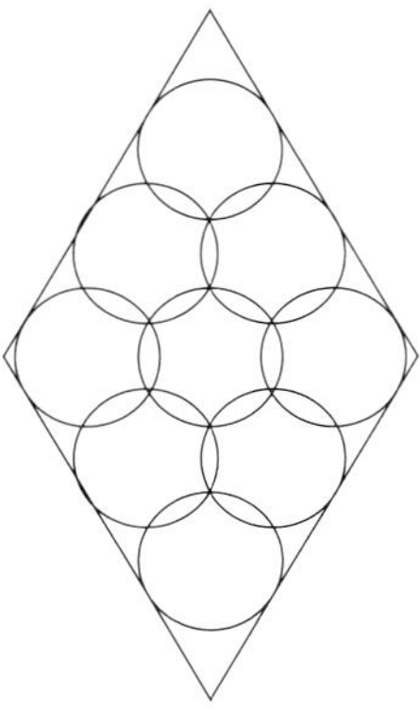

**142**

6in (15.25cm) 300%

12in (30.5cm) 600%

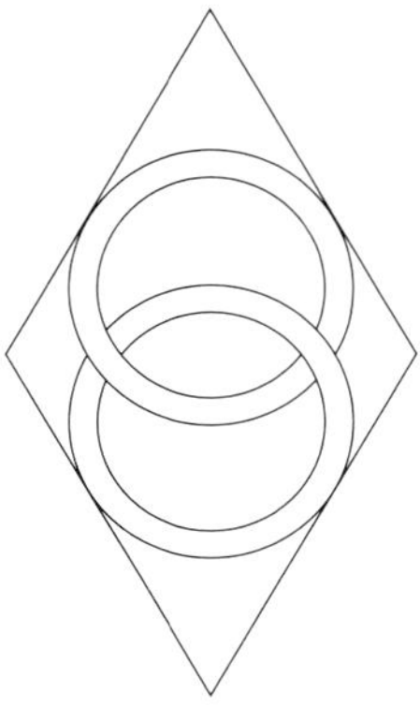

**143**

8in (20.3cm) 400%

10in (25.4cm) 500%

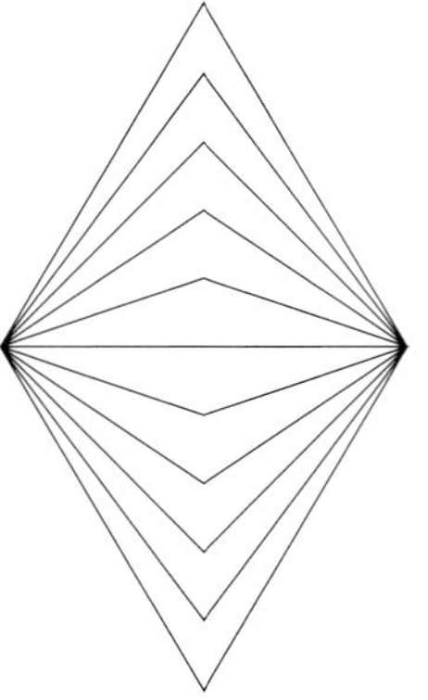

**144a**

5in (12.7cm) 250%

8in (20.3cm) 400%

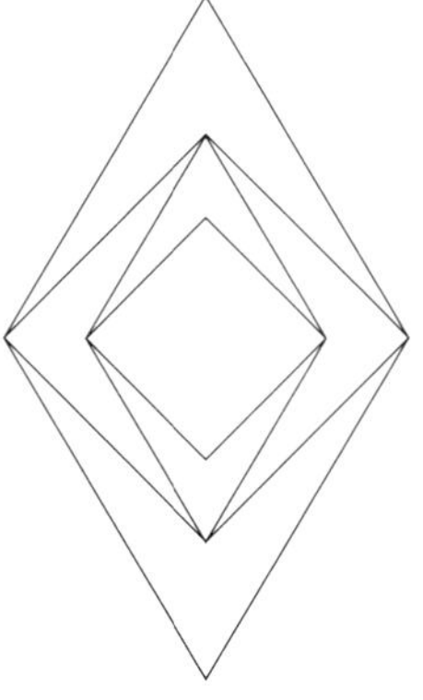

**144b**

6in (15.25cm) 300%

8in (20.3cm) 400%

**145**

(2½in (6.4cm)) to 6in (15.25cm) 240%

(2½in (6.4cm)) to 8in (20.3cm) 320%

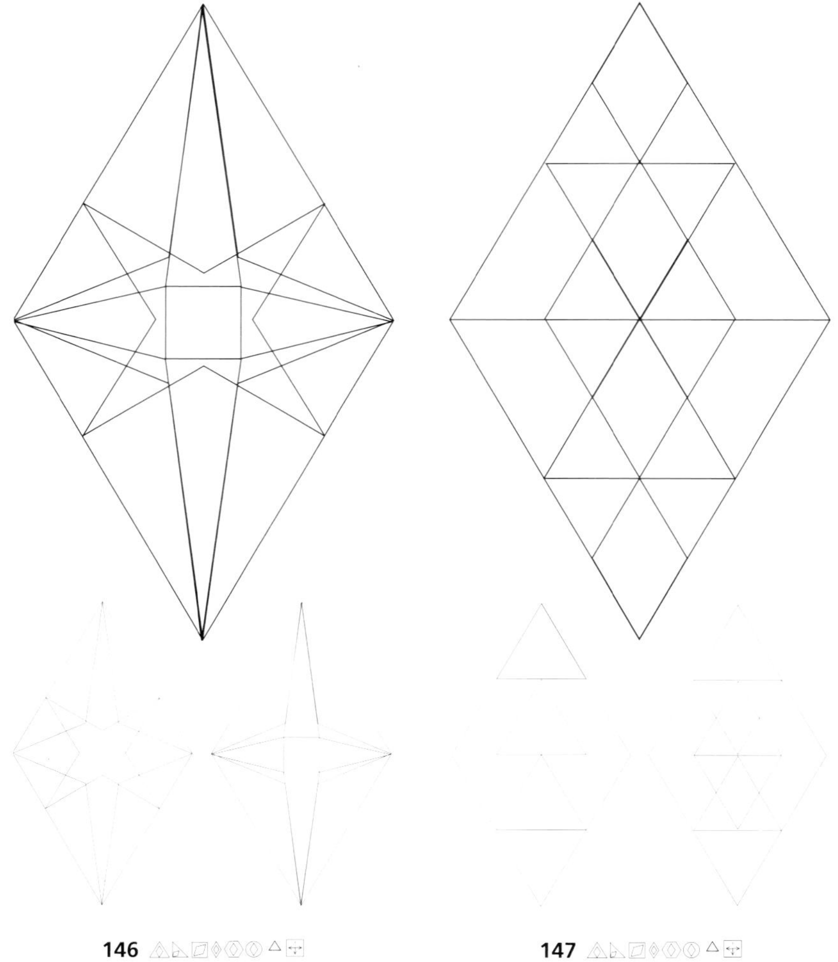

**146**

⟼ 8in (20.3cm) 400%

⟼ 10in (25.4cm) 500%

**147**

⟼ 6in (15.25cm) 300%

⟼ 8in (20.3cm) 400%

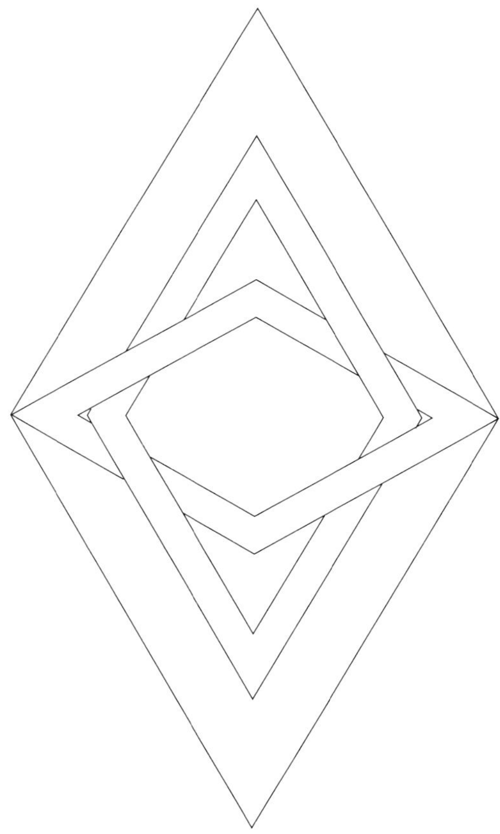

**148**

(2½in (6.4cm)) to 6in (15.25cm) 240%

(2½in (6.4cm)) to 10in (25.4cm) 400%

## Kites

Kites are not symmetrical top and bottom and can vary quite a lot. The most common example is an equilateral triangle as a base and a right angle triangle or half a square as a top. Look at the chapters on triangles and squares (pages 40–87) for further inspiration.

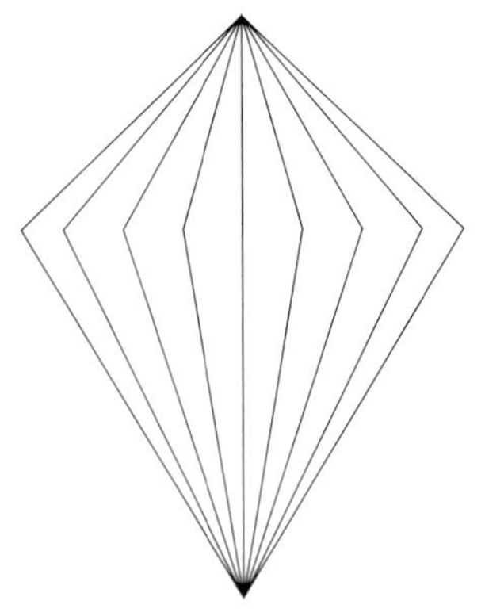

**149**
4in (10.2cm) 200%
6in (15.25cm) 300%

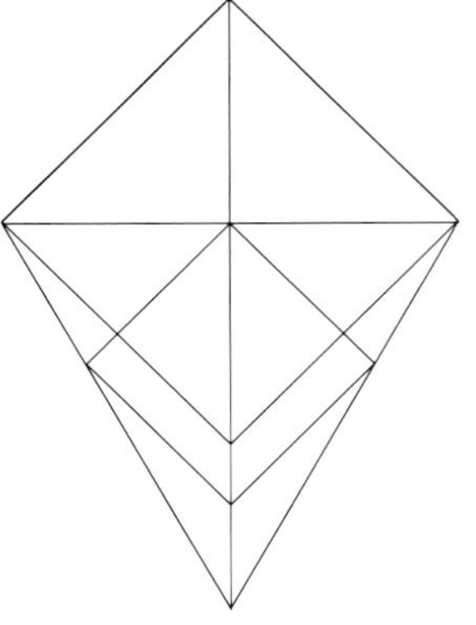

**150a**
6in (15.25cm) 300%
8in (20.3cm) 400%

**150b**
6in (15.25cm) 300%
8in (20.3cm) 400%

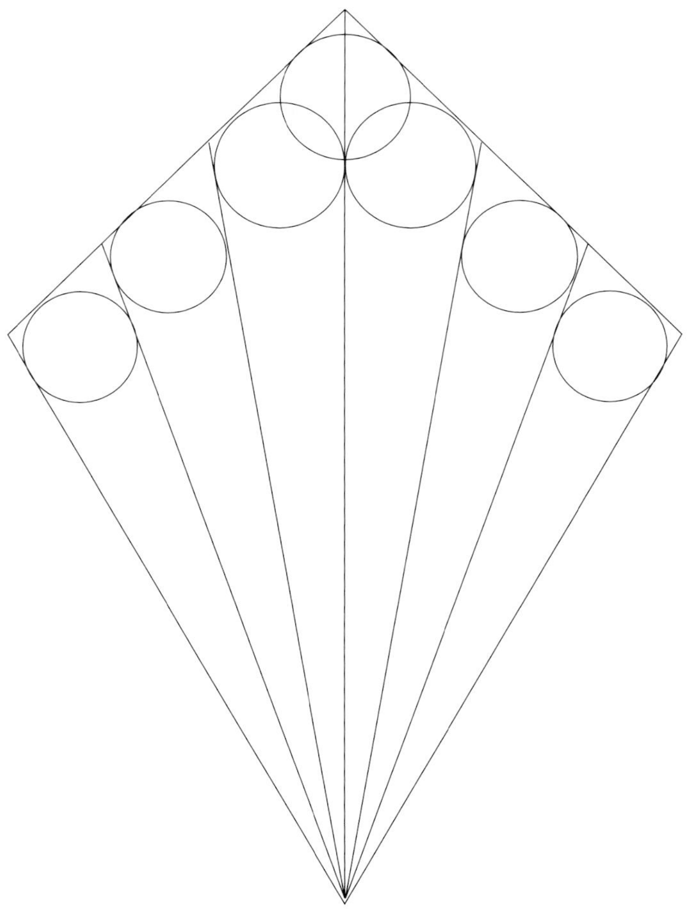

**151**

⟷ (3½in (8.9cm)) to 10in (25.4cm) 285%

⟷ (3½in (8.9cm)) to 12in (30.5cm) 480%

**152**

↔ (3½in (8.9cm)) to 10in (25.4cm) 285%

↔ (3½in (8.9cm)) to 12in (30.5cm) 480%

ALL PATTERNS ARE STANDARD 2IN (5CM) OR 4IN (10.2CM) UNLESS OTHERWISE STATED

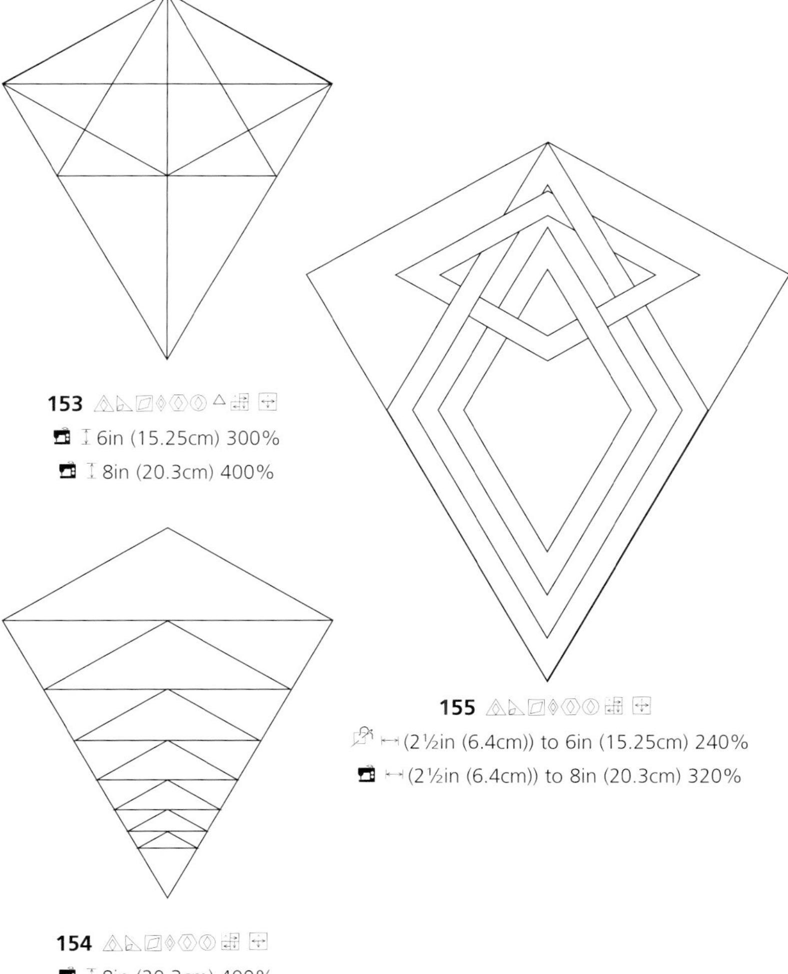

**153**

6in (15.25cm) 300%

8in (20.3cm) 400%

**154**

8in (20.3cm) 400%

10in (25.4cm) 500%

**155**

(2½in (6.4cm)) to 6in (15.25cm) 240%

(2½in (6.4cm)) to 8in (20.3cm) 320%

# Pentagons

These are multi-sided shapes with equal sides and and angles. They can be used as single designs, but they are more useful because their sides can be used as angles of symmetry.

## Pentagons

Five-sided shapes when combined form a five-pointed star (see number 157). Designs with a symmetry of either five or ten elements can easily be adapted to fit.

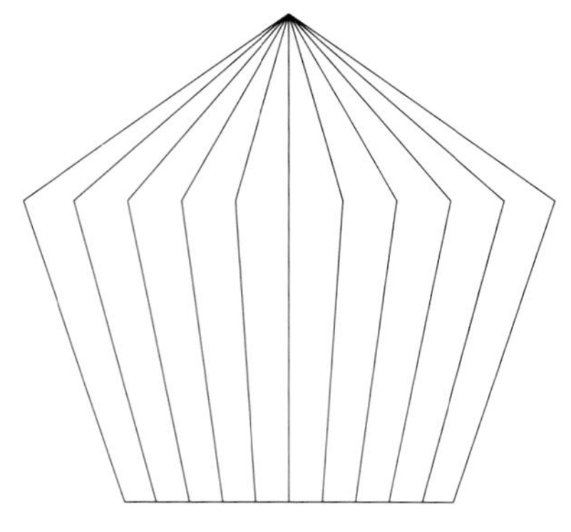

**156**

⟷ 4in (10.2cm) 200%

⟷ 5in (12.7cm) 250%

**157**

⟷ 4in (10.2cm) 200%

⟷ 6in (15.25cm) 300%

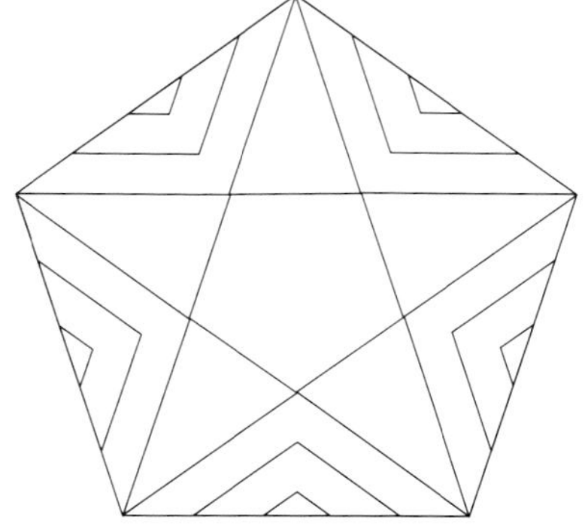

**158**

⟷ 4in (10.2cm) 200%

⟷ 6in (15.25cm) 300%

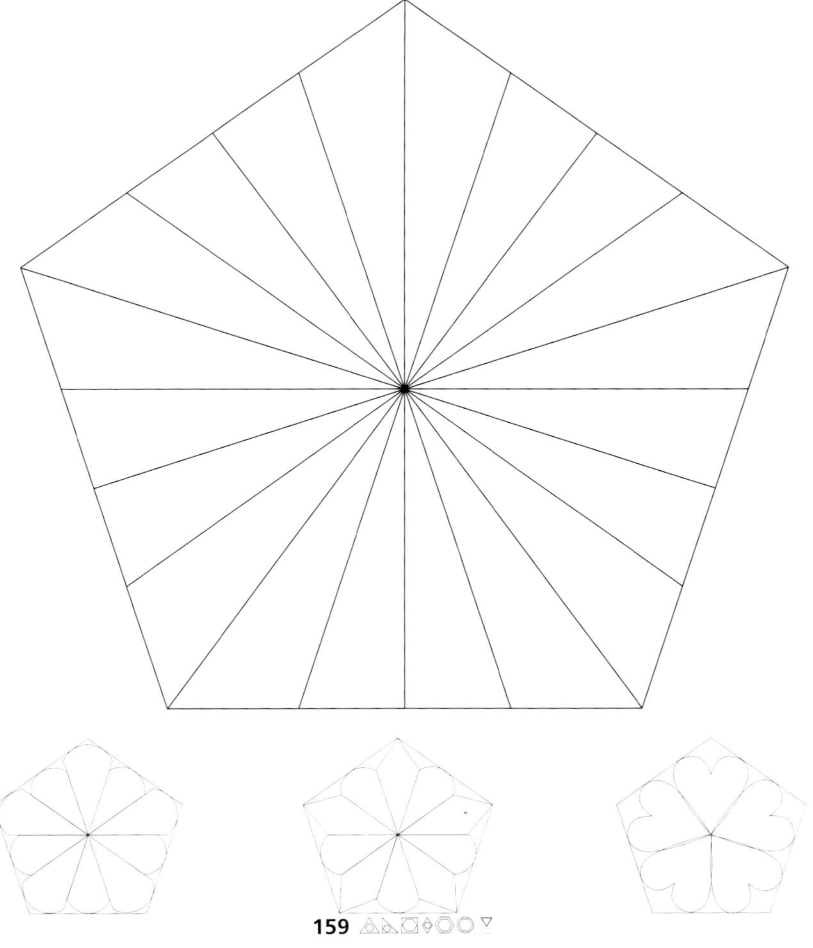

**159**

↦ 16in (40.6cm) 400%

↦ 20in (50.8cm) 500%

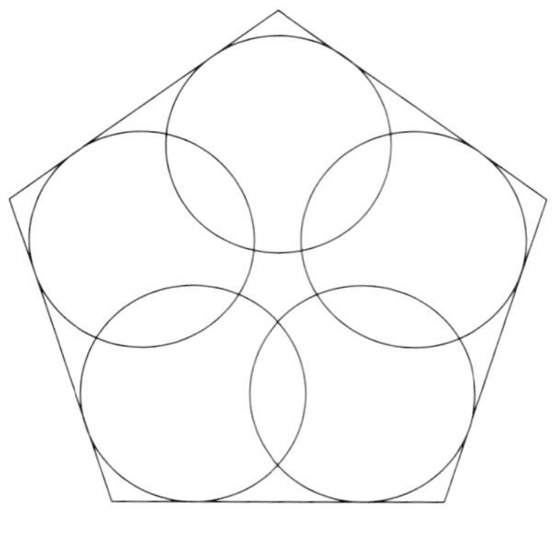

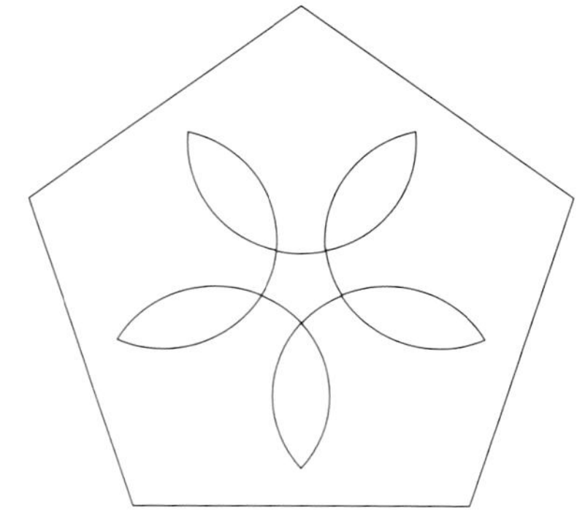

**160a** 

⟼ 4in (10.2cm) 200%

⟼ 5in (12.7cm) 250%

**160b**

⟼ 4in (10.2cm) 200%

⟼ 5in (12.7cm) 250%

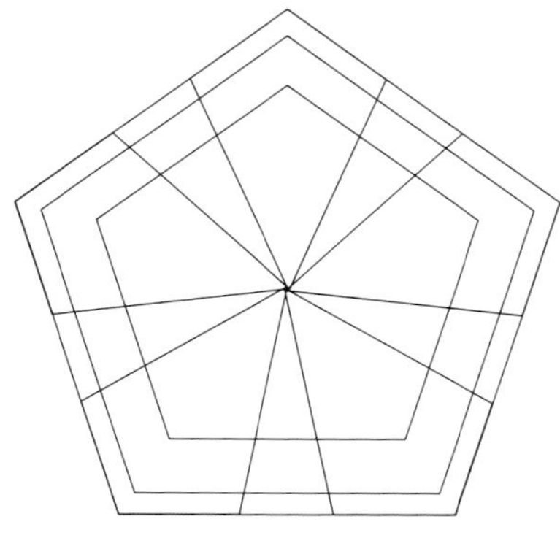

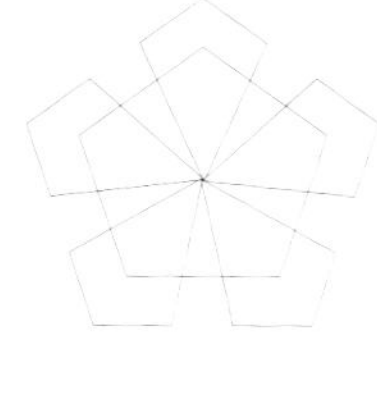

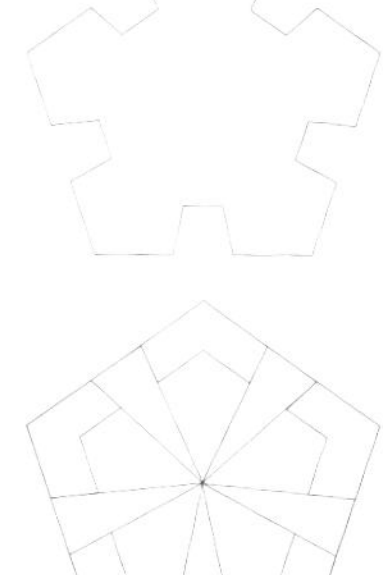

**161**

⟼ 8in (20.3cm) 400%

⟼ 10in (25.4cm) 500%

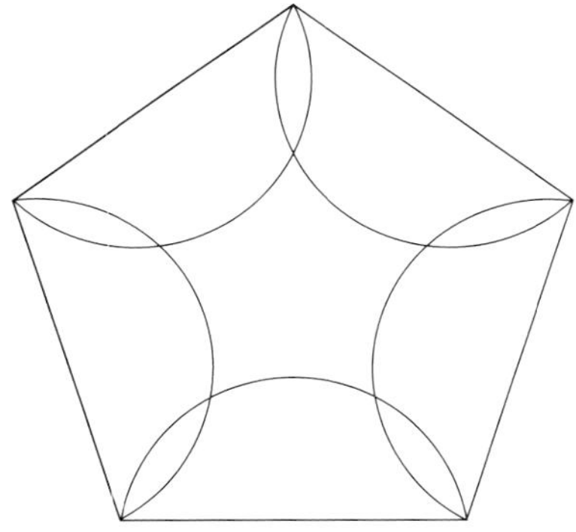

**162**

⟷ 4in (10.2cm) 200%

⟷ 5in (12.7cm) 250%

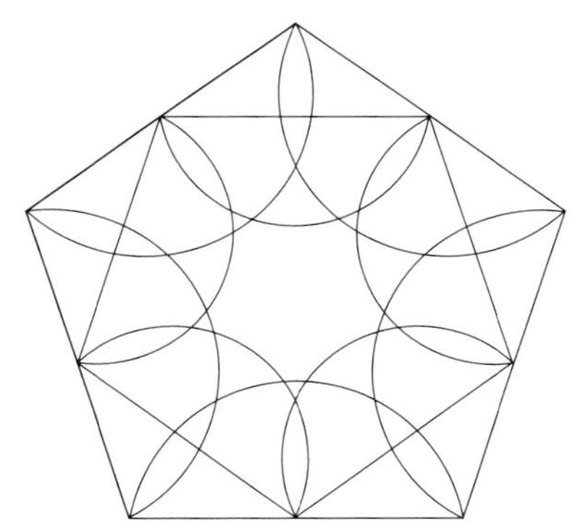

**163**

⟷ 6in (15.25cm) 300%

⟷ 8in (20.3cm) 400%

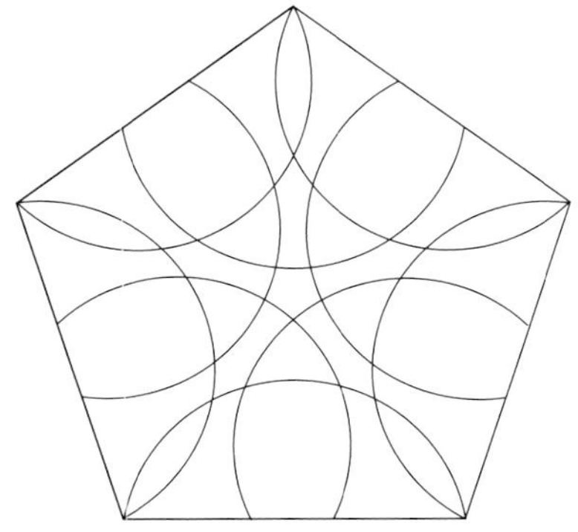

**164**

⟷ 8in (20.3cm) 400%

⟷ 10in (25.4cm) 500%

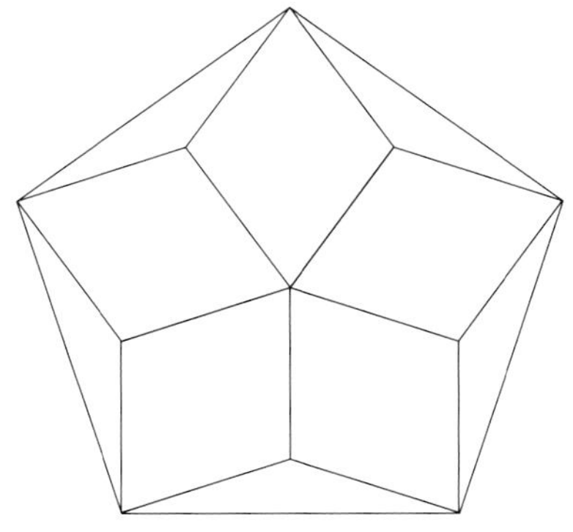

**165**

⟷ 4in (10.2cm) 200%

⟷ 5in (12.7cm) 250%

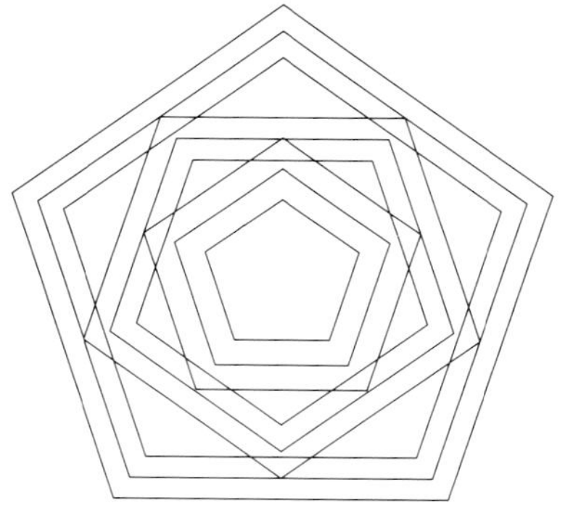

**166**

⟷ 6in (15.25cm) 300%

⟷ 8in (20.3cm) 400%

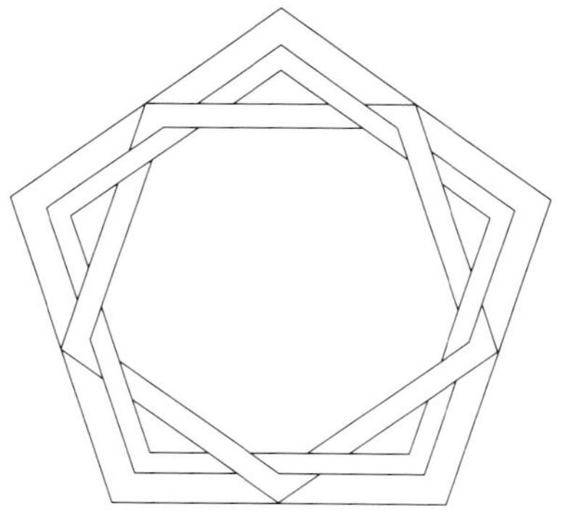

**167**

⟷ 6in (15.25cm) 300%

⟷ 8in (20.3cm) 400%

**168**

⟷ 8in (20.3cm) 400%

⟷ 10in (25.4cm) 500%

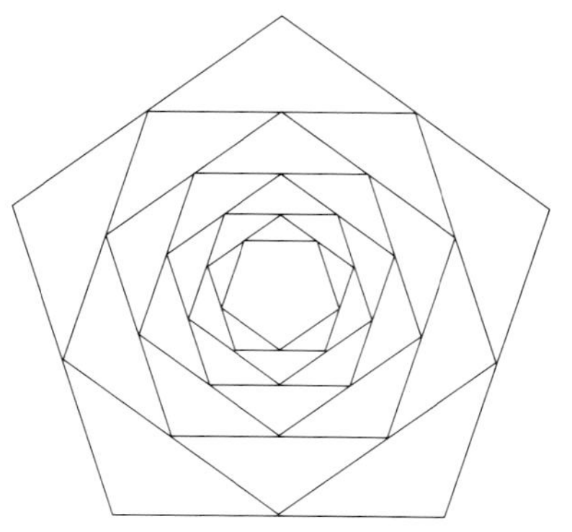

**169**

⟷ 6in (15.25cm) 300%

⟷ 8in (20.3cm) 400%

ALL PATTERNS ARE STANDARD 2IN (5CM) OR 4IN (10.2CM) UNLESS OTHERWISE STATED

## Hexagons

This very popular block shape is also found a lot in quilting. It is made up of six equilateral triangles so look at the triangle designs (see page 40). Any design with a symmetry of three, six, or twelve elements can also be adapted to fit a hexagon.

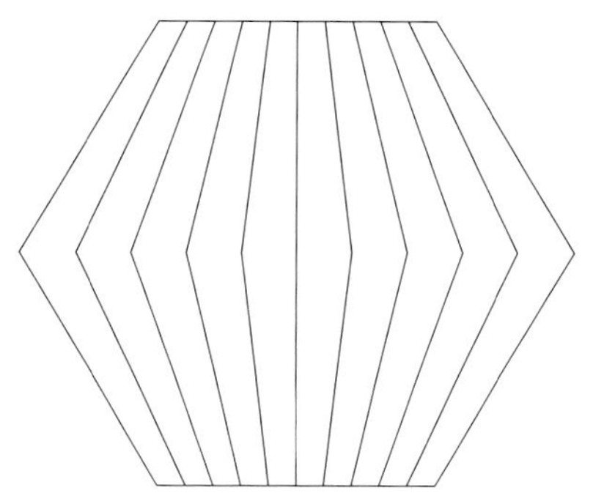

**170**

↔ 4in (10.2cm) 200%

↔ 5in (12.7cm) 250%

**171**

↔ 6in (15.25cm) 300%

↔ 8in (20.3cm) 400%

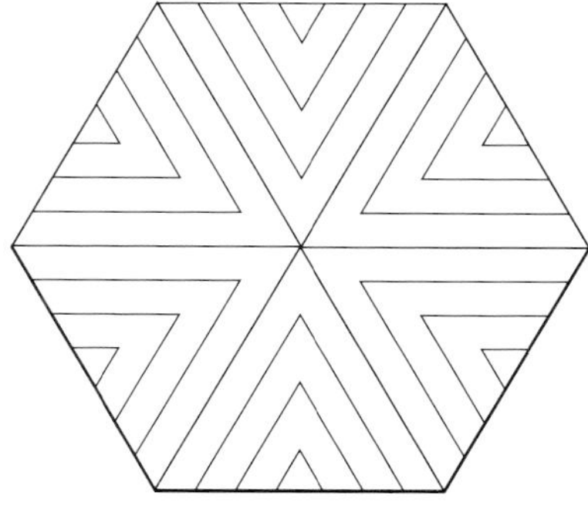

**172**

↔ 10in (25.4cm) 500%

↔ 12in (30.5cm) 600%

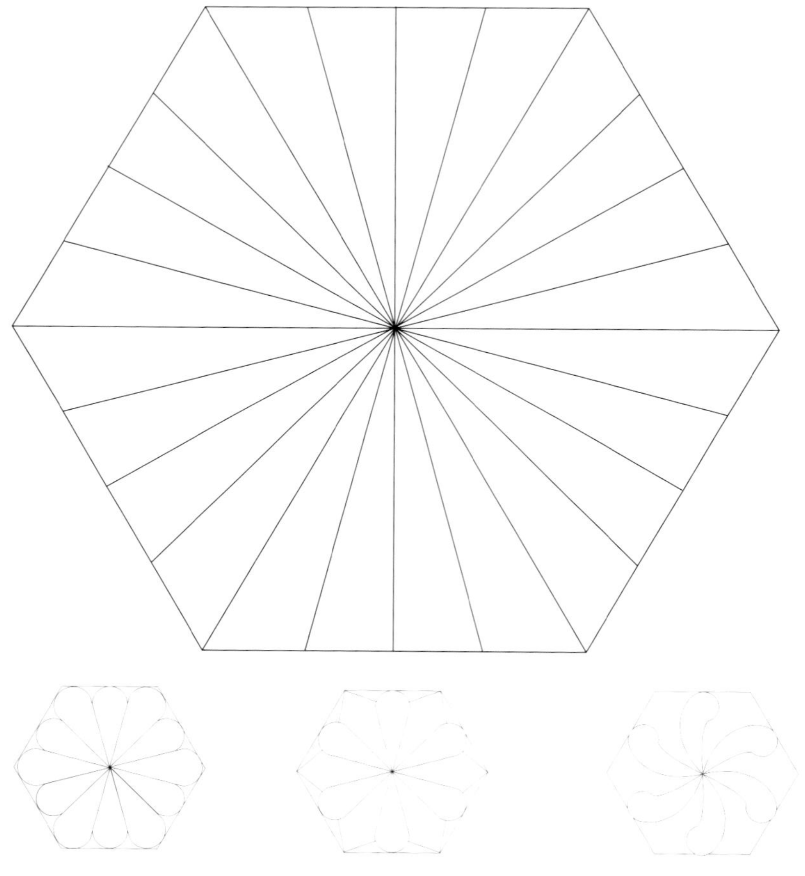

**173**

↦ 16in (40.6cm) 400%

↦ 20in (50.8cm) 500%

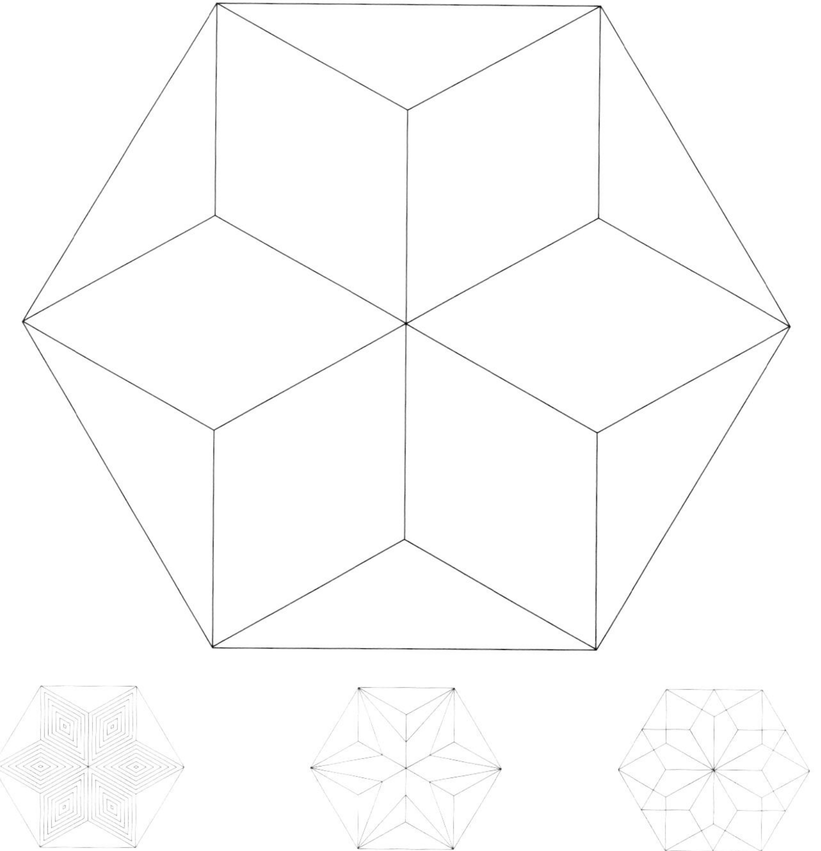

**174**

⟼ 16in (40.6cm) 400%

⟼ 20in (50.8cm) 500%

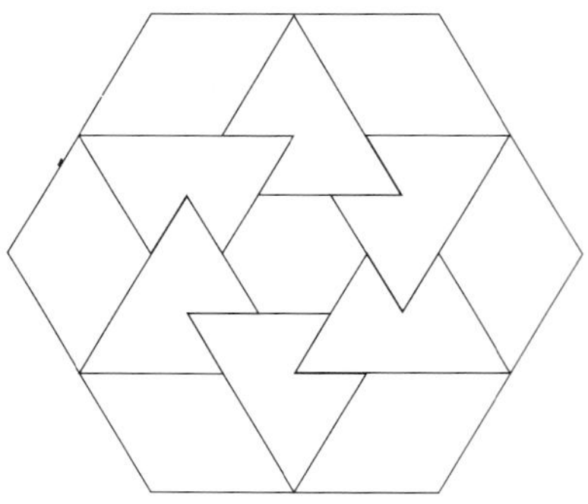

**175**

6in (15.25cm) 300%

8in (20.3cm) 400%

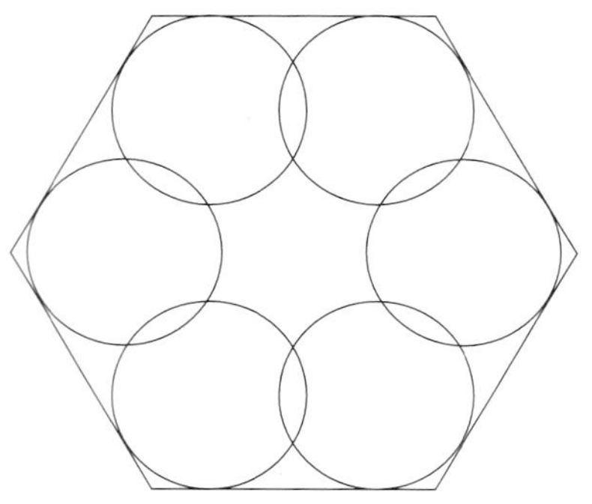

**176**

6in (15.25cm) 300%

8in (20.3cm) 400%

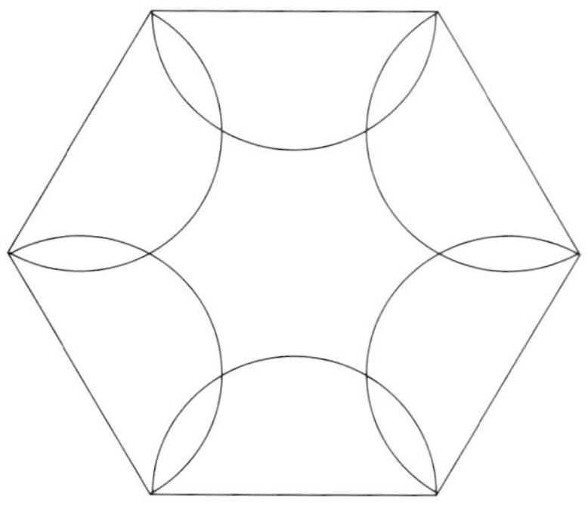

**177**

4in (10.2cm) 200%

8in (20.3cm) 400%

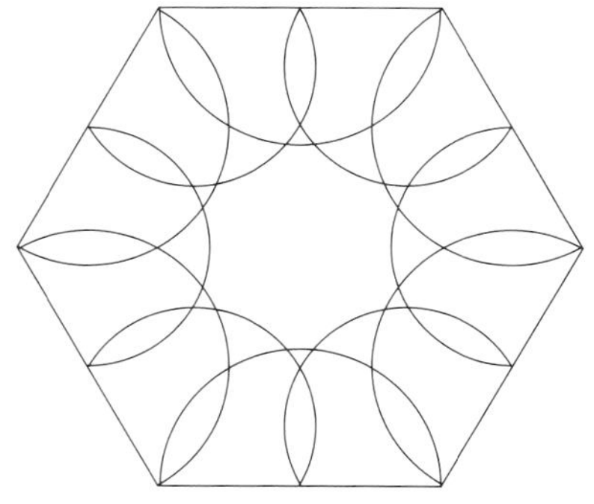

**178**

6in (15.25cm) 300%

8in (20.3cm) 400%

ALL PATTERNS ARE STANDARD 2IN (5CM) OR 4IN (10.2CM) UNLESS OTHERWISE STATED

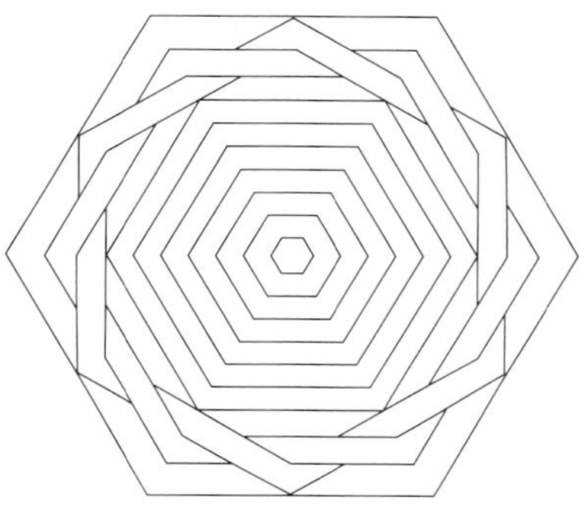

**179**

6in (15.25cm) 300%

8in (20.3cm) 400%

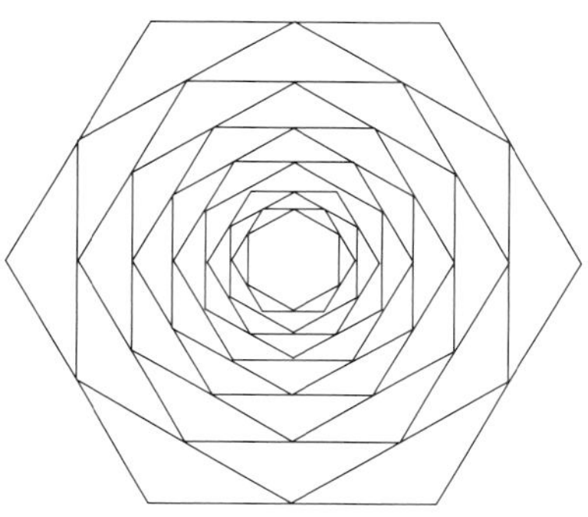

**180**

6in (15.25cm) 300%

8in (20.3cm) 400%

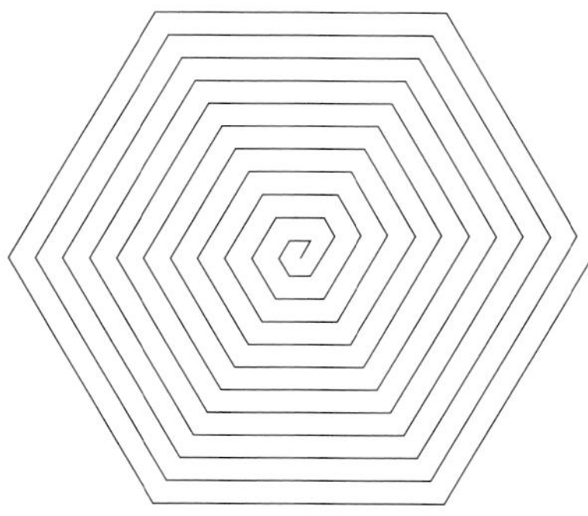

**181**

10in (25.4cm) 500%

12in (30.5cm) 600%

**182**

10in (25.4cm) 500%

12in (30.5cm) 600%

## Octagons

This eight sided shape can be tessellated quite easily or makes an excellent focal point. It is made up of rotated triangles that are easily adapted from equilateral triangles by enlarging them with different percentages for the horizontal and vertical measurement. Any design that can be divided into four, eight, or sixteen can be adapted to fit an octagon.

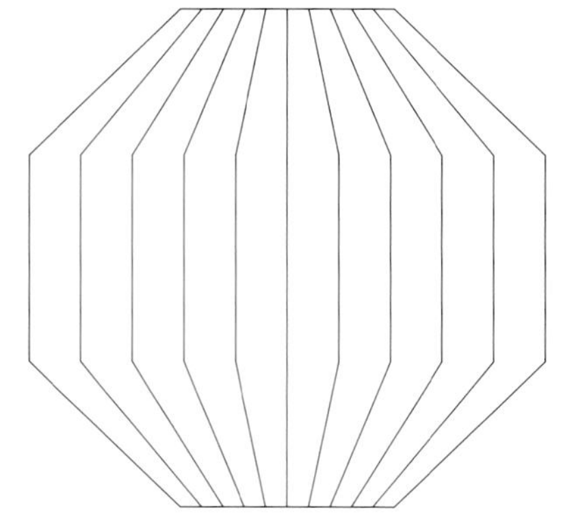

**183**

4in (10.2cm) 200%

6in (15.25cm) 300%

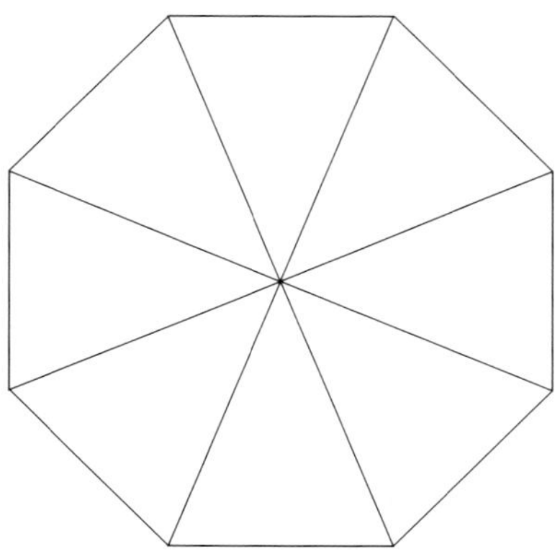

**184a**

4in (10.2cm) 200%

6in (15.25cm) 300%

**184b**

6in (15.25cm) 300%

8in (20.3cm) 400%

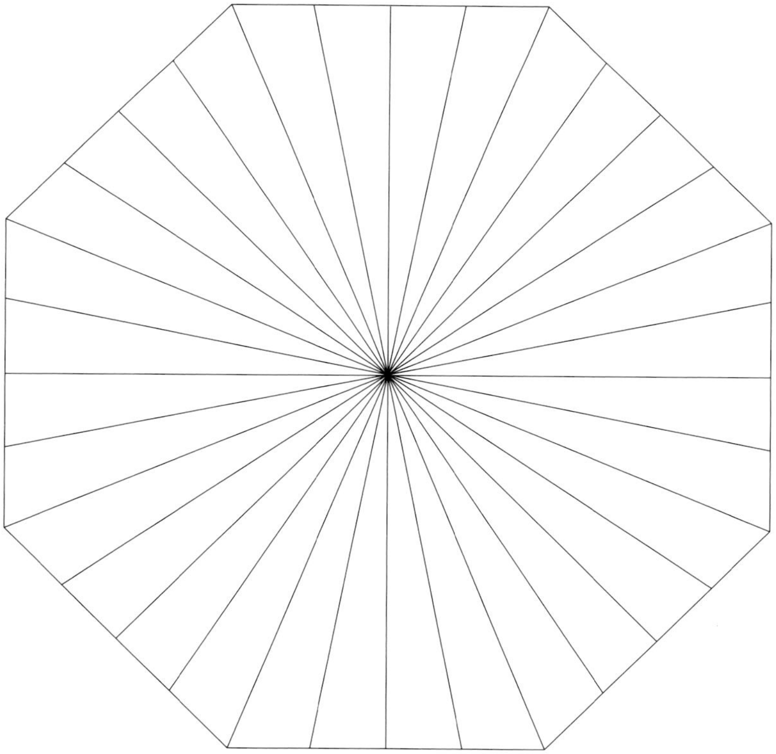

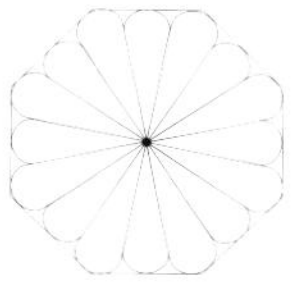

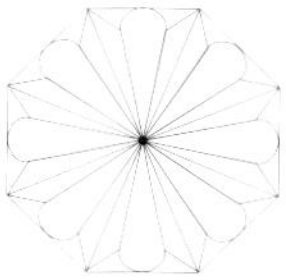

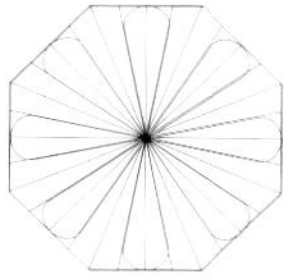

185 

16in (40.6cm) 400%

20in (50.8cm) 500%

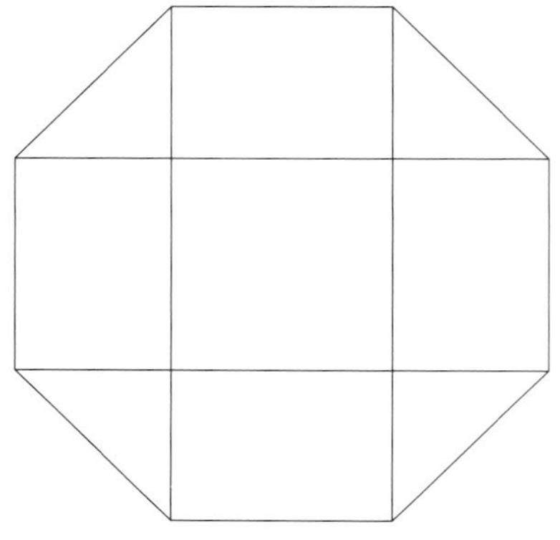

**186a**

⟼ 4in (10.2cm) 200%

⟼ 5in (12.7cm) 250%

**186b**

⟼ 6in (15.25cm) 300%

⟼ 8in (20.3cm) 400%

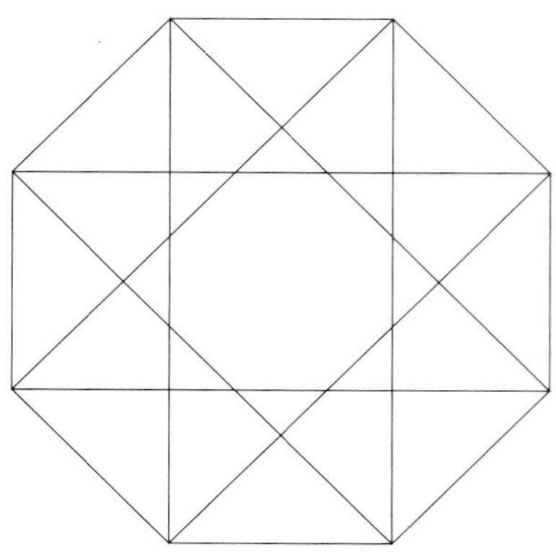

**187**

⟼ 4in (10.2cm) 200%

⟼ 5in (12.7cm) 250%

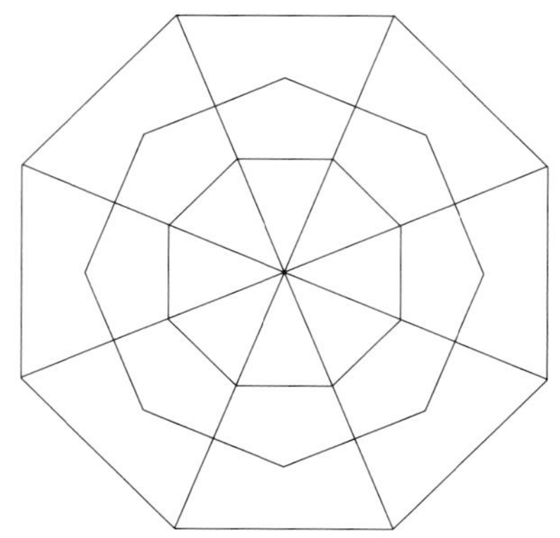

**188**

⟼ 4in (10.2cm) 200%

⟼ 5in (12.7cm) 250%

**189a**
⟷ 6in (15.25cm) 300%
⟷ 8in (20.3cm) 400%

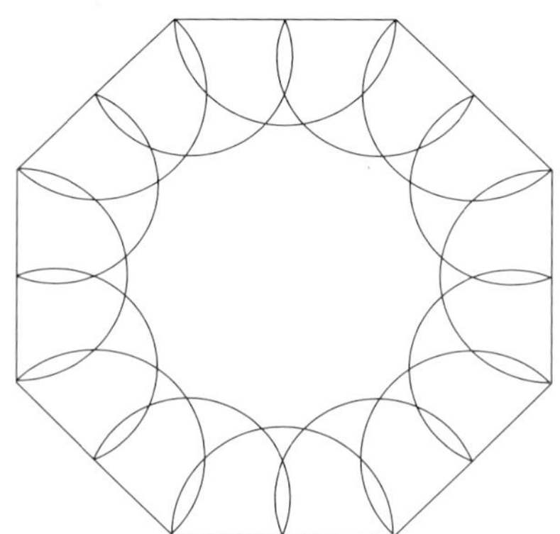

**189b**
⟷ 6in (15.25cm) 300%
⟷ 8in (20.3cm) 400%

**189c**
⟷ 4in (10.2cm) 200%
⟷ 6in (15.25cm) 300%

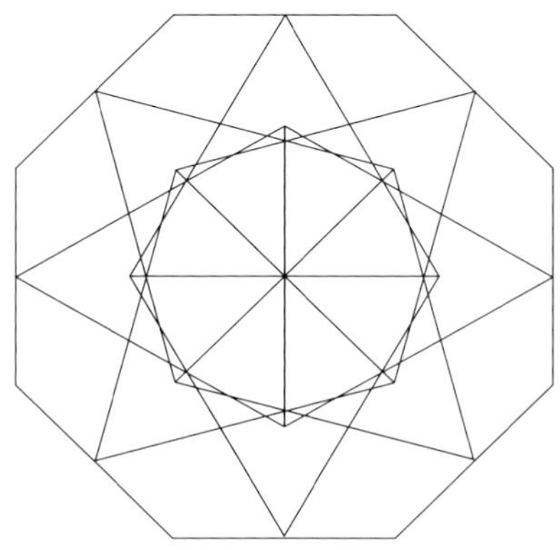

**190**
⟷ 10in (25.4cm) 500%
⟷ 12in (30.5cm) 600%

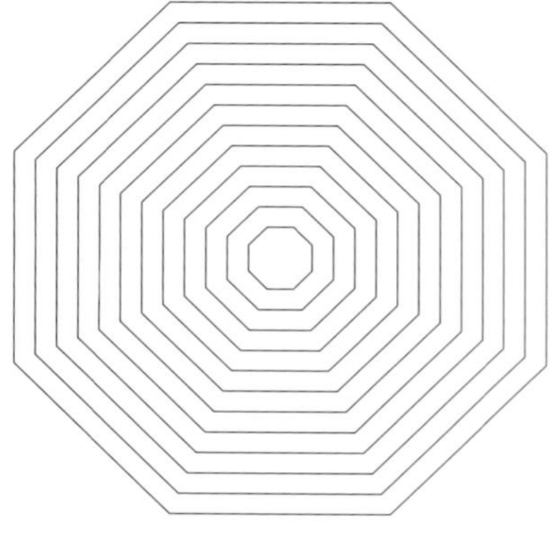

**191**

6in (15.25cm) 300%

8in (20.3cm) 400%

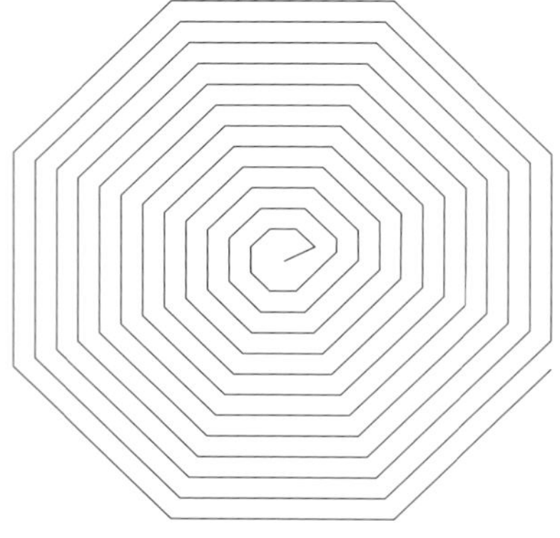

**192**

10in (25.4cm) 500%

12in (30.5cm) 600%

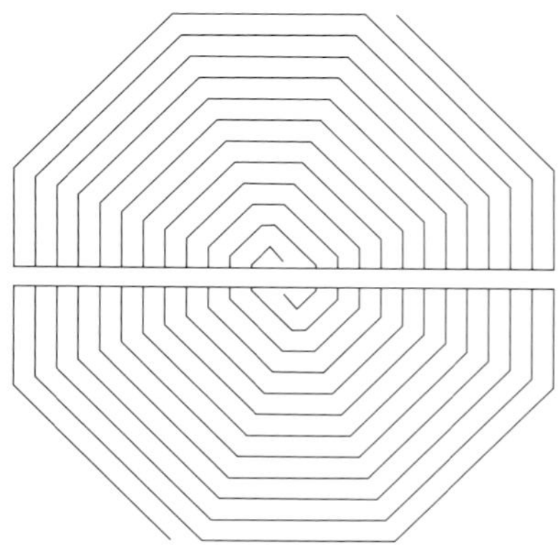

**193**

10in (25.4cm) 500%

12in (30.5cm) 600%

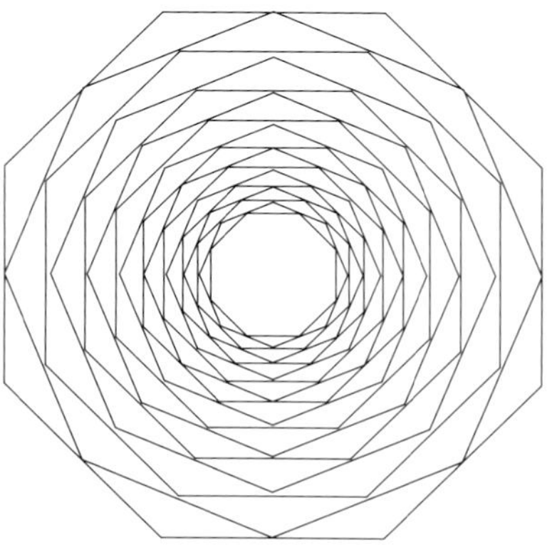

**194a**

12in (30.5cm) 600%

15in (38.1cm) 750%

ALL PATTERNS ARE STANDARD 2IN (5CM) OR 4IN (10.2CM) UNLESS OTHERWISE STATED

**194b**

16in (40.6cm) 400%

20in (50.8cm) 500%

# Circles

Circles have infinite symmetry and can be divided any number of ways. Circles are useful motifs for creating a focal point and adapt well to any design.

The radiating designs are traditionally made by folding a disc of paper. However, more complex divisions are also included in this chapter.

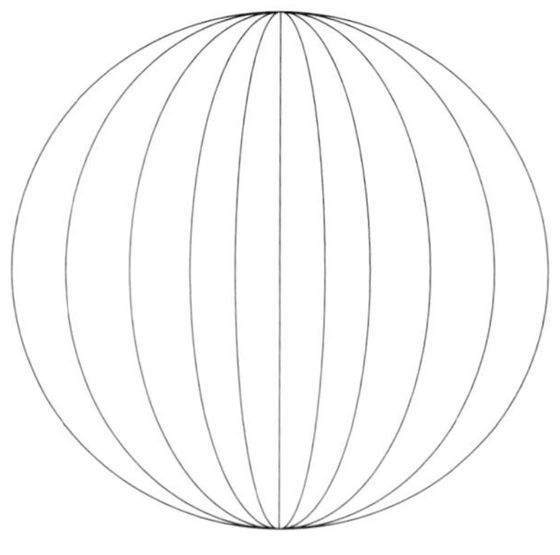

**195**

⟷ 4in (10.2cm) 200%

⟷ 5in (12.7cm) 250%

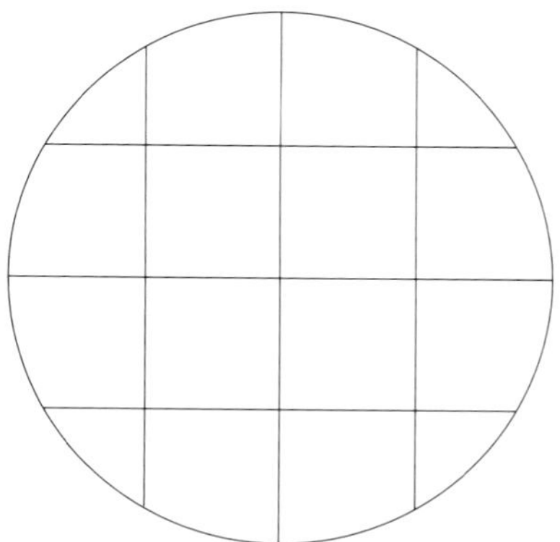

**196a**

⟷ 4in (10.2cm) 200%

⟷ 5in (12.7cm) 250%

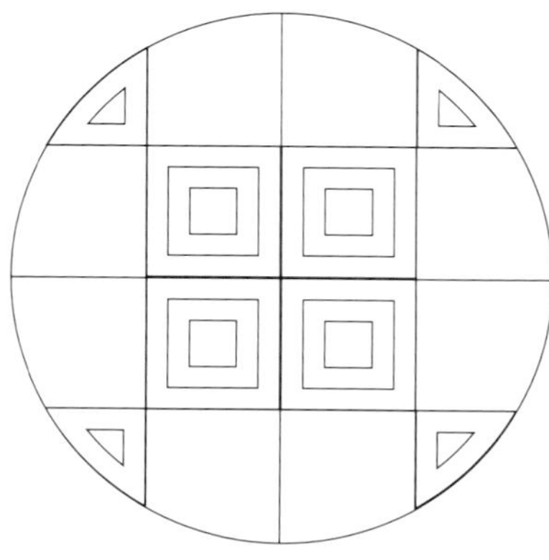

**196b**

⟷ 4in (10.2cm) 200%

⟷ 6in (15.25cm) 300%

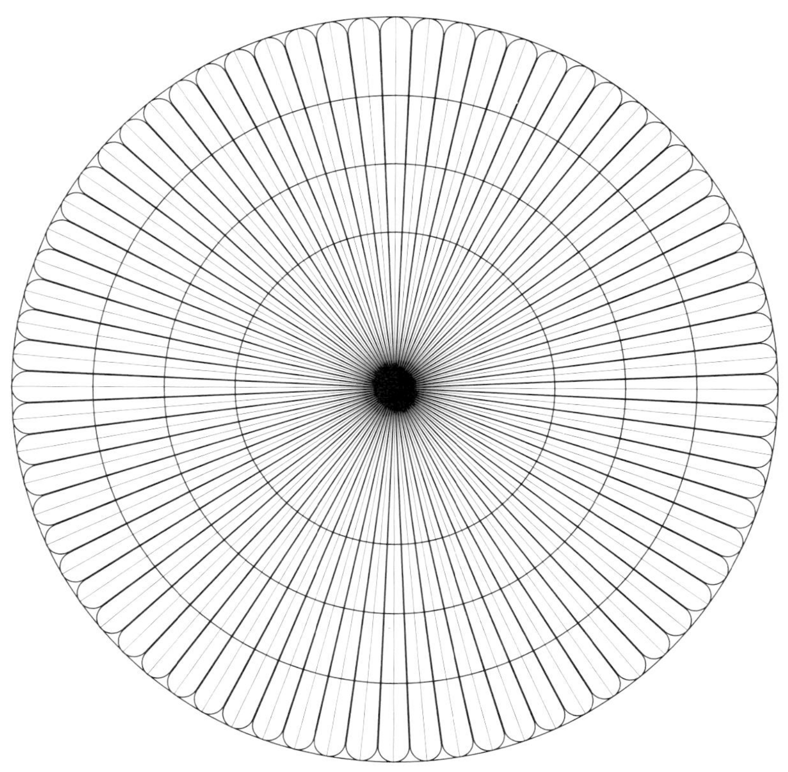

**197**

24in (61cm) 600%

30in (76.2cm) 750%

**198a**

↦ 4in (10.2cm) 200%

↦ 5in (12.7cm) 250%

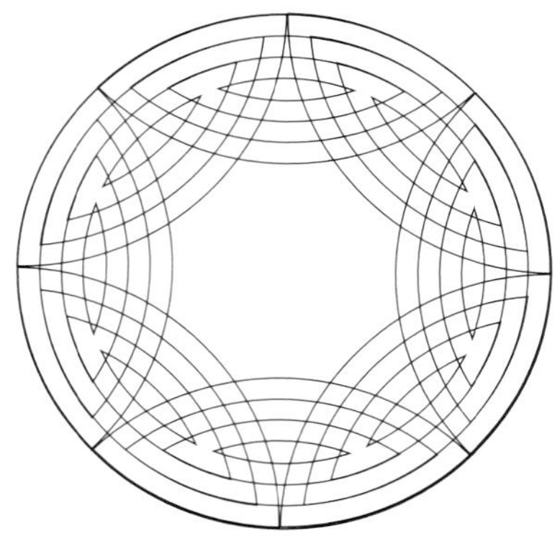

**198b**

↦ 6in (15.25cm) 300%

↦ 8in (20.3cm) 400%

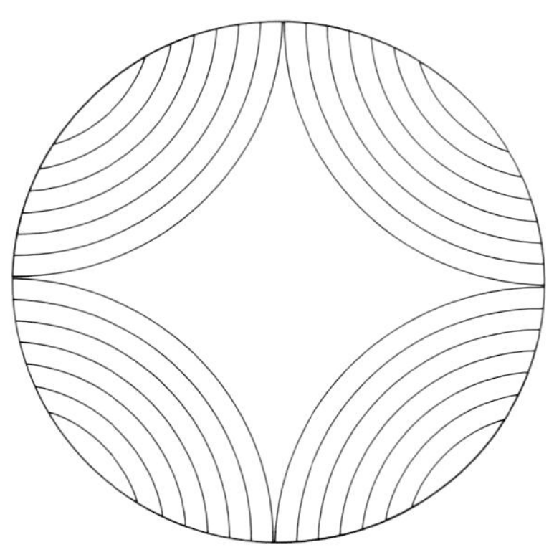

**199a**

↦ 6in (15.25cm) 300%

↦ 8in (20.3cm) 400%

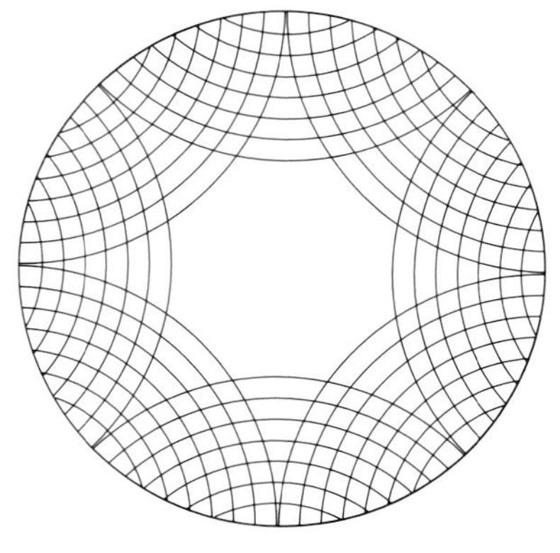

**199b**

↦ 10in (25.4cm) 500%

↦ 12in (30.5cm) 600%

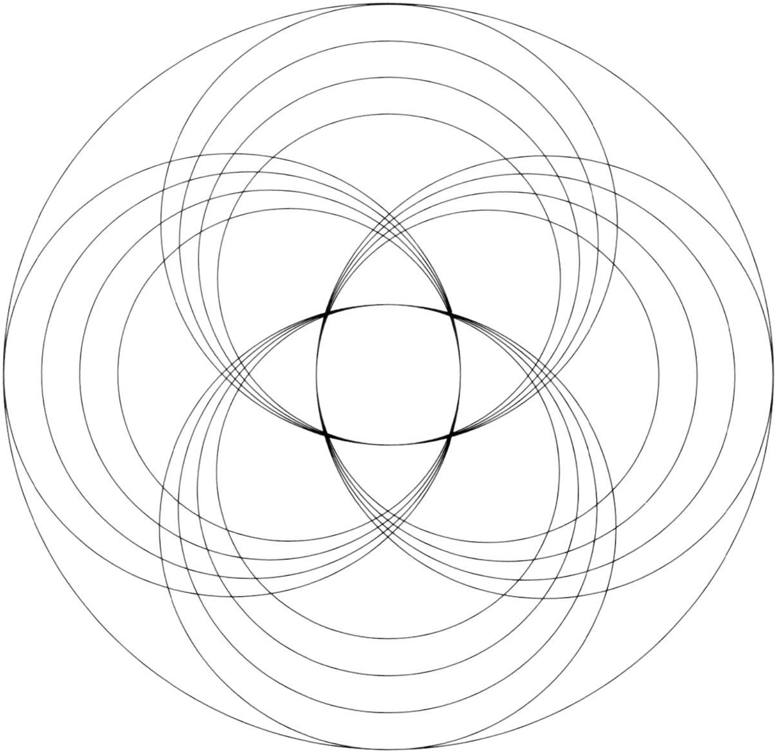

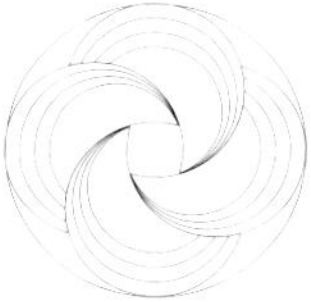

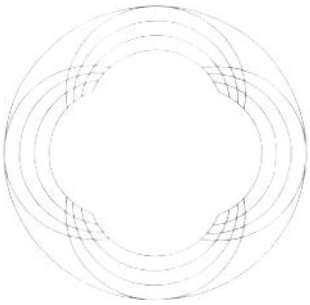

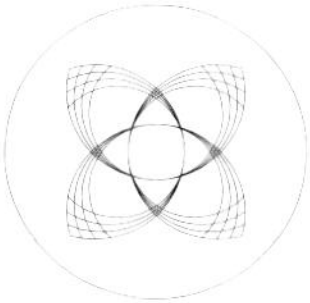

**200** 

⟼ 20in (50.8cm) 500%

⟼ 24in (61cm) 600%

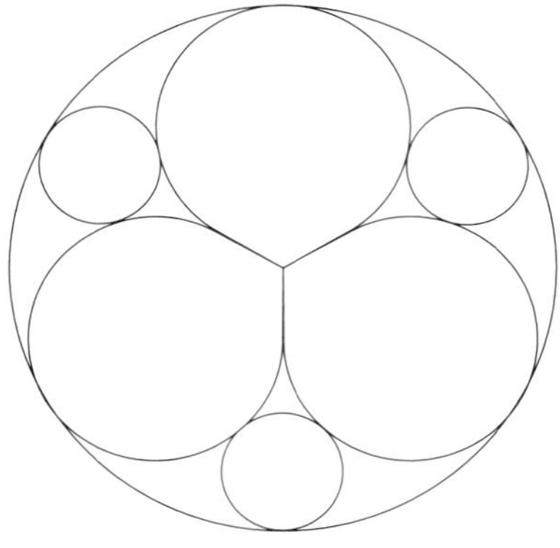

**201a**

⟼ 4in (10.2cm) 200%

⟼ 5in (12.7cm) 250%

**201b**

⟼ 6in (15.25cm) 300%

⟼ 8in (20.3cm) 400%

**202**

⟼ 10in (25.4cm) 500%

⟼ 12in (30.5cm) 600%

**203**

⟼ 6in (15.25cm) 300%

⟼ 8in (20.3cm) 400%

ALL PATTERNS ARE STANDARD 2IN (5CM) OR 4IN (10.2CM) UNLESS OTHERWISE STATED

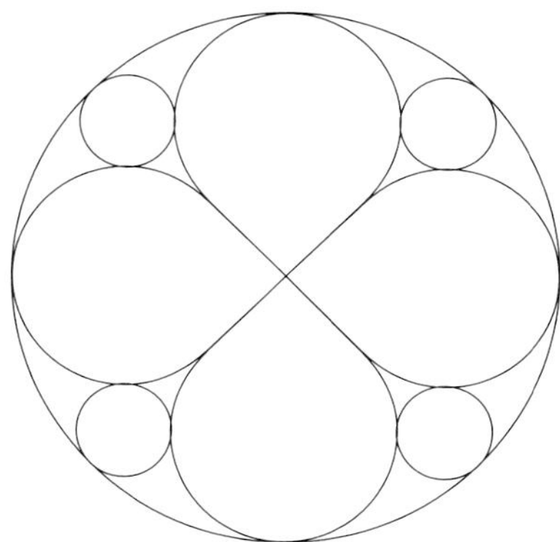

**204a**

4in (10.2cm) 200%

5in (12.7cm) 250%

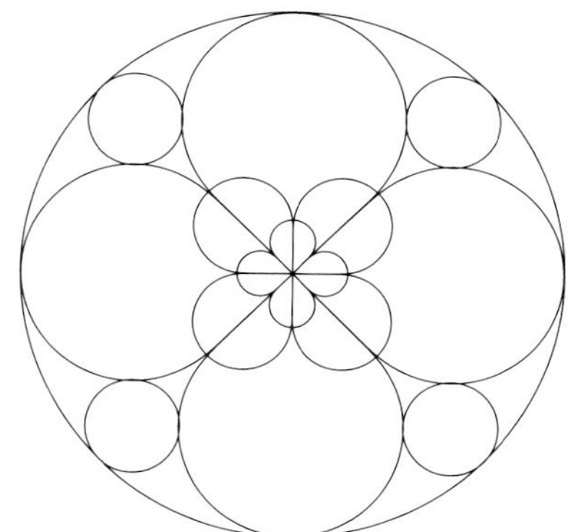

**204b**

8in (20.3cm) 400%

10in (25.4cm) 500%

**205**

6in (15.25cm) 300%

8in (20.3cm) 400%

**206**

6in (15.25cm) 300%

8in (20.3cm) 400%

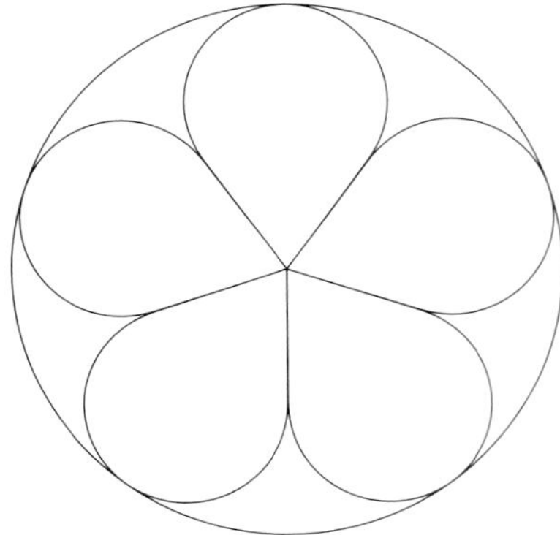

**207**

4in (10.2cm) 200%

5in (12.7cm) 250%

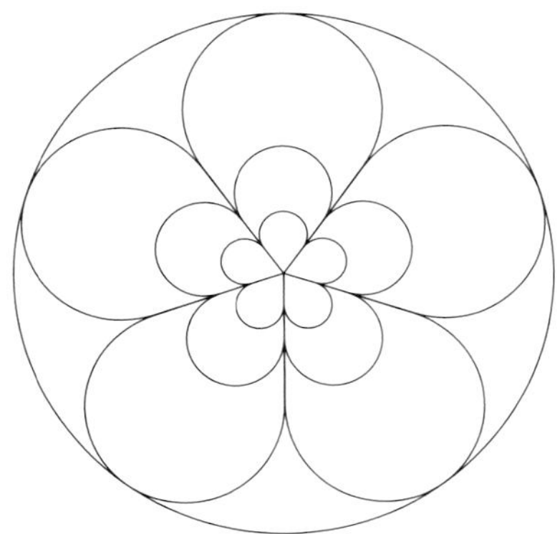

**208**

6in (15.25cm) 300%

8in (20.3cm) 400%

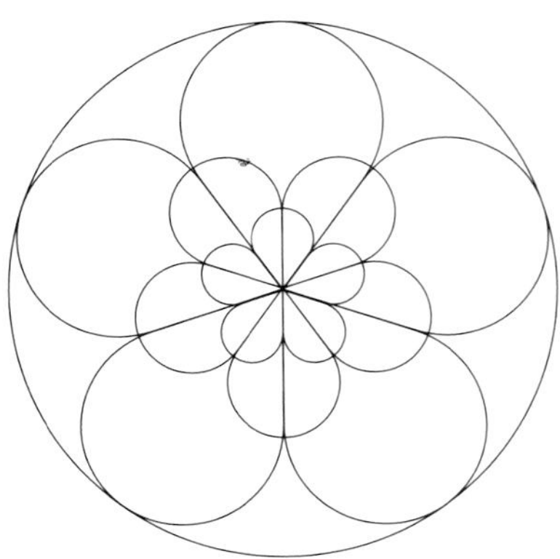

**209**

6in (15.25cm) 300%

8in (20.3cm) 400%

**210**

8in (20.3cm) 400%

10in (25.4cm) 500%

ALL PATTERNS ARE STANDARD 2IN (5CM) OR 4IN (10.2CM) UNLESS OTHERWISE STATED

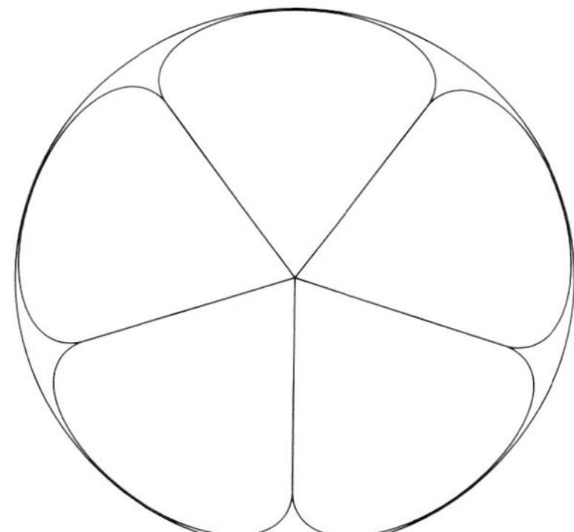

**211**

⟼ 4in (10.2cm) 200%

⟼ 5in (12.7cm) 250%

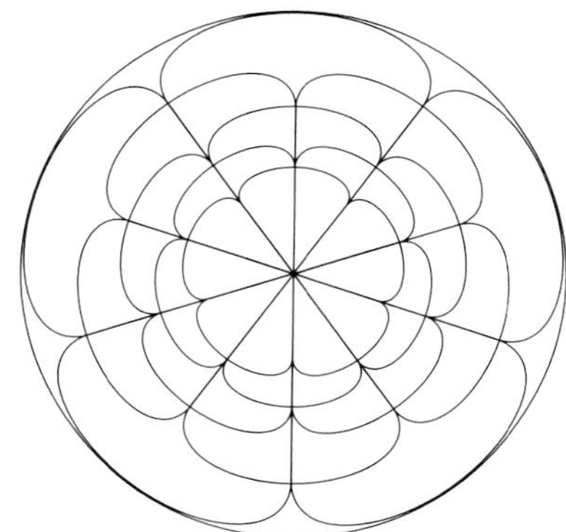

**212**

⟼ 6in (15.25cm) 300%

⟼ 8in (20.3cm) 400%

**213**

⟼ 10in (25.4cm) 500%

⟼ 12in (30.5cm) 600%

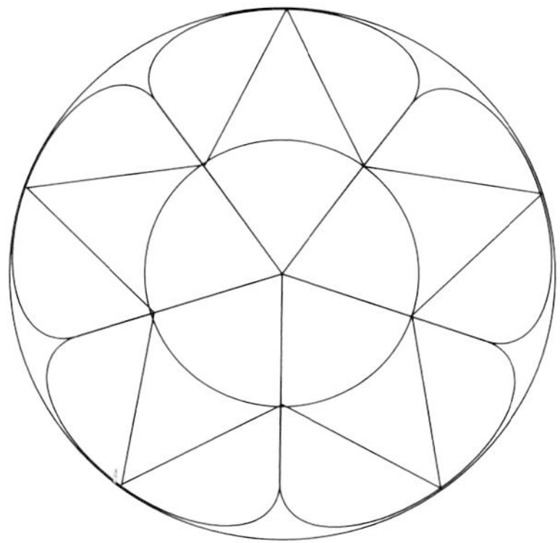

**214**

⟼ 6in (15.25cm) 300%

⟼ 8in (20.3cm) 400%

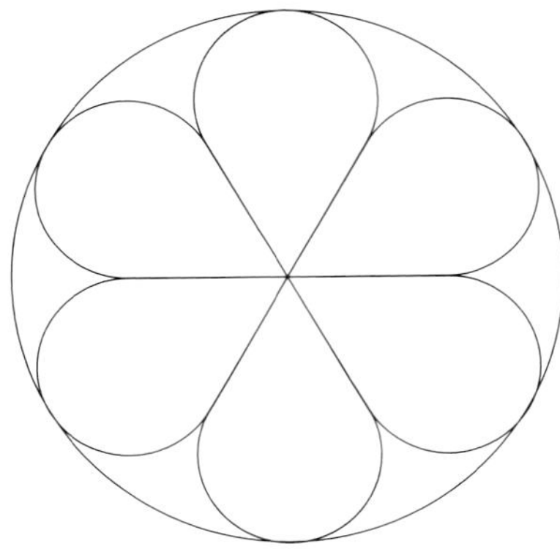

**215**

⟼ 4in (10.2cm) 200%

⟼ 5in (12.7cm) 250%

**216**

⟼ 6in (15.25cm) 300%

⟼ 8in (20.3cm) 400%

**217**

⟼ 6in (15.25cm) 300%

⟼ 8in (20.3cm) 400%

**218**

⟼ 8in (20.3cm) 400%

⟼ 10in (25.4cm) 500%

ALL PATTERNS ARE STANDARD 2IN (5CM) OR 4IN (10.2CM) UNLESS OTHERWISE STATED

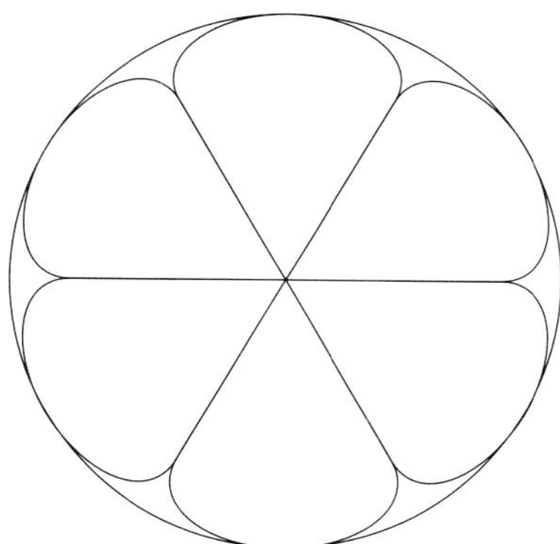

**219**

⟷ 4in (10.2cm) 200%

⟷ 5in (12.7cm) 250%

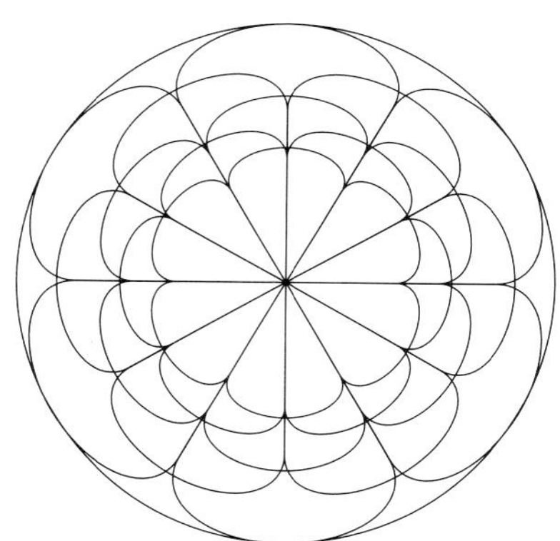

**220**

⟷ 10in (25.4cm) 500%

⟷ 12in (30.5cm) 600%

**221**

⟷ 10in (25.4cm) 500%

⟷ 12in (30.5cm) 600%

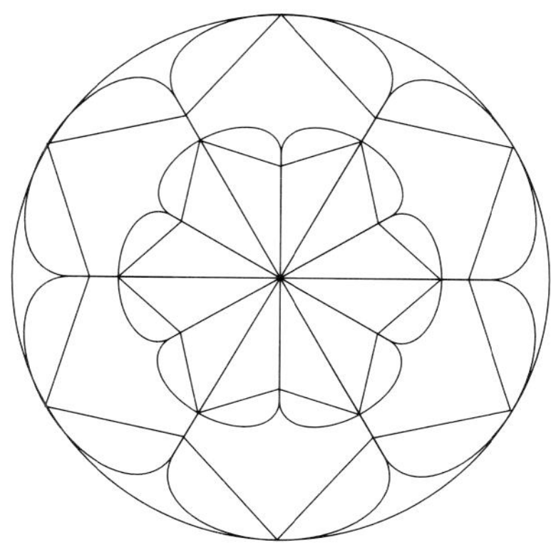

**222**

⟷ 6in (15.25cm) 300%

⟷ 8in (20.3cm) 400%

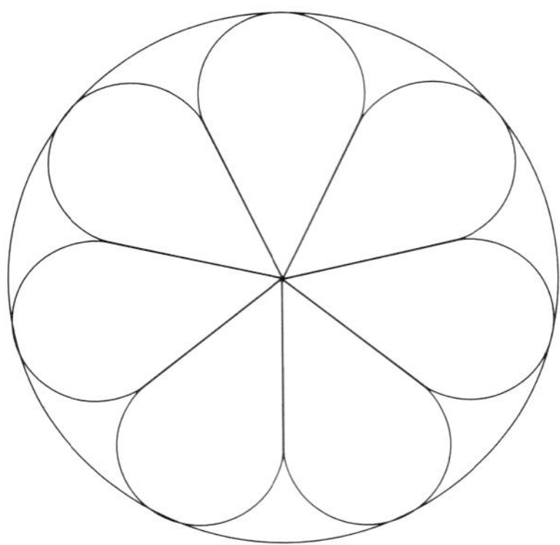

**223**

⟼ 4in (10.2cm) 200%

⟼ 6in (15.25cm) 300%

**224**

⟼ 6in (15.25cm) 300%

⟼ 8in (20.3cm) 400%

**225**

⟼ 6in (15.25cm) 300%

⟼ 8in (20.3cm) 400%

**226**

⟼ 12in (30.5cm) 600%

⟼ 15in (38.1cm) 750%

ALL PATTERNS ARE STANDARD 2IN (5CM) OR 4IN (10.2CM) UNLESS OTHERWISE STATED

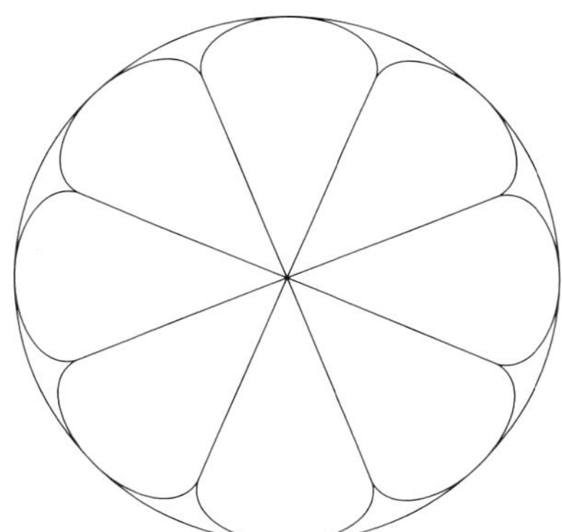

**227**

⟼ 4in (10.2cm) 200%

⟼ 5in (12.7cm) 250%

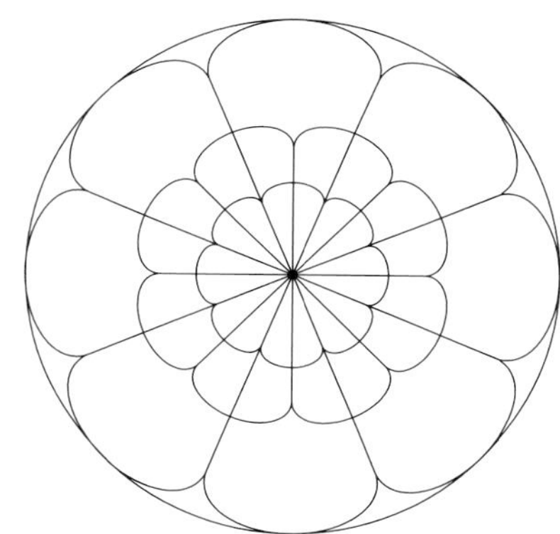

**228**

⟼ 6in (15.25cm) 300%

⟼ 8in (20.3cm) 400%

**229**

⟼ 6in (15.25cm) 300%

⟼ 8in (20.3cm) 400%

**230**

⟼ 12in (30.5cm) 600%

⟼ 15in (38.1cm) 750%

**231**

⟼ 4in (10.2cm) 200%

⟼ 8in (20.3cm) 400%

**232**

⟼ 8in (20.3cm) 400%

⟼ 10in (25.4cm) 500%

**233**

⟼ 6in (15.25cm) 300%

⟼ 8in (20.3cm) 400%

**234**

⟼ 8in (20.3cm) 400%

⟼ 10in (25.4cm) 500%

**235**

⟼ 6in (15.25cm) 300%

⟼ 8in (20.3cm) 400%

**236**

⟼ 6in (15.25cm) 300%

⟼ 8in (20.3cm) 400%

**237**

⟼ 8in (20.3cm) 400%

⟼ 10in (25.4cm) 500%

**238**

⟼ 12in (30.5cm) 600%

⟼ 15in (38.1cm) 750%

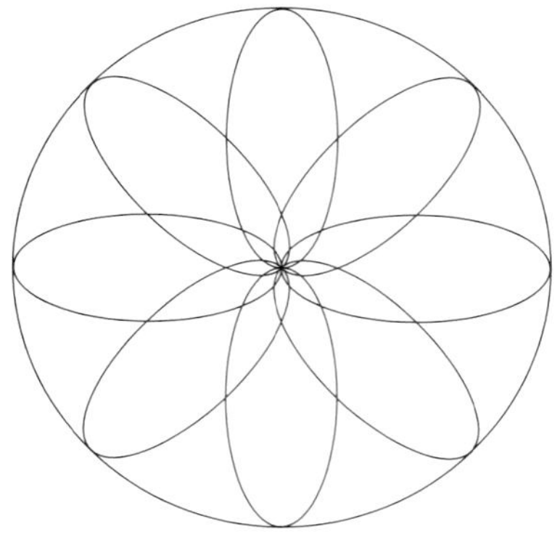

**239**

⟼ 5in (12.7cm) 250%

⟼ 8in (20.3cm) 400%

**240**

⟼ 8in (20.3cm) 400%

⟼ 10in (25.4cm) 500%

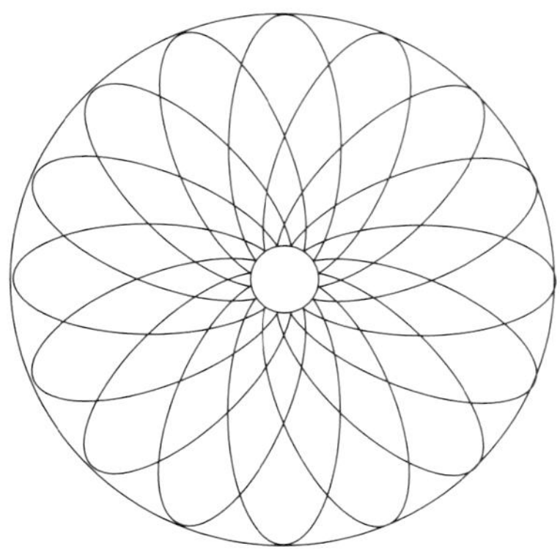

**241**

⟼ 12in (30.5cm) 600%

⟼ 15in (38.1cm) 750%

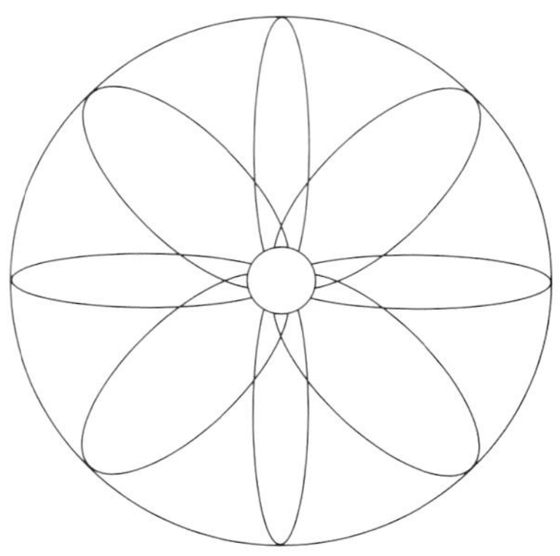

**242**

⟼ 5in (12.7cm) 250%

⟼ 8in (20.3cm) 400%

ALL PATTERNS ARE STANDARD 2IN (5CM) OR 4IN (10.2CM) UNLESS OTHERWISE STATED

**243**

20in (50.8cm) 500%

24in (61cm) 600%

**244**

⟼ 4in (10.2cm) 200%

⟼ 6in (15.25cm) 300%

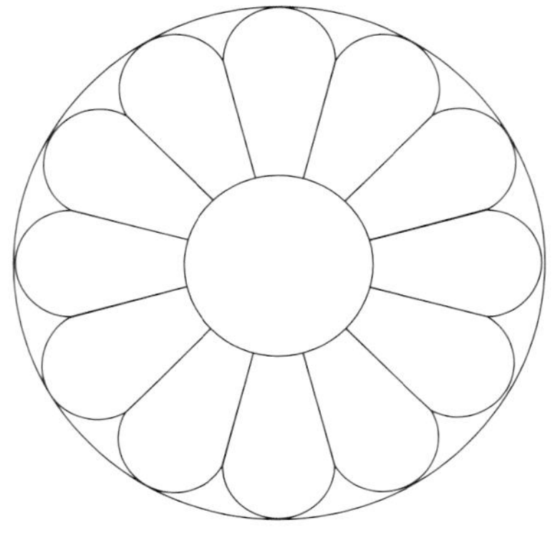

**245**

⟼ 6in (15.25cm) 300%

⟼ 8in (20.3cm) 400%

**246**

⟼ 8in (20.3cm) 400%

⟼ 10in (25.4cm) 500%

**247**

⟼ 8in (20.3cm) 400%

⟼ 10in (25.4cm) 500%

ALL PATTERNS ARE STANDARD 2IN (5CM) OR 4IN (10.2CM) UNLESS OTHERWISE STATED

**248**

⟷ 4in (10.2cm) 200%

⟷ 6in (15.25cm) 300%

**249**

⟷ 8in (20.3cm) 400%

⟷ 10in (25.4cm) 500%

**250**

⟷ 8in (20.3cm) 400%

⟷ 10in (25.4cm) 500%

**251**

⟷ 10in (25.4cm) 500%

⟷ 12in (30.5cm) 600%

**252**

⟼ 6in (15.25cm) 300%

⟼ 8in (20.3cm) 400%

**253**

⟼ 6in (15.25cm) 300%

⟼ 8in (20.3cm) 400%

**254**

⟼ 6in (15.25cm) 300%

⟼ 8in (20.3cm) 400%

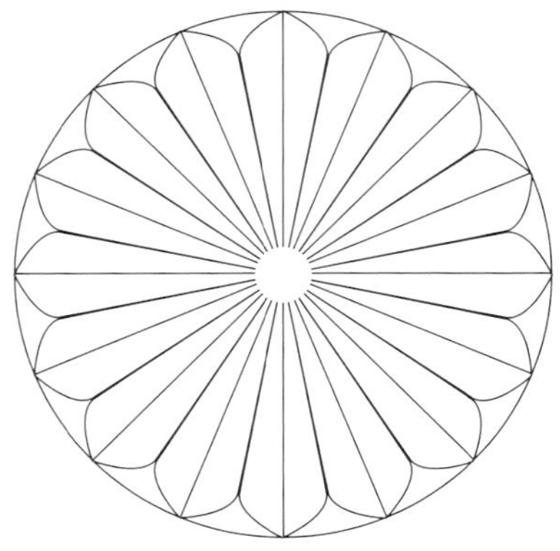

**255**

⟼ 8in (20.3cm) 400%

⟼ 10in (25.4cm) 500%

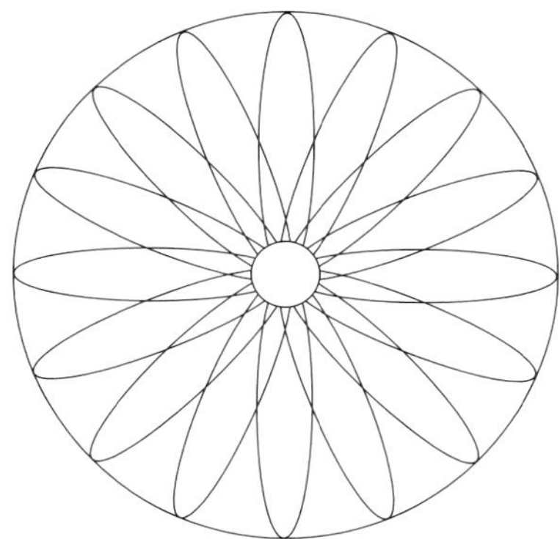

**256**

⟼ 6in (15.25cm) 300%

⟼ 8in (20.3cm) 400%

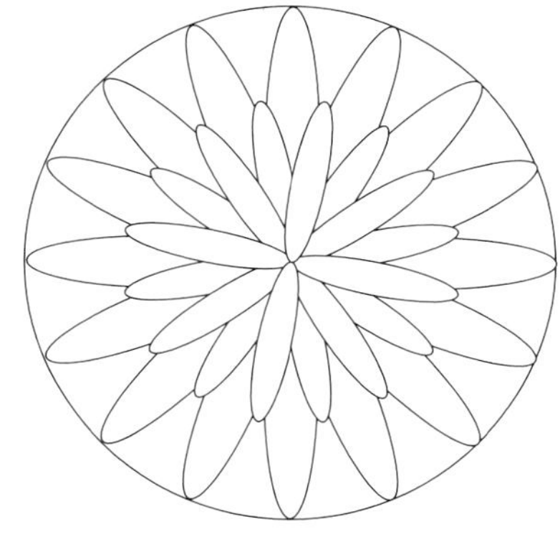

**257**

⟼ 8in (20.3cm) 400%

⟼ 10in (25.4cm) 500%

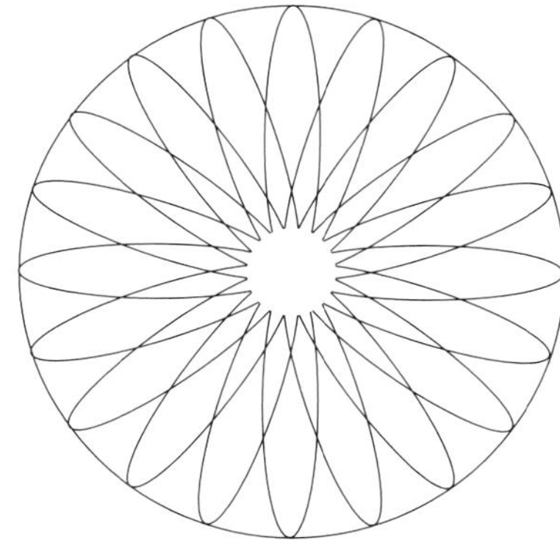

**258**

⟼ 8in (20.3cm) 400%

⟼ 10in (25.4cm) 500%

**259**

⟼ 4in (10.2cm) 200%

⟼ 6in (15.25cm) 300%

**260**

⟷ 8in (20.3cm) 400%

⟷ 10in (25.4cm) 500%

**261**

⟷ 8in (20.3cm) 400%

⟷ 10in (25.4cm) 500%

**262**

⟷ 10in (25.4cm) 500%

⟷ 12in (30.5cm) 600%

**263**

⟷ 10in (25.4cm) 500%

⟷ 12in (30.5cm) 600%

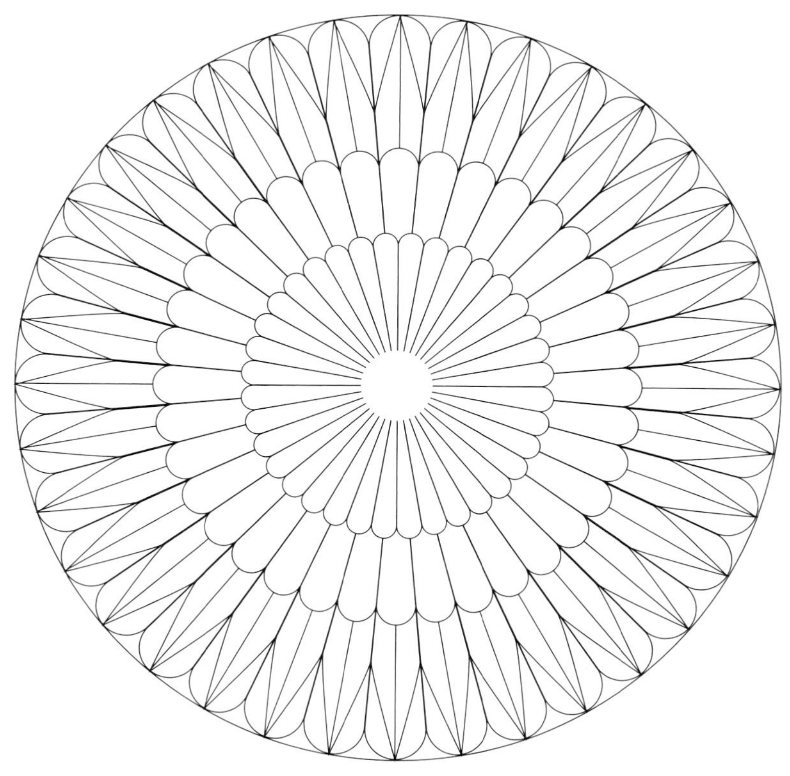

**264**

24in (61cm) 600%

30in (76.2cm) 750%

**265**

4in (10.2cm) 200%

8in (20.3cm) 400%

**266**

5in (12.7cm) 250%

8in (20.3cm) 400%

**267**

6in (15.25cm) 300%

8in (20.3cm) 400%

**268**

8in (20.3cm) 400%

10in (25.4cm) 500%

ALL PATTERNS ARE STANDARD 2IN (5CM) OR 4IN (10.2CM) UNLESS OTHERWISE STATED

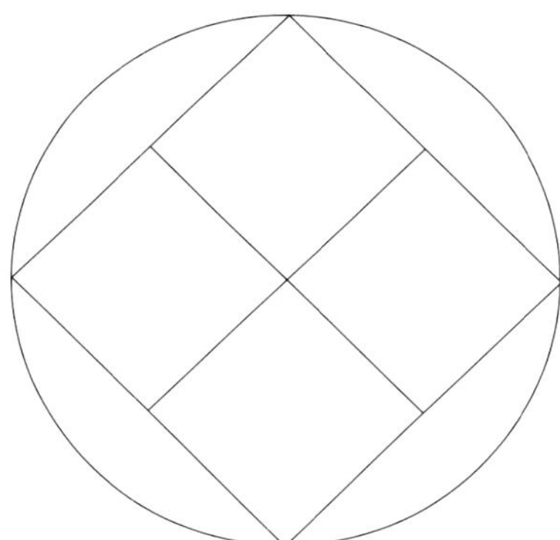

**269**

⟼ 5in (12.7cm) 250%

⟼ 8in (20.3cm) 400%

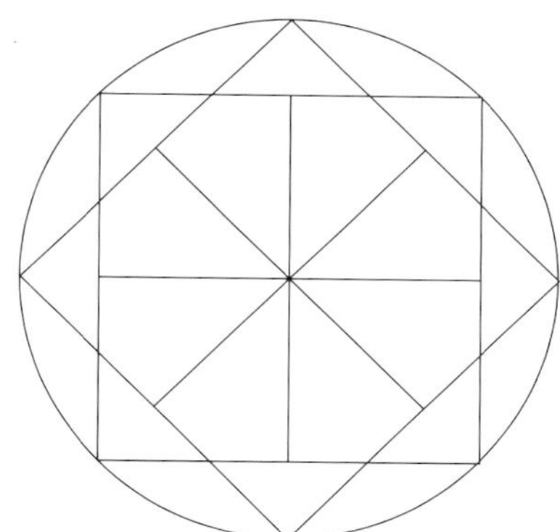

**270**

⟼ 6in (15.25cm) 300%

⟼ 8in (20.3cm) 400%

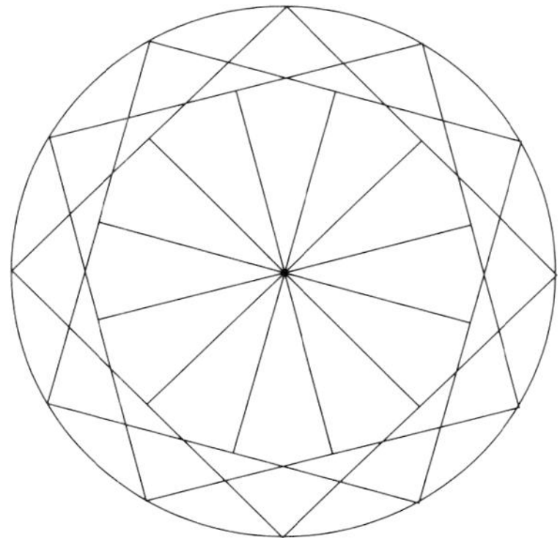

**271**

⟼ 8in (20.3cm) 400%

⟼ 10in (25.4cm) 500%

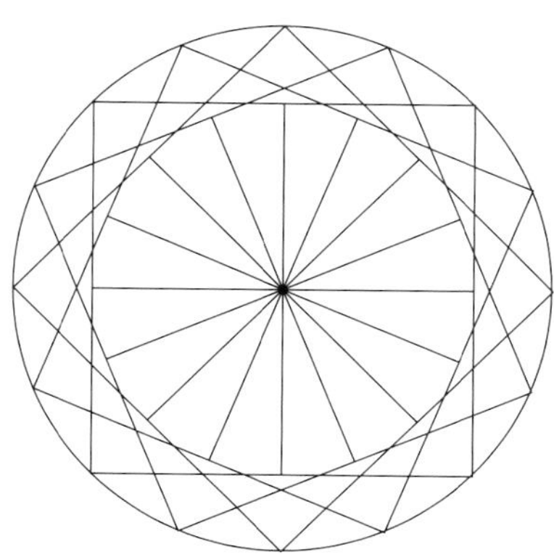

**272**

⟼ 10in (25.4cm) 500%

⟼ 12in (30.5cm) 600%

**273**

↔ 5in (12.7cm) 250%

↔ 8in (20.3cm) 400%

**274**

↔ 6in (15.25cm) 300%

↔ 8in (20.3cm) 400%

**275**

↔ 8in (20.3cm) 400%

↔ 10in (25.4cm) 500%

**276**

↔ 4in (10.2cm) 200%

↔ 6in (15.25cm) 300%

ALL PATTERNS ARE STANDARD 2IN (5CM) OR 4IN (10.2CM) UNLESS OTHERWISE STATED

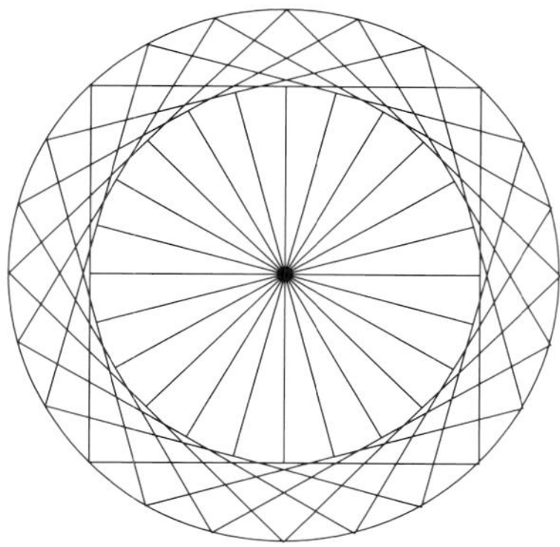

**277**

↔ 8in (20.3cm) 400%

↔ 10in (25.4cm) 500%

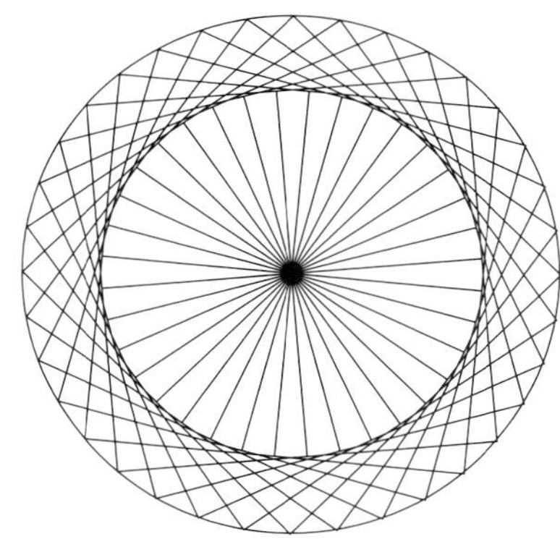

**278**

↔ 12in (30.5cm) 600%

↔ 15in (38.1cm) 750%

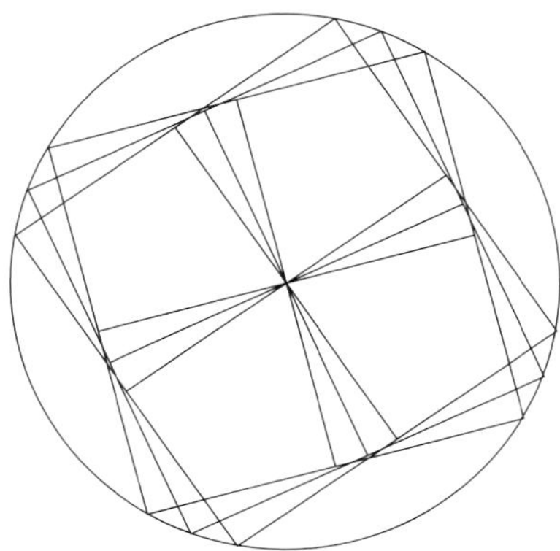

**279**

↔ 6in (15.25cm) 300%

↔ 8in (20.3cm) 400%

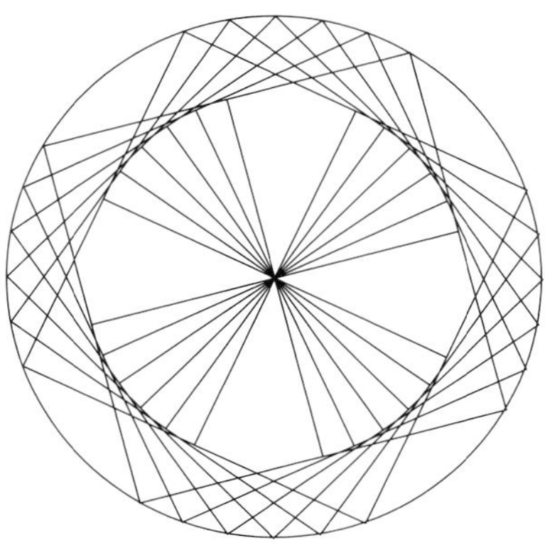

**280**

↔ 8in (20.3cm) 400%

↔ 10in (25.4cm) 500%

**281**

5in (12.7cm) 250%

8in (20.3cm) 400%

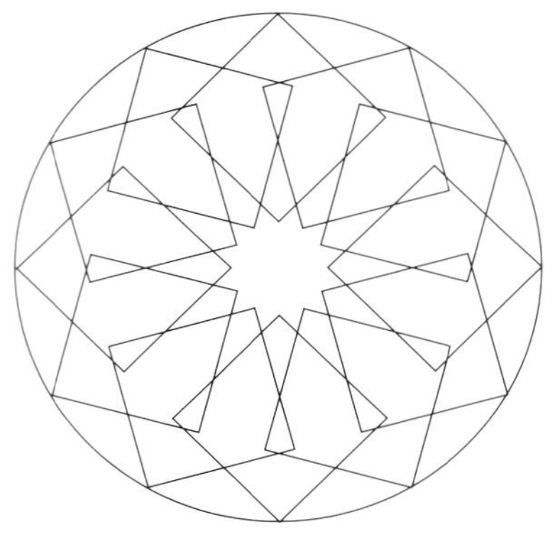

**282**

6in (15.25cm) 300%

8in (20.3cm) 400%

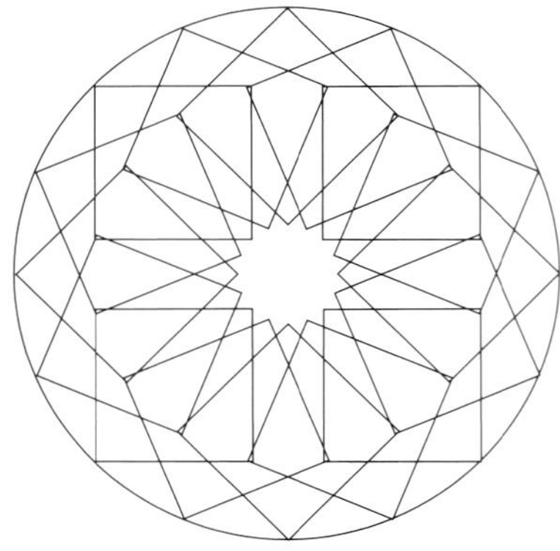

**283**

10in (25.4cm) 500%

12in (30.5cm) 600%

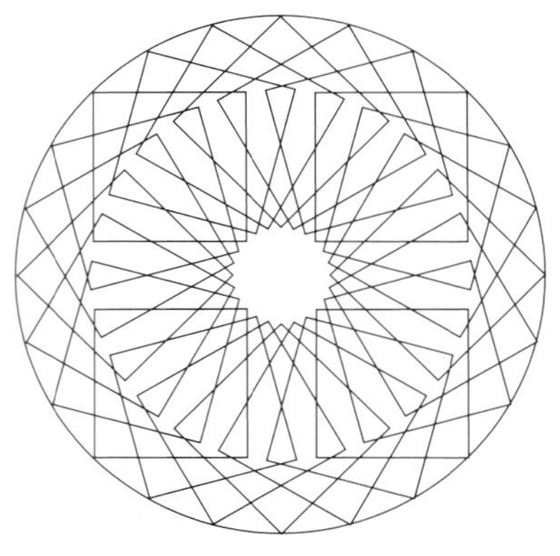

**284**

12in (30.5cm) 600%

15in (38.1cm) 750%

ALL PATTERNS ARE STANDARD 2IN (5CM) OR 4IN (10.2CM) UNLESS OTHERWISE STATED

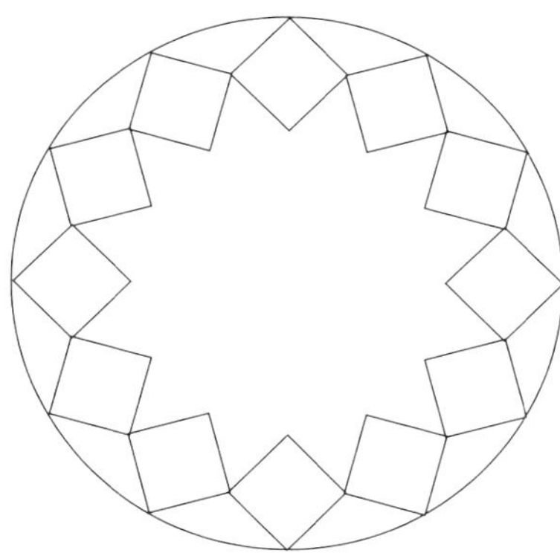

**285**

⟼ 5in (12.7cm) 250%

⟼ 8in (20.3cm) 400%

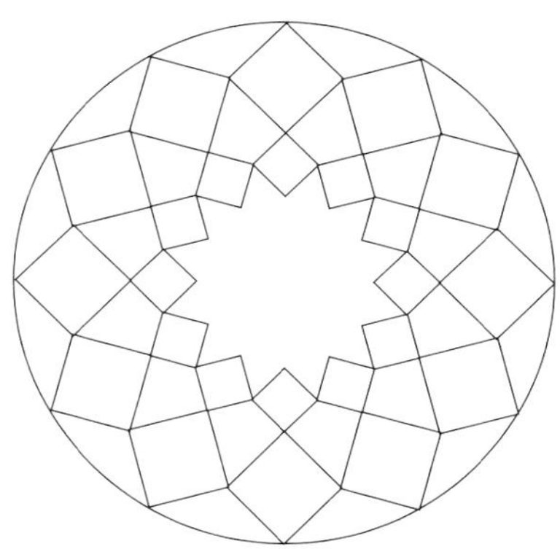

**286**

⟼ 8in (20.3cm) 400%

⟼ 10in (25.4cm) 500%

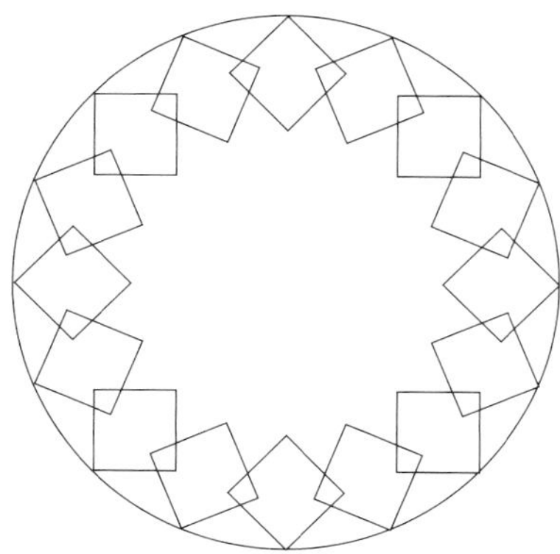

**287**

⟼ 5in (12.7cm) 250%

⟼ 8in (20.3cm) 400%

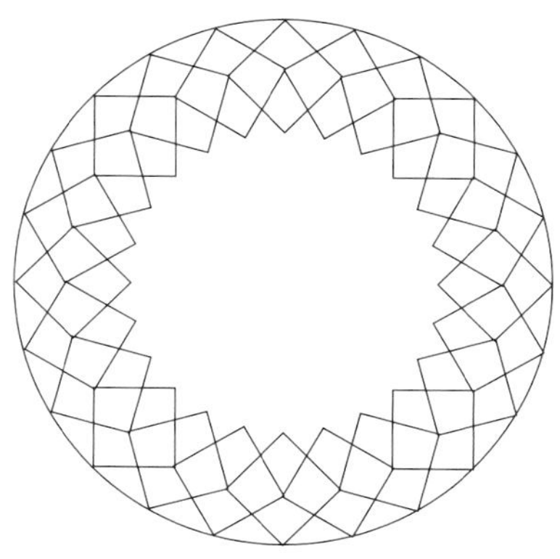

**288**

⟼ 12in (30.5cm) 600%

⟼ 15in (38.1cm) 750%

**289**

6in (15.25cm) 300%

8in (20.3cm) 400%

**290**

6in (15.25cm) 300%

8in (20.3cm) 400%

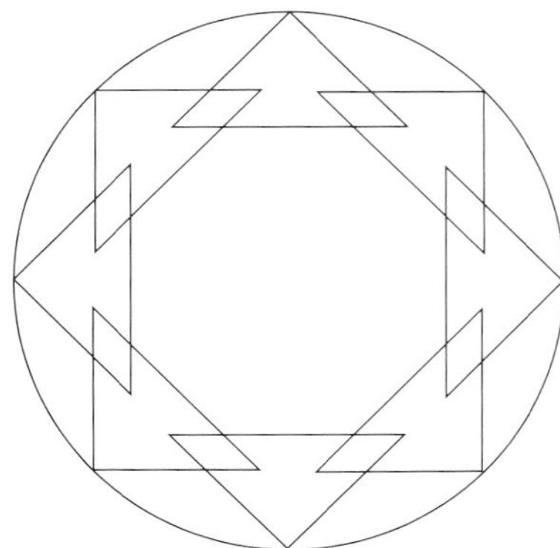

**291**

5in (12.7cm) 250%

8in (20.3cm) 400%

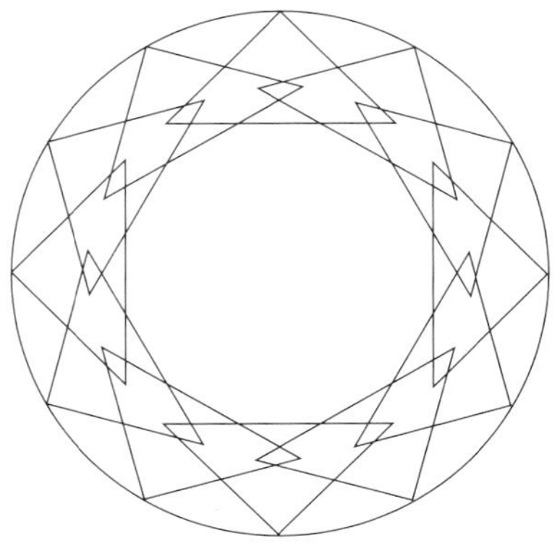

**292**

10in (25.4cm) 500%

12in (30.5cm) 600%

ALL PATTERNS ARE STANDARD 2IN (5CM) OR 4IN (10.2CM) UNLESS OTHERWISE STATED

**293**
6in (15.25cm) 300%
8in (20.3cm) 400%

**294**
8in (20.3cm) 400%
10in (25.4cm) 500%

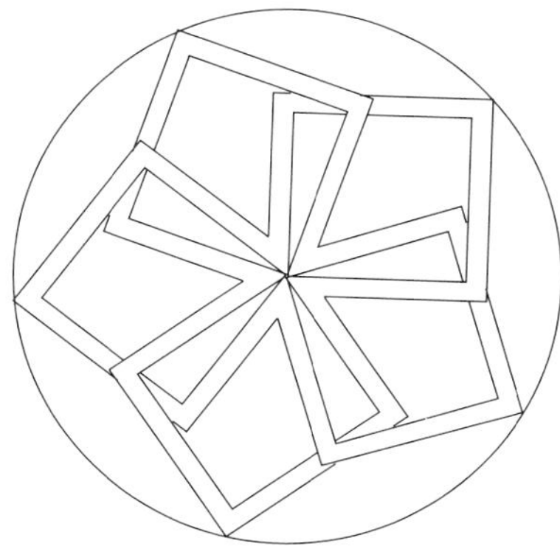

**295**
6in (15.25cm) 300%
8in (20.3cm) 400%

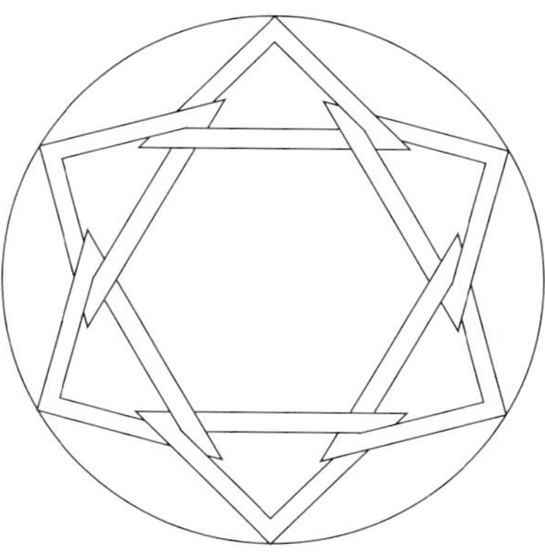

**296**
6in (15.25cm) 300%
10in (25.4cm) 500%

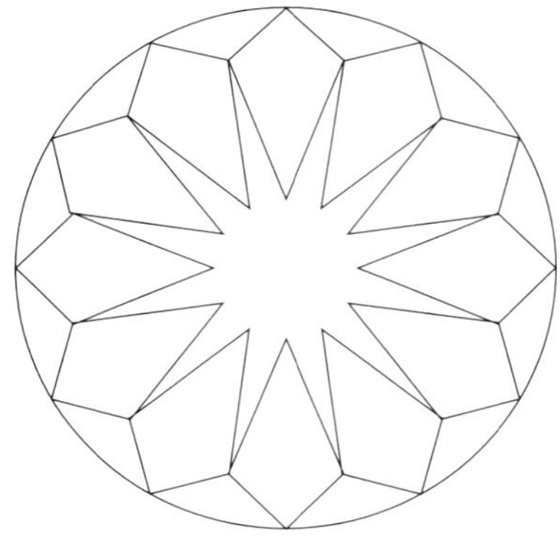

**297**

⟷ 5in (12.7cm) 250%

⟷ 8in (20.3cm) 400%

**298**

⟷ 8in (20.3cm) 400%

⟷ 10in (25.4cm) 500%

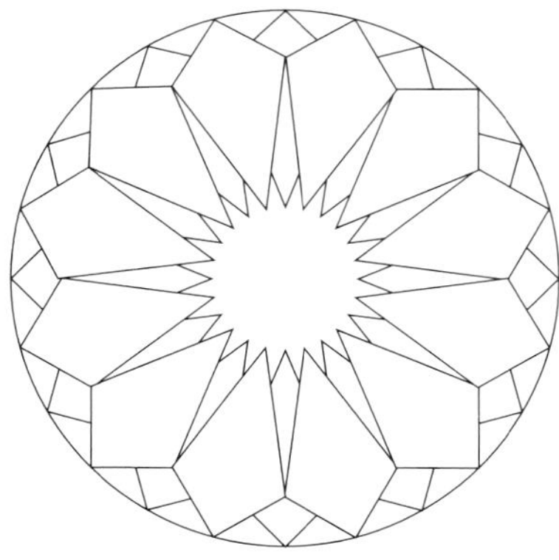

**299**

⟷ 8in (20.3cm) 400%

⟷ 10in (25.4cm) 500%

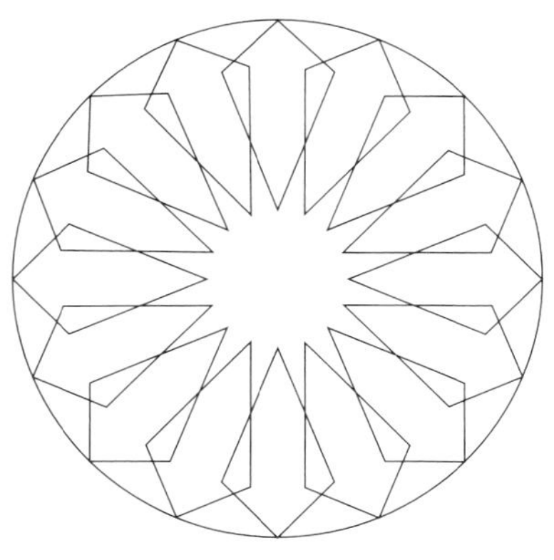

**300**

⟷ 6in (15.25cm) 300%

⟷ 8in (20.3cm) 400%

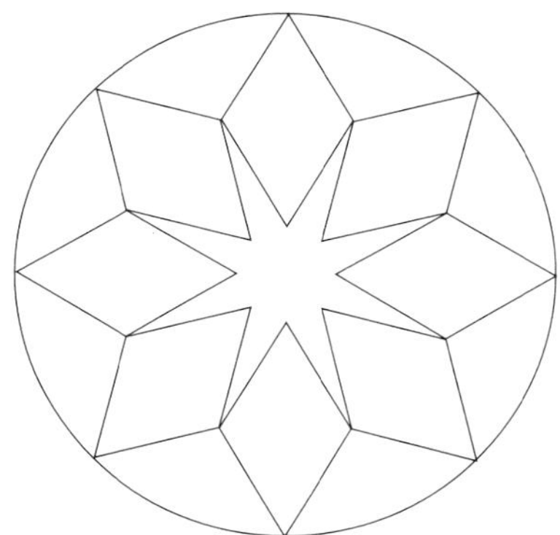

**301**

↔ 5in (12.7cm) 250%

↔ 8in (20.3cm) 400%

**302**

↔ 6in (15.25cm) 300%

↔ 8in (20.3cm) 400%

**303**

↔ 6in (15.25cm) 300%

↔ 8in (20.3cm) 400%

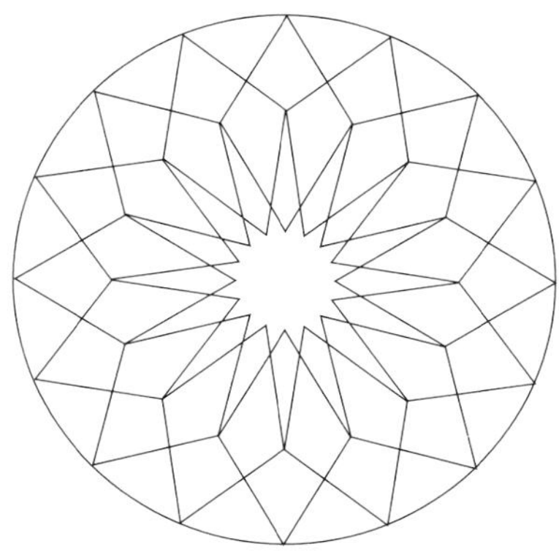

**304**

↔ 10in (25.4cm) 500%

↔ 12in (30.5cm) 600%

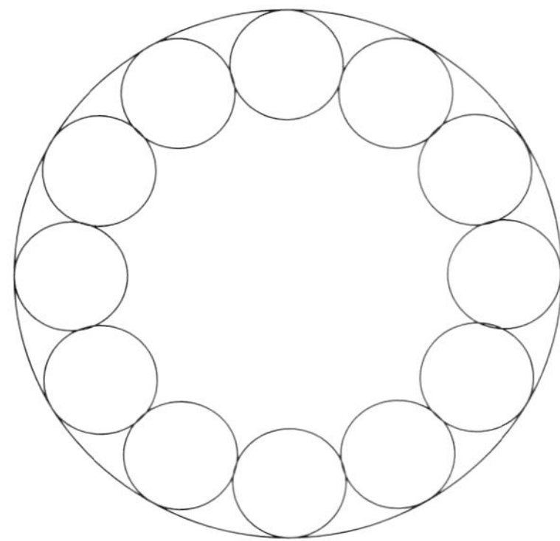

**305**

⟼ 5in (12.7cm) 250%

⟼ 8in (20.3cm) 400%

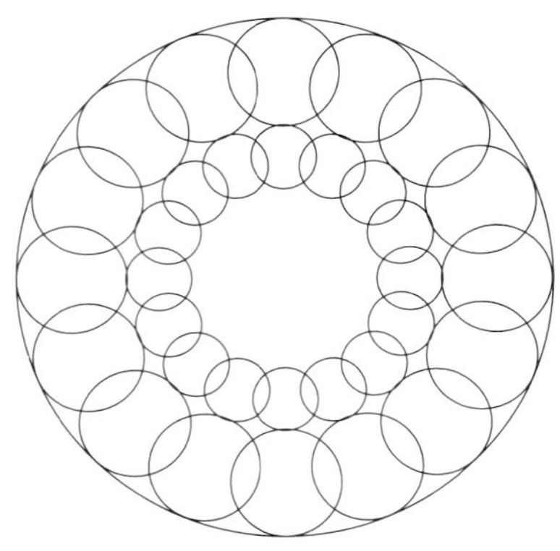

**306**

⟼ 8in (20.3cm) 400%

⟼ 10in (25.4cm) 500%

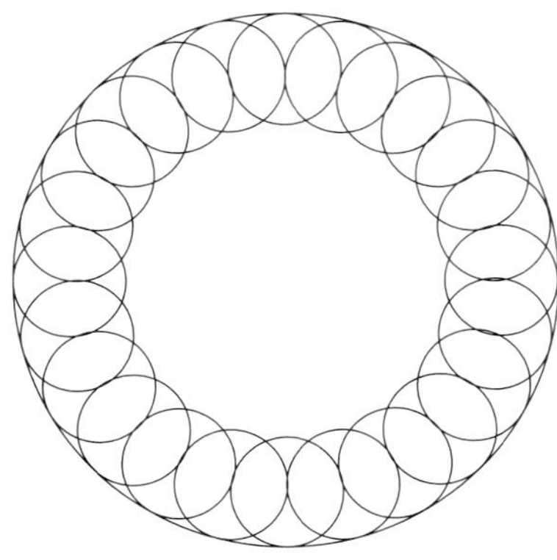

**307**

⟼ 10in (25.4cm) 500%

⟼ 12in (30.5cm) 600%

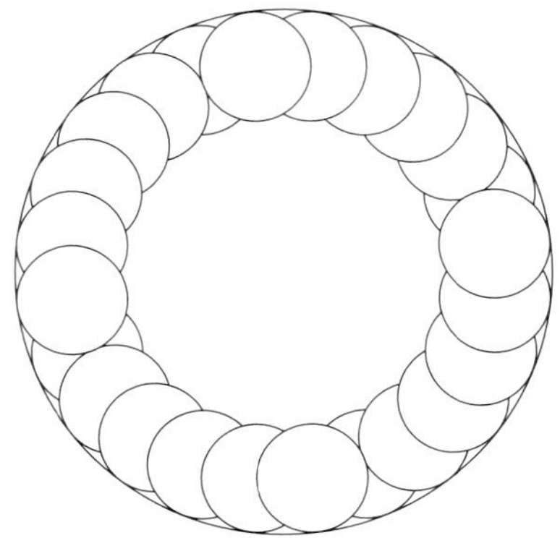

**308**

⟼ 6in (15.25cm) 300%

⟼ 8in (20.3cm) 400%

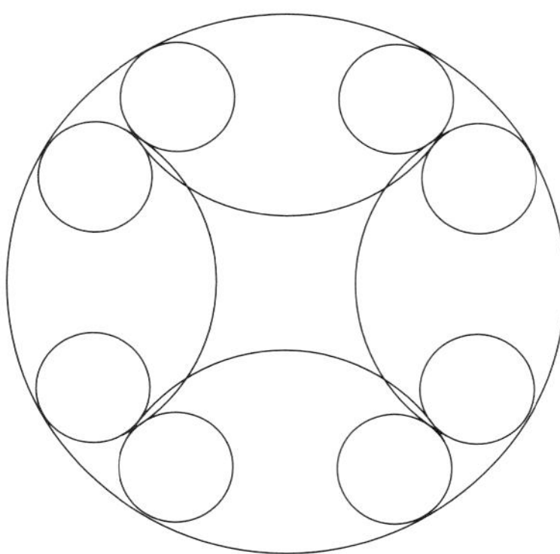

**309**

⟷ 5in (12.7cm) 250%

⟷ 8in (20.3cm) 400%

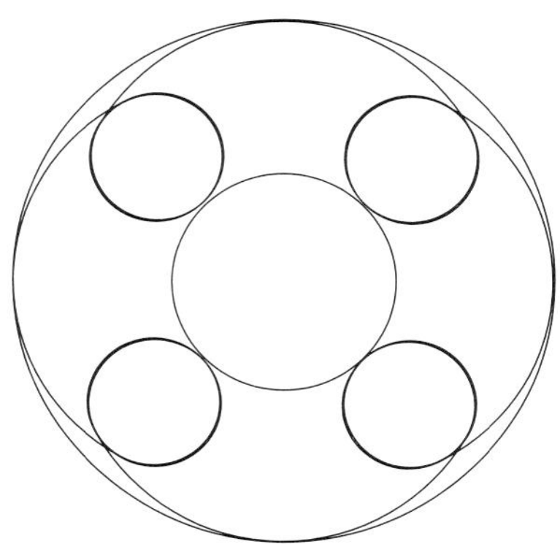

**310**

⟷ 4in (10.2cm) 200%

⟷ 8in (20.3cm) 400%

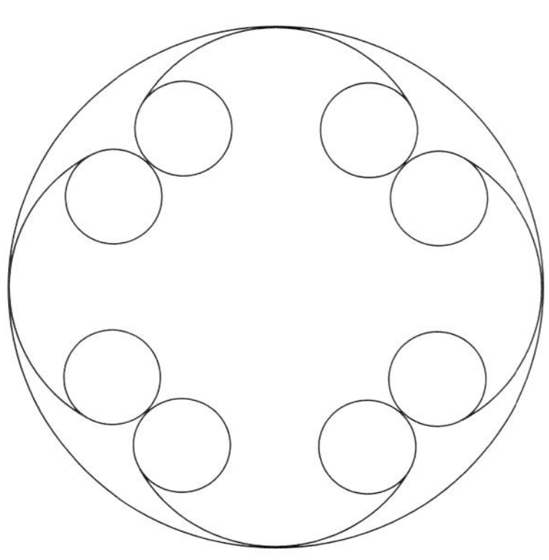

**311**

⟷ 6in (15.25cm) 300%

⟷ 8in (20.3cm) 400%

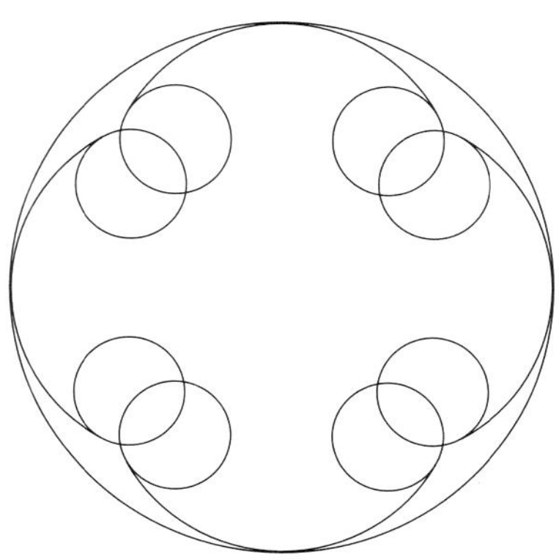

**312**

⟷ 8in (20.3cm) 400%

⟷ 10in (25.4cm) 500%

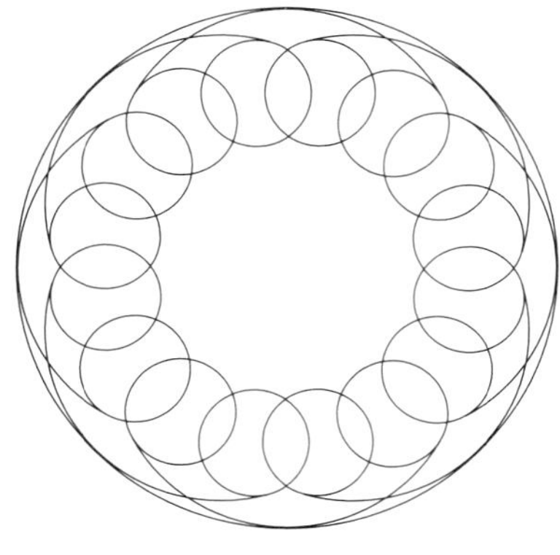

**313**

⟷ 8in (20.3cm) 400%

⟷ 10in (25.4cm) 500%

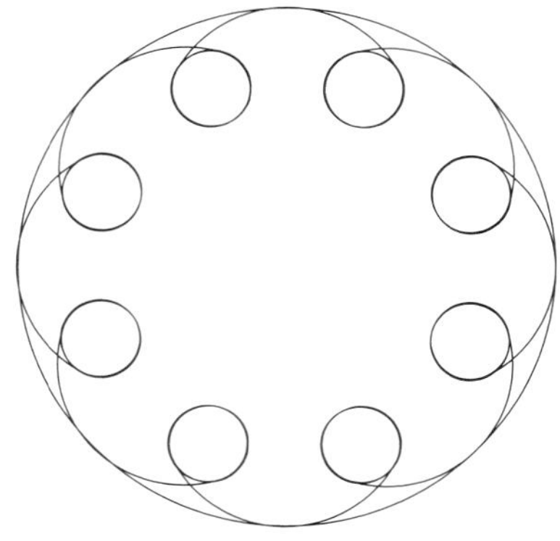

**314**

⟷ 6in (15.25cm) 300%

⟷ 8in (20.3cm) 400%

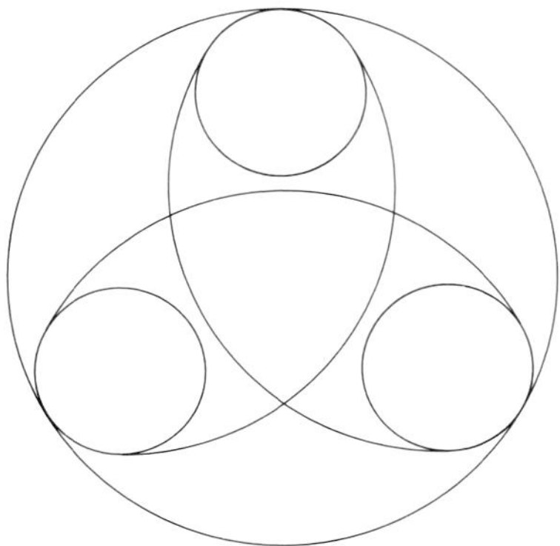

**315**

⟷ 5in (12.7cm) 250%

⟷ 8in (20.3cm) 400%

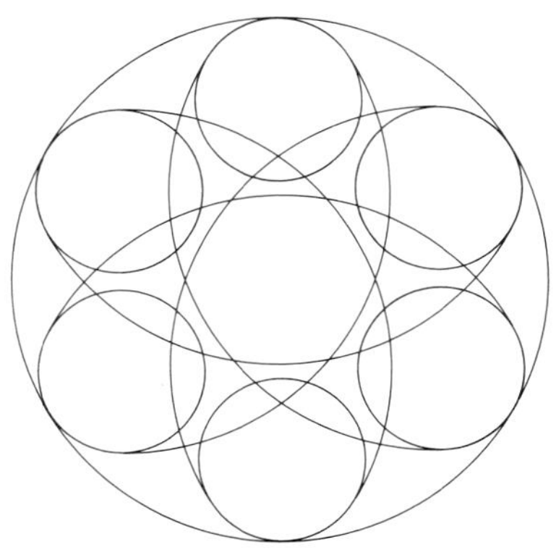

**316**

⟷ 8in (20.3cm) 400%

⟷ 10in (25.4cm) 500%

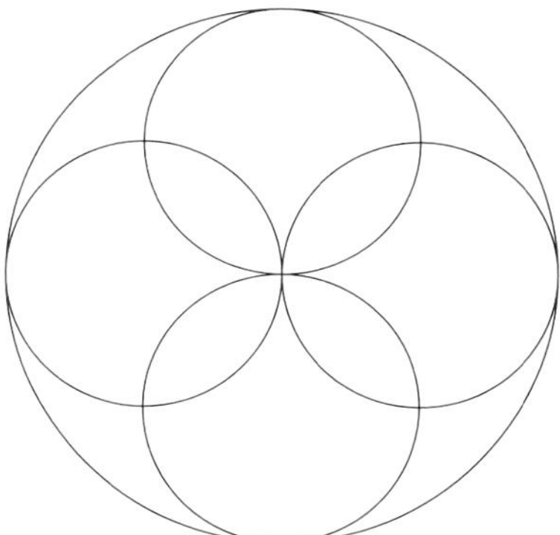

**317**

⟷ 5in (12.7cm) 250%

⟷ 8in (20.3cm) 400%

**318**

⟷ 6in (15.25cm) 300%

⟷ 8in (20.3cm) 400%

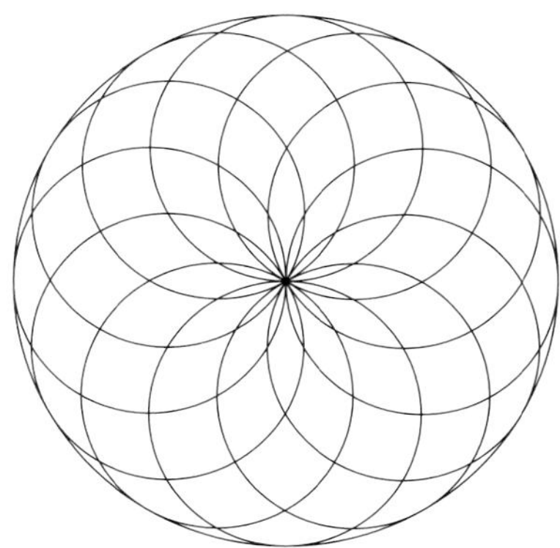

**319**

⟷ 10in (25.4cm) 500%

⟷ 12in (30.5cm) 600%

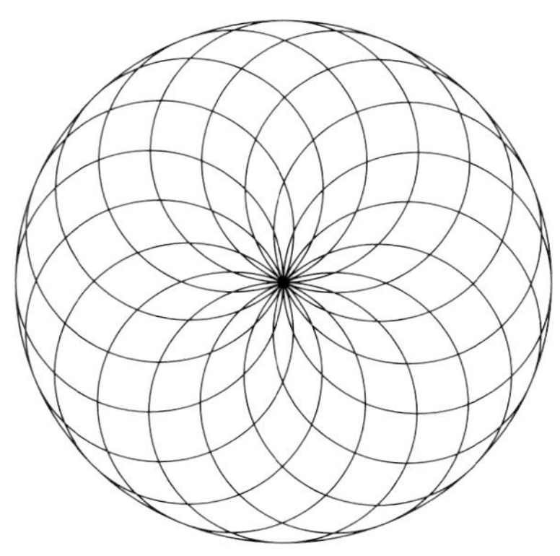

**320**

⟷ 15in (38.1cm) 750%

⟷ 18in (45.7cm) 900%

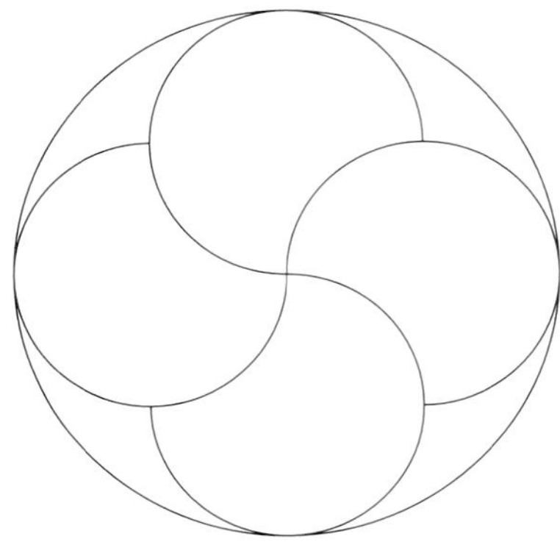

**321**
⟷ 4in (10.2cm) 200%
⟷ 8in (20.3cm) 400%

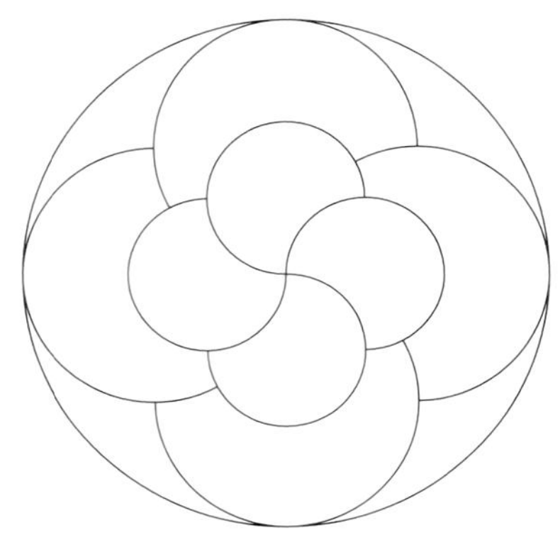

**322**
⟷ 5in (12.7cm) 250%
⟷ 8in (20.3cm) 400%

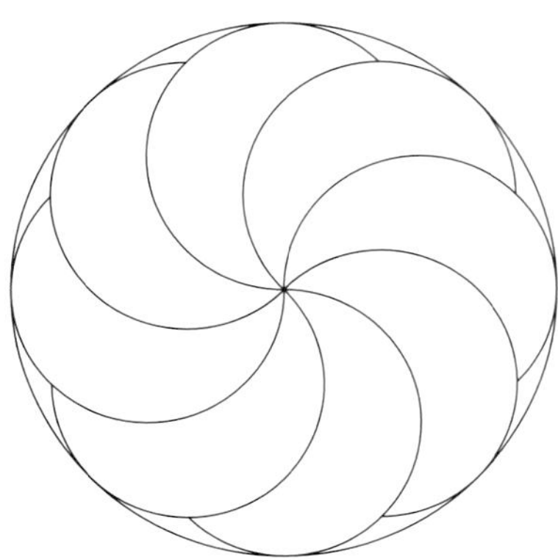

**323**
⟷ 6in (15.25cm) 300%
⟷ 8in (20.3cm) 400%

**324**
⟷ 8in (20.3cm) 400%
⟷ 12in (30.5cm) 600%

**325**
↦ 6in (15.25cm) 300%
↦ 8in (20.3cm) 400%

**326**
↦ 8in (20.3cm) 400%
↦ 12in (30.5cm) 600%

**327**
↦ 6in (15.25cm) 300%
↦ 8in (20.3cm) 400%

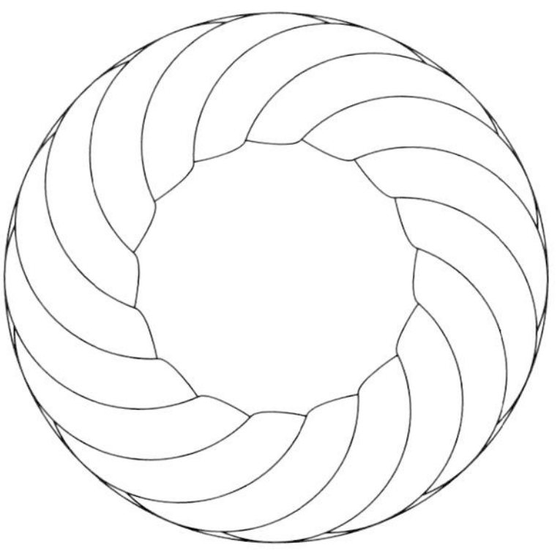

**328**
↦ 6in (15.25cm) 300%
↦ 8in (20.3cm) 400%

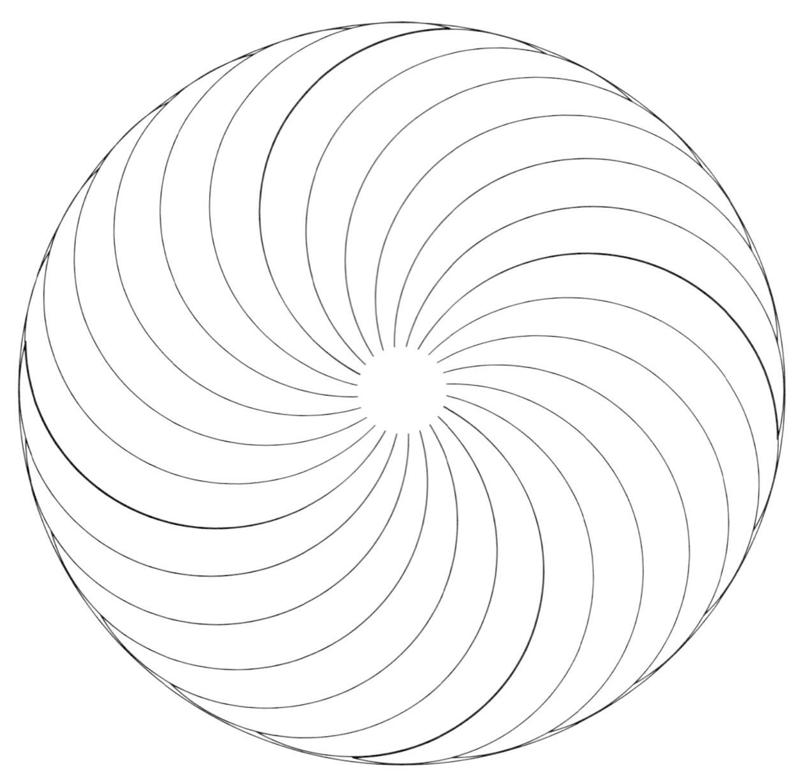

**329**

16in (40.6cm) 400%

30in (76.2cm) 750%

ALL PATTERNS ARE STANDARD 2IN (5CM) OR 4IN (10.2CM) UNLESS OTHERWISE STATED

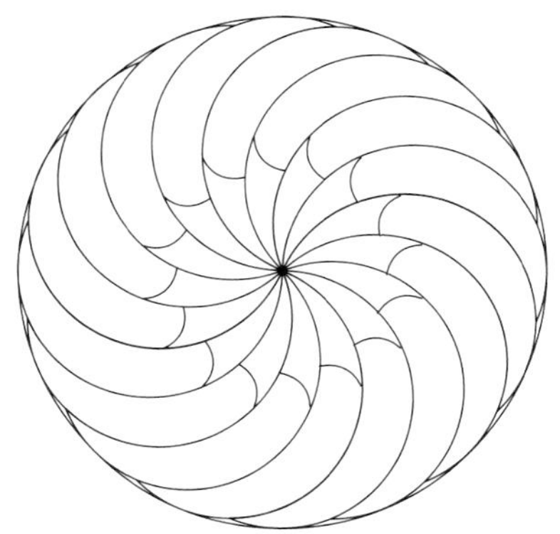

**330**

⟷ 8in (20.3cm) 400%

⟷ 12in (30.5cm) 600%

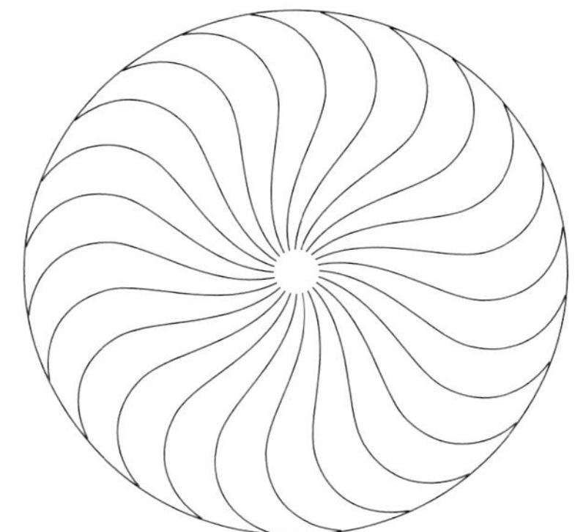

**331**

⟷ 6in (15.25cm) 300%

⟷ 8in (20.3cm) 400%

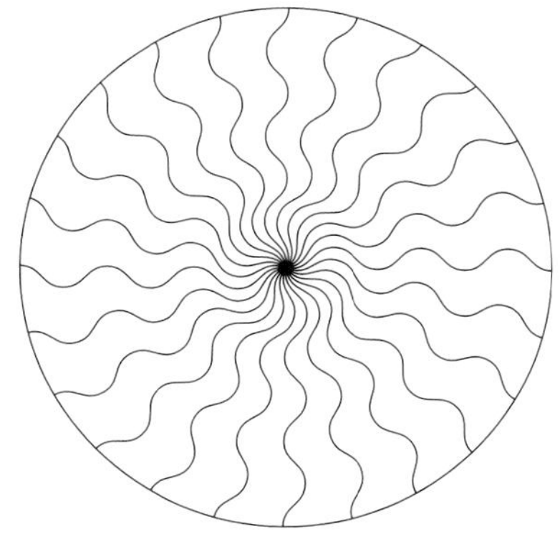

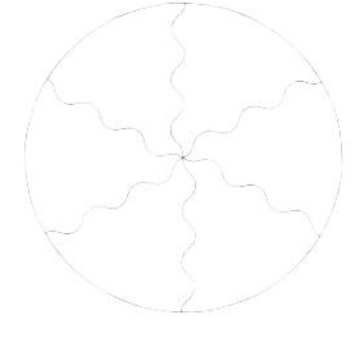

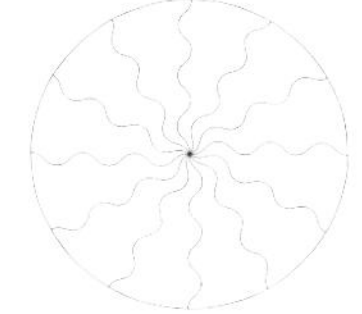

**332**

⟷ 5in (12.7cm) 250%

⟷ 12in (30.5cm) 600%

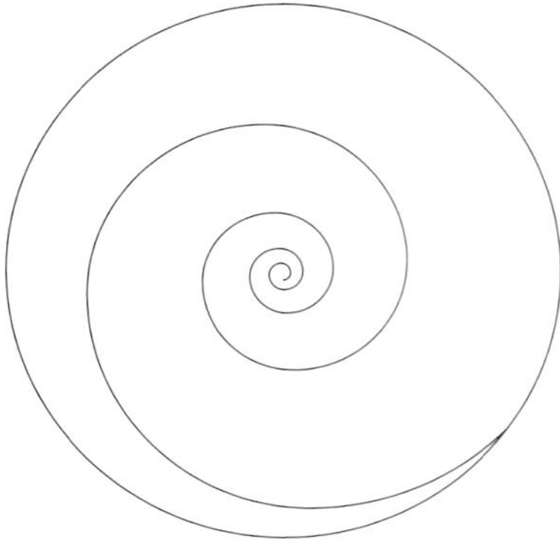

**333**

5in (12.7cm) 250%

8in (20.3cm) 400%

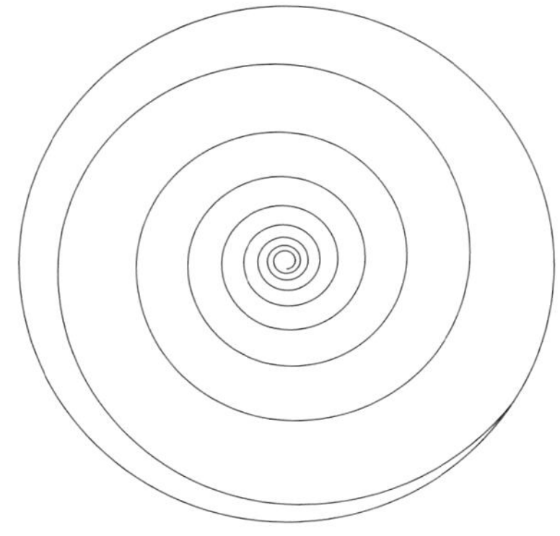

**334**

8in (20.3cm) 400%

10in (25.4cm) 500%

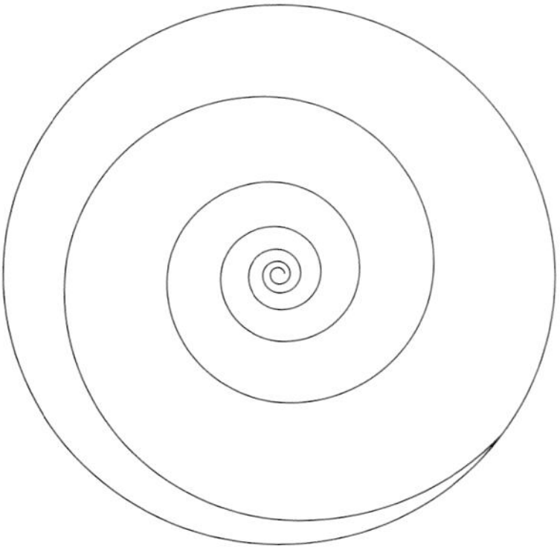

**335**

5in (12.7cm) 250%

8in (20.3cm) 400%

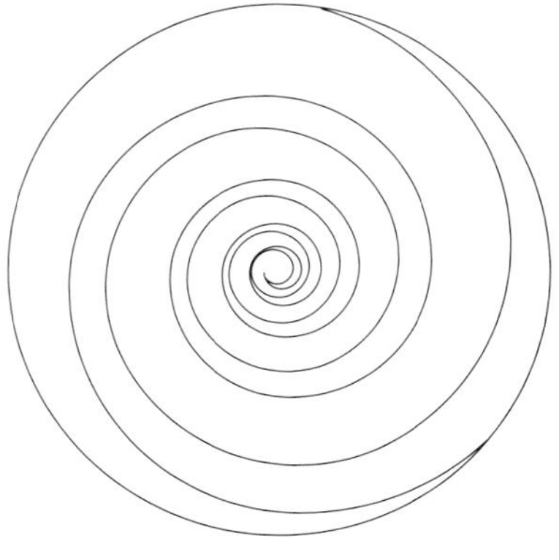

**336**

8in (20.3cm) 400%

10in (25.4cm) 500%

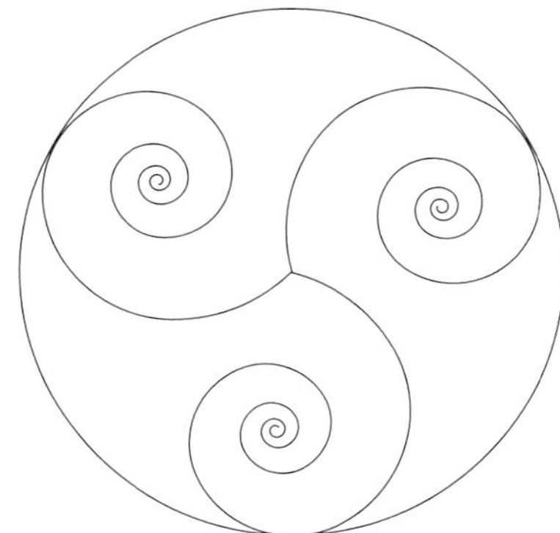

**337**

4in (10.2cm) 200%

8in (20.3cm) 400%

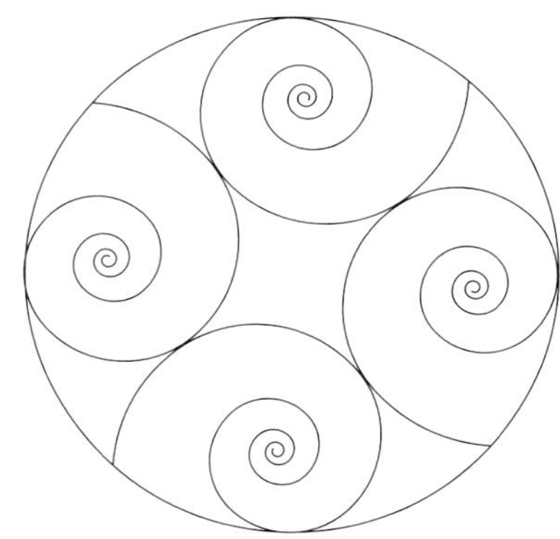

**338**

6in (15.25cm) 300%

8in (20.3cm) 400%

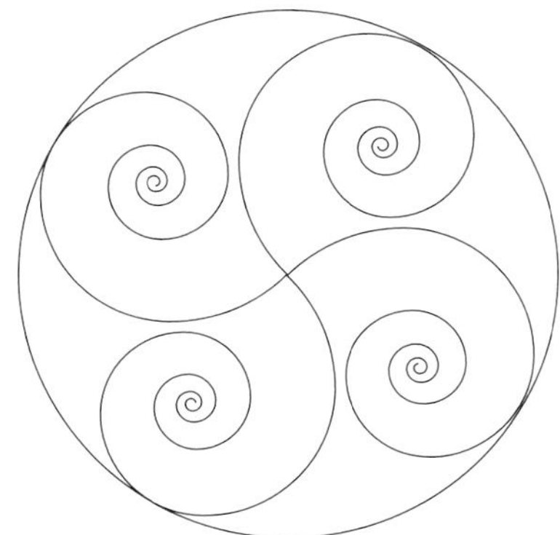

**339**

6in (15.25cm) 300%

8in (20.3cm) 400%

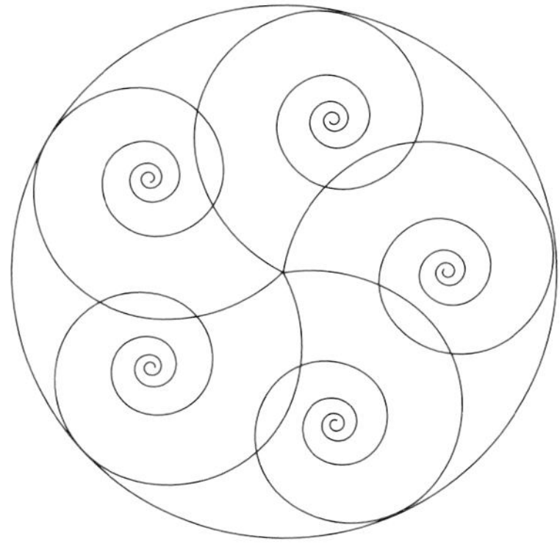

**340**

8in (20.3cm) 400%

10in (25.4cm) 500%

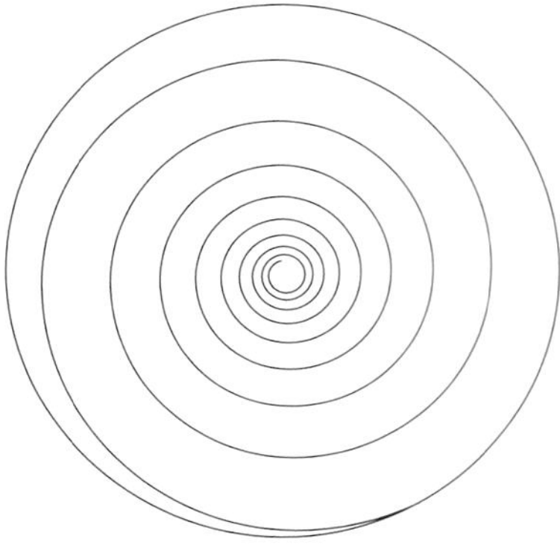

**341**

⟼ 8in (20.3cm) 400%

⟼ 10in (25.4cm) 500%

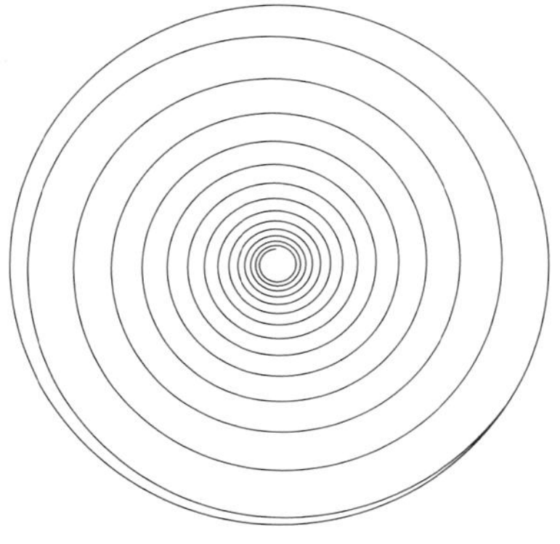

**342**

⟼ 12in (30.5cm) 600%

⟼ 15in (38.1cm) 750%

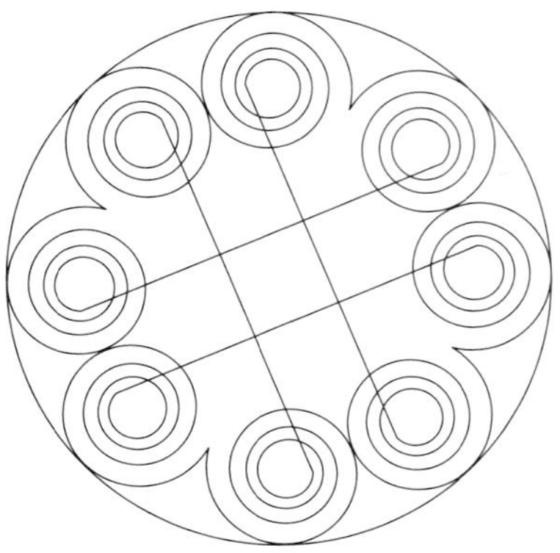

**343**

⟼ 8in (20.3cm) 400%

⟼ 10in (25.4cm) 500%

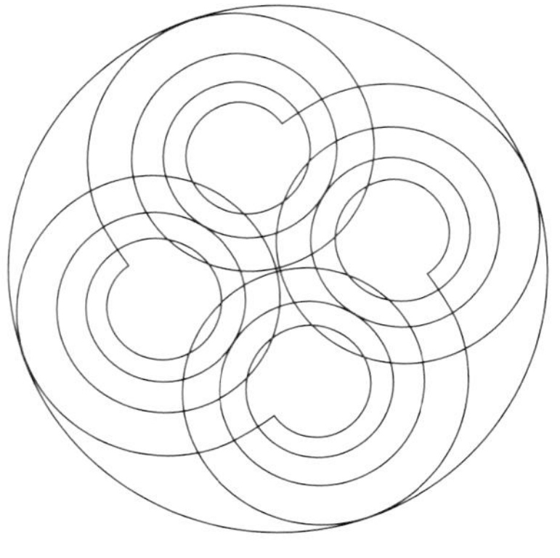

**344**

⟼ 8in (20.3cm) 400%

⟼ 10in (25.4cm) 500%

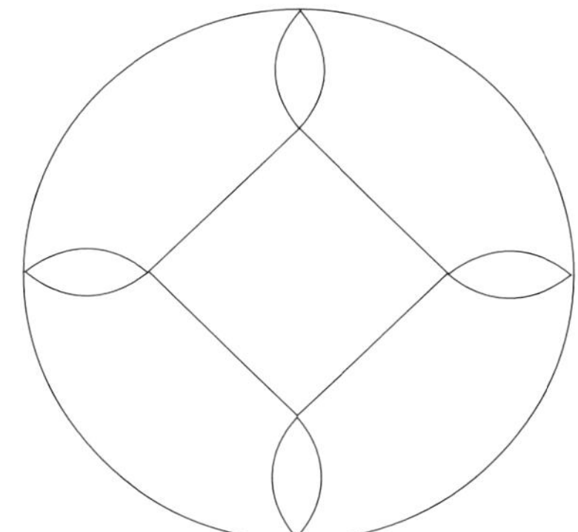

**345** 

4in (10.2cm) 200%

8in (20.3cm) 400%

**346**

5in (12.7cm) 250%

6in (15.25cm) 300%

**347**

6in (15.25cm) 300%

8in (20.3cm) 400%

**348**

8in (20.3cm) 400%

10in (25.4cm) 500%

**349**

⟷ 20in (50.8cm) 500%

⟷ 24in (61cm) 600%

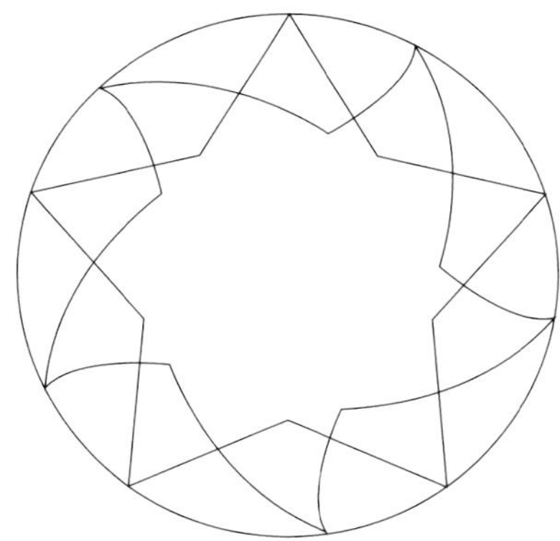

**350**

⟼ 5in (12.7cm) 250%

⟼ 8in (20.3cm) 400%

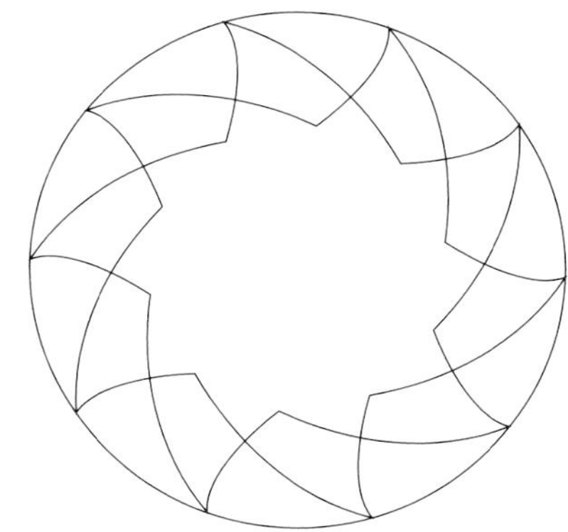

**351**

⟼ 8in (20.3cm) 400%

⟼ 10in (25.4cm) 500%

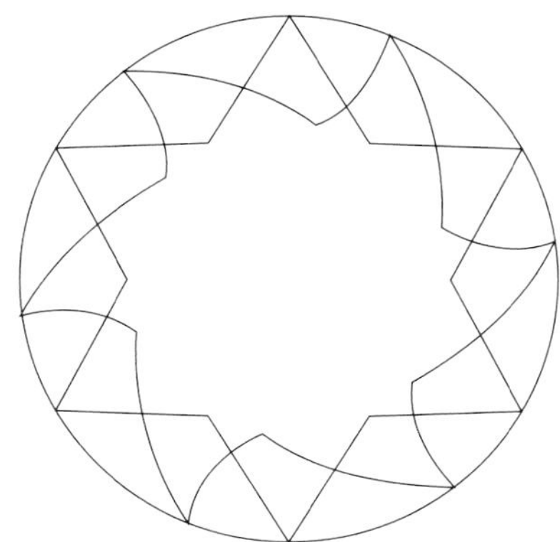

**352**

⟼ 5in (12.7cm) 250%

⟼ 8in (20.3cm) 400%

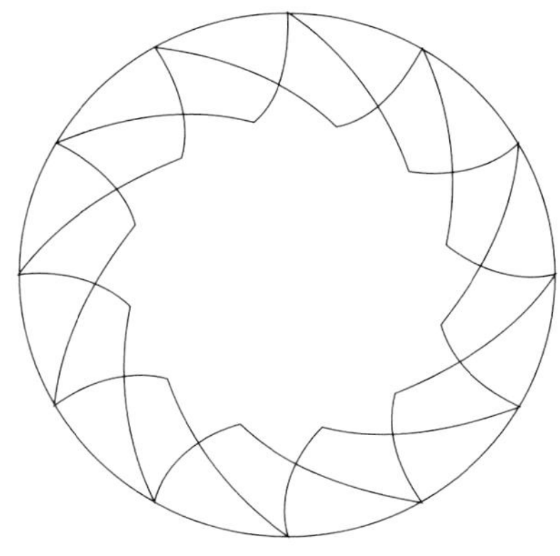

**353**

⟼ 8in (20.3cm) 400%

⟼ 10in (25.4cm) 500%

**354**

⟼ 5in (12.7cm) 250%

⟼ 8in (20.3cm) 400%

**355**

⟼ 8in (20.3cm) 400%

⟼ 10in (25.4cm) 500%

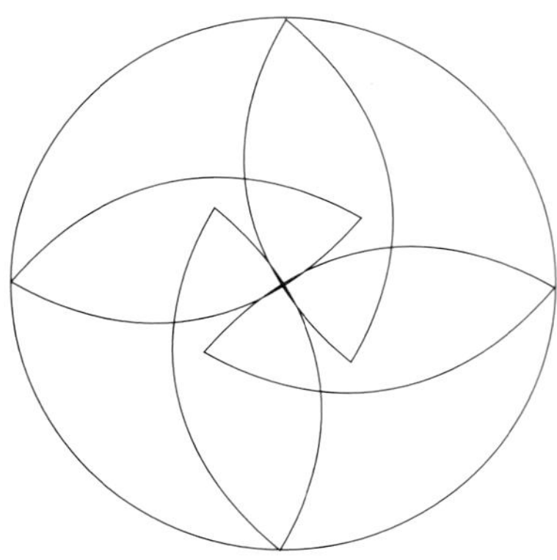

**356**

⟼ 5in (12.7cm) 250%

⟼ 8in (20.3cm) 400%

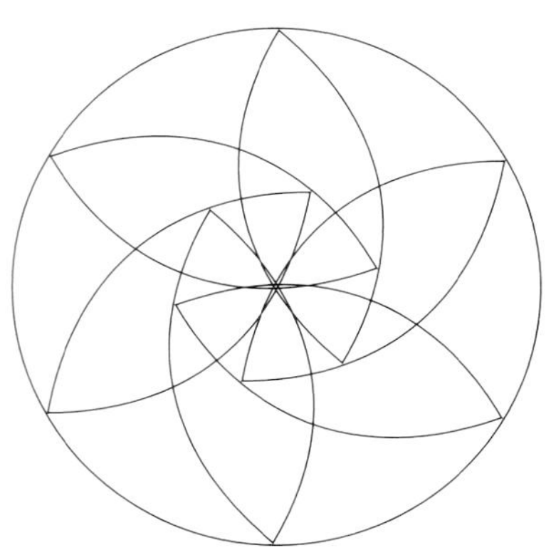

**357**

⟼ 6in (15.25cm) 300%

⟼ 8in (20.3cm) 400%

ALL PATTERNS ARE STANDARD 2IN (5CM) OR 4IN (10.2CM) UNLESS OTHERWISE STATED

**358**

6in (15.25cm) 300%

8in (20.3cm) 400%

**359**

6in (15.25cm) 300%

12in (30.5cm) 600%

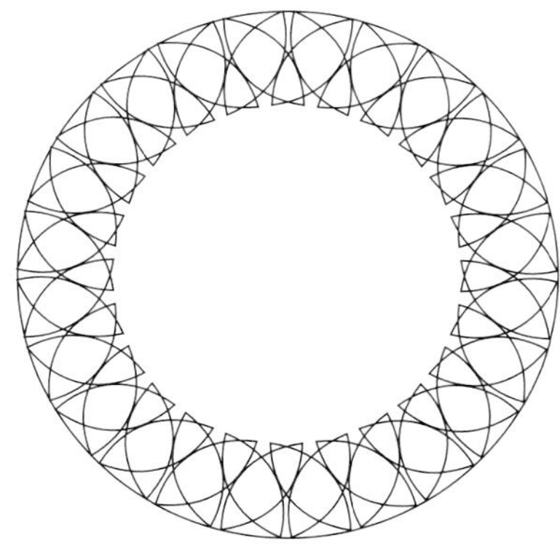

**360**

6in (15.25cm) 300%

16in (40.6cm) 800%

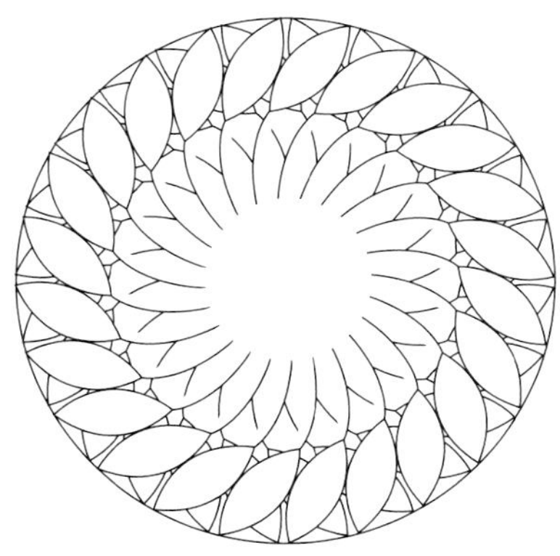

**361**

6in (15.25cm) 300%

12in (30.5cm) 600%

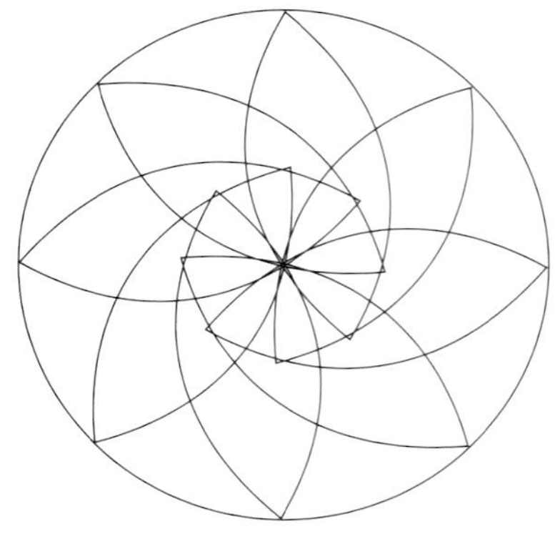

**362**

↦ 6in (15.25cm) 300%

↦ 8in (20.3cm) 400%

**363**

↦ 6in (15.25cm) 300%

↦ 8in (20.3cm) 400%

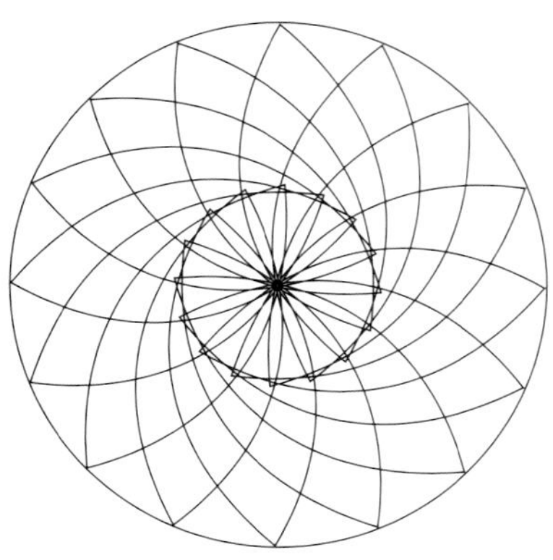

**364**

↦ 12in (30.5cm) 600%

↦ 18in (45.7cm) 900%

**365**

↦ 6in (15.25cm) 300%

↦ 16in (40.6cm) 800%

ALL PATTERNS ARE STANDARD 2IN (5CM) OR 4IN (10.2CM) UNLESS OTHERWISE STATED

**366**

20in (50.8cm) 500%

30in (76.2cm) 750%

**367**

20in (50.8cm) 500%

30in (76.2cm) 750%

**368**

6in (15.25cm) 300%

8in (20.3cm) 400%

**369**

10in (25.4cm) 500%

12in (30.5cm) 600%

**370**

6in (15.25cm) 300%

12in (30.5cm) 600%

**371**

6in (15.25cm) 300%

10in (25.4cm) 500%

**372**

6in (15.25cm) 300%

8in (20.3cm) 400%

**373**

6in (15.25cm) 300%

10in (25.4cm) 500%

**374**

5in (12.7cm) 250%

12in (30.5cm) 600%

**375**

6in (15.25cm) 300%

8in (20.3cm) 400%

ALL PATTERNS ARE STANDARD 2IN (5CM) OR 4IN (10.2CM) UNLESS OTHERWISE STATED

**376**

6in (15.25cm) 300%

10in (25.4cm) 500%

**377**

6in (15.25cm) 300%

8in (20.3cm) 400%

**378**

8in (20.3cm) 400%

12in (30.5cm) 600%

**379**

8in (20.3cm) 400%

12in (30.5cm) 600%

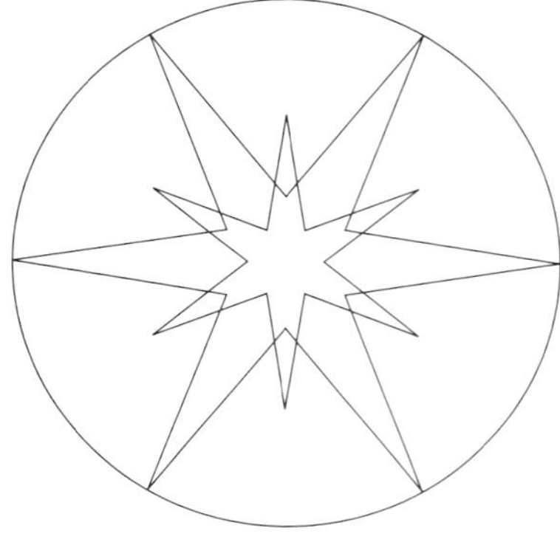

**380**

6in (15.25cm) 300%

8in (20.3cm) 400%

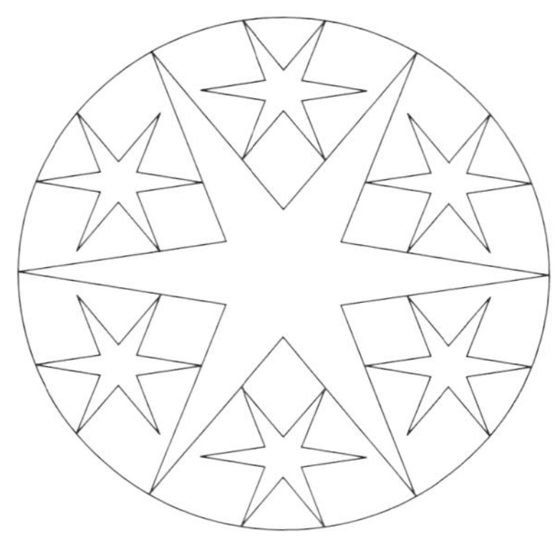

**381**

8in (20.3cm) 400%

10in (25.4cm) 500%

**382**

8in (20.3cm) 400%

10in (25.4cm) 500%

**383**

8in (20.3cm) 400%

10in (25.4cm) 500%

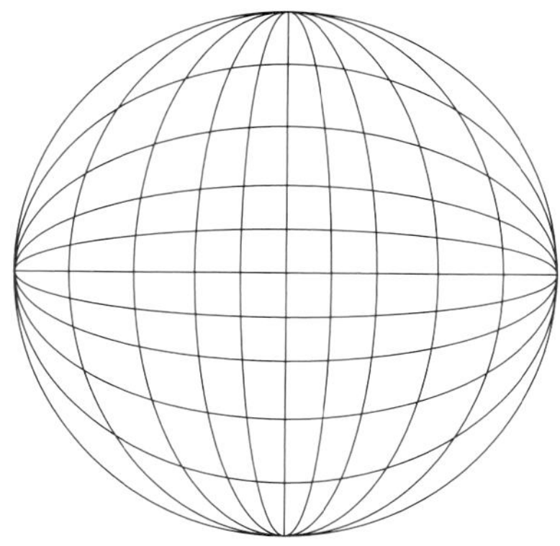

**384**

⟼ 6in (15.25cm) 300%

⟼ 8in (20.3cm) 400%

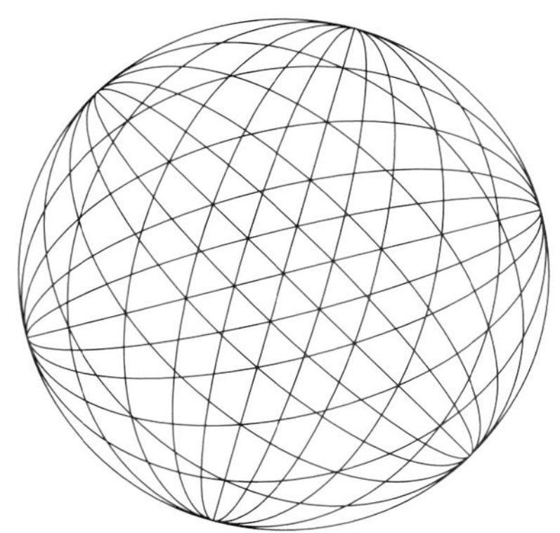

**385**

⟼ 15in (38.1cm) 750%

⟼ 16in (40.6cm) 800%

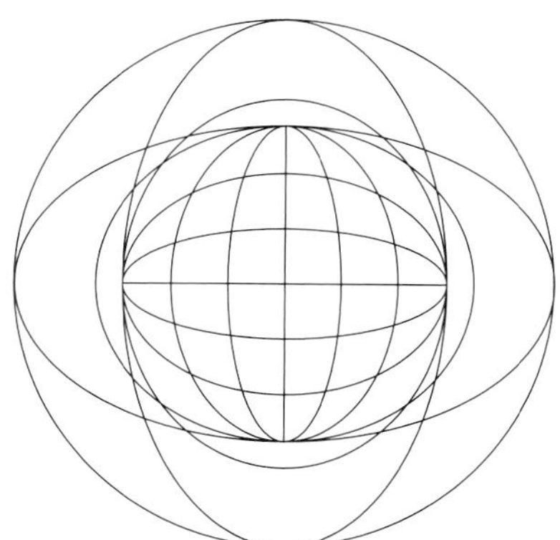

**386**

⟼ 8in (20.3cm) 400%

⟼ 10in (25.4cm) 500%

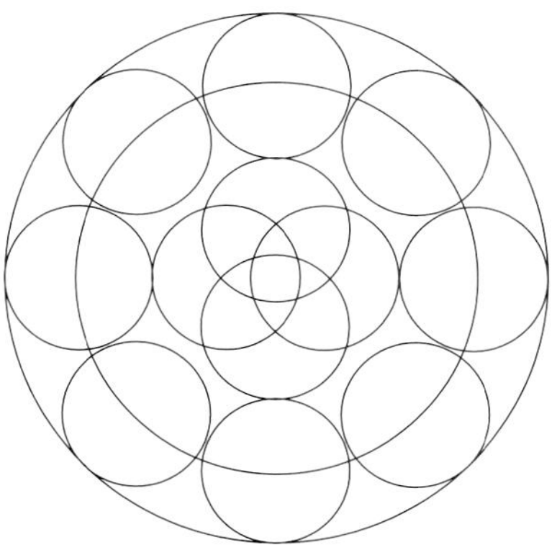

**387**

⟼ 8in (20.3cm) 400%

⟼ 10in (25.4cm) 500%

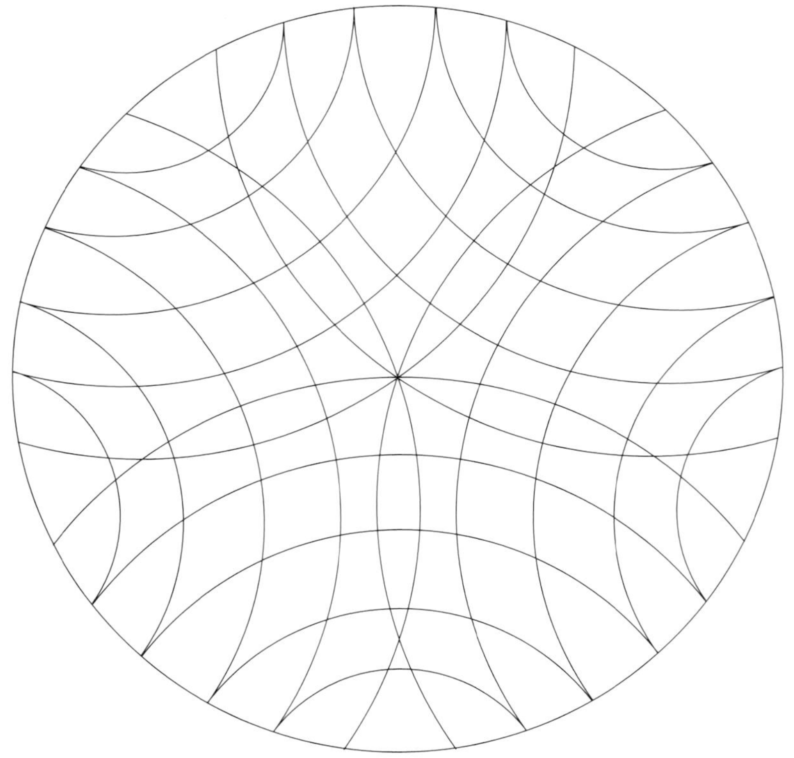

**388**

16in (40.6cm) 400%

24in (61cm) 600%

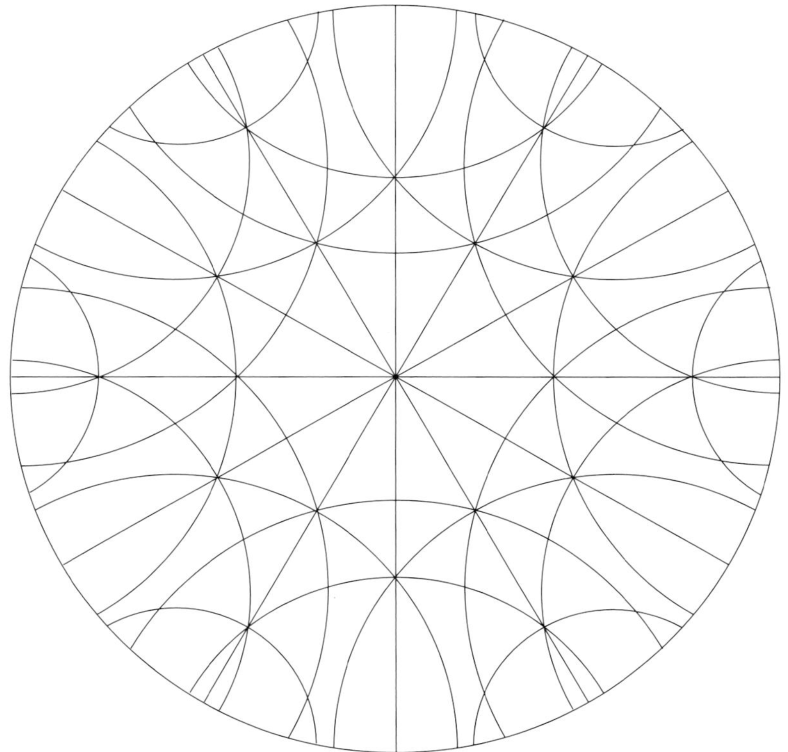

**389**

↔ 20in (50.8cm) 500%

↔ 30in (76.2cm) 750%

# Stars

Stars are versatile shapes and only a small selection is shown here. As for the circular motifs, designs have been included with numbers of points not easily achieved by traditional methods of drafting, but with useful lines of symmetry. If a star shape looks like a promising motif or the design calls for a shape with a certain number of lines of symmetry (but the star shape isn't quite right), experiment with the proportions of the points by moving the inner points either nearer or farther from the center point until the desired result is achieved.

More ideas for stars designs can be found in the chapter on circles (see pages 116–173).

**390**

8in (20.3cm) 400%

10in (25.4cm) 500%

**391**

8in (20.3cm) 400%

10in (25.4cm) 500%

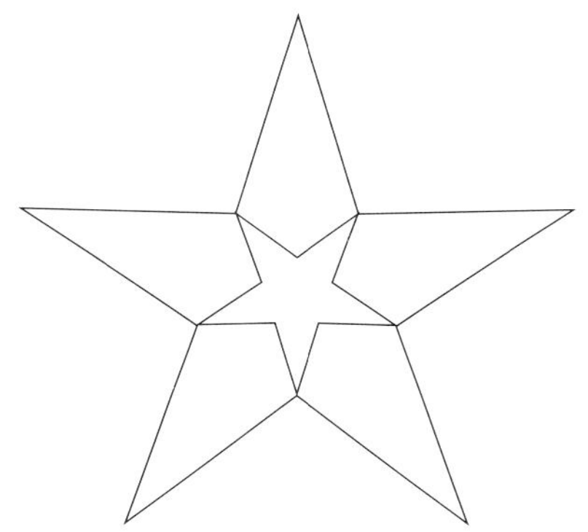

**392**

⟷ 4in (10.2cm) 200%

⟷ 5in (12.7cm) 250%

**393**

⟷ 6in (15.25cm) 300%

⟷ 8in (20.3cm) 400%

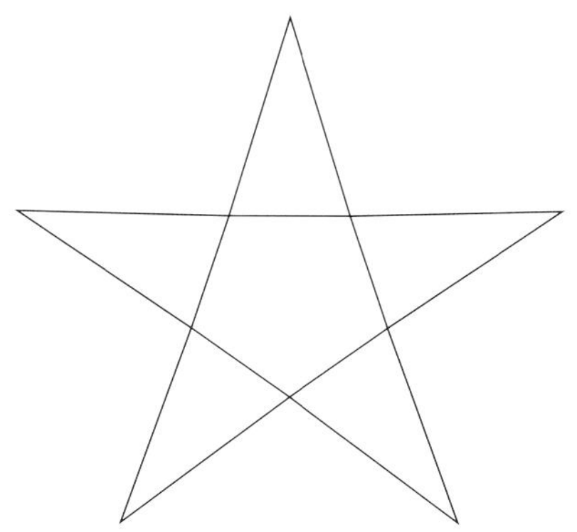

**394**

⟷ 4in (10.2cm) 200%

⟷ 5in (12.7cm) 250%

**395**

⟷ 8in (20.3cm) 400%

⟷ 10in (25.4cm) 500%

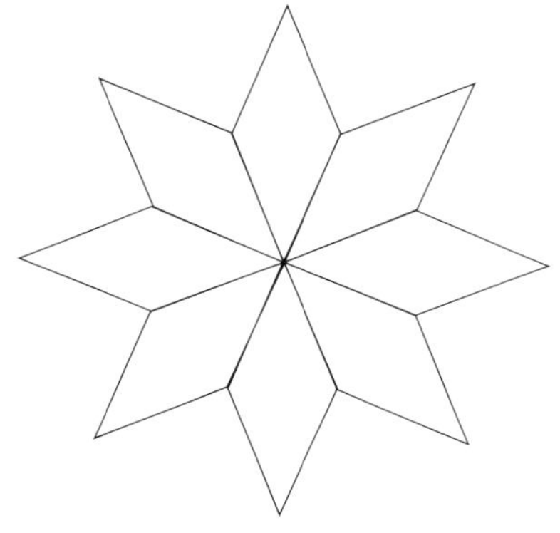

**396**

⟼ 4in (10.2cm) 200%

⟼ 5in (12.7cm) 250%

**397**

⟼ 6in (15.25cm) 300%

⟼ 8in (20.3cm) 400%

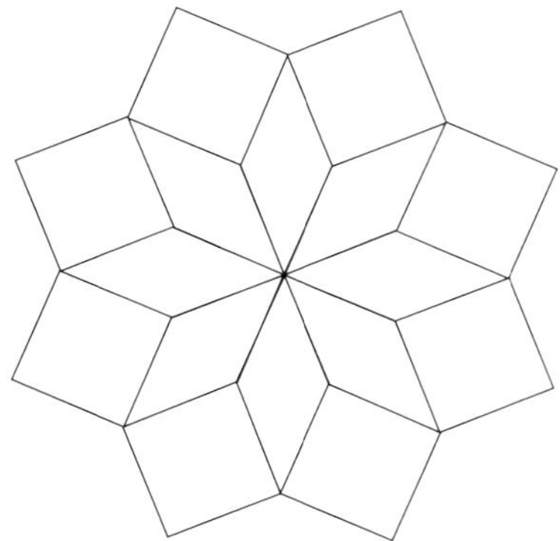

**398**

⟼ 4in (10.2cm) 200%

⟼ 5in (12.7cm) 250%

**399**

⟼ 12in (30.5cm) 600%

⟼ 15in (38.1cm) 750%

**400**

8in (20.3cm) 400%

10in (25.4cm) 500%

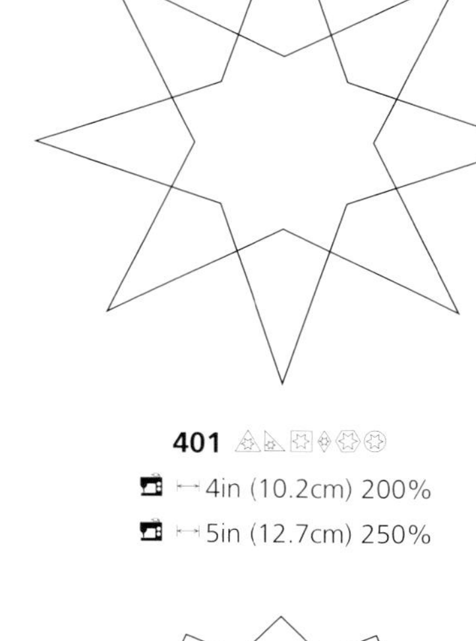

**401**

4in (10.2cm) 200%

5in (12.7cm) 250%

**402**

6in (15.25cm) 300%

8in (20.3cm) 400%

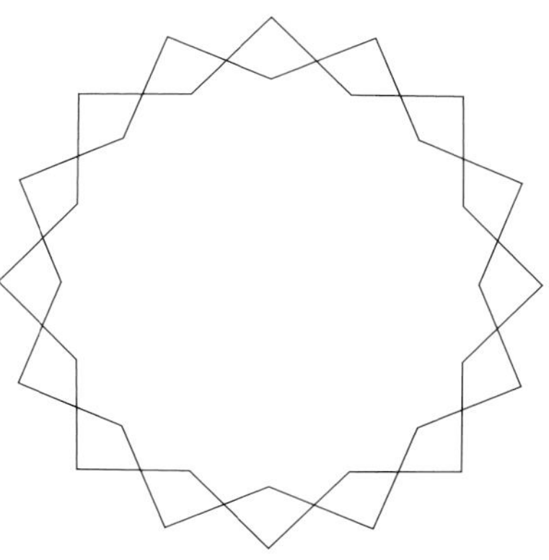

**403**

6in (15.25cm) 300%

8in (20.3cm) 400%

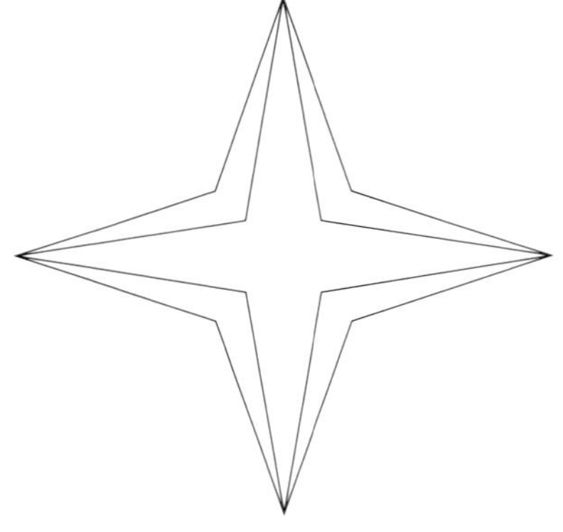

**404**

⟷ 4in (10.2cm) 200%

⟷ 5in (12.7cm) 250%

**405**

⟷ 4in (10.2cm) 200%

⟷ 5in (12.7cm) 250%

**406**

⟷ 6in (15.25cm) 300%

⟷ 8in (20.3cm) 400%

**407**

⟷ 8in (20.3cm) 400%

⟷ 10in (25.4cm) 500%

ALL PATTERNS ARE STANDARD 2IN (5CM) OR 4IN (10.2CM) UNLESS OTHERWISE STATED

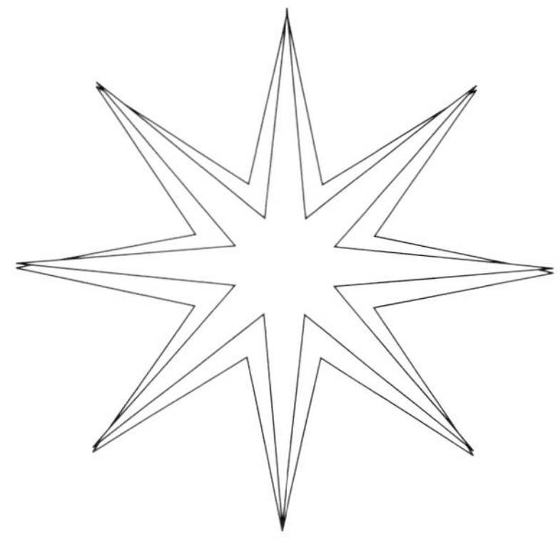

**408**

⟷ 6in (15.25cm) 300%

⟷ 8in (20.3cm) 400%

**409**

⟷ 6in (15.25cm) 300%

⟷ 8in (20.3cm) 400%

**410**

⟷ 10in (25.4cm) 500%

⟷ 12in (30.5cm) 600%

**411**

⟷ 10in (25.4cm) 500%

⟷ 12in (30.5cm) 600%

**412**

⟷ 6in (15.25cm) 300%

⟷ 8in (20.3cm) 400%

**413**

⟷ 8in (20.3cm) 400%

⟷ 10in (25.4cm) 500%

**414**

⟷ 12in (30.5cm) 600%

⟷ 15in (38.1cm) 750%

**415**

⟷ 12in (30.5cm) 600%

⟷ 15in (38.1cm) 750%

**416**

16in (40.6cm) 400%

20in (50.8cm) 500%

**417**

16in (40.6cm) 400%

20in (50.8cm) 500%

**418**

16in (40.6cm) 400%

20in (50.8cm) 500%

**419**

⟼ 4in (10.2cm) 200%

⟼ 5in (12.7cm) 250%

**420**

⟼ 6in (15.25cm) 300%

⟼ 8in (20.3cm) 400%

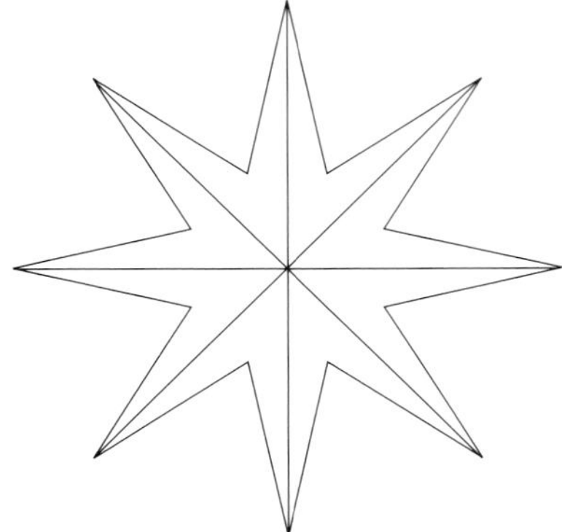

**421**

⟼ 6in (15.25cm) 300%

⟼ 8in (20.3cm) 400%

**422**

⟼ 6in (15.25cm) 300%

⟼ 8in (20.3cm) 400%

ALL PATTERNS ARE STANDARD 2IN (5CM) OR 4IN (10.2CM) UNLESS OTHERWISE STATED

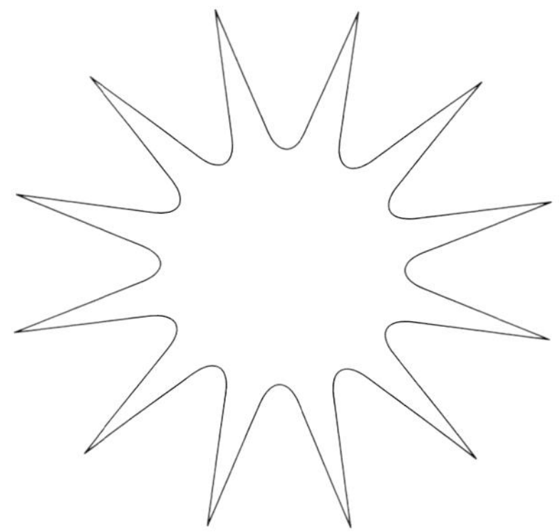

**423**

4in (10.2cm) 200%

5in (12.7cm) 250%

**424**

6in (15.25cm) 300%

8in (20.3cm) 400%

**425**

6in (15.25cm) 300%

8in (20.3cm) 400%

**426**

10in (25.4cm) 500%

12in (30.5cm) 600%

# Hearts

Hearts often appear in quilting designs, used singly or in groups. Long used as a traditional symbol of love and marriage, it was considered unlucky for a young woman to stitch this symbol in her quilt if she were not engaged or married. Originally the paper template was created by folding a piece of paper in half and cutting a rough feather shape. Hearts work well in most other shapes and can be adapted to fill an awkward space. Note that two circle motifs will easily fit in the space in the top of a heart shape.

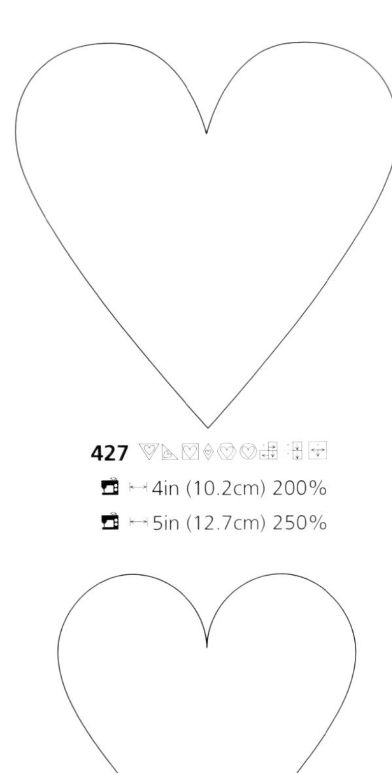

**427**

4in (10.2cm) 200%

5in (12.7cm) 250%

**428**

4in (10.2cm) 200%

6in (15.25cm) 300%

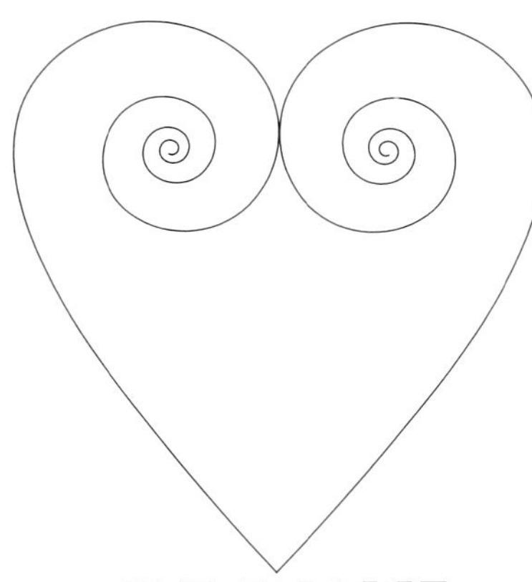

**429**

6in (15.25cm) 300%

8in (20.3cm) 400%

**430**

8in (20.3cm) 400%

10in (25.4cm) 500%

**431**

6in (15.25cm) 300%

8in (20.3cm) 400%

**432**

8in (20.3cm) 400%

10in (25.4cm) 500%

**433**

15in (38.1cm) 375%

18in (45.7cm) 450%

ALL PATTERNS ARE STANDARD 2IN (5CM) OR 4IN (10.2CM) UNLESS OTHERWISE STATED

**434**

6in (15.25cm) 300%

8in (20.3cm) 400%

**435**

6in (15.25cm) 300%

8in (20.3cm) 400%

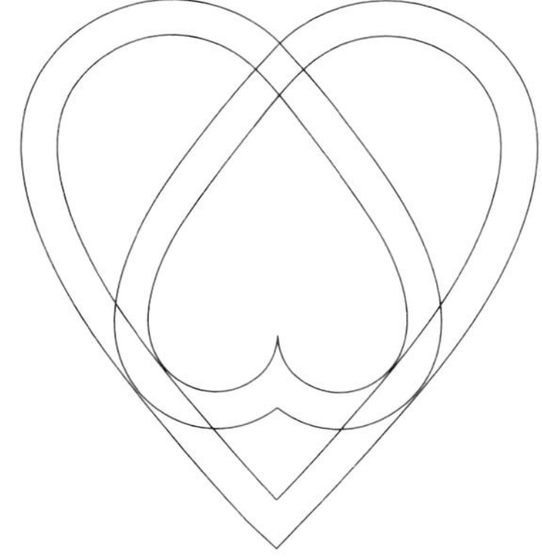

**436**

8in (20.3cm) 400%

10in (25.4cm) 500%

**437**

10in (25.4cm) 500%

12in (30.5cm) 600%

**438**

(2¼in (5.6cm)) to 6¾in (15.25cm) 300%

(2¼in (5.6cm)) to 8in (20.3cm) 400%

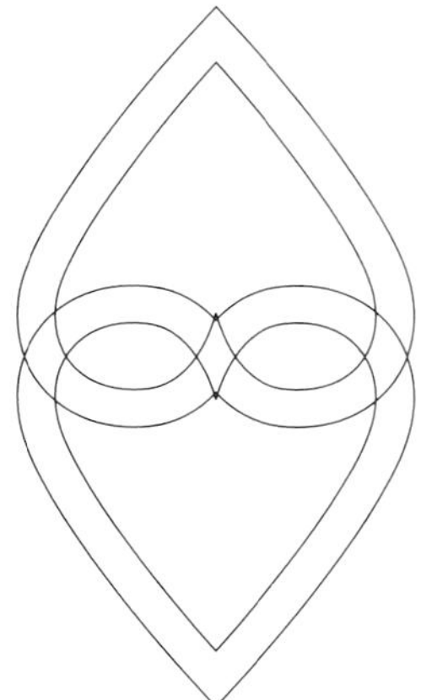

**439** 

(2¼in (5.6cm)) to 6¾in (15.25cm) 300%

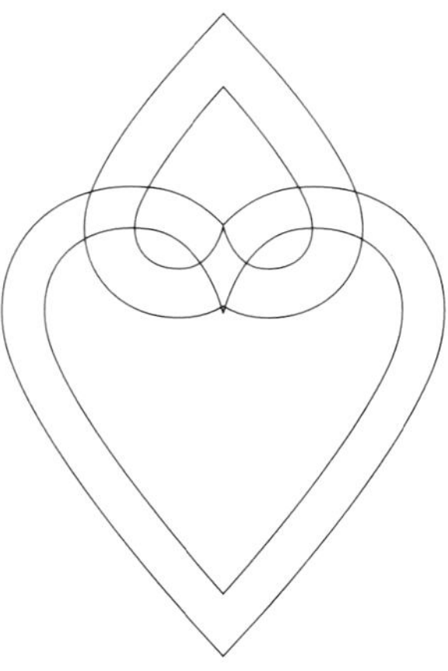

**440**

(2¼in (5.6cm)) to 6¾in (15.25cm) 300%

**441**

⟼ 15in (38.1cm) 375%

⟼ 18in (45.7cm) 450%

**442**

⟷ 6in (15.25cm) 300%

⟷ 8in (20.3cm) 400%

**443**

⟷ 6in (15.25cm) 300%

⟷ 8in (20.3cm) 400%

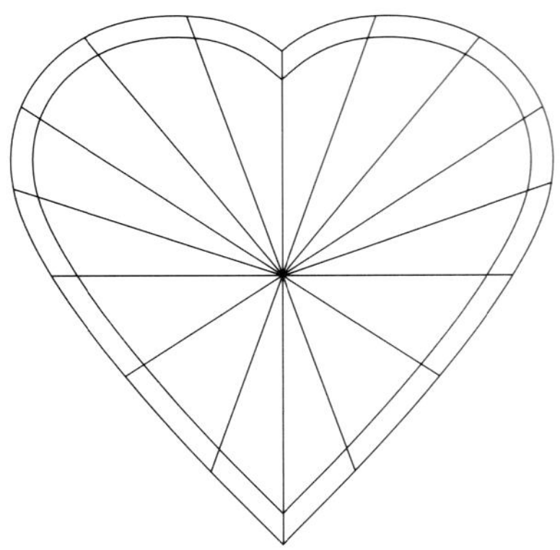

**444**

⟷ 6in (15.25cm) 300%

⟷ 8in (20.3cm) 400%

**445**

⟷ 10in (25.4cm) 500%

⟷ 12in (30.5cm) 600%

ALL PATTERNS ARE STANDARD 2IN (5CM) OR 4IN (10.2CM) UNLESS OTHERWISE STATED

**446**

15in (38.1cm) 375%

18in (45.7cm) 450%

# Pictorial motifs

Traditional quilting motifs include a range of pictorial designs that are based on nature and everyday objects. In particular, floral patterns can be found in abundance, and the good news is that they are very forgiving for those who don't have highly sophisticated drawing skills.

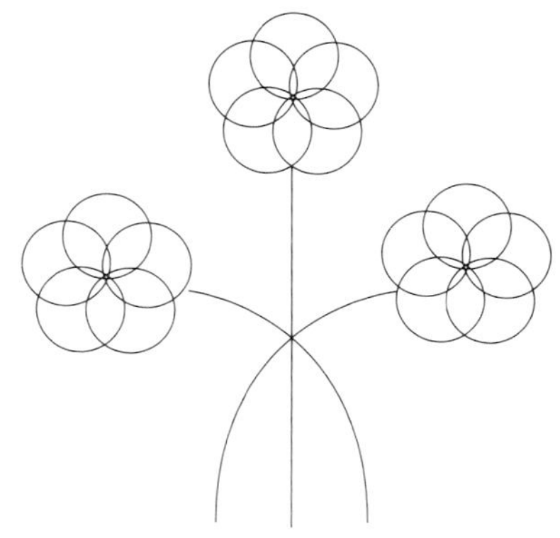

**447**

6in (15.25cm) 300%

8in (20.3cm) 400%

## Florals

Stylized flowers are based on geometric designs. For more ideas and variations see the previous pages. Remember to be flexible and look at the overall shape of one flower and perhaps consider adding elements of another.

**448**

6in (15.25cm) 300%

8in (20.3cm) 400%

**449**

8in (20.3cm) 400%

10in (25.4cm) 500%

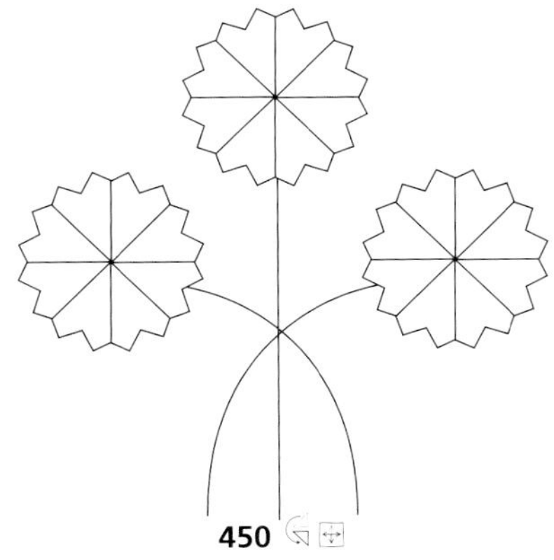

**450**

6in (15.25cm) 300%

8in (20.3cm) 400%

**451**

10in (25.4cm) 500%

12in (30.5cm) 600%

**452**

6in (15.25cm) 300%

8in (20.3cm) 400%

**453**

5in (12.7cm) 250%

8in (20.3cm) 400%

ALL PATTERNS ARE STANDARD 2IN (5CM) OR 4IN (10.2CM) UNLESS OTHERWISE STATED

**458**

⟷ 5in (12.7cm) 250%

⟷ 8in (20.3cm) 400%

**459**

⟷ 10in (25.4cm) 500%

⟷ 12in (30.5cm) 600%

**460**

⟷ 6in (15.25cm) 300%

⟷ 8in (20.3cm) 400%

**461**

⟷ 8in (20.3cm) 400%

⟷ 10in (25.4cm) 500%

**462a**

⟷ 6in (15.25cm) 300%

⟷ 10in (25.4cm) 500%

**462b**

⟷ 6in (15.25cm) 300%

⟷ 8in (20.3cm) 400%

**462c**

⟷ (1½ in (3.8cm)) to 5in (12.7cm) 333%

⟷ (1½ in (3.8cm)) to 6in (15.25cm) 400%

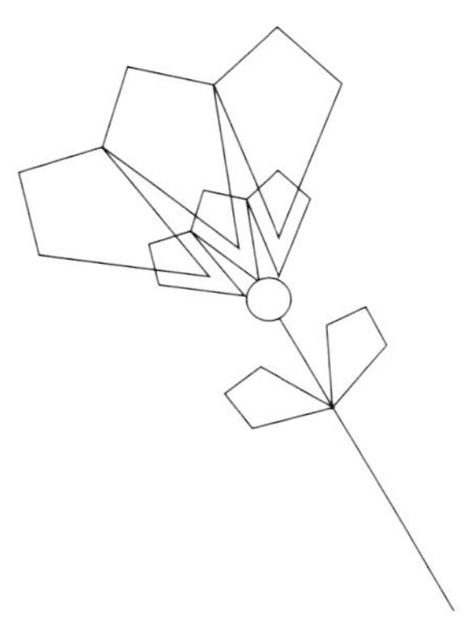

463

6in (15.25cm) 300%

8in (20.3cm) 400%

464

6in (15.25cm) 300%

8in (20.3cm) 400%

465

6in (15.25cm) 300%

8in (20.3cm) 400%

466

4in (10.2cm) 200%

6in (15.25cm) 300%

**467**

⟷ 6in (15.25cm) 300%

⟷ 8in (20.3cm) 400%

**468a**

⟷ 10in (25.4cm) 500%

⟷ 12in (30.5cm) 600%

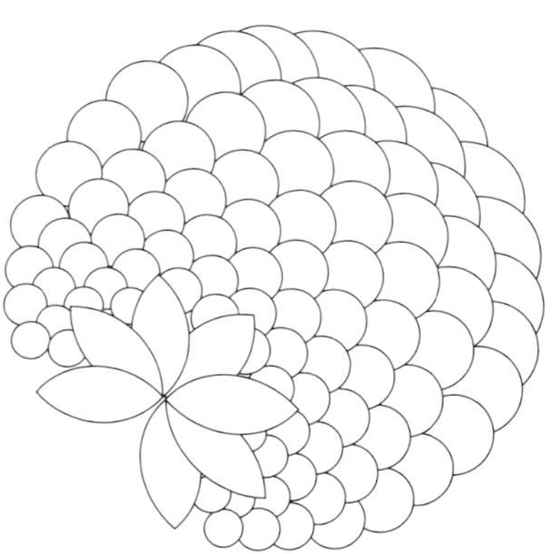

**468b**

⟷ 10in (25.4cm) 500%

⟷ 12in (30.5cm) 600%

**469**

⟷ 6in (15.25cm) 300%

⟷ 8in (20.3cm) 400%

ALL PATTERNS ARE STANDARD 2IN (5CM) OR 4IN (10.2CM) UNLESS OTHERWISE STATED

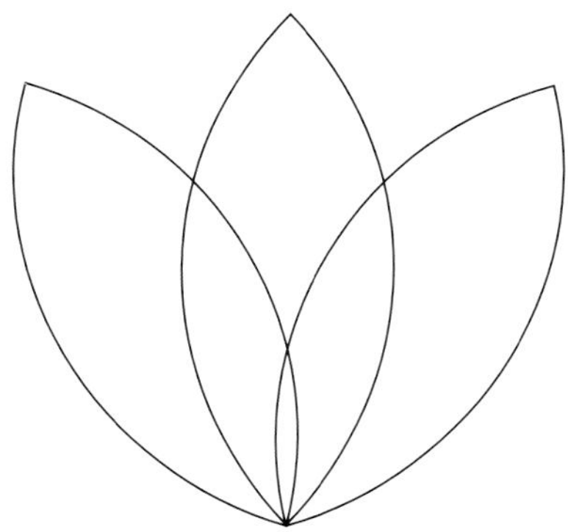

**470**
4in (10.2cm) 200%
5in (12.7cm) 250%

**471**
6in (15.25cm) 300%
8in (20.3cm) 400%

**472a**
8in (20.3cm) 400%
10in (25.4cm) 500%

**472b**
12in (30.5cm) 600%
15in (38.1cm) 750%

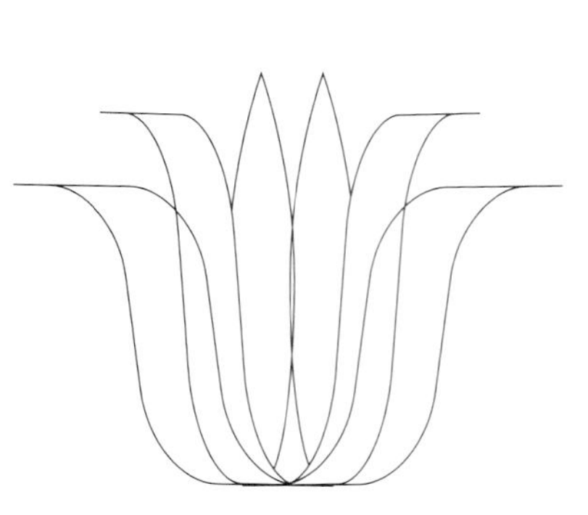

**473**
↦ 6in (15.25cm) 300%
↦ 8in (20.3cm) 400%

**474**
↦ 6in (15.25cm) 300%
↦ 8in (20.3cm) 400%

**475a**
↦ 6in (15.25cm) 300%
↦ 8in (20.3cm) 400%

**475b**
↦ 6in (15.25cm) 300%
↦ 8in (20.3cm) 400%

**476a**

⟼ 4in (10.2cm) 200%

⟼ 5in (12.7cm) 250%

**476b**

⟼ 6in (15.25cm) 300%

⟼ 8in (20.3cm) 400%

**477**

⟼ 8in (20.3cm) 400%

⟼ 10in (25.4cm) 500%

**478**

⟼ 4in (10.2cm) 200%

⟼ 5in (12.7cm) 250%

**479**

6in (15.25cm) 300%

8in (20.3cm) 400%

**480a**

6in (15.25cm) 300%

8in (20.3cm) 400%

**480b**

10in (25.4cm) 500%

12in (30.5cm) 600%

ALL PATTERNS ARE STANDARD 2IN (5CM) OR 4IN (10.2CM) UNLESS OTHERWISE STATED

**481a**

⟷ 5in (12.7cm) 250%

⟷ 8in (20.3cm) 400%

**481b**

⟷ 8in (20.3cm) 400%

⟷ 10in (25.4cm) 500%

**481c**

⟷ 8in (20.3cm) 400%

⟷ 10in (25.4cm) 500%

**482**

⟷ 6in (15.25cm) 300%

⟷ 8in (20.3cm) 400%

**483**

5in (12.7cm) 250%

8in (20.3cm) 400%

**484**

6in (15.25cm) 300%

8in (20.3cm) 400%

**485**

6in (15.25cm) 300%

8in (20.3cm) 400%

**486**

8in (20.3cm) 400%

10in (25.4cm) 500%

**487**

⟷ 24in (61cm) 600%

⟷ 30in (76.2cm) 750%

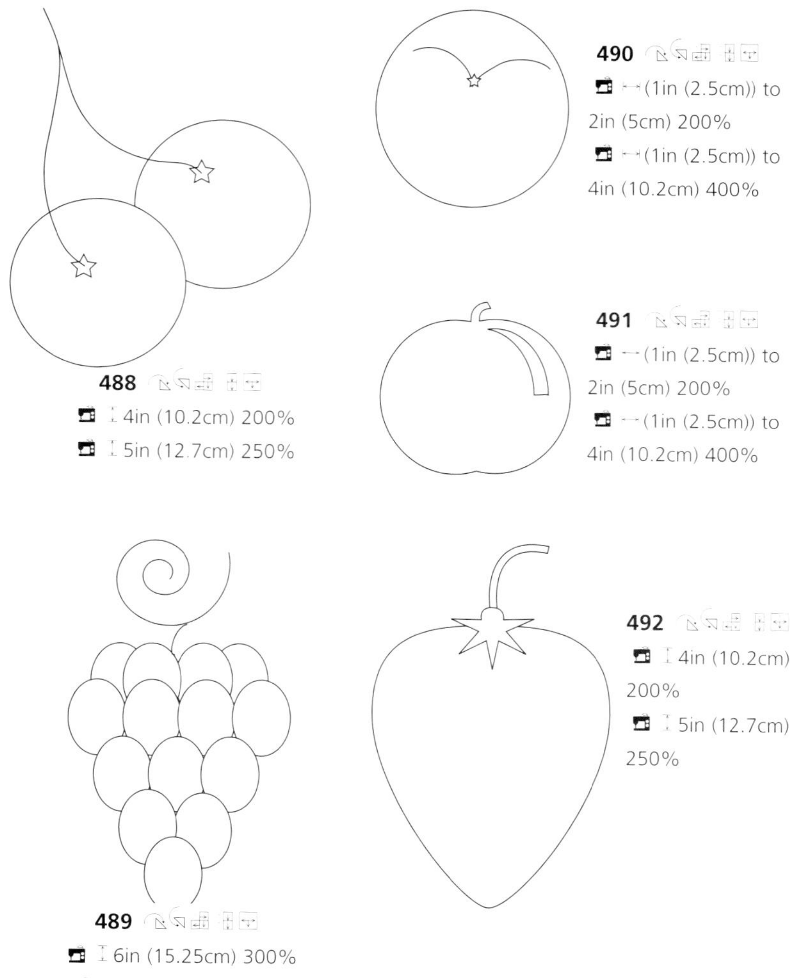

**488**
4in (10.2cm) 200%
5in (12.7cm) 250%

**489**
6in (15.25cm) 300%
8in (20.3cm) 400%

**490**
(1in (2.5cm)) to 2in (5cm) 200%
(1in (2.5cm)) to 4in (10.2cm) 400%

**491**
(1in (2.5cm)) to 2in (5cm) 200%
(1in (2.5cm)) to 4in (10.2cm) 400%

**492**
4in (10.2cm) 200%
5in (12.7cm) 250%

**493**

30in (76.2cm) 750%

32in (81.3cm) 800%

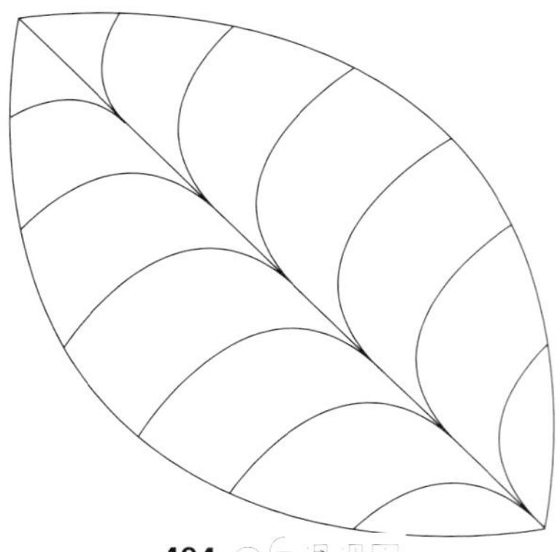

**494**

4in (10.2cm) 200%

5in (12.7cm) 250%

**495**

4in (10.2cm) 200%

5in (12.7cm) 250%

**496**

4in (10.2cm) 200%

5in (12.7cm) 250%

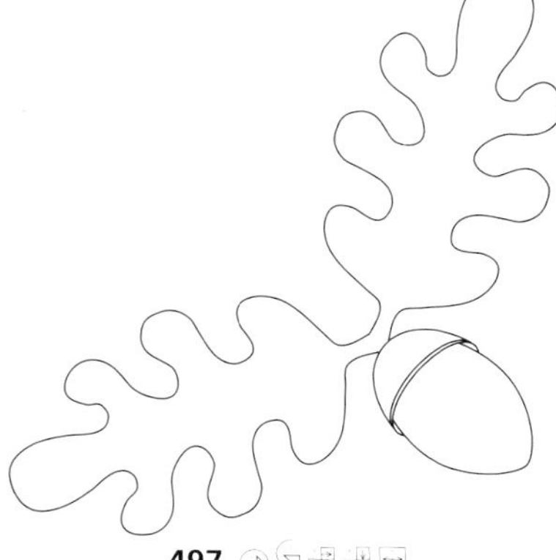

**497**

4in (10.2cm) 200%

5in (12.7cm) 250%

**498**

⟷ 4in (10.2cm) 200%

⟷ 5in (12.7cm) 250%

**499**

⟷ 10in (25.4cm) 500%

⟷ 12in (30.5cm) 600%

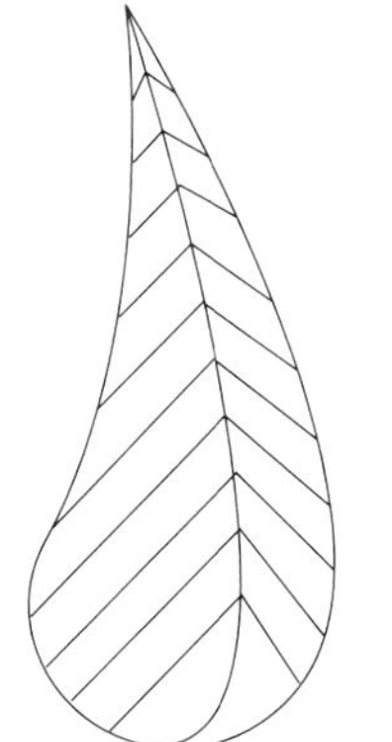

**500**

⟷ 6in (15.25cm) 300%

⟷ 8in (20.3cm) 400%

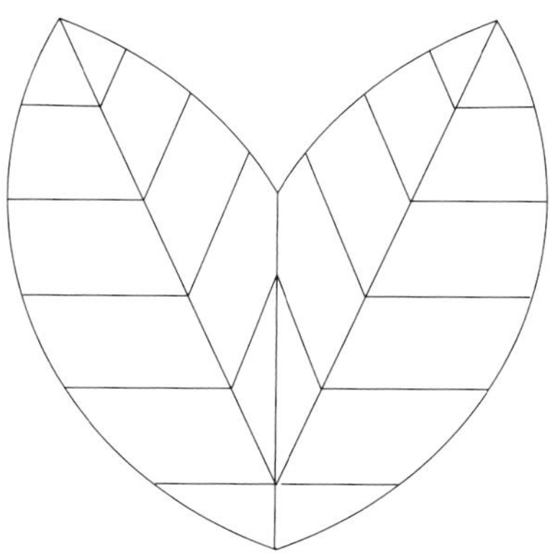

**501**

⟷ 4in (10.2cm) 200%

⟷ 5in (12.7cm) 250%

**502**

6in (15.25cm) 300%

8in (20.3cm) 400%

**503**

6in (15.25cm) 300%

8in (20.3cm) 400%

**504**

6in (15.25cm) 300%

8in (20.3cm) 400%

**506**

4in (10.2cm) 200%

6in (15.25cm) 300%

**507**

⟷ 12in (30.5cm) 600%

⟷ 15in (38.1cm) 750%

**508**

⟷ 8in (20.3cm) 400%

⟷ 10in (25.4cm) 500%

**509**

24in (61cm) 600%

30in (76.2cm) 750%

ALL PATTERNS ARE STANDARD 2IN (5CM) OR 4IN (10.2CM) UNLESS OTHERWISE STATED

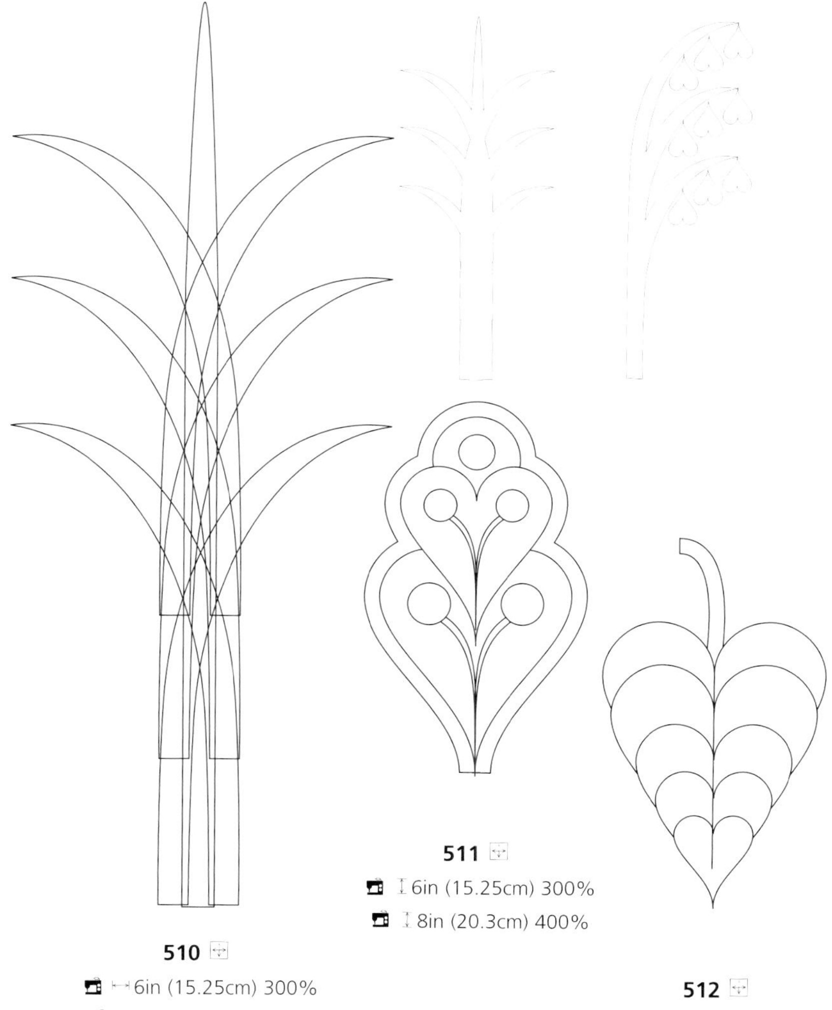

**510**

↔ 6in (15.25cm) 300%

↔ 8in (20.3cm) 400%

**511**

↕ 6in (15.25cm) 300%

↕ 8in (20.3cm) 400%

**512**

↕ 4in (10.2cm) 200%

↕ 6in (15.25cm) 300%

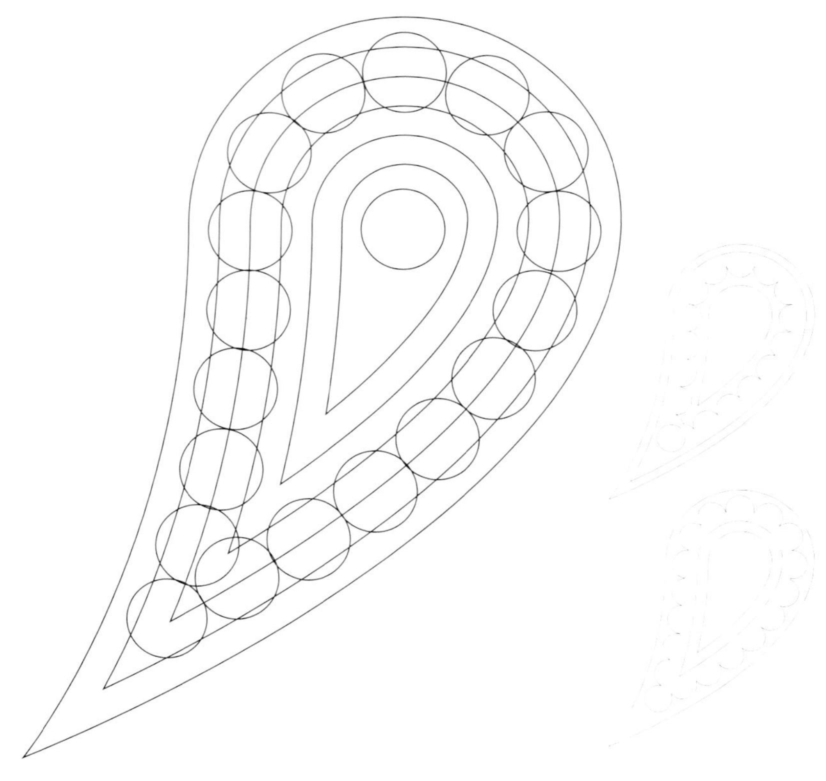

**513**

20in (50.8cm) 500%

24in (61cm) 600%

**514**

⟷ 6in (15.25cm) 300%

⟷ 8in (20.3cm) 400%

**516**

⟷ 6in (15.25cm) 300%

⟷ 8in (20.3cm) 400%

**517**

⟷ 4in (10.2cm) 200%

⟷ 5in (12.7cm) 250%

**518**

⟷ 4in (10.2cm) 200%

⟷ 5in (12.7cm) 250%

## Animals and birds

Birds and butterflies can be found in a variety of shapes and sizes on traditional quilts. The butterfly, in particular, lends itself to geometric designs and patterns because its simple shape is easy to draw convincingly. Look at the geometric patterns in earlier chapters for ideas on how to fill the areas within the shapes.

Small insects can also be found, often hidden among the foliage of floral designs. Stitch the wings quite densely with a slightly lighter thread to replicate the delicate shimmer of the wings; keep the body shapes to bold outlines for a three-dimensional effect.

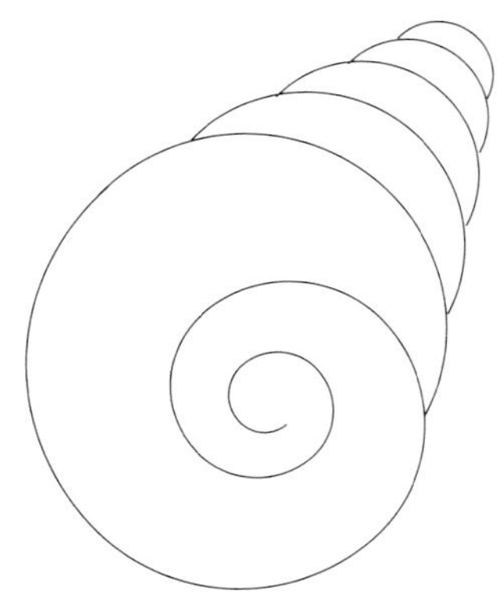

**519**

6in (15.25cm) 300%

8in (20.3cm) 400%

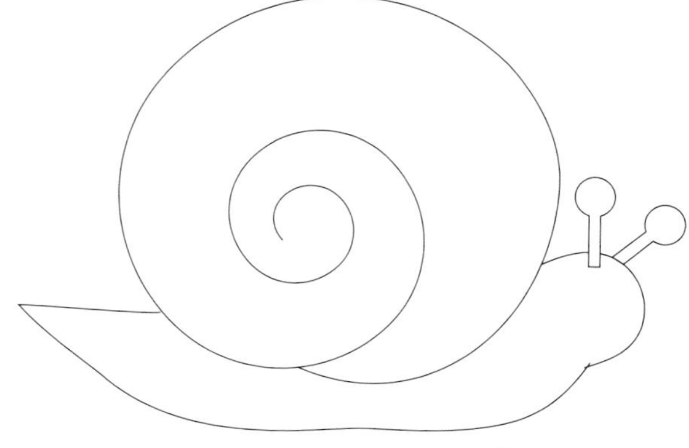

**520**

6in (15.25cm) 300%

8in (20.3cm) 400%

**521**

4in (10.2cm) 200%

8in (20.3cm) 400%

**522**

5in (12.7cm) 250%

8in (20.3cm) 400%

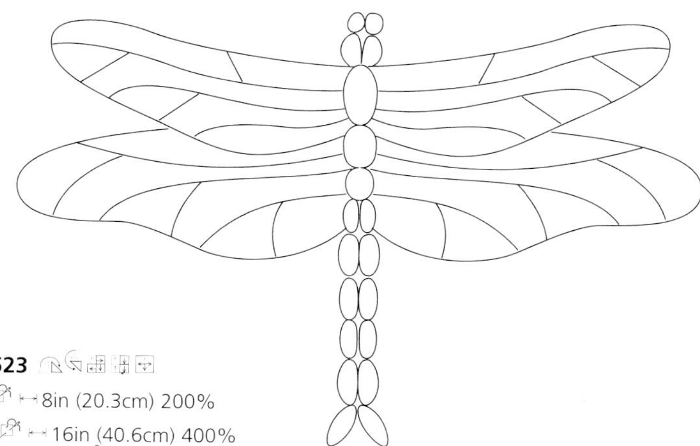

**523**

8in (20.3cm) 200%

16in (40.6cm) 400%

**524**

⟼ 4in (10.2cm) 200%

⟼ 8in (20.3cm) 400%

**525**

⟼ 6in (15.25cm) 300%

⟼ 8in (20.3cm) 400%

**526**

⟼ 6in (15.25cm) 300%

⟼ 8in (20.3cm) 400%

**527**

⟼ 6in (15.25cm) 300%

⟼ 8in (20.3cm) 400%

ALL PATTERNS ARE STANDARD 2IN (5CM) OR 4IN (10.2CM) UNLESS OTHERWISE STATED

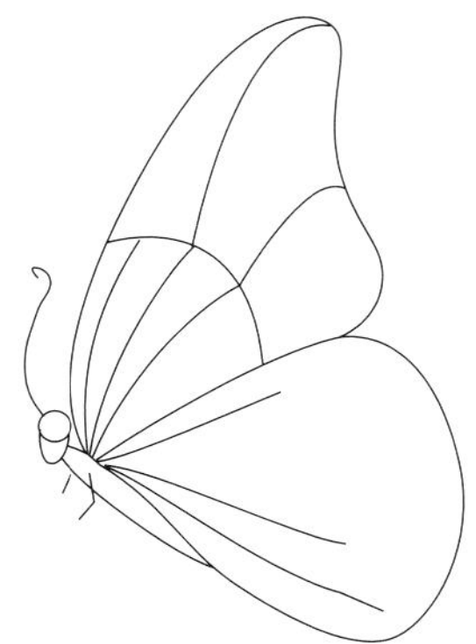

**528**

6in (15.25cm) 300%

8in (20.3cm) 400%

**529**

6in (15.25cm) 300%

8in (20.3cm) 400%

**530**

6in (15.25cm) 300%

8in (20.3cm) 400%

**531a**

(3in (7.6cm)) to 6in (15.25cm) 200%

(3in (7.6cm)) to 8in (20.3cm) 266%

**531b, 531c, 531d**

Enlargements as for above

**532**

(3in (7.6cm)) to 8in (20.3cm) 266%

(3in (7.6cm)) to 10in (25.4cm) 333%

**533**

(3in (7.6cm)) to 6in (15.25cm) 200%

(3in (7.6cm)) to 8in (20.3cm) 266%

**534**

16in (40.6cm) 400%

20in (50.8cm) 500%

**535**

6in (15.25cm) 300%

8in (20.3cm) 400%

**536**

6in (15.25cm) 300%

8in (20.3cm) 400%

ALL PATTERNS ARE STANDARD 2IN (5CM) OR 4IN (10.2CM) UNLESS OTHERWISE STATED

**537**

16in (40.6cm) 400%

20in (50.8cm) 500%

## Baskets, bows, and containers

Baskets and containers are the perfect vehicle for a central floral motif on a wholecloth or a on-point square. Look at the baskets and containers carefully and mix the shapes and texture to suit your design.

Bows are always fun and easy to adapt to any shape. Extend the ends, increase the loops, and have fun with this very adaptable motif.

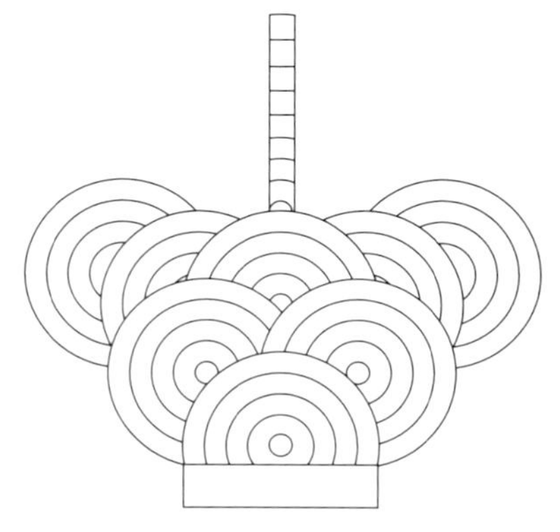

**538**

6in (15.25cm) 300%

8in (20.3cm) 400%

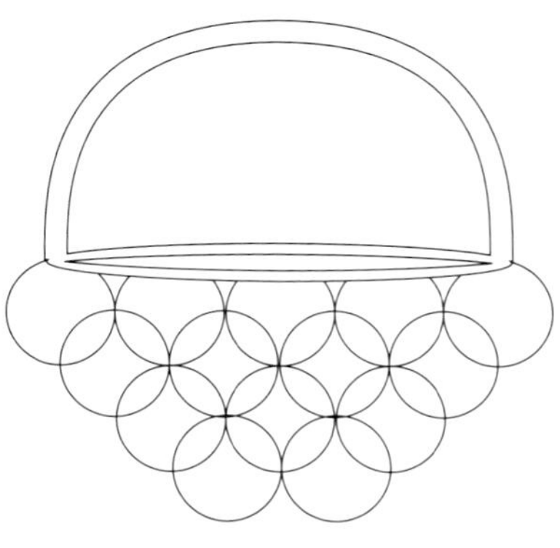

**539a**

6in (15.25cm) 300%

8in (20.3cm) 400%

**539b**

6in (15.25cm) 300%

8in (20.3cm) 400%

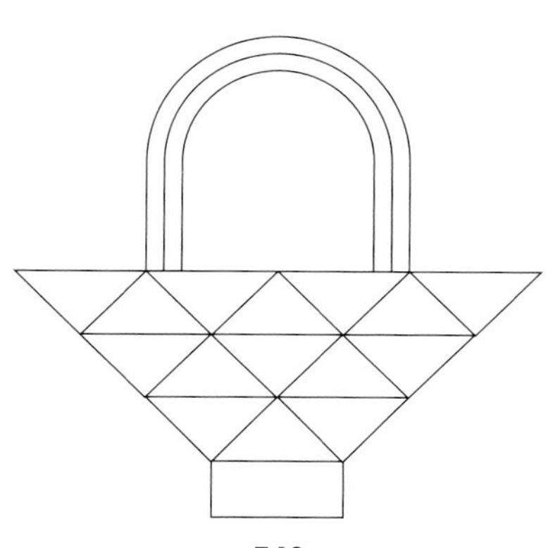

**540**

⟼ 6in (15.25cm) 300%

⟼ 8in (20.3cm) 400%

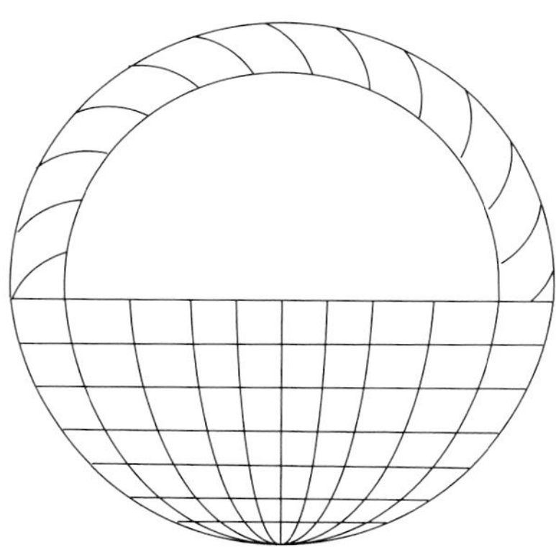

**541**

⟼ 6in (15.25cm) 300%

⟼ 8in (20.3cm) 400%

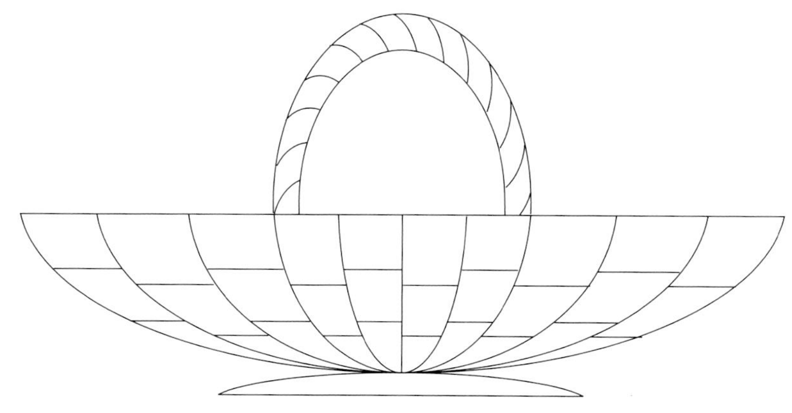

**542**

⟼ 16in (40.6cm) 400%

⟼ 20in (50.8cm) 500%

**543**

⟷ 20in (50.8cm) 500%

⟷ 24in (61cm) 600%

ALL PATTERNS ARE STANDARD 2IN (5CM) OR 4IN (10.2CM) UNLESS OTHERWISE STATED

**544**

⟷ 5in (12.7cm) 250%

⟷ 6in (15.25cm) 300%

**545**

⟷ 6in (15.25cm) 300%

⟷ 8in (20.3cm) 400%

**546**

⟷ 4in (10.2cm) 200%

⟷ 8in (20.3cm) 400%

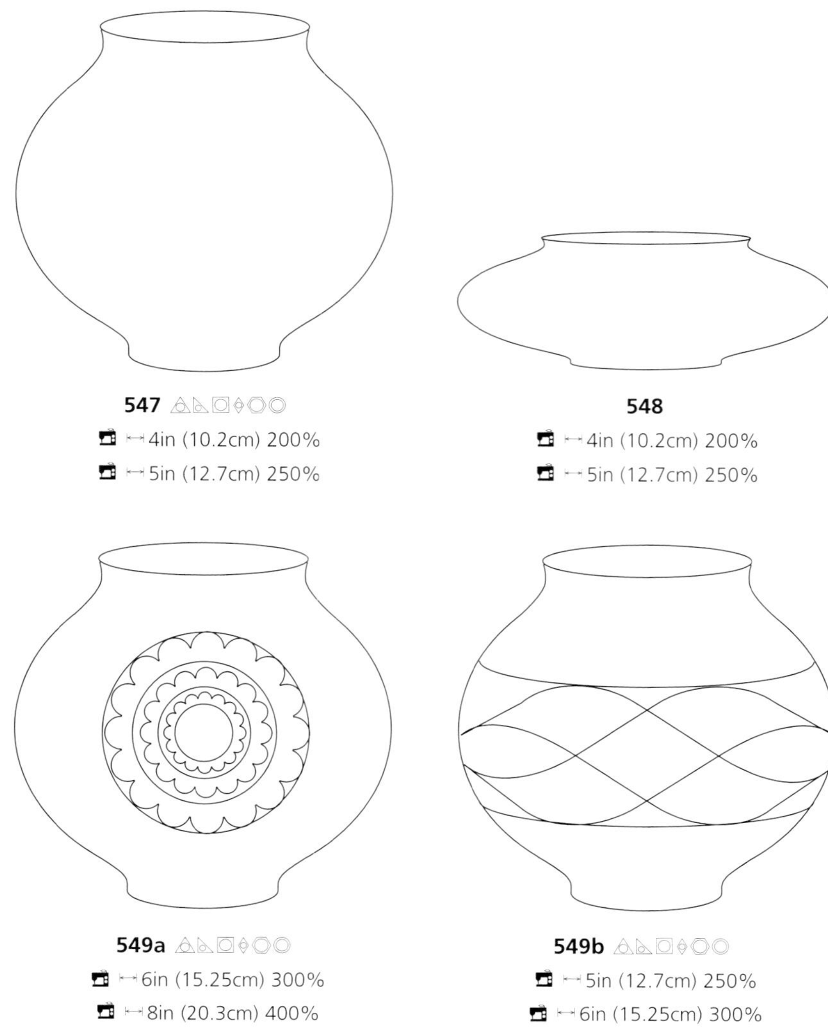

**547**

4in (10.2cm) 200%

5in (12.7cm) 250%

**548**

4in (10.2cm) 200%

5in (12.7cm) 250%

**549a**

6in (15.25cm) 300%

8in (20.3cm) 400%

**549b**

5in (12.7cm) 250%

6in (15.25cm) 300%

ALL PATTERNS ARE STANDARD 2IN (5CM) OR 4IN (10.2CM) UNLESS OTHERWISE STATED

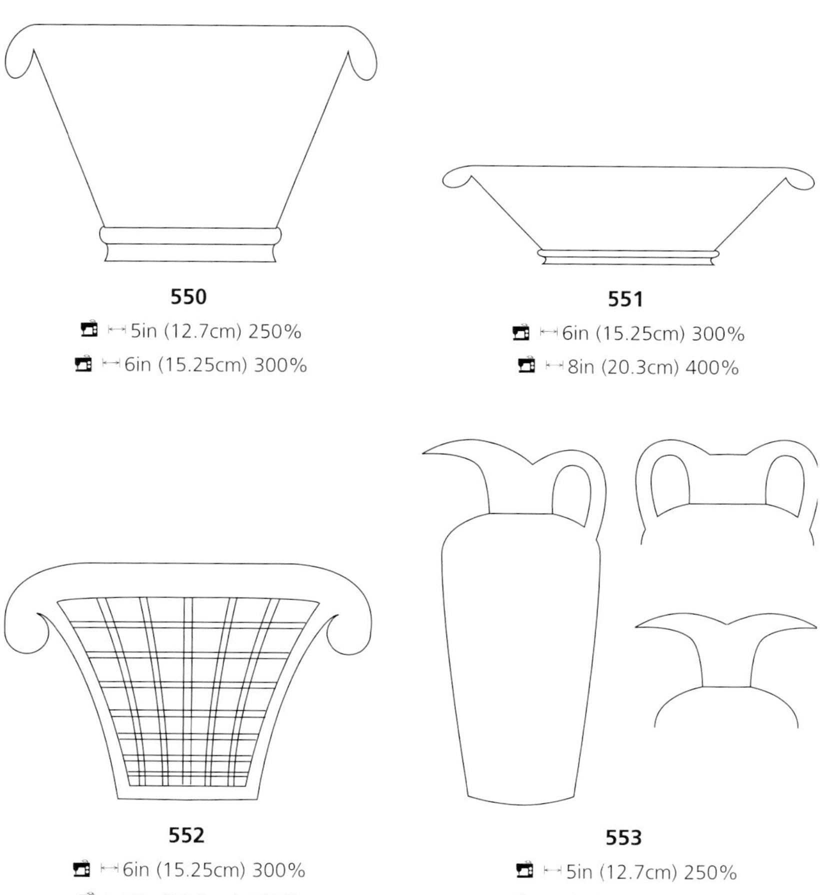

**550**

5in (12.7cm) 250%

6in (15.25cm) 300%

**551**

6in (15.25cm) 300%

8in (20.3cm) 400%

**552**

6in (15.25cm) 300%

8in (20.3cm) 400%

**553**

5in (12.7cm) 250%

6in (15.25cm) 300%

## Feathers and fans

Traditionally drawn using a penny or the thumb as a template, feathers are a particular favorite in Amish quilts and the quilts of northern England. The designs that follow may look too complex for a small motif, but look at them carefully and combine two feathers to simplify the designs. At the end of the chapter are some feather designs that are perhaps not the traditional quilter's feather but nevertheless interesting.

This chapter also includes some feather designs 584 and 585 that are larger than those elsewhere to reduce the percentage enlargements. See the chapter of geometric circular designs (page 116) for more ideas.

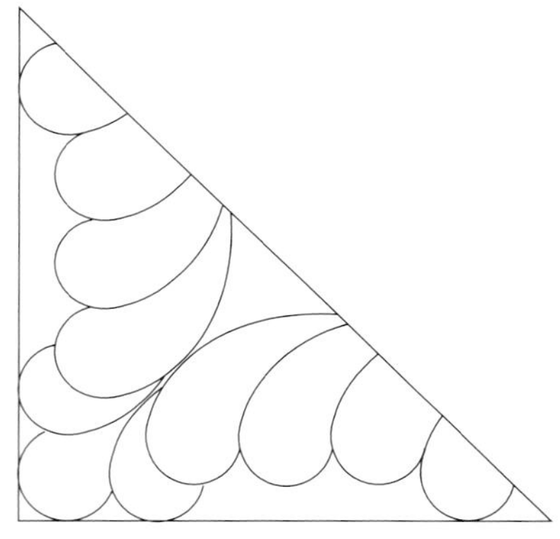

**554**

↔ 6in (15.25cm) 300%

↔ 8in (20.3cm) 400%

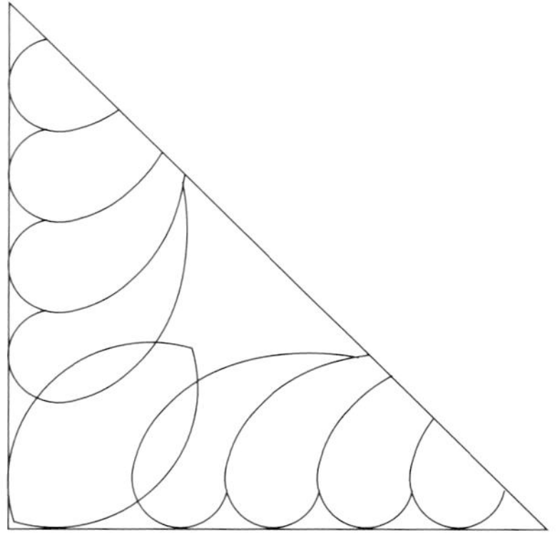

**555**

↔ 6in (15.25cm) 300%

↔ 8in (20.3cm) 400%

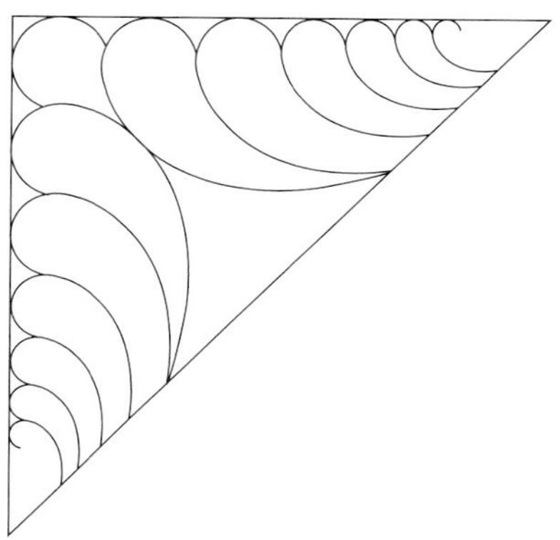

**556**

⟷ 6in (15.25cm) 300%

⟷ 8in (20.3cm) 400%

**557**

⟷ 4in (10.2cm) 200%

⟷ 6in (15.25cm) 300%

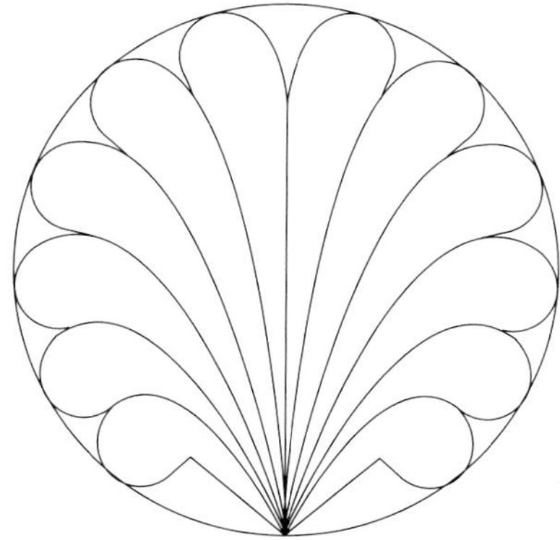

**558**

⟷ 6in (15.25cm) 300%

⟷ 8in (20.3cm) 400%

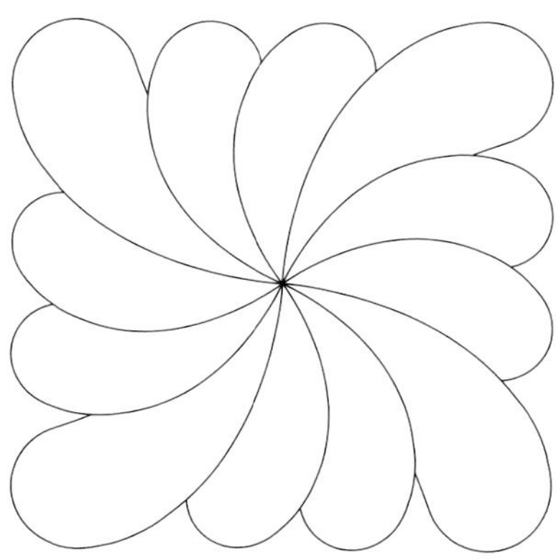

**559**

⟷ 8in (20.3cm) 400%

⟷ 10in (25.4cm) 500%

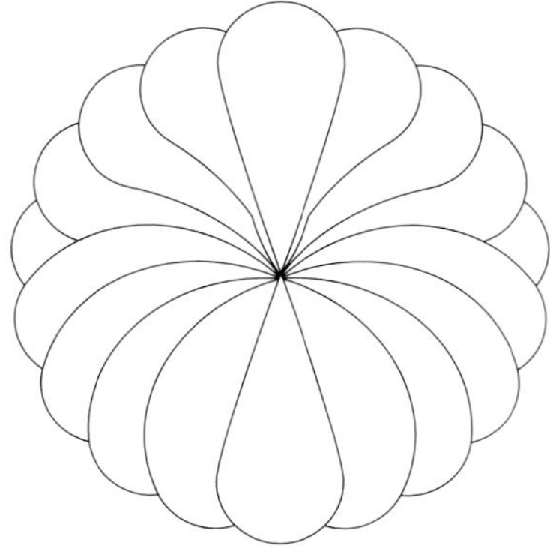

**560a**

⟷ 6in (15.25cm) 300%

⟷ 8in (20.3cm) 400%

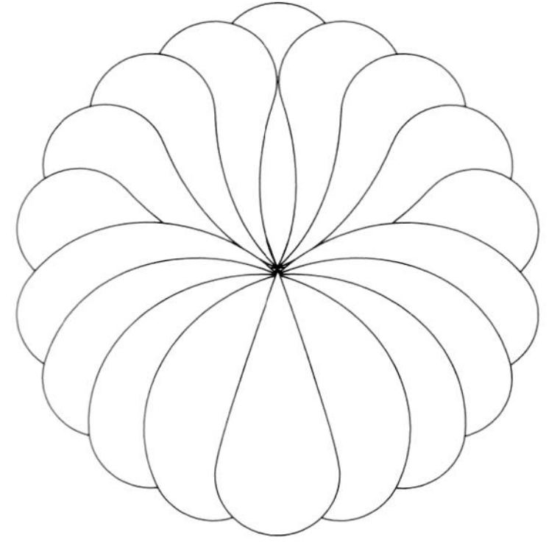

**560b**

⟷ 6in (15.25cm) 300%

⟷ 8in (20.3cm) 400%

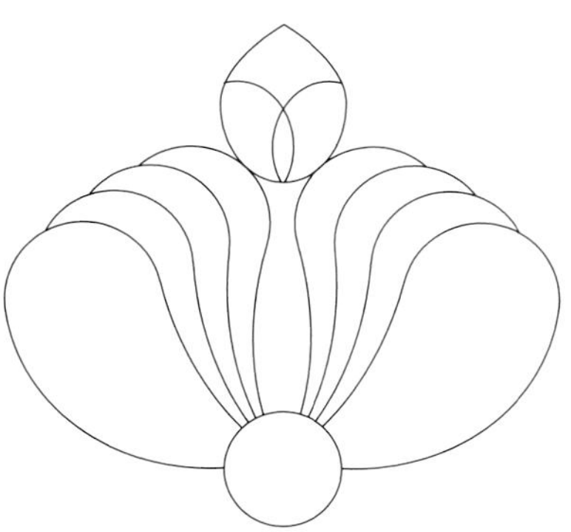

**561**

⟷ 6in (15.25cm) 300%

⟷ 8in (20.3cm) 400%

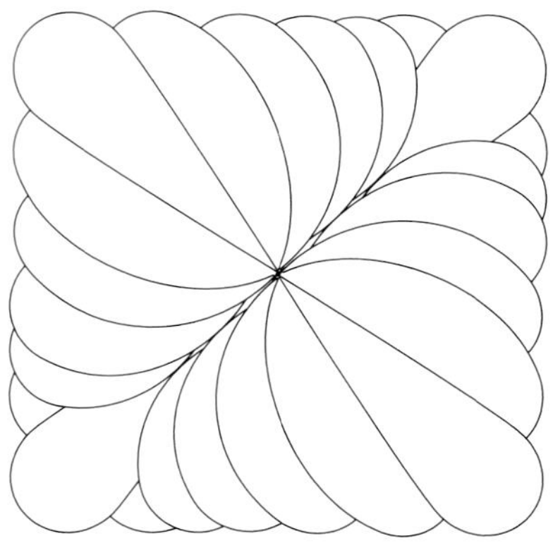

**562**

⟷ 10in (25.4cm) 500%

⟷ 12in (30.5cm) 600%

**563**

16in (40.6cm) 400%

20in (50.8cm) 500%

**564**

30in (76.2cm) 750%

32in (81.3cm) 800%

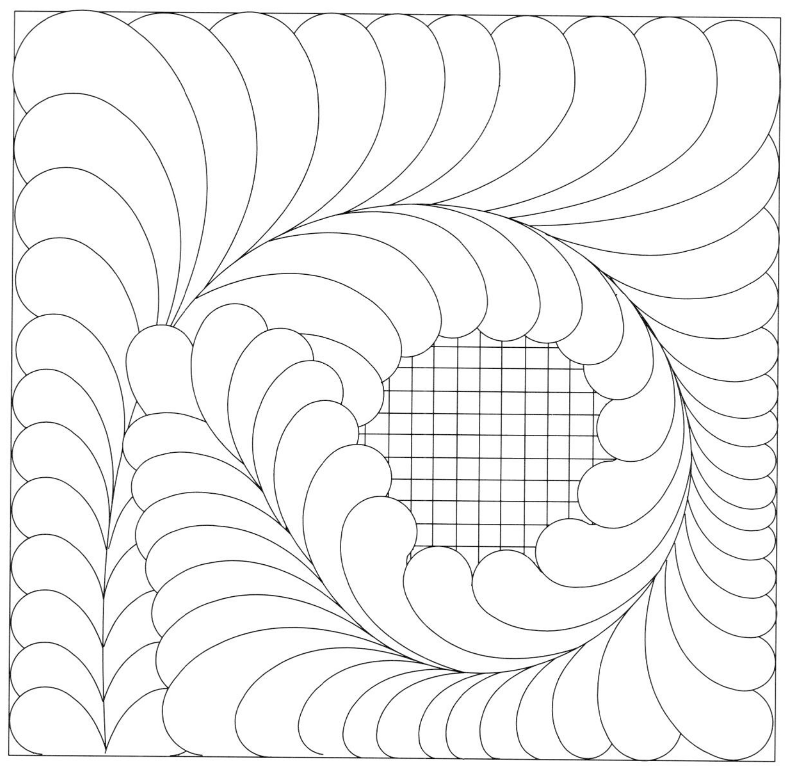

**565**

⟼ 32in (81.3cm) 800%

⟼ 36in (91.4cm) 900%

**566**

16in (40.6cm) 400%

20in (50.8cm) 500%

ALL PATTERNS ARE STANDARD 2IN (5CM) OR 4IN (10.2CM) UNLESS OTHERWISE STATED

**567**

16in (40.6cm) 400%

20in (50.8cm) 500%

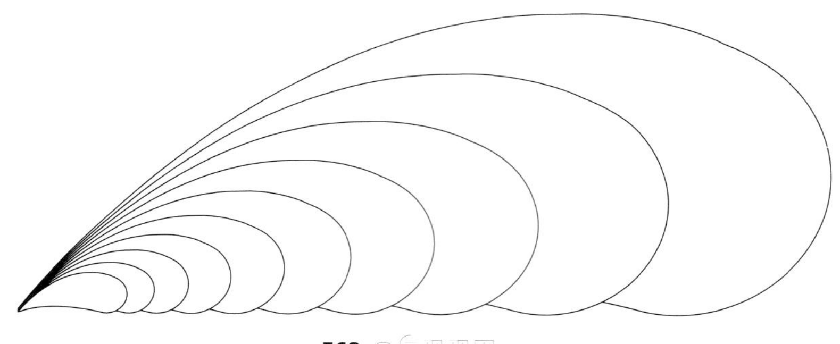

**568**

↔ 16in (40.6cm) 400%

↔ 20in (50.8cm) 500%

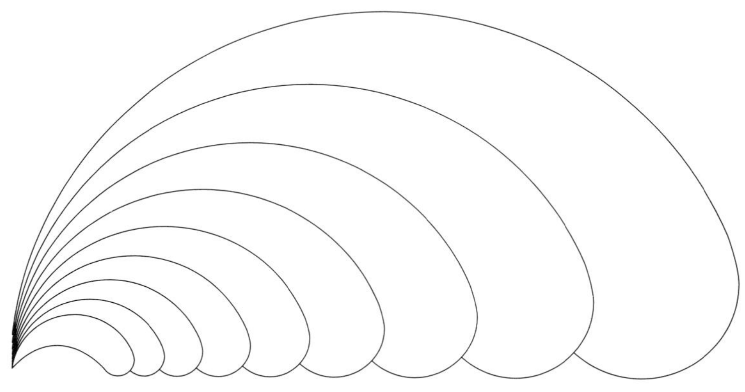

**569**

↕ 6in (15.25cm) 300%

↕ 8in (20.3cm) 400%

ALL PATTERNS ARE STANDARD 2IN (5CM) OR 4IN (10.2CM) UNLESS OTHERWISE STATED

**570**

↔ (3in (7.6cm)) to 6in (15.25cm) 300%

↔ (3in (7.6cm)) to 8in (20.3cm) 266%

**571**

↔ (3in (7.6cm)) to 6in (15.25cm) 200%

↔ (3in (7.6cm)) to 8in (20.3cm) 266%

**572**

↔ (3in (7.6cm)) to 6in (15.25cm) 200%

↔ (3in (7.6cm)) to 8in (20.3cm) 266%

**573a**

16in (40.6cm) 400%

24in (61cm) 600%

ALL PATTERNS ARE STANDARD 2IN (5CM) OR 4IN (10.2CM) UNLESS OTHERWISE STATED

**573b**

16in (40.6cm) 400%

24in (61cm) 600%

**574a**

16in (40.6cm) 400%

24in (61cm) 600%

**574b**

⟷ 20in (50.8cm) 500%

⟷ 24in (61cm) 600%

**575a**

16in (40.6cm) 400%

20in (50.8cm) 500%

ALL PATTERNS ARE STANDARD 2IN (5CM) OR 4IN (10.2CM) UNLESS OTHERWISE STATED

**575b**

24in (61cm) 600%

30in (76.2cm) 750%

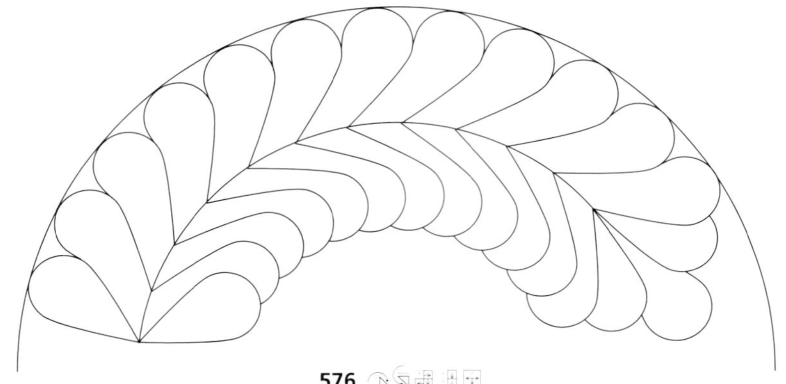

**576**
6in (15.25cm) 300%
8in (20.3cm) 400%

**577**
5in (12.7cm) 250%
12in (30.5cm) 600%

ALL PATTERNS ARE STANDARD 2IN (5CM) OR 4IN (10.2CM) UNLESS OTHERWISE STATED

**578**

16in (40.6cm) 400%

20in (50.8cm) 500%

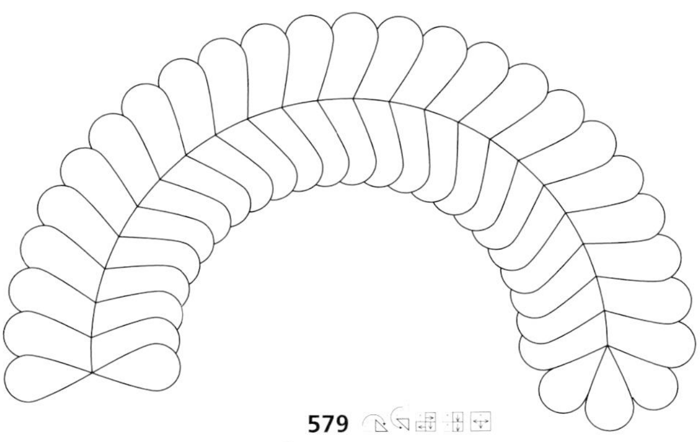

**579**

16in (40.6cm) 400%

20in (50.8cm) 500%

**580**

↔ 16in (40.6cm) 400%

↔ 20in (50.8cm) 500%

**581**

↔ 16in (40.6cm) 400%

↔ 24in (61cm) 600%

**582**

↔ 16in (40.6cm) 400%

↔ 24in (61cm) 600%

ALL PATTERNS ARE STANDARD 2IN (5CM) OR 4IN (10.2CM) UNLESS OTHERWISE STATED

**583**

16in (40.6cm) 400%

24in (61cm) 600%

**584**

↦ 16in (40.6cm) 400%

↦ 20in (50.8cm) 500%

**585**

16in (40.6cm) 400%

20in (50.8cm) 500%

**586a**

⟷ 16in (40.6cm) 400%

⟷ 20in (50.8cm) 500%

**586b**

⟷ 16in (40.6cm) 400%

⟷ 20in (50.8cm) 500%

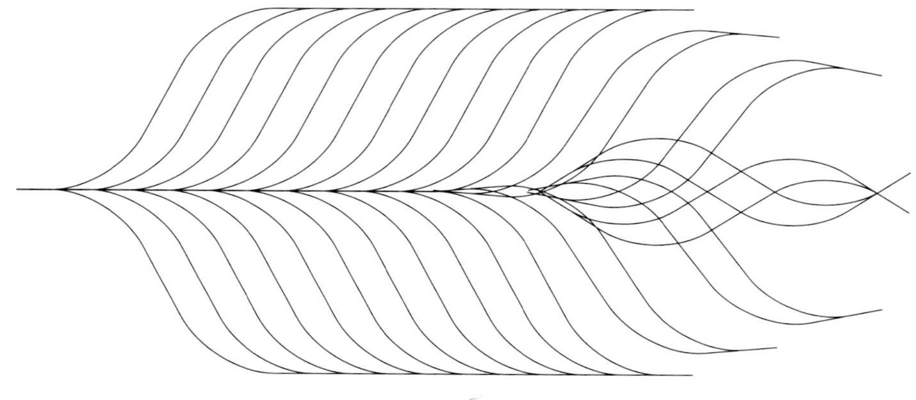

**587**

6in (15.25cm) 300%

8in (20.3cm) 400%

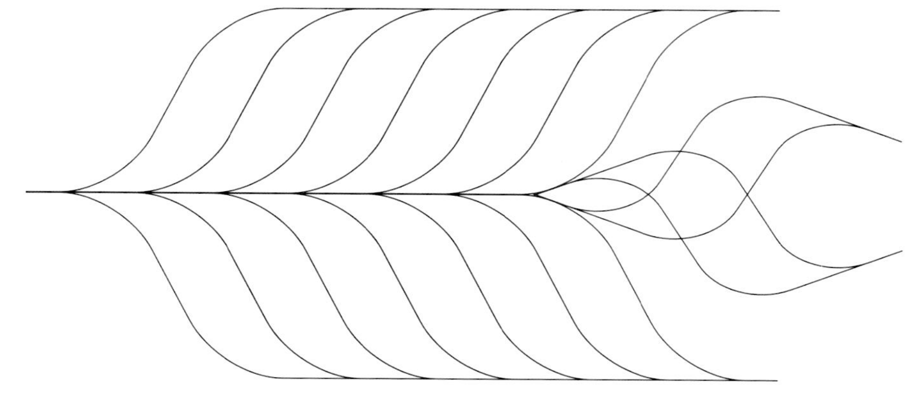

**588a**

8in (20.3cm) 400%

10in (25.4cm) 500%

**588b**

16in (40.6cm) 400%

20in (50.8cm) 500%

# Borders and edgings

Borders and edgings can be an important frame for a quilt, but can also be used in stripes from the top to the bottom of a quilt. They can be used as wide as 18in (45.7cm) or simplified for motifs 2in (5cm) across. Often quick to quilt using a sewing machine, they can be combined alongside each other, used to repeat part of a motif that appears elsewhere, or to introduce a new theme.

Look carefully at the designs in this chapter and also look through the repeat and filler patterns chapter (see page 310) to find other designs that can be easily adapted to create borders.

**589a**

⟷(1in (2.5cm)) to 6in (15.25cm) 600%

**589b**

(1in (2.5cm)) to 8in (20.3cm) 800%

**589c**

(1in (2.5cm)) to 8in (20.3cm) 800%

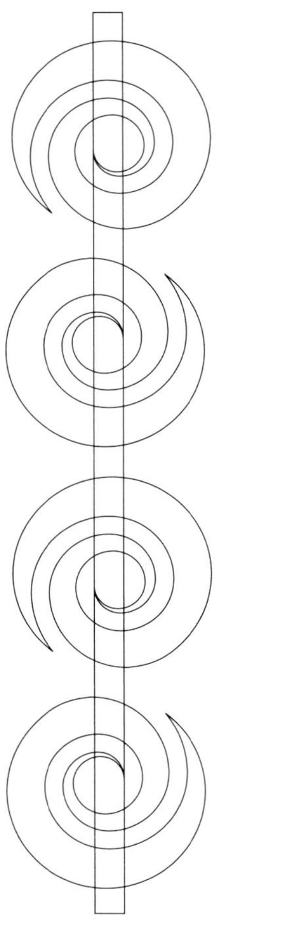

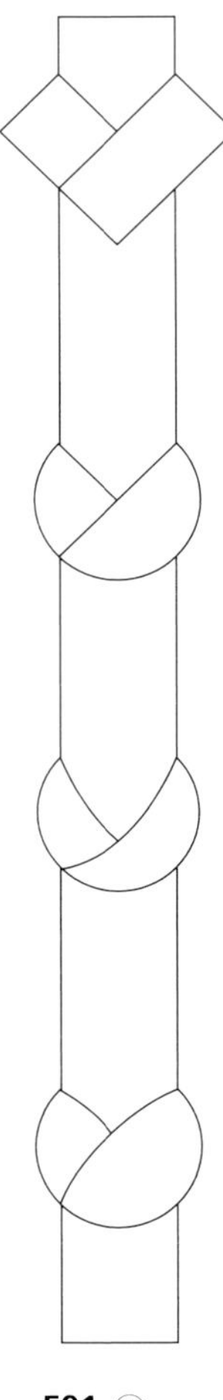

**590a**

(1in (2.5cm)) to 6in (15.25cm) 600%

**590b**

(1in (2.5cm)) to 6in (15.25cm) 600%

**591**

(1in (2.5cm)) to 4in (10.2cm) 400%

ALL PATTERNS ARE STANDARD 2IN (5CM) OR 4IN (10.2CM) UNLESS OTHERWISE STATED

**592a**

(1in (2.5cm)) to
6in (15.25cm) 600%

**592b**

(1in (2.5cm)) to
8in (20.3cm) 800%

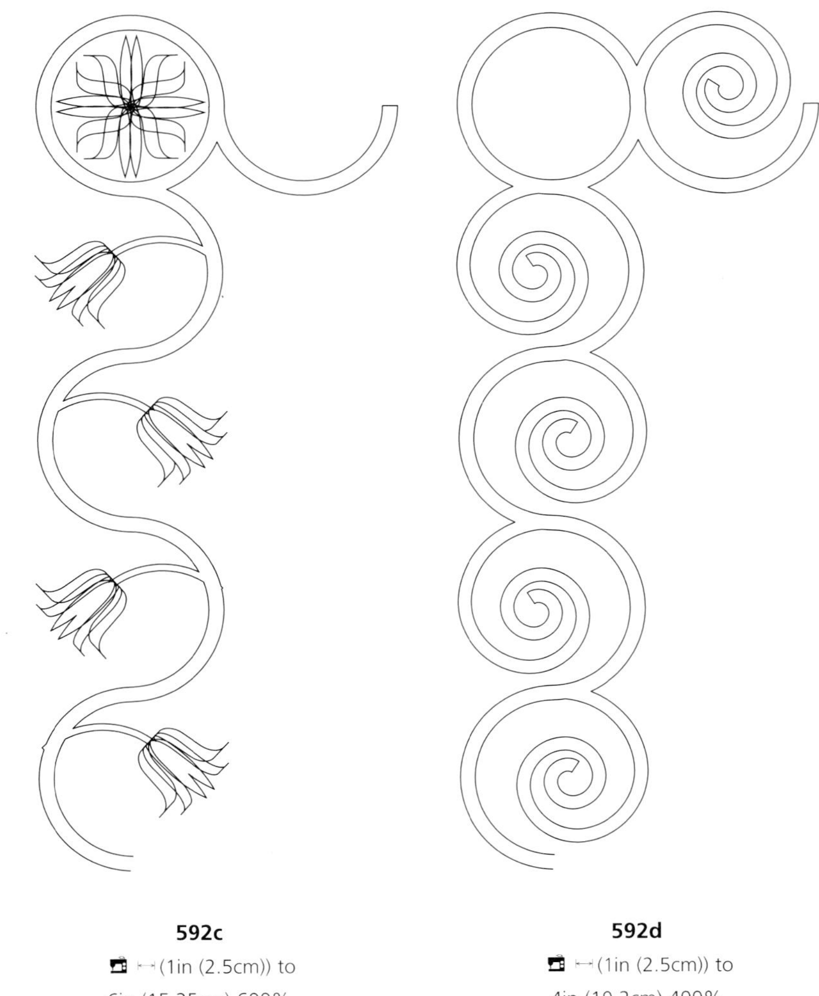

**592c**

⊶(1in (2.5cm)) to
6in (15.25cm) 600%

**592d**

⊶(1in (2.5cm)) to
4in (10.2cm) 400%

**593**
(¾in (1.9cm)) to 6in (15.25cm) 800%

**594a**
(1in (2.5cm)) to 6in (15.25cm) 600%

**594b**
(1in (2.5cm)) to 4in (10.2cm) 400%

**595a**

(⅝in (1.6cm)) to 6in (15.25cm) 960%

**595b**

(⅝in (1.6cm)) to 6in (15.25cm) 960%

**596**

(½in (1.3cm)) to 4in (10.2cm) 800%

**597a**

(1in (2.5cm)) to 4in (10.2cm) 400%

**597b**

(1in (2.5cm)) to 6in (15.25cm) 600%

**597c**

(1in (2.5cm)) to 4in (10.2cm) 400%

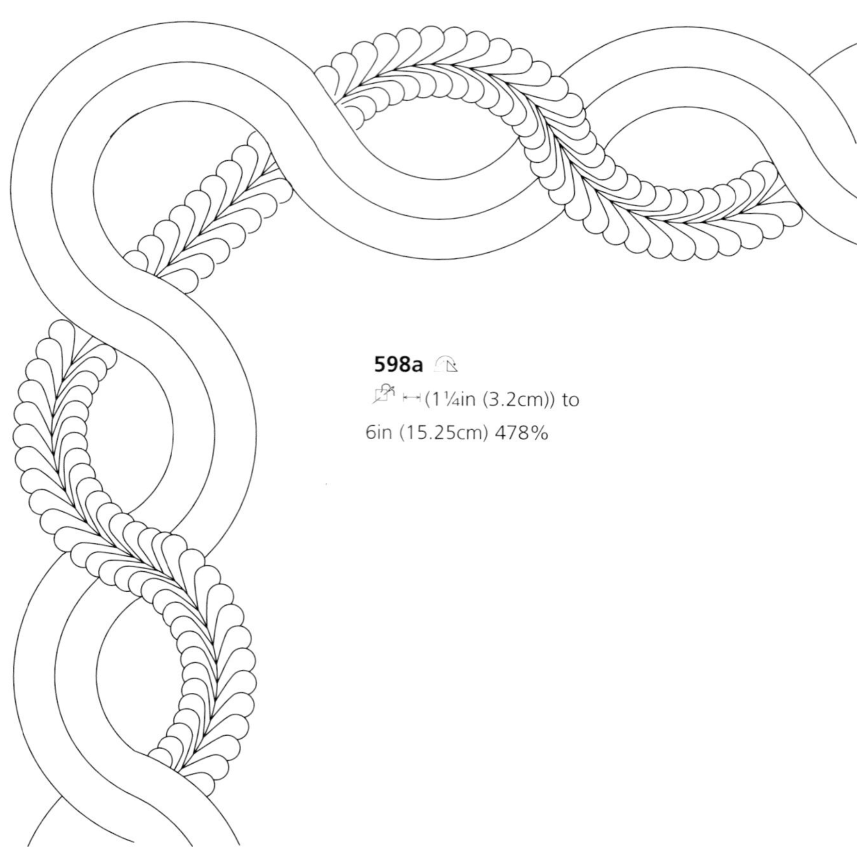

**598a**

(1¼in (3.2cm)) to 6in (15.25cm) 478%

**598b**

(2in (5cm)) to

6in (15.25cm) 300%

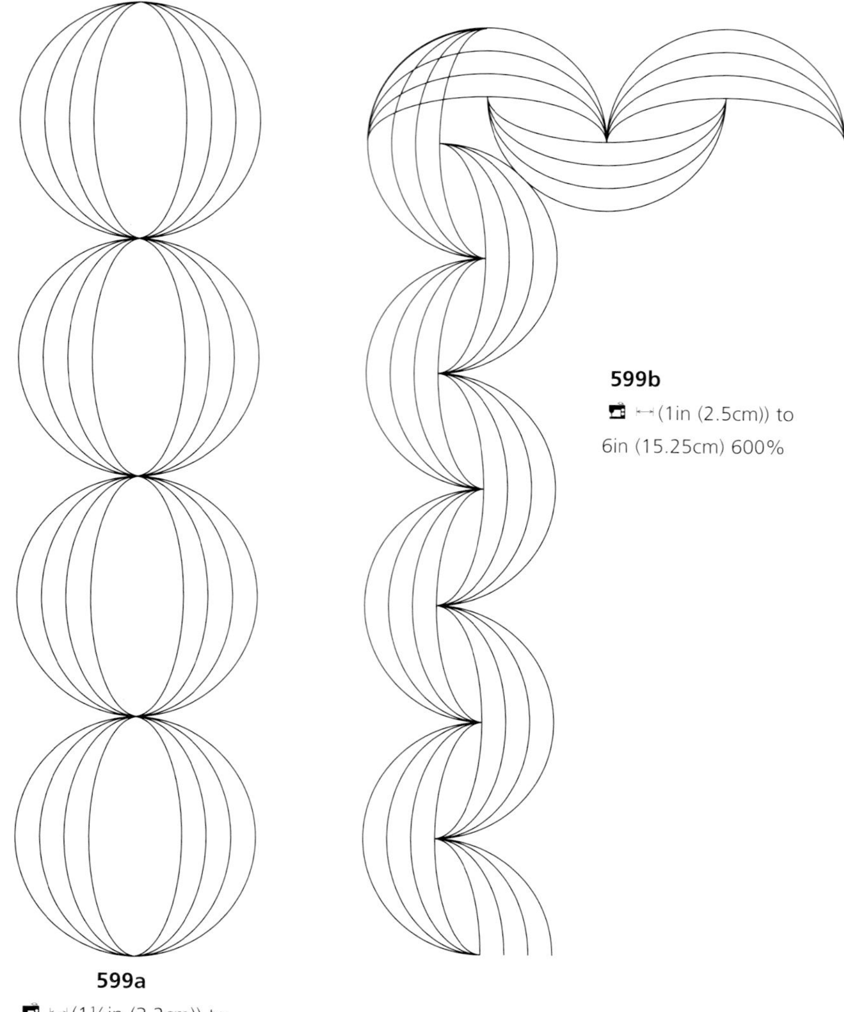

**599b**

⟼(1in (2.5cm)) to 6in (15.25cm) 600%

**599a**

⟼(1¼in (3.2cm)) to 6in (15.25cm) 480%

ALL PATTERNS ARE STANDARD 2IN (5CM) OR 4IN (10.2CM) UNLESS OTHERWISE STATED

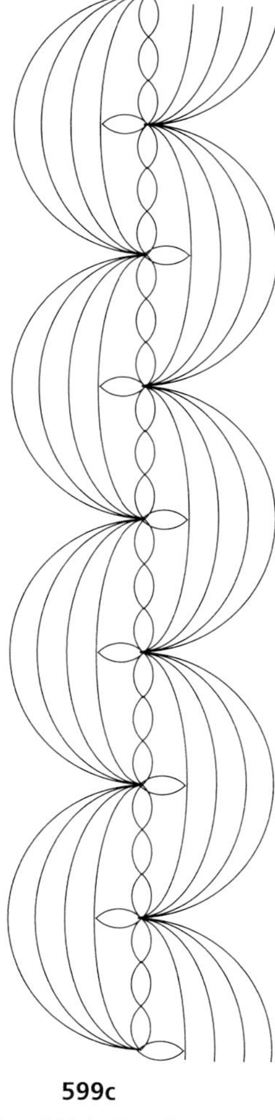

**599c**

⟼(1 1/16in (3cm)) to
6in (15.25cm) 508%

**600**

⟼(1 3/8in (3.5cm)) to
6in (15.25cm) 436%

**601a**

(⅞in (2.2cm)) to 4in (10.2cm) 457%

**601b**

(⅞in (2.2cm)) to 6in (15.25cm) 685%

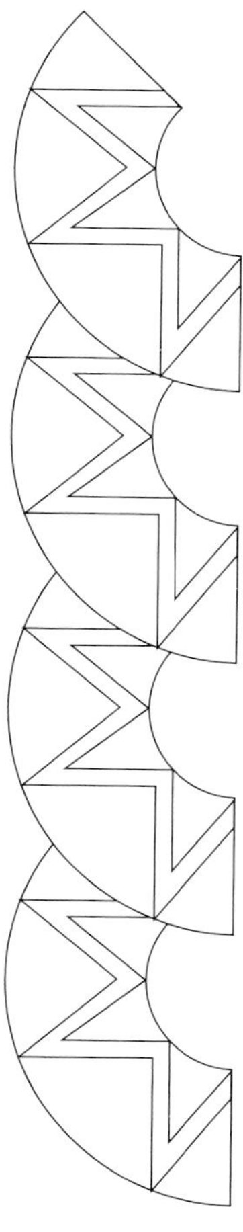

**601c**

(⅞in (2.2cm)) to 6in (15.25cm) 685%

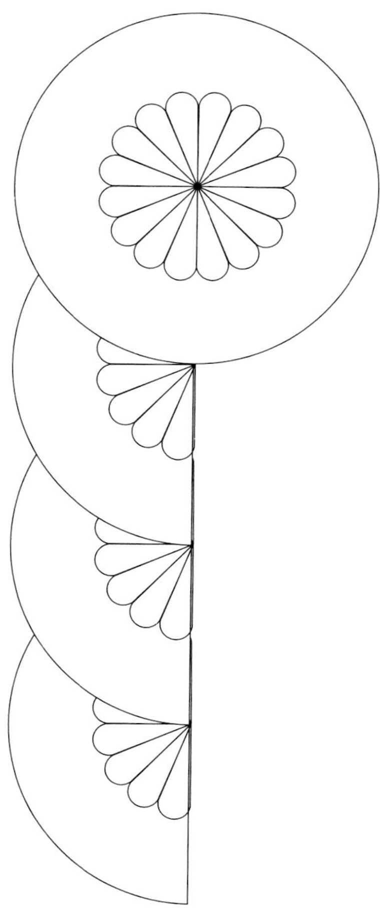

**602**

(⅞in (2.2cm)) to 6in (15.25cm) 685%

**603**

⟼(1in (2.5cm)) to
4in (10.2cm) 400%

**604**

⟼(1in (2.5cm)) to
6in (15.25cm) 600%

**605**
(½in (1.3cm)) to 4in (10.2cm) 800%

**606**
(⅝in (1.6cm)) to 6in (15.25cm) 960%

**607**
(⅝in (1.6cm)) to 6in (15.25cm) 960%

**608**

(1in (2.5cm)) to 6in (15.25cm) 600%

**609**

(1in (2.5cm)) to 4in (10.2cm) 400%

ALL PATTERNS ARE STANDARD 2IN (5CM) OR 4IN (10.2CM) UNLESS OTHERWISE STATED

**610**

(1in (2.5cm)) to 6in (15.25cm) 600%

**611**

(1in (2.5cm)) to 8in (20.3cm) 800%

**612a**

⟼(1in (2.5cm)) to 6in (15.25cm) 600%

**612b**

⟼(1in (2.5cm)) to 8in (20.3cm) 800%

**613**

⟼(1in (2.5cm)) to 4in (10.2cm) 400%

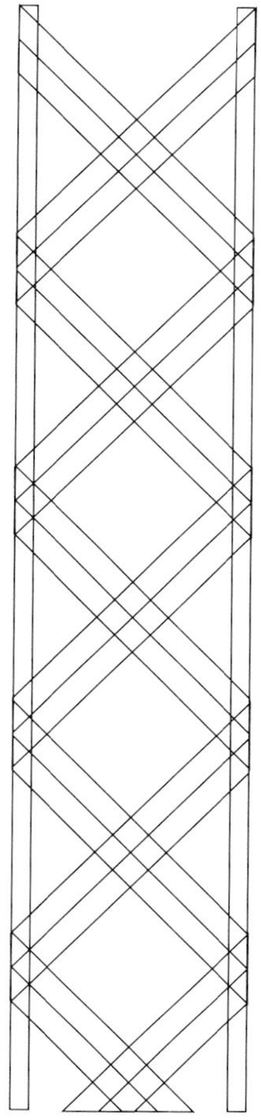

**614a**

⟼(1in (2.5cm)) to 6in (15.25cm) 600%

**614b**

⟼(1in (2.5cm)) to 6in (15.25cm) 600%

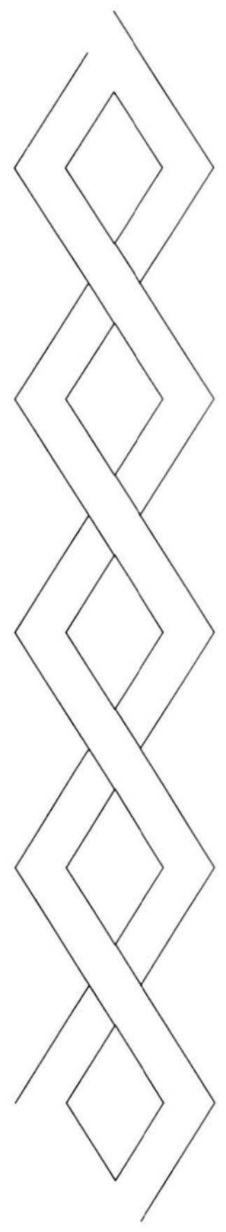

**615a**

⟼(¾in (1.9cm)) to
4in (10.2cm) 533%
(see **570** for corner)

**615b**

⟼(1¼in (3.2cm)) to
6in (15.25cm) 480%
(see **570** for corner)

**616a**

(½in (1.3cm)) to 4in (10.2cm) 400%

**616b**

(1in (2.5cm)) to 6in (15.25cm) 600%

**616c**

(⅝in (1.6cm)) to 6in (15.25cm) 960%

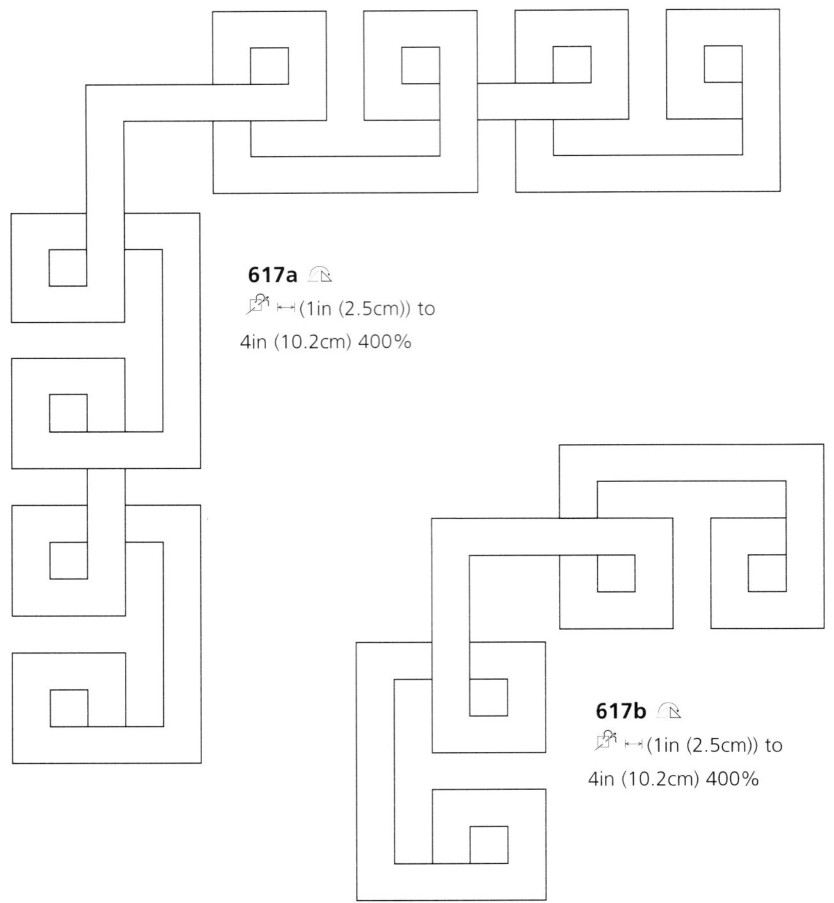
617a
(1in (2.5cm)) to
4in (10.2cm) 400%
617b
(1in (2.5cm)) to
4in (10.2cm) 400%

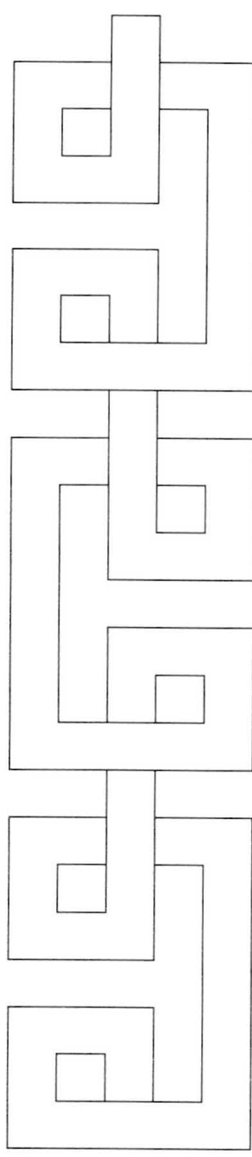

**617c**

(1in (2.5cm)) to 4in (10.2cm) 400%

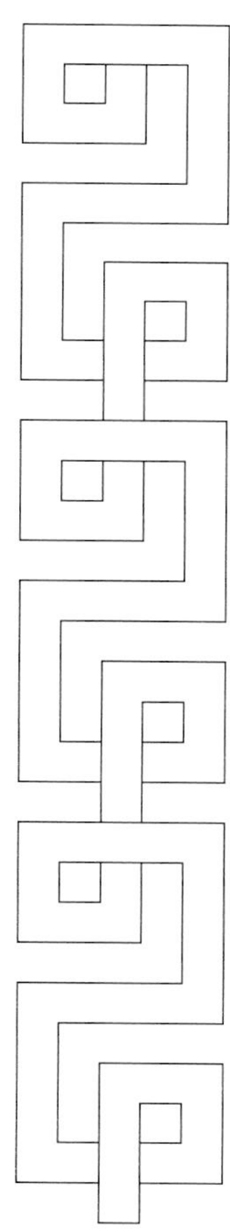

**618**

(¾in (1.9cm)) to 4in (10.2cm) 400%

**619a**
↦ (1in (2.5cm)) to
6in (15.25cm) 600%

**619b**
↦ (1⅝in (4.1cm)) to
6in (15.25cm) 369%

**620**
↦ (1in (2.5cm)) to
6in (15.25cm) 600%

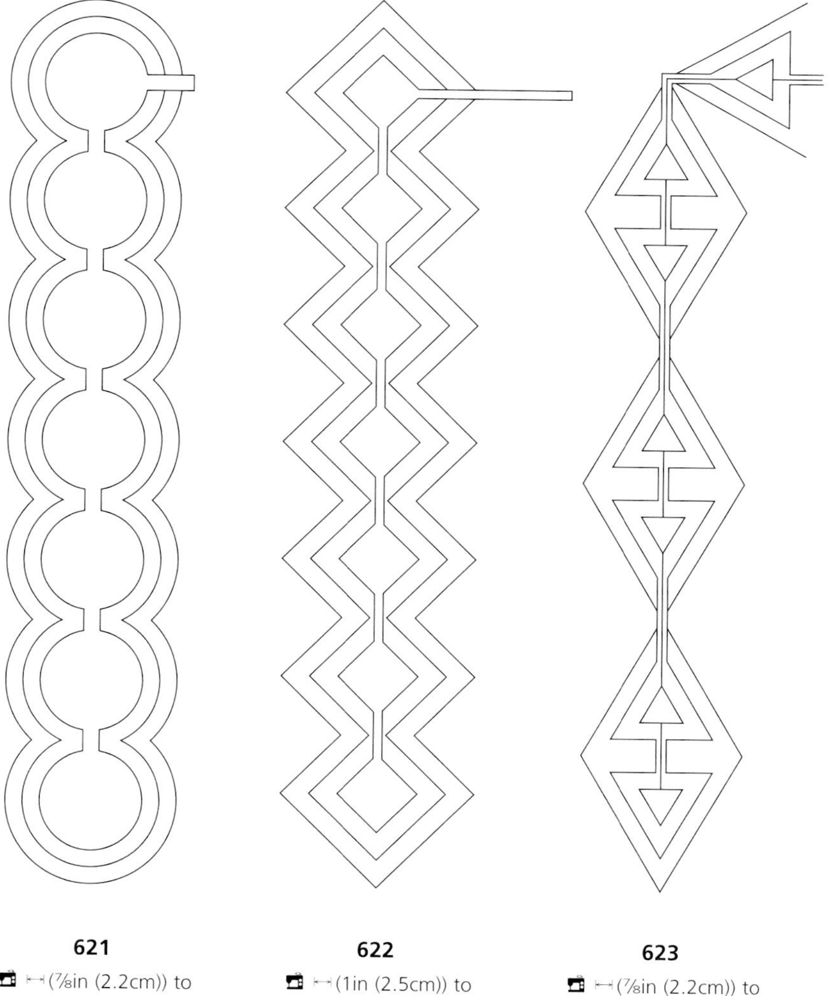

**621**

⟼(7⁄8in (2.2cm)) to 6in (15.25cm) 686%

**622**

⟼(1in (2.5cm)) to 8in (20.3cm) 800%

**623**

⟼(7⁄8in (2.2cm)) to 8in (20.3cm) 914%

**624**

 ⊢⊣(1¼in (3.2cm)) to 6in (15.25cm) 480%

(see **616** for corner)

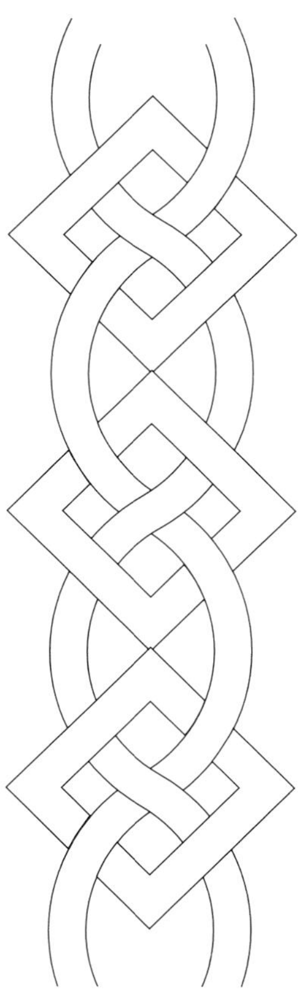

**625**

⊢⊣(1¼in (3.2cm)) to 8in (20.3cm) 640%

(see **616** for corner)

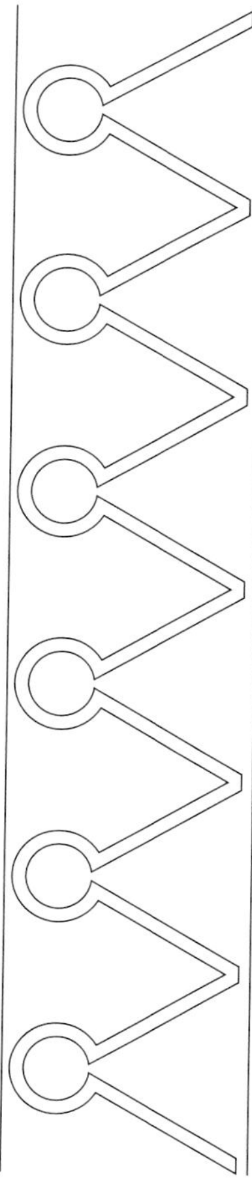

**626a**

(1in (2.5cm)) to
6in (15.25cm) 600%

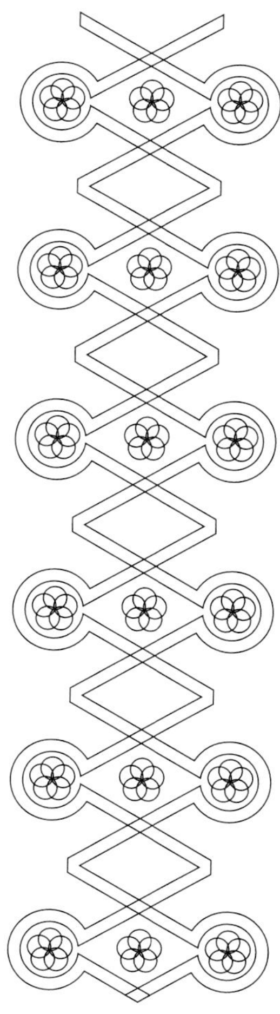

**626b**

(1¼in (3.2cm)) to
6in (15.25cm) 480%

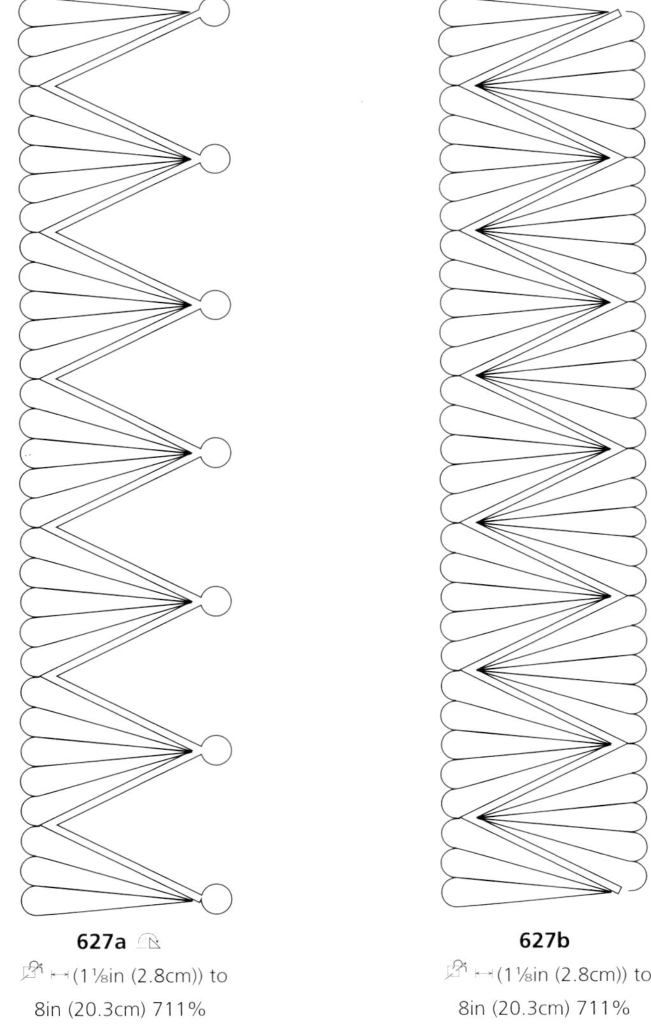

**627a**

(1⅛in (2.8cm)) to 8in (20.3cm) 711%

**627b**

(1⅛in (2.8cm)) to 8in (20.3cm) 711%

ALL PATTERNS ARE STANDARD 2IN (5CM) OR 4IN (10.2CM) UNLESS OTHERWISE STATED

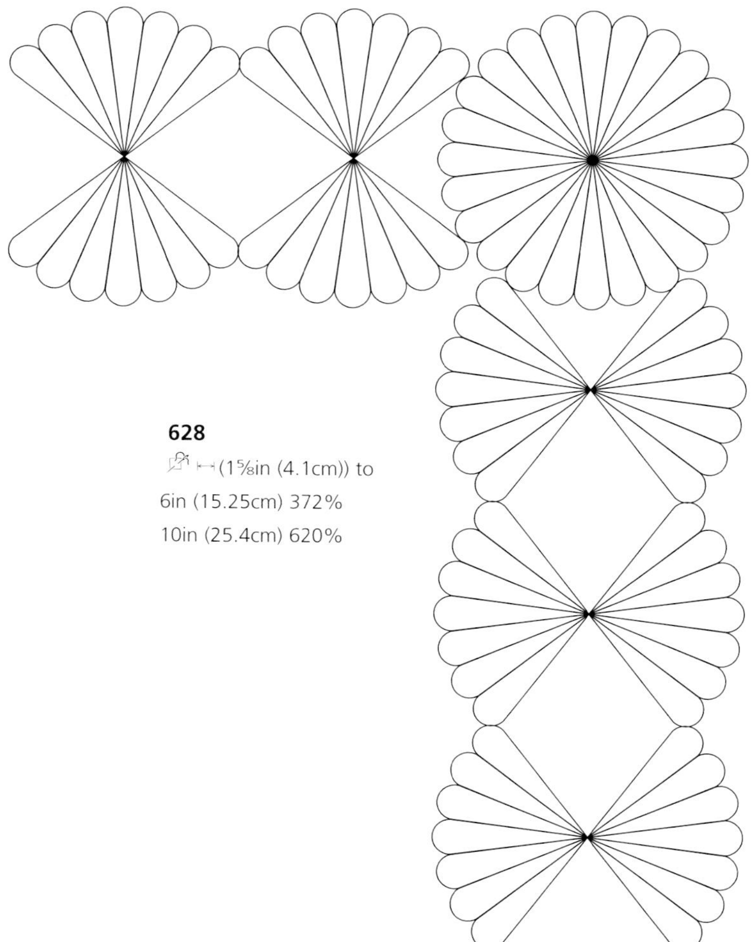

**628**

↦ (1⅝in (4.1cm)) to
6in (15.25cm) 372%
10in (25.4cm) 620%

**629**

↦ (1¾in (4.4cm)) to
8in (20.3cm) 457%
(see **628** for corner)

**630**

↦ (1¾in (4.4cm)) to
8in (20.3cm) 462%
(see **628** for corner)

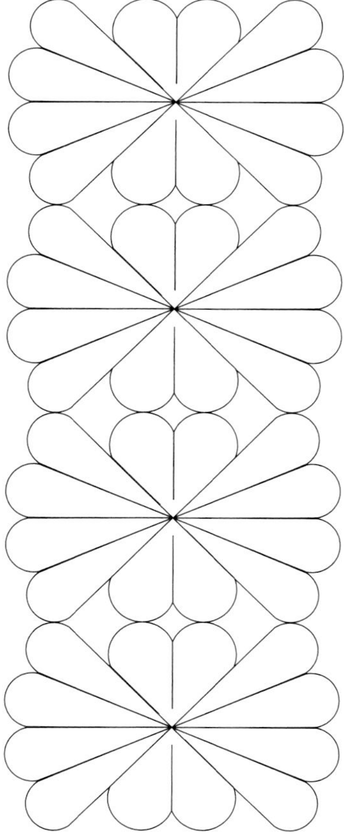

**631**

(1¾in (4.4cm)) to
8in (20.3cm) 462%
(see **628** for corner)

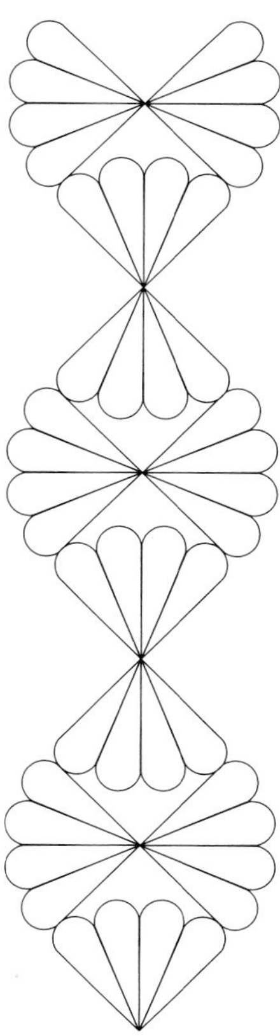

**632**

(1⅛in (2.8cm)) to
6in (15.25cm) 533%
(see **628** for corner)

**633**

(1in (2.5cm)) to 4in (10.2cm) 400%

**634**

(1in (2.5cm)) to 6in (15.25cm) 600%

**635**

(1in (2.5cm)) to 6in (15.25cm) 600%

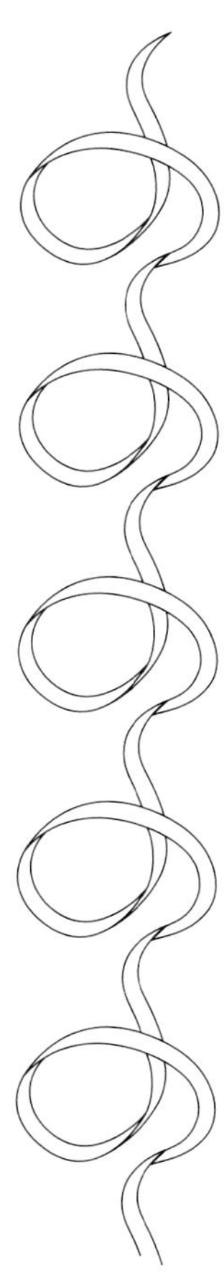

**636a**

(¾in (1.9cm)) to 4in (10.2cm) 533%

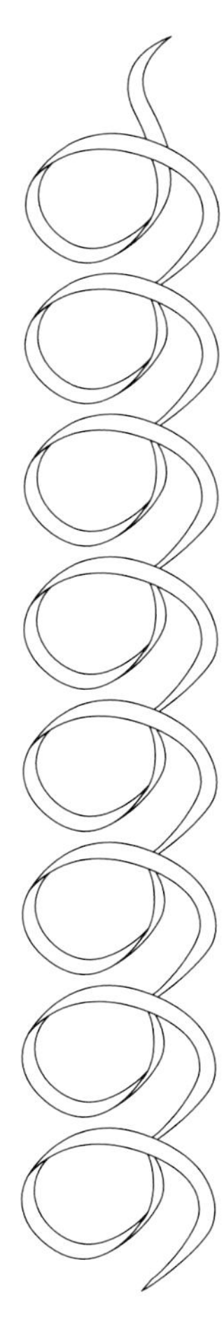

**636b**

(¾in (1.9cm)) to 4in (10.2cm) 533%

**636c**

(1in (2.5cm)) to 6in (15.25cm) 600%

**637a**

(⅝in (1.6cm)) to
4in (10.2cm) 640%

**637b**

(⅝in (1.6cm)) to
4in (10.2cm) 640%

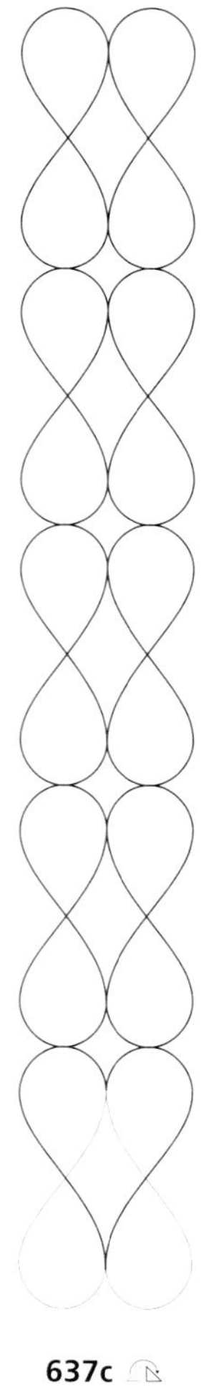

**637c**

(⅝in (1.6cm)) to
6in (15.25cm) 960%

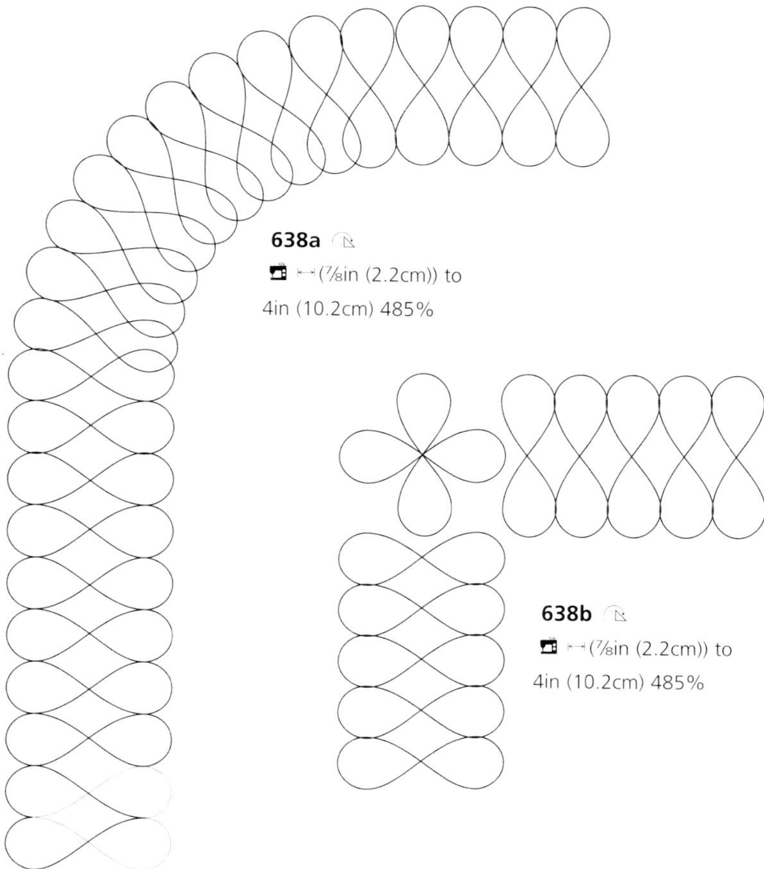

**638a**

↔ (⅞in (2.2cm)) to 4in (10.2cm) 485%

**638b**

↔ (⅞in (2.2cm)) to 4in (10.2cm) 485%

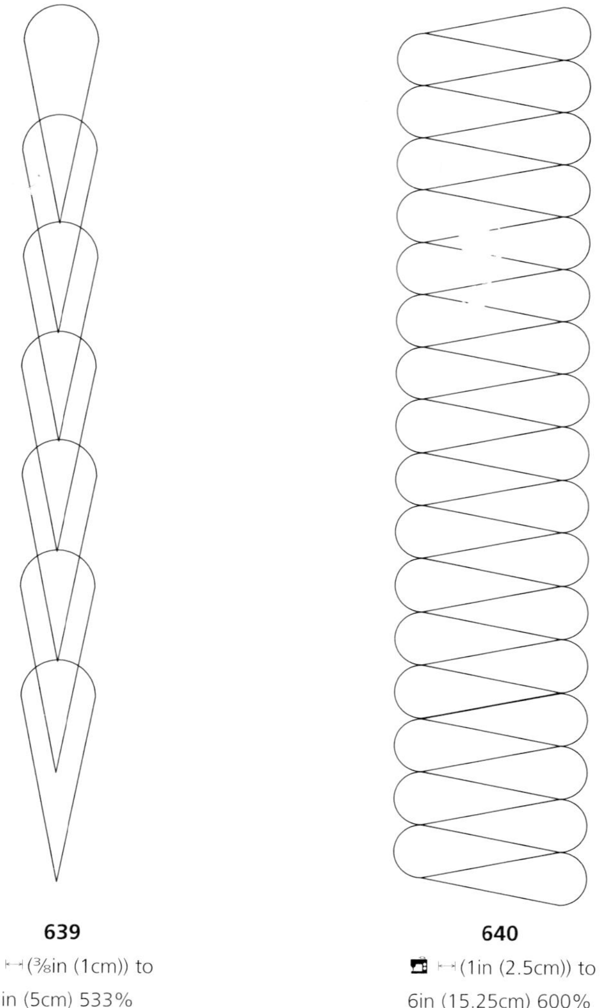

**639**

⟼ (⅜in (1cm)) to 2in (5cm) 533%

**640**

⟼ (1in (2.5cm)) to 6in (15.25cm) 600%

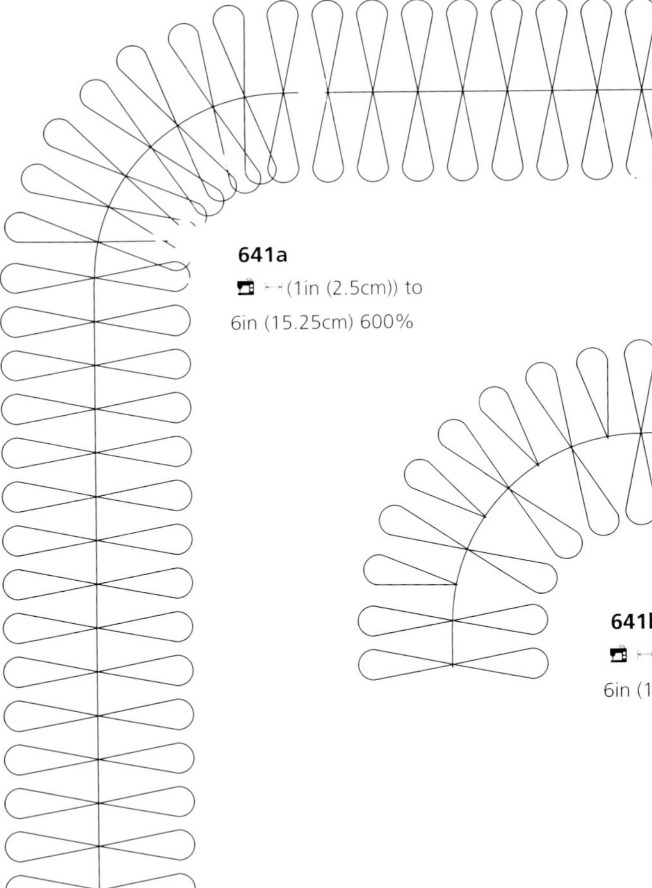

**641a**

(1in (2.5cm)) to 6in (15.25cm) 600%

**641b**

(1in (2.5cm)) to 6in (15.25cm) 600%

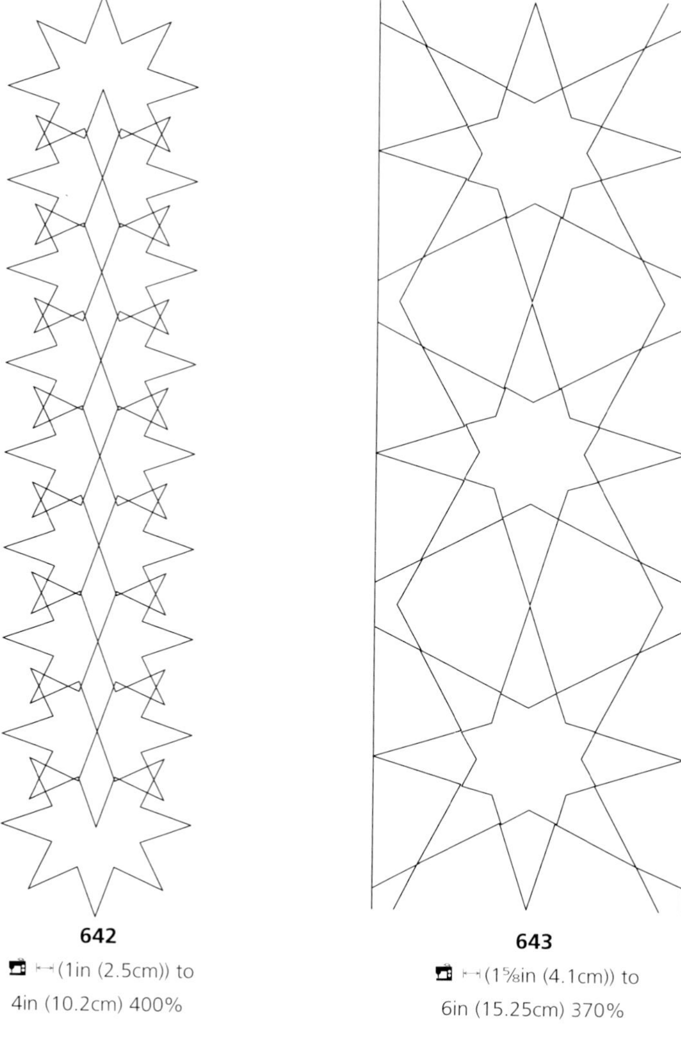

**642**

(1in (2.5cm)) to 4in (10.2cm) 400%

**643**

(1⅝in (4.1cm)) to 6in (15.25cm) 370%

ALL PATTERNS ARE STANDARD 2IN (5CM) OR 4IN (10.2CM) UNLESS OTHERWISE STATED

**644**

⟼ (1in (2.5cm)) to 6in (15.25cm) 600%

**645**

⟼ (1in (2.5cm)) to 6in (15.25cm) 600%

**646**

⟼ (1in (2.5cm)) to 6in (15.25cm) 600%

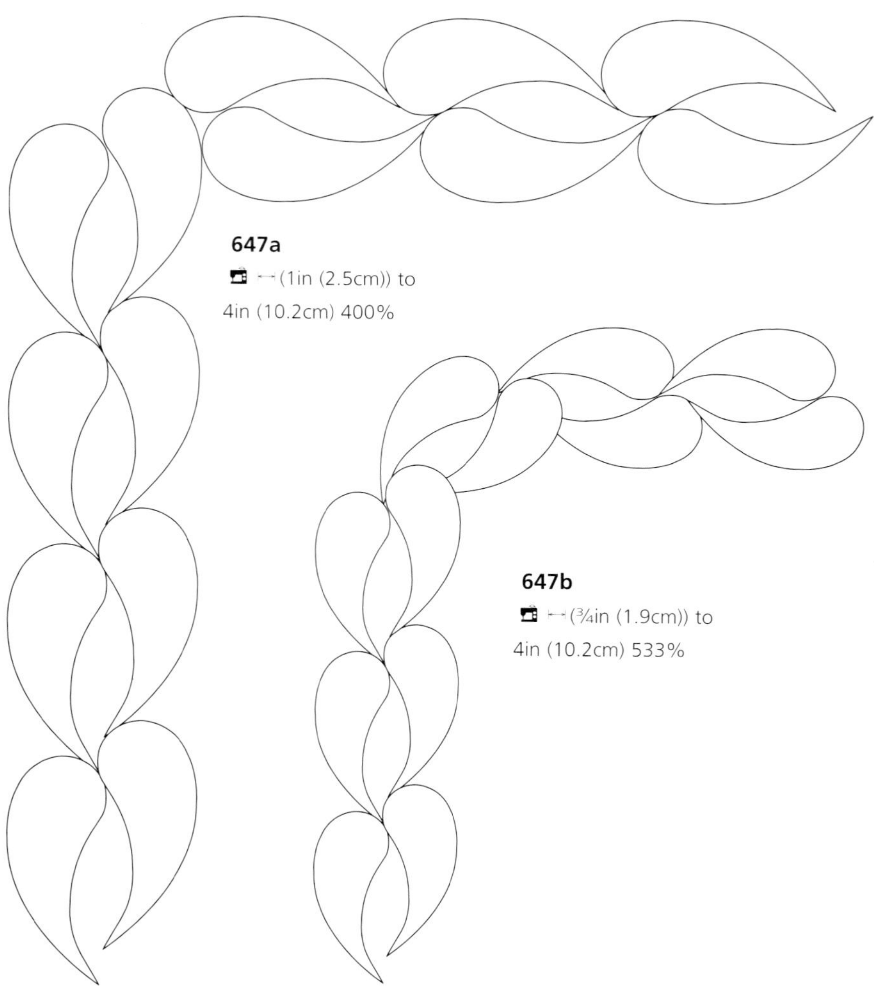

**647a**

⟷(1in (2.5cm)) to 4in (10.2cm) 400%

**647b**

⟷(¾in (1.9cm)) to 4in (10.2cm) 533%

**647c**

⟷(1in (2.5cm)) to 6in (15.25cm) 600%

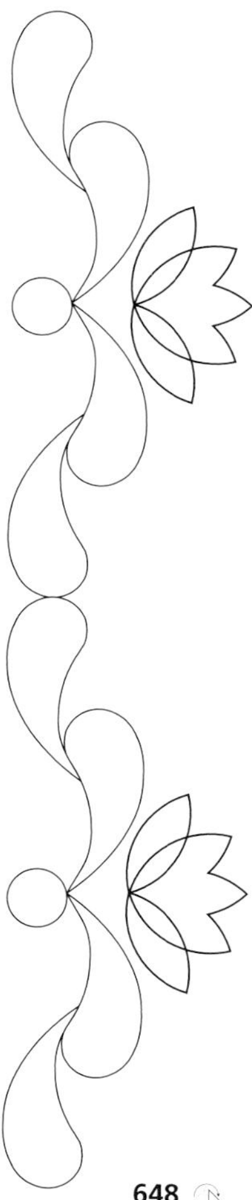

**648**

⟷(1in (2.5cm)) to 8in (20.3cm) 800%

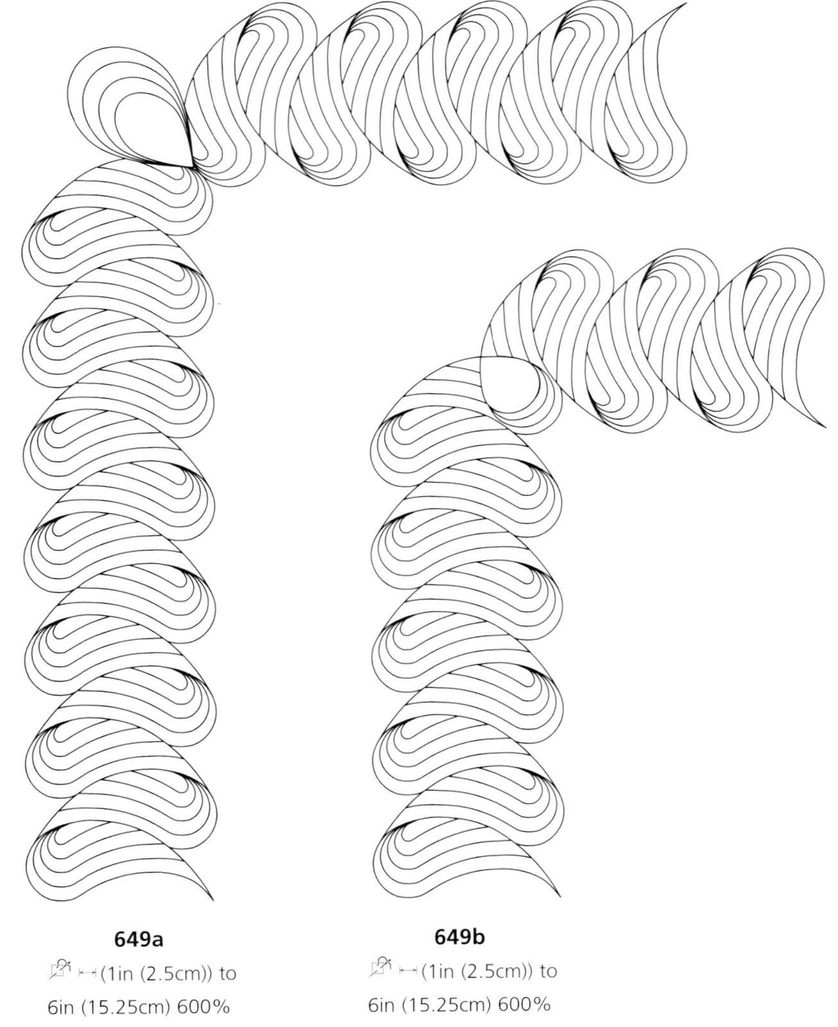

**649a**

↦ (1in (2.5cm)) to 6in (15.25cm) 600%

**649b**

↦ (1in (2.5cm)) to 6in (15.25cm) 600%

**649c**

⟷ (1in (2.5cm)) to 6in (15.25cm) 600%

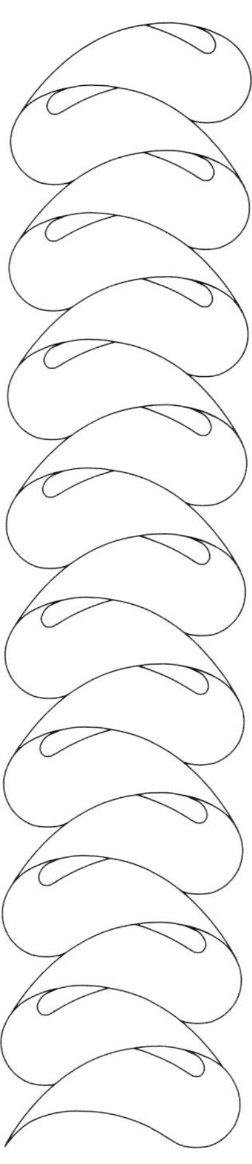

**649d**

⟷ (1in (2.5cm)) to 4in (10.2cm) 400%

**650**

(1in (2.5cm)) to
6in (15.25cm) 600%

**651**

(1½in (3.8cm)) to
6in (15.25cm) 400%

ALL PATTERNS ARE STANDARD 2IN (5CM) OR 4IN (10.2CM) UNLESS OTHERWISE STATED

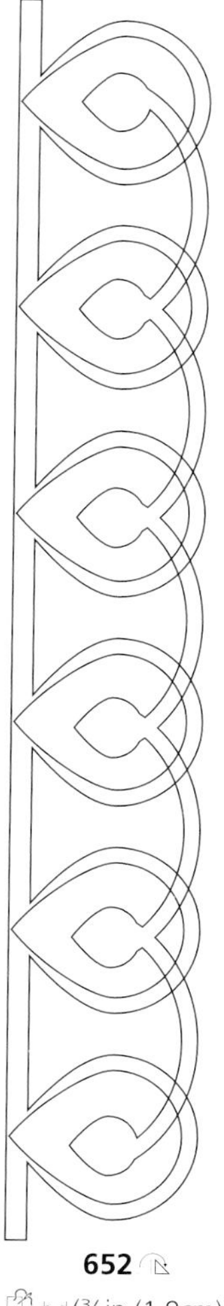

**652**

(¾in (1.9cm)) to 6in (15.25cm) 800%

**653**

(⅝in (1.6cm)) to 4in (10.2cm) 640%

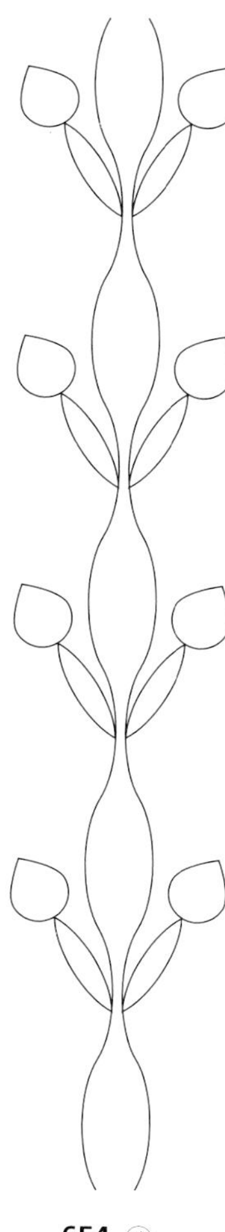

**654**

(⅞in (2.2cm)) to 4in (10.2cm) 457%

**655**

(1⅜in (3.5cm)) to 6in (15.25cm) 436%

**656**

(1⅜in (3.5cm)) to 8in (20.3cm) 582%

**657**
⟼(⅝in (1.6cm)) to 6in (15.25cm) 960%

**658**
⟼(⅞in (2.2cm)) to 6in (15.25cm) 686%

**659**
⟼(1in (2.5cm)) to 8in (20.3cm) 800%

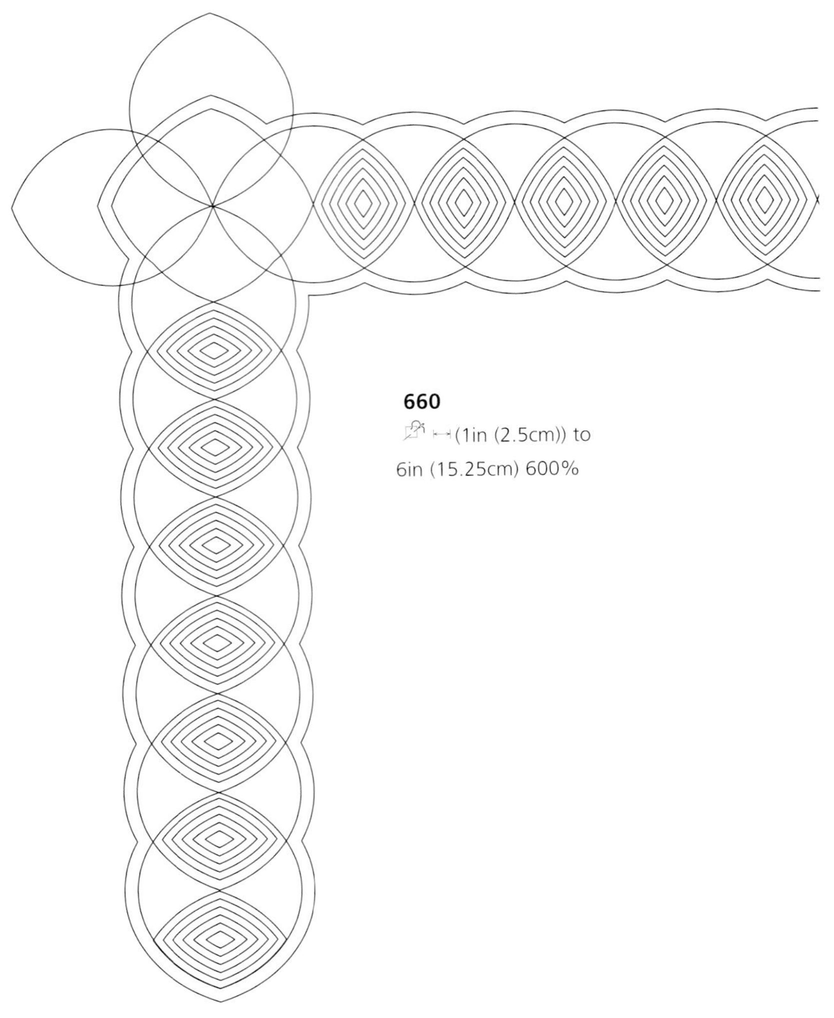

**660**

⟷(1in (2.5cm)) to 6in (15.25cm) 600%

**661a**

⇹ ↦(1in (2.5cm)) to 8in (20.3cm) 800%

**661b**

⇹ ↦(1in (2.5cm)) to 8in (20.3cm) 800%

# Filler patterns

Filler patterns have a variety of uses. They secure the three layers of the quilt in the background areas between motifs, or the simpler filler patterns can be used to make parts of a motif recede or flatten, adding emphasis to other sections of the motif.

Quilters have traditionally used a very narrow palette of geometric designs; these are shown at the beginning of this chapter. Note that they are shown at a smaller size because they are often more easily drawn using a quilter's ruler, which has the angles conveniently marked. However, the development of continuous single-line patterns for the sewing machine and the influences of sashiko have made an impact; now a myriad of patterns are quite commonly seen. Because these patterns are not necessarily as easy to mark on the fabric as the traditional patterns, most of the patterns in this chapter are accompanied by a single unit of the design to use for making a template.

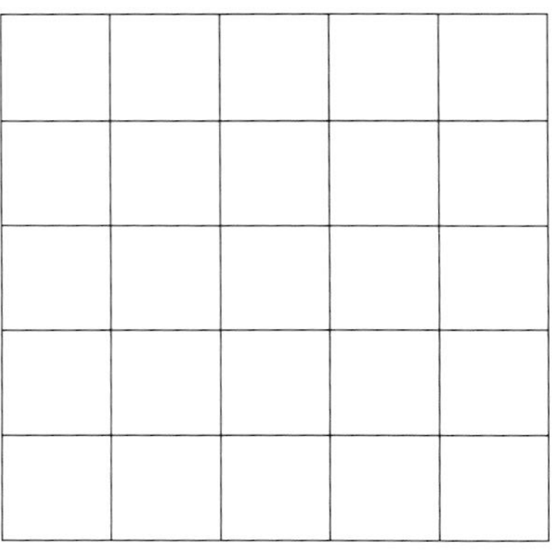

**662**

⟷ 18in (45.7cm) 900%

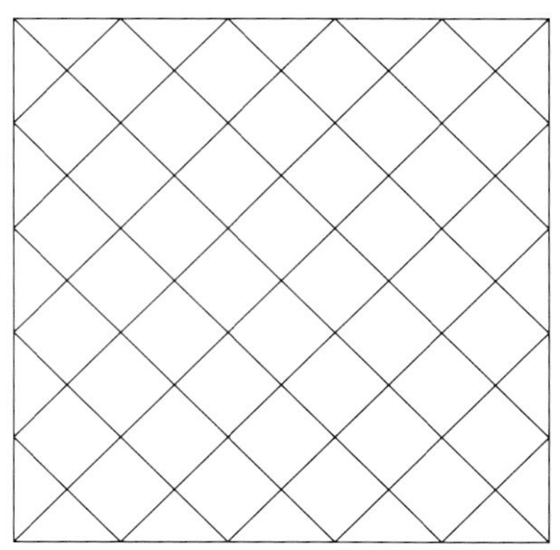

**663**

⟷ 18in (45.7cm) 900%

**664**

18in (45.7cm) 900%

**665**

18in (45.7cm) 900%

**666**

18in (45.7cm) 900%

**667**

18in (45.7cm) 900%

**668**

⟼ 18in (45.7cm) 900%

**669**

⟼ 18in (45.7cm) 900%

**670**

⟼ 18in (45.7cm) 900%

**671**

⟼ 18in (45.7cm) 900%

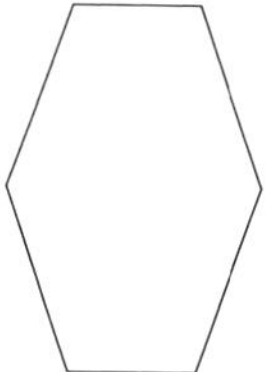

**672a**

This elongated hexagon can be used as a template or as a guide to position parallel strips of masking tape.

(unit is 1in (2.5cm)) to
2in (5cm) 200%
4in (10.2cm) 400%
6in (15.25cm) 600%

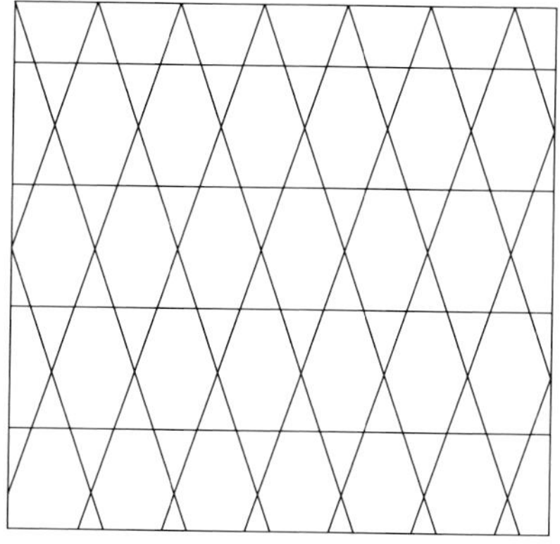

**672b**

The negative triangle shapes within this pattern can also be emphasized.

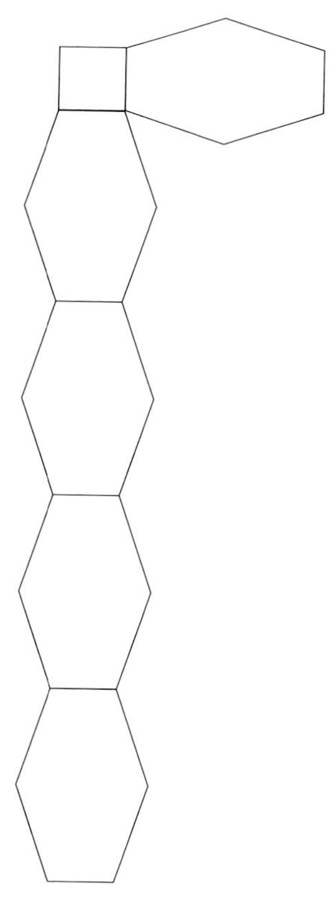

**672c**

(⅝in (1.6cm)) to
2in (5cm) 320%
4in (10.2cm) 640%

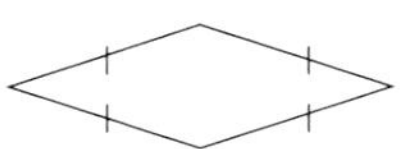

**673a**

A classic filler shape, this distorted diamond looks very different if rotated through 90 degrees.

(unit is 1in (2.5cm)) to

2in (5cm) 200%

4in (10.2cm) 400%

6in (15.25cm) 600%

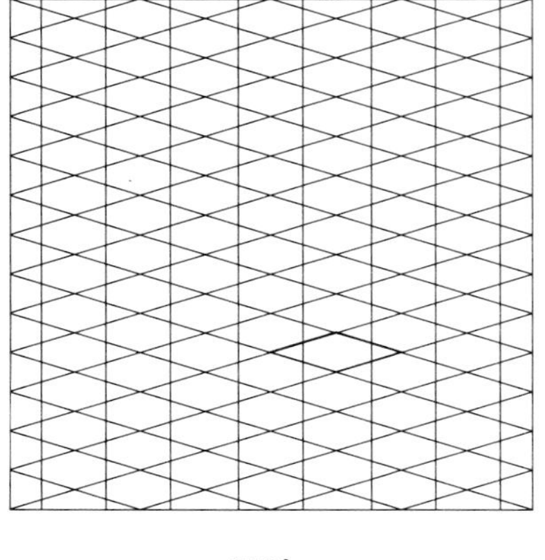

**673b**

(see **673a**) The vertical lines help prevent sagging and allows the patterns to be used larger.

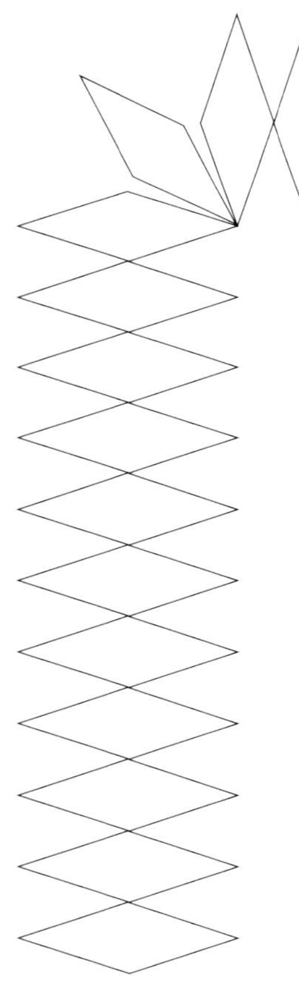

**673c**

(1in (2.5cm)) to

2in (5cm) 200%

4in (10.2cm) 400%

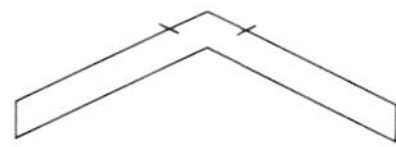

**674a**

This shape can be used as a template or as a homemade protractor for strips of masking tape.

⟷ (unit is 1in (2.5cm)) to
2in (5cm) 200%
4in (10.2cm) 400%
6in (15.25cm) 600%

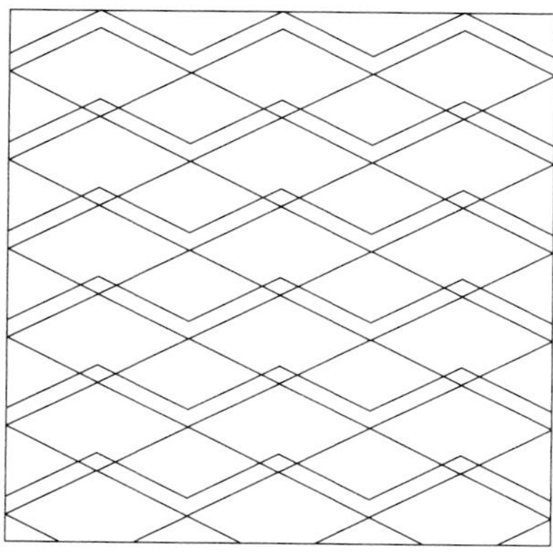

**674b**

⟷ (see **674a**) When the motif is combined with a single-line repeat of the template, it has an art deco feel.

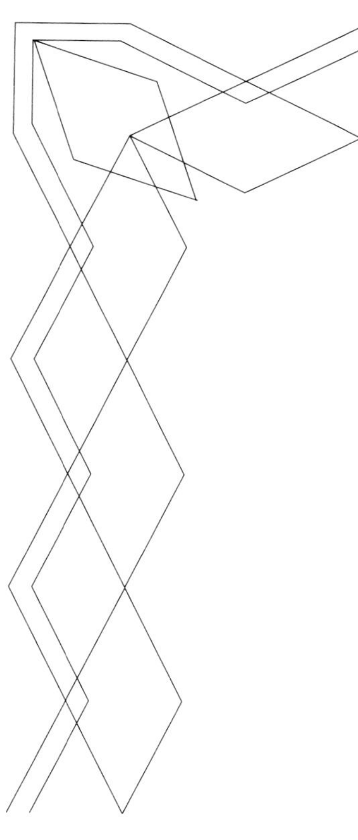

**674c**

⟷ (⅞in (2.2cm)) to
4in (10.2cm) 454%
6in (15.25cm) 690%

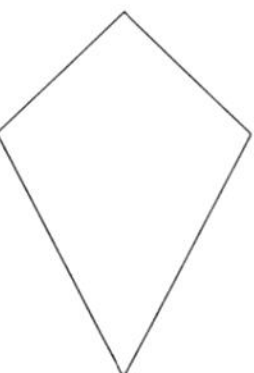

**675a**

The kite is a popular theme in quilting, and it is sometimes useful to extend it to the border. However, if this shape is used at the larger sizes, sagging could be a problem.

(unit is 1in (2.5cm)) to
4in (10.2cm) 400%
6in (15.25cm) 600%

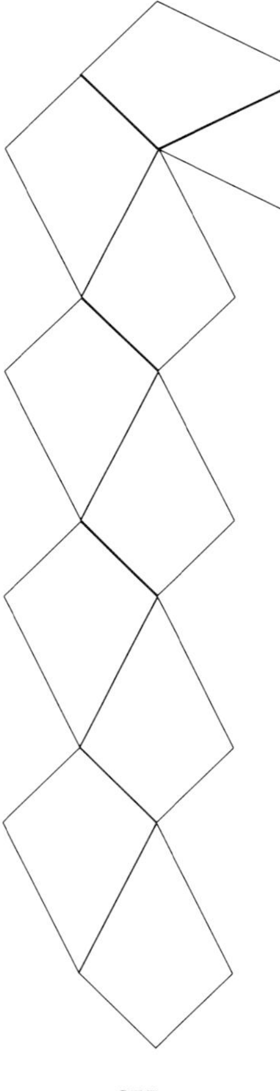

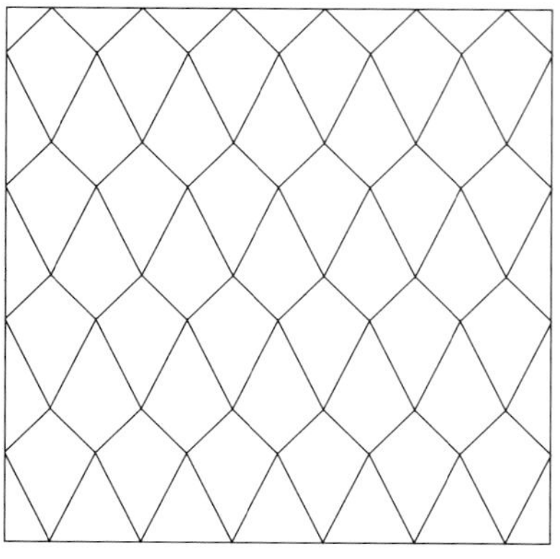

**675b**

(see **675a**) This pattern is very simple but quite mesmerizing.

**675c**

(1in (2.5cm)) to
4in (10.2cm) 400%
6in (15.25cm) 600%

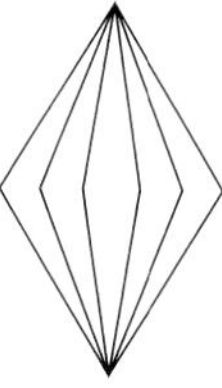

**676a**

The lines contained within this diamond make it suitable to be used larger. Do not stitch individual shapes but chains of shapes.

(unit is 1in (2.5cm)) to
6in (15.25cm) 600%
8in (20.3cm) 800%

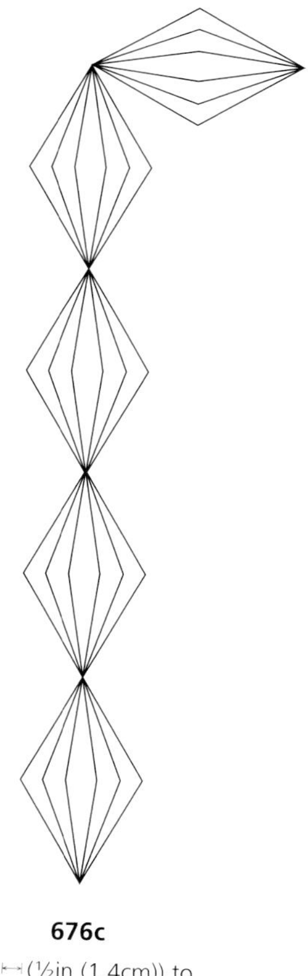

**676c**

(½in (1.4cm)) to
2in (5cm) 400%
4in (10.2cm) 800%

**676b**

An additional motif may be required in the negative shape.

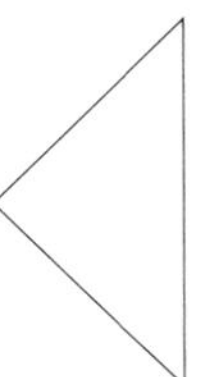

**677a**

This right-angle triangle can be used to echo piecing in quilt tops, making an interesting border or a contrasting stitched pattern.

(unit is 1in (2.5cm)) to
2in (5cm) 200%
4in (10.2cm) 400%
6in (15.25cm) 600%

**677b**

(see **677a**) The horizontal lines can be removed to create a zig-zag pattern.

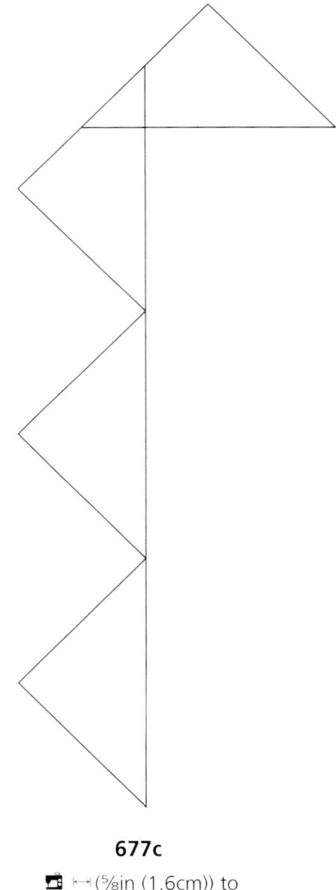

**677c**

(⅝in (1.6cm)) to
2in (5cm) 320%
4in (10.2cm) 640%

**677d**

(⅜in (1cm)) to
2in (5cm) 530%
3in (7.6cm)790%

**677e**

(⅞in (2.2cm)) to
4in (10.2cm) 464%
6in (15.25cm) 693%

**677f**

(⅞in (2.2cm)) to
5in (12.7cm) 577%
6in (15.25cm) 693%

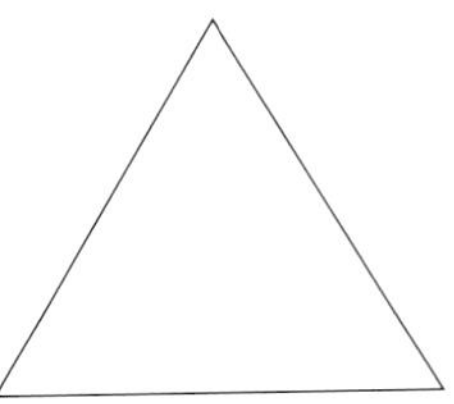

**678a**

This equilateral triangle is equally useful as a filler or a border. If the shape does not overlap itself, an additional filler or motif may be required.

(unit is 1in (2.5cm)) to
4in (10.2cm) 400%
6in (15.25cm) 600%

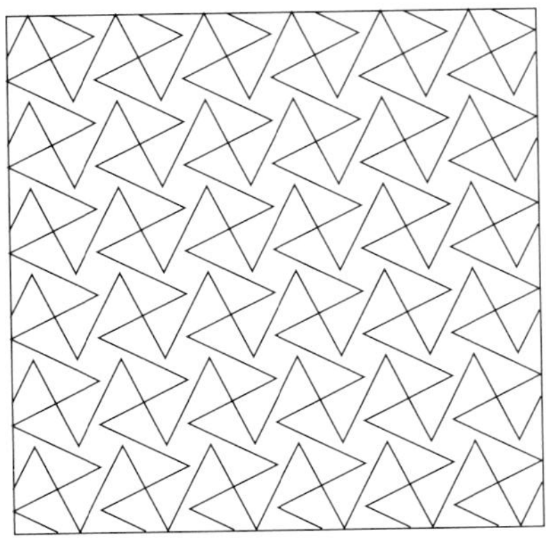

**678b**

(see **678a**) This pattern is simply two zig-zag patterns at right-angles to each other.

**678c**

(⅝in (1.6cm)) to
2in (5cm) 320%
4in (10.2cm) 640%

**678d**

(⅝in (1.6cm)) to
3in (7.6cm) 475%
5in (12.7cm) 794%

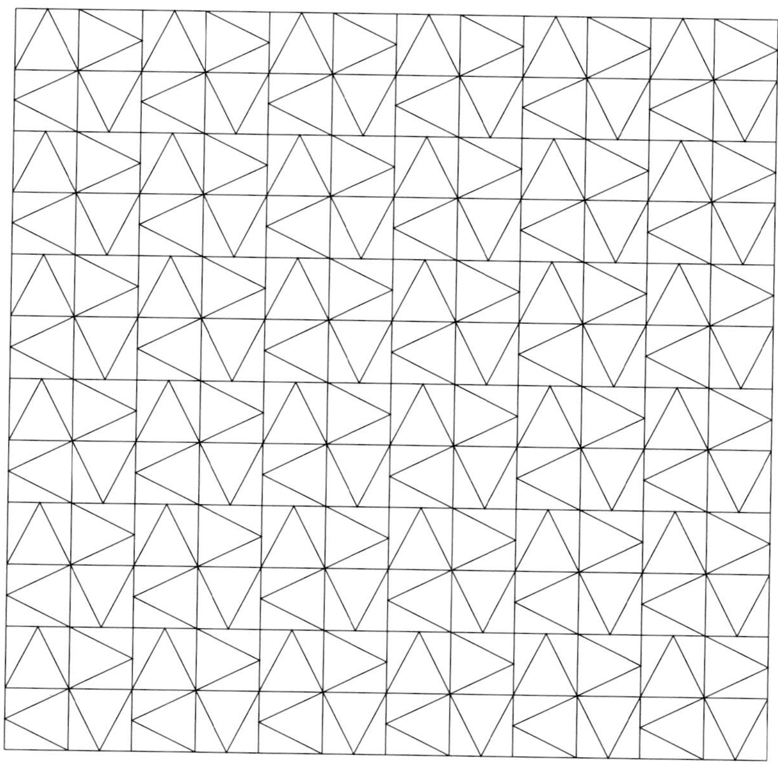

**679**

(see **678a**) This pattern is the zig-zag pattern of **678b** with horizontal and vertical rules.

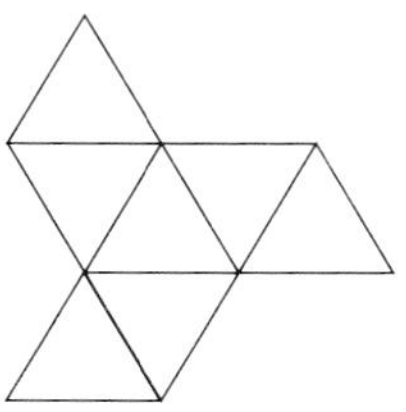

**680a**

This shape is made up of equilateral triangles as shown. This a very flexible shape that looks good with a motif in its center.

(unit is 1in (2.5cm)) to
4in (10.2cm) 400%
6in (15.25cm) 600%

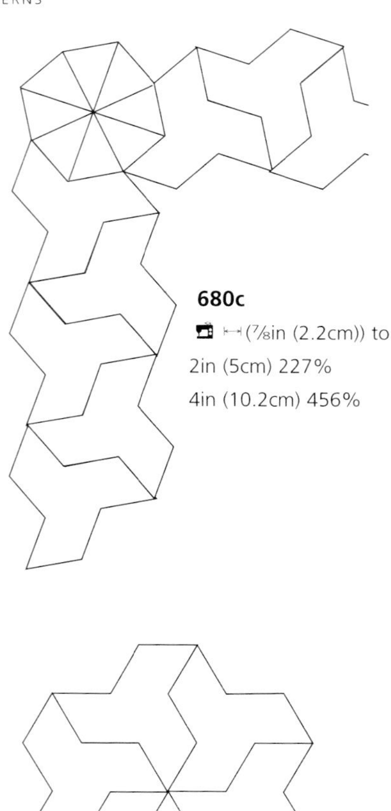

**680c**

(⅞in (2.2cm)) to
2in (5cm) 227%
4in (10.2cm) 456%

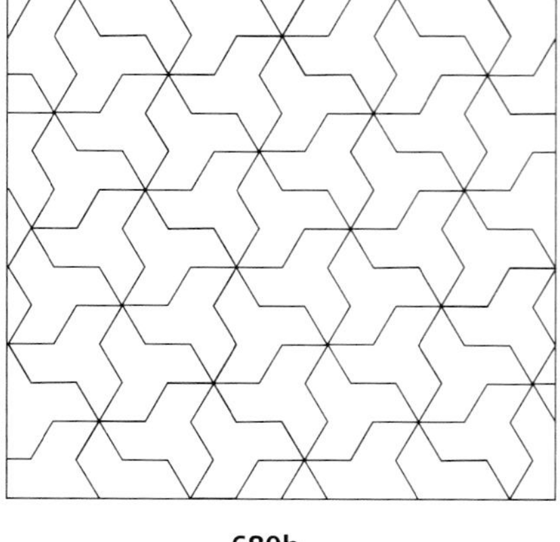

**680b**

(see **680a**) Contrasting thread can be used for opposing lines of stitching.

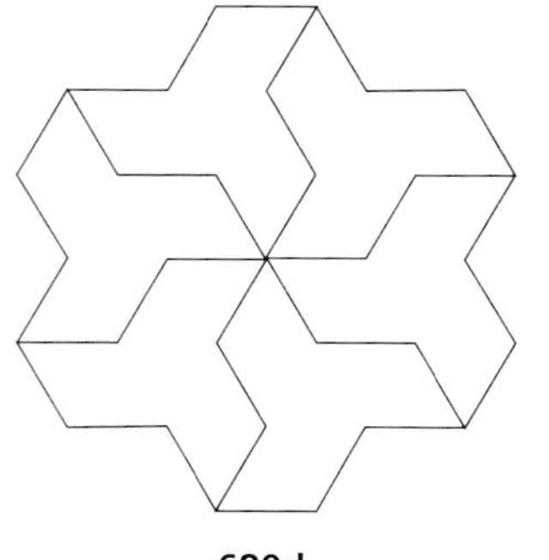

**680d**

(see **640a**)

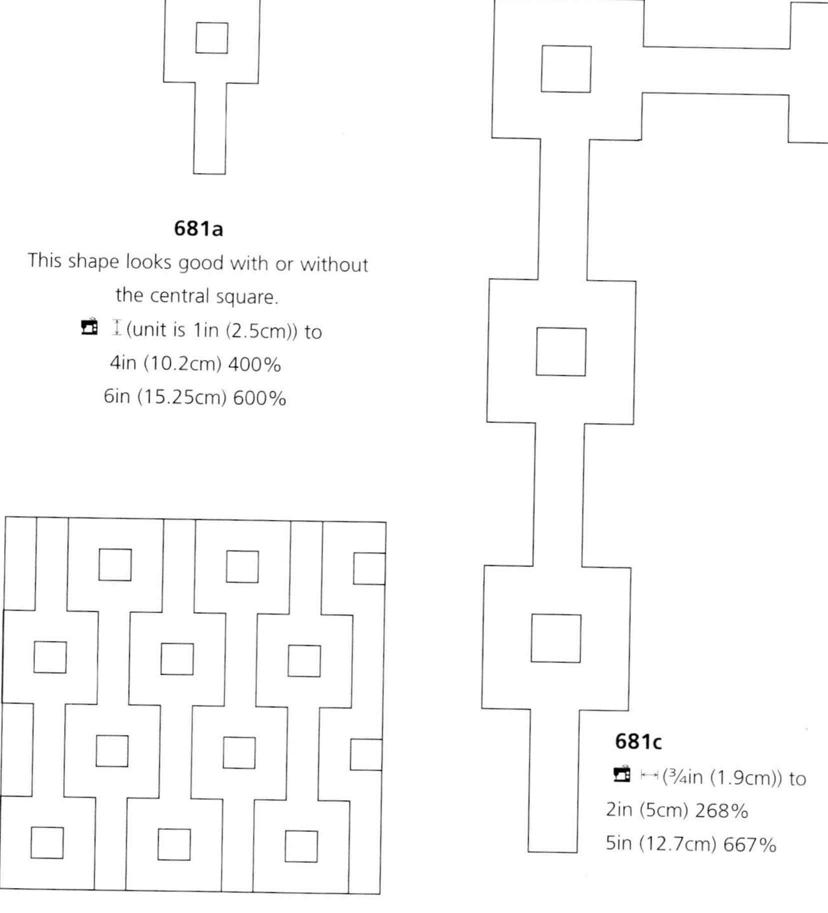

**681a**

This shape looks good with or without the central square.

(unit is 1in (2.5cm)) to
4in (10.2cm) 400%
6in (15.25cm) 600%

**681c**

(¾in (1.9cm)) to
2in (5cm) 268%
5in (12.7cm) 667%

**681b**

(see **681a**) Consider dispensing with the inner square for a different look.

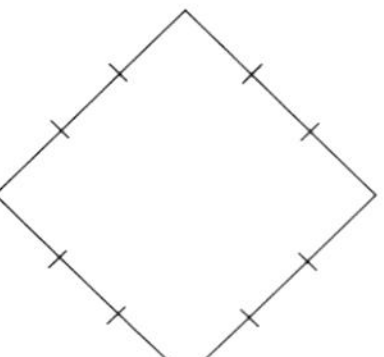

**682a**

The classic square shape can be used in a variety of ways. Remember to look for long lines of stitching within any filler pattern rather than stitching the outline of the individual squares.

(unit is 1in (2.5cm)) to
4in (10.2cm) 400%
6in (15.25cm) 600%

**682b**

(see **682a**) The negative shapes within this pattern can also be emphasized.

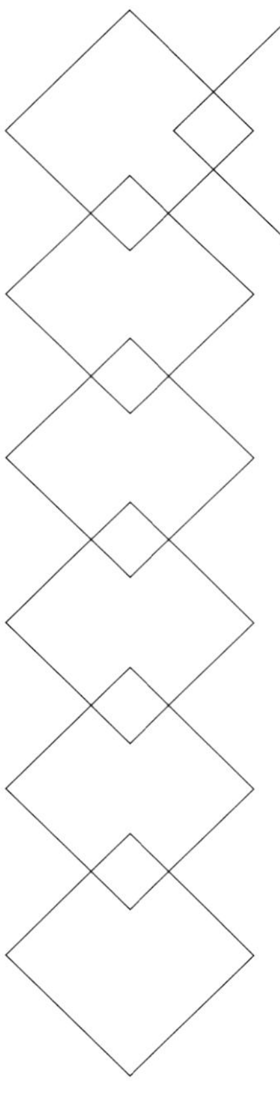

**682c**

(1in (2.5cm)) to
2in (5cm) 200%
4in (10.2cm) 400%

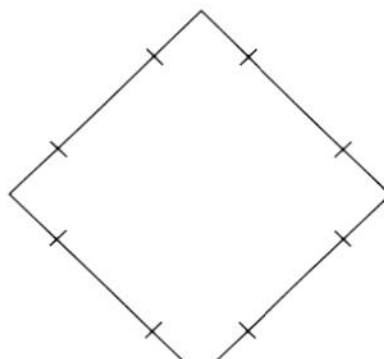

**682d**

Compare this pattern with **681a** and note how the different proportions can alter the overall effect.

(unit is 1in (2.5cm)) to
2in (5cm) 200%
4in (10.2cm) 400%
6in (15.25cm) 600%

**682e**

(see **682d**) This pattern has a variety of negative shapes and can be used as an overall structure for further motifs.

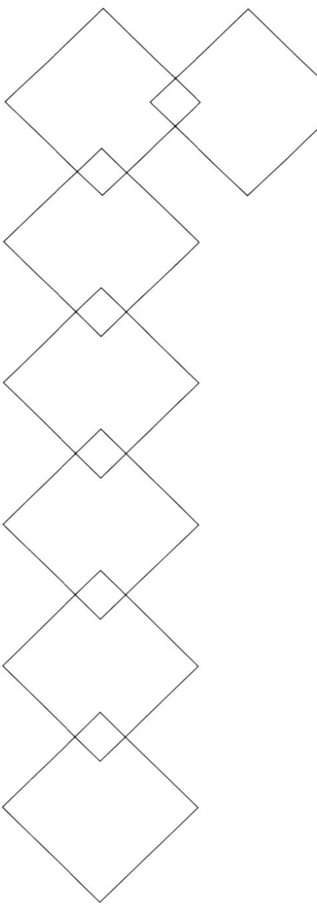

**682f**

(1in (2.5cm)) to
2in (5cm) 200%
4in (10.2cm) 400%

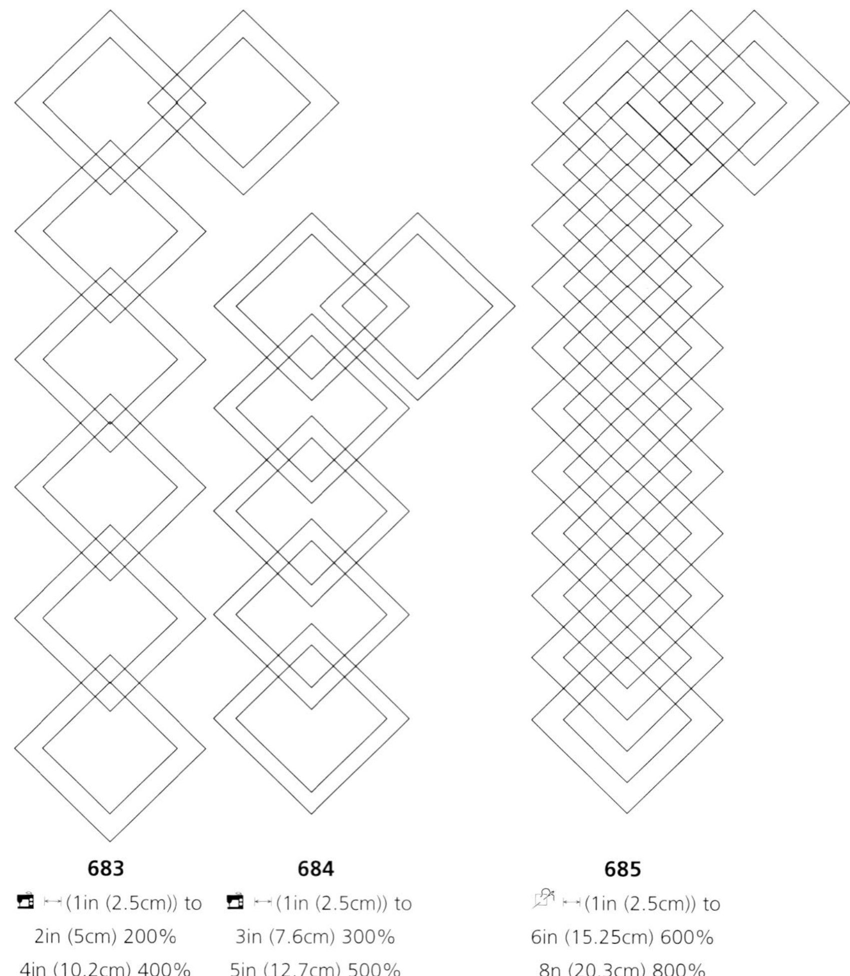

**683**

⟼(1in (2.5cm)) to
2in (5cm) 200%
4in (10.2cm) 400%

**684**

⟼(1in (2.5cm)) to
3in (7.6cm) 300%
5in (12.7cm) 500%

**685**

⟼(1in (2.5cm)) to
6in (15.25cm) 600%
8n (20.3cm) 800%

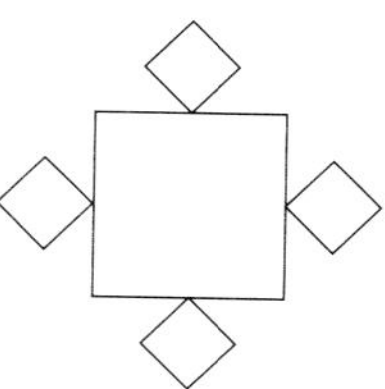

**686a**

This motif is slightly more complicated, but it can be an interesting overall quilting structure for other designs.

(unit is 1in (2.5cm)) to 6in (15.25cm) 600%

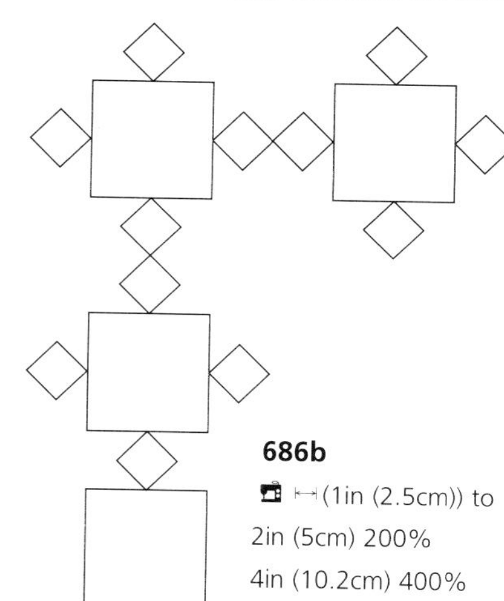

**686b**

(1in (2.5cm)) to
2in (5cm) 200%
4in (10.2cm) 400%

**686c**

(see **686a**) Self-contained motifs can be stitched in each medium and large square.

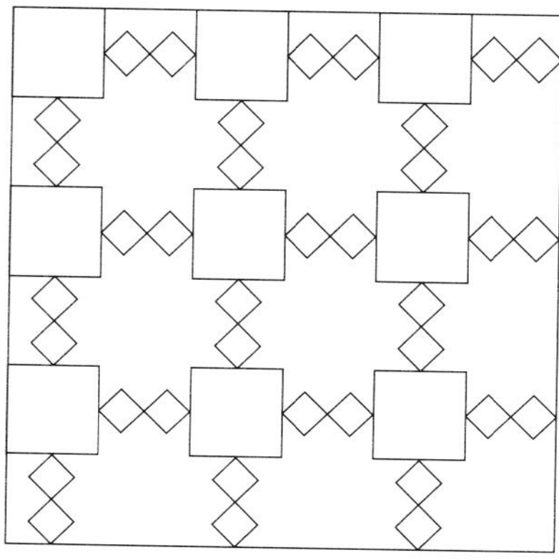

**686d**

(see **686a**) The negative star shape should not be ignored.

**687a**

This shape is made up of two squares; this means that the longer length is twice the shorter edge.

(unit is 1in (2.5cm)) to
2in (5cm) 200%
4in (10.2cm) 400%
6in (15.25cm) 600%

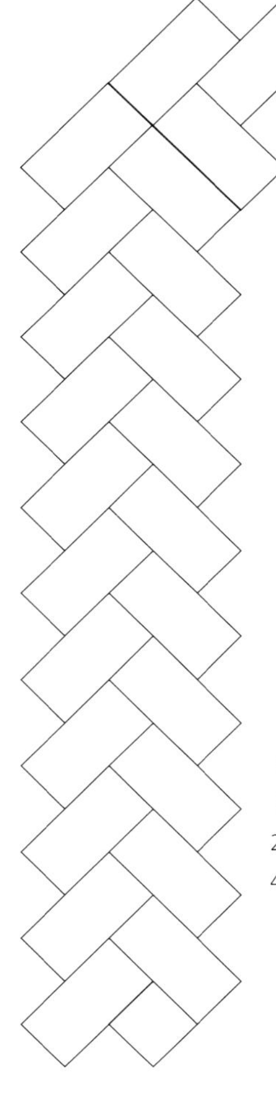

**687c**

(1in (2.5cm)) to
2in (5cm) 200%
4in (10.2cm) 400%

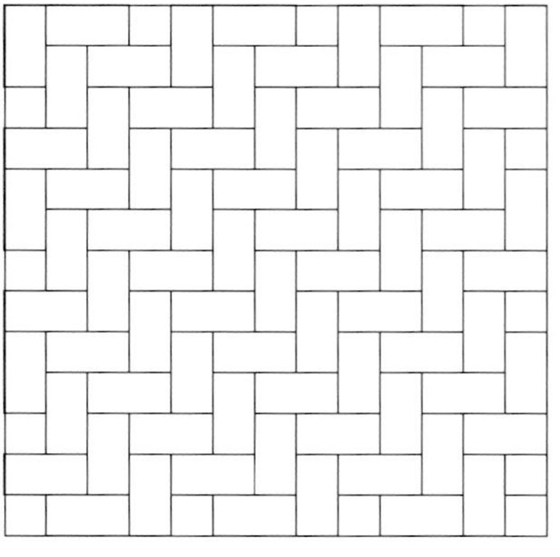

**687b**

(see **687a**) A classic herringbone pattern can be created.

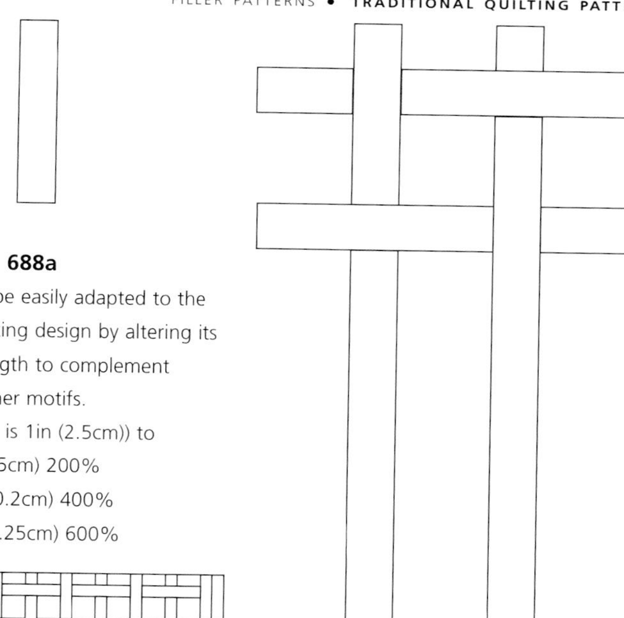

**688a**

This shape can be easily adapted to the needs of the quilting design by altering its width or length to complement other motifs.

(unit is 1in (2.5cm)) to
2in (5cm) 200%
4in (10.2cm) 400%
6in (15.25cm) 600%

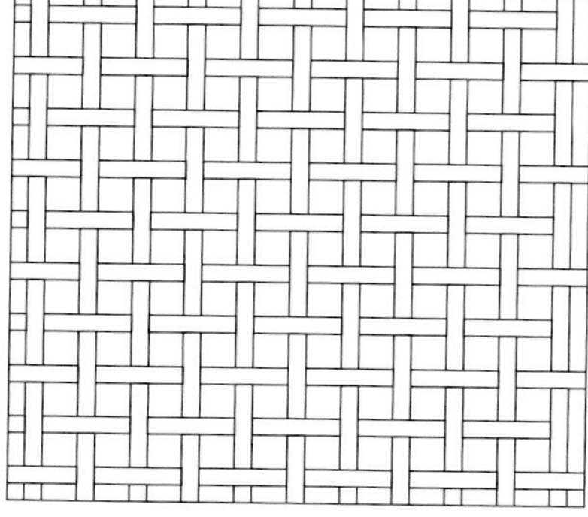

**688b**

(see **688a**) This basket weave pattern has a square negative shape that can be further embellished.

**688c**

(1in (2.5cm)) to
2in (5cm) 200%
4in (10.2cm) 400%

**689a**

This shape is made up of five squares, which makes it easy to draw and stitch. To achieve the perfect corner when machine quilting, match the length of one edge to an exact number of stitches.

(unit is 1in (2.5cm)) to
2in (5cm) 200%
4in (10.2cm) 400%

**689b**

(see **689a**) Depending on the scale that is used, the center of each cross shape may need an additional motif.

**689c**

(1in (2.5cm)) to
4in (10.2cm) 400%
6in (15.25cm) 600%

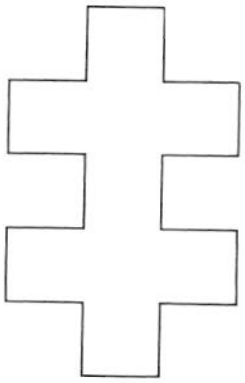

**690a**

This shape is made up of two overlapping **689** shapes and shares many of its advantages.

(unit is 1in (2.5cm)) to
2in (5cm) 200%
4in (10.2cm) 400%
6in (15.25cm) 600%

**690b**

(see **690a**) This pattern can be very dominant and works better if it is further emphasized with contrasting thread.

**690c**

(1in (2.5cm)) to
4in (10.2cm) 400%
6in (15.25cm) 600%

**691a**

Although this shape is made up of squares, the center square can be replaced by any motif that would suit the quilting.

(unit is 1in (2.5cm)) to
2in (5cm) 200%
4in (10.2cm) 400%
6in (15.25cm) 600%

**691b**

(see **691a**) This pattern looks good using contrasting threads.

**691c**

(¾in (1.9cm)) to
2in (5cm) 266%
4in (10.2cm) 533%

**691d**

(⅞in (2.2cm)) to
2in (5cm) 228%
4in (10.2cm) 458%

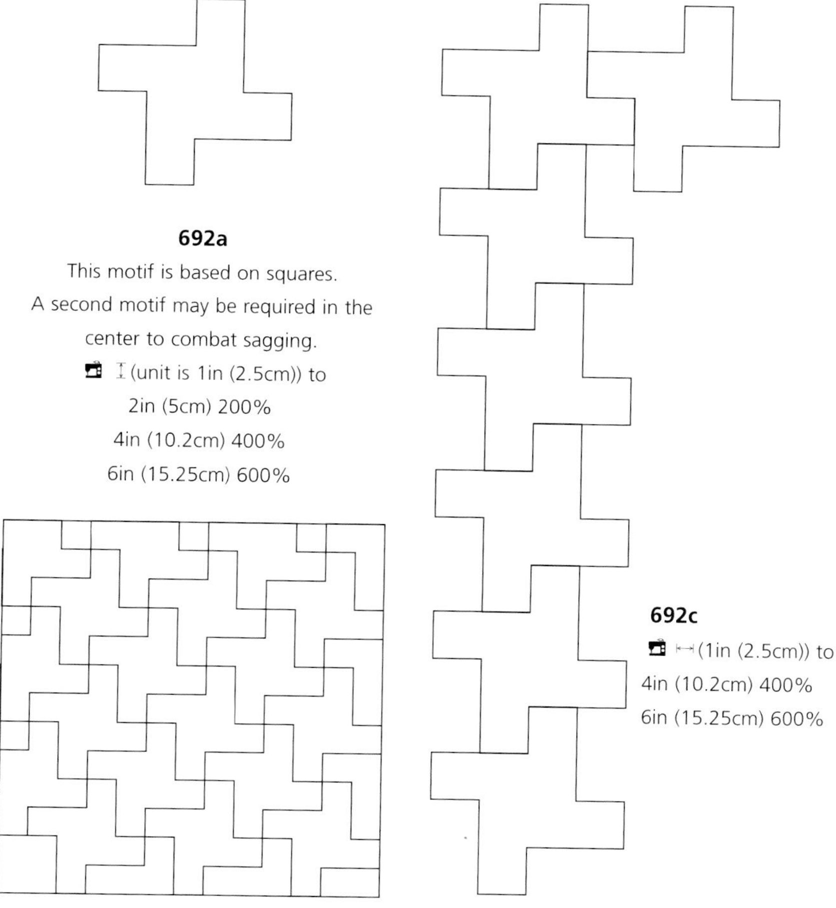

**692a**

This motif is based on squares.
A second motif may be required in the center to combat sagging.

(unit is 1in (2.5cm)) to
2in (5cm) 200%
4in (10.2cm) 400%
6in (15.25cm) 600%

**692c**

(1in (2.5cm)) to
4in (10.2cm) 400%
6in (15.25cm) 600%

**692b**

(see **692a**) The longer lengths of straight stitching make this quicker to machine stitch than previous designs.

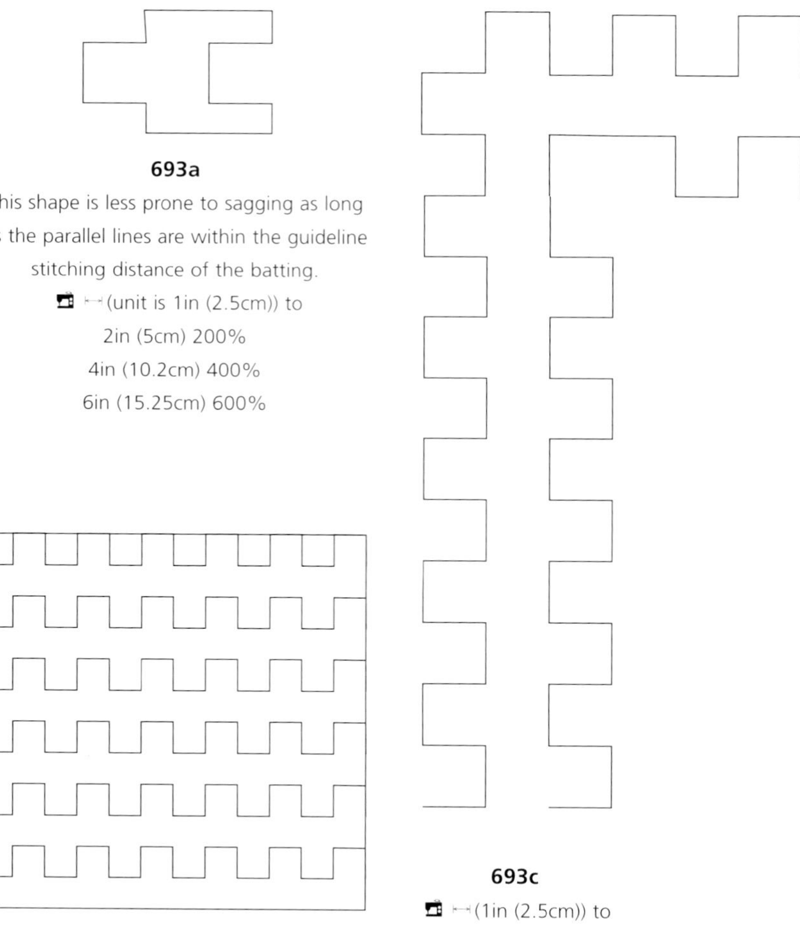

**693a**

This shape is less prone to sagging as long as the parallel lines are within the guideline stitching distance of the batting.

(unit is 1in (2.5cm)) to
2in (5cm) 200%
4in (10.2cm) 400%
6in (15.25cm) 600%

**693b**

(see **693a**) Use the horizontal lines to visually add width to a design or rotate it 90 degrees to add length.

**693c**

(1in (2.5cm)) to
2in (5cm) 200%
4in (10.2cm) 400%

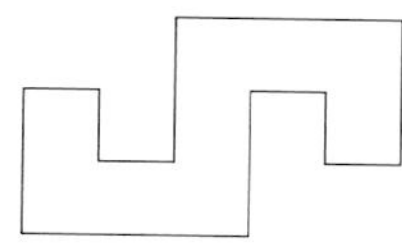

**694a**

This shape is easy to draw onto the fabric, although it is a bit laborious to stitch; however, it does reward its efforts with a subtle Oriental feel.

⟷ (unit is 1in (2.5cm)) to
2in (5cm) 200%
4in (10.2cm) 400%
6in (15.25cm) 600%

**694b**

⟷ (see **694a**) A dominant design that should either be emphasized or used in small blocks or panels.

**694c**

⟷ (1in (2.5cm)) to
2in (5cm) 200%
4in (10.2cm) 400%

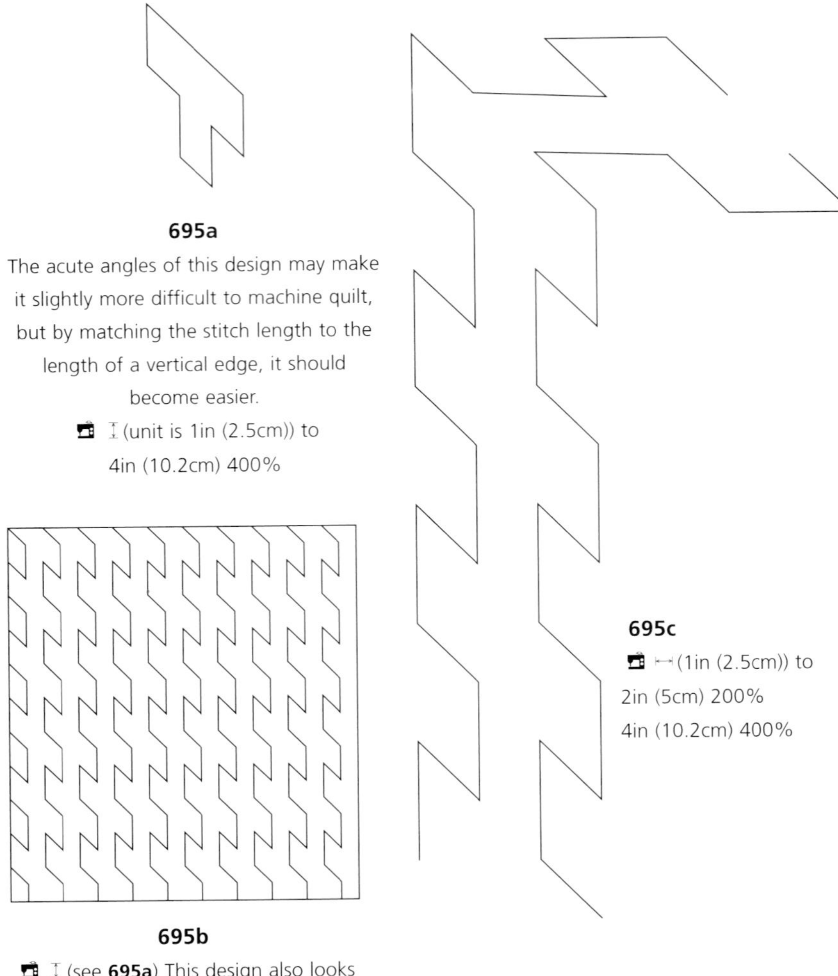

**695a**

The acute angles of this design may make it slightly more difficult to machine quilt, but by matching the stitch length to the length of a vertical edge, it should become easier.

(unit is 1in (2.5cm)) to
4in (10.2cm) 400%

**695b**

(see **695a**) This design also looks good rotated 45 degrees.

**695c**

(1in (2.5cm)) to
2in (5cm) 200%
4in (10.2cm) 400%

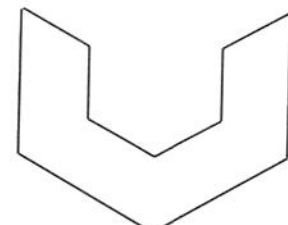

**696a**

This more complex shape looks best when it is used larger and is a feature pattern on a panel of plain fabric.

⟷(unit is 1in (2.5cm)) to
4in (10.2cm) 400%
6in (15.25cm) 600%

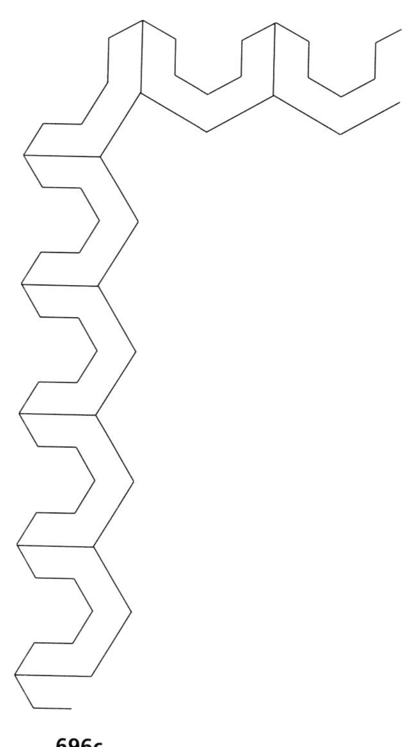

**696c**

⟷(⅝in (1.6cm)) to
2in (5cm) 320%
4in (10.2cm) 640%

**696b**

⟷(see **696a**) To make this pattern easier to machine sew link the vertical lines as on the right of the pattern.

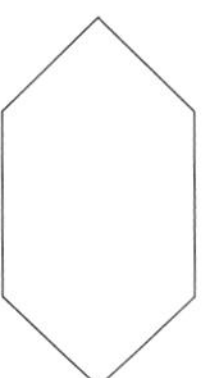

**697a**

This shape is equally useful as a filler or as a border. It is made up of two squares on point with connecting parallel lines; however, these proportions may be altered.

(unit is 1in (2.5cm)) to
4in (10.2cm) 400%
6in (15.25cm) 600%

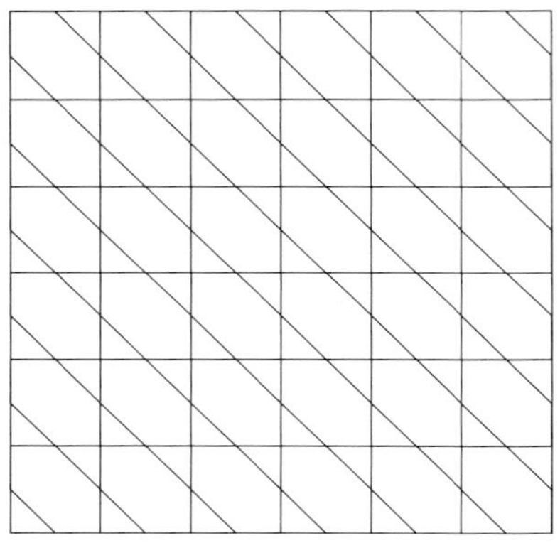

**697b**

(see **697a**) This filler pattern is based on a square grid.

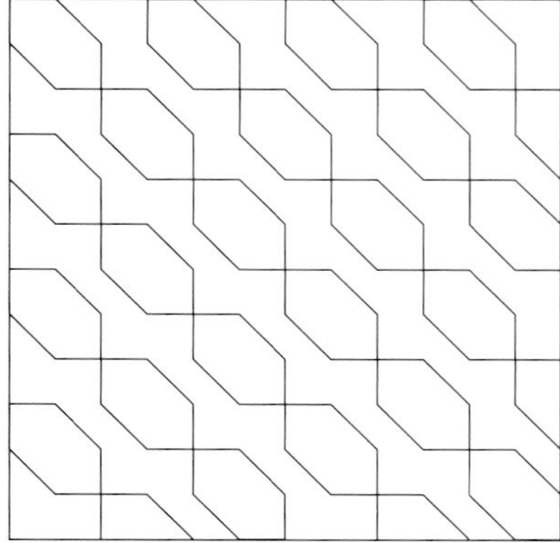

**697c**

(see **697a**) The negative shapes within this pattern may also be emphasized.

**697d**

(see **697a**) This filler contains a potential zigzag border pattern.

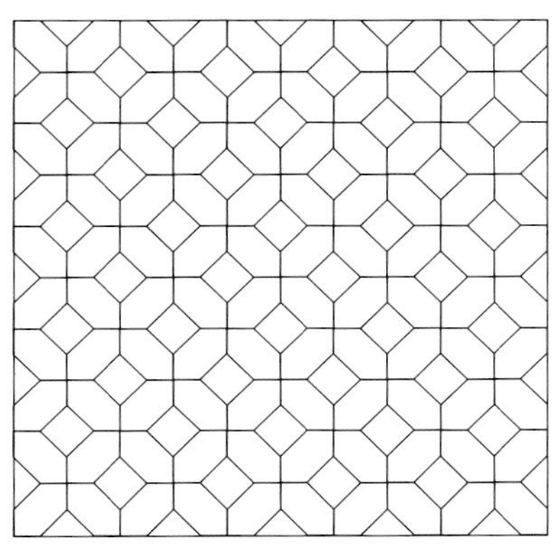

**697e**

(see **697a**) The square shapes in this pattern can be further embellished.

**697f**

(see **697a**) This pattern will require a second motif in the negative shape to avoid sagging.

**698**

(⅝in (1.6cm)) to
4in (10.2cm) 640%
6in (15.25cm) 960%

**699**

(⅝in (1.6cm)) to
5in (12.7cm) 800%
6in (15.25cm) 960%

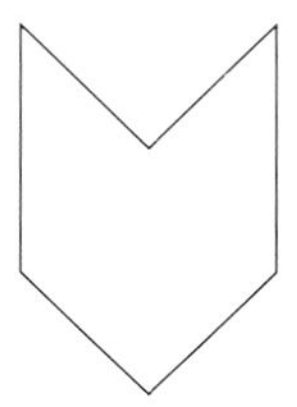

**700a**

This shape combines the two diamond shapes of **697a** .

(unit is 1in (2.5cm)) to
2in (5cm) 200%
4in (10.2cm) 400%
6in (15.25cm) 600%

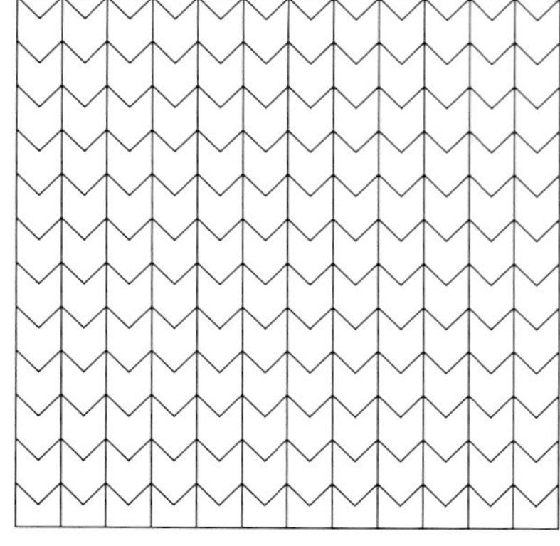

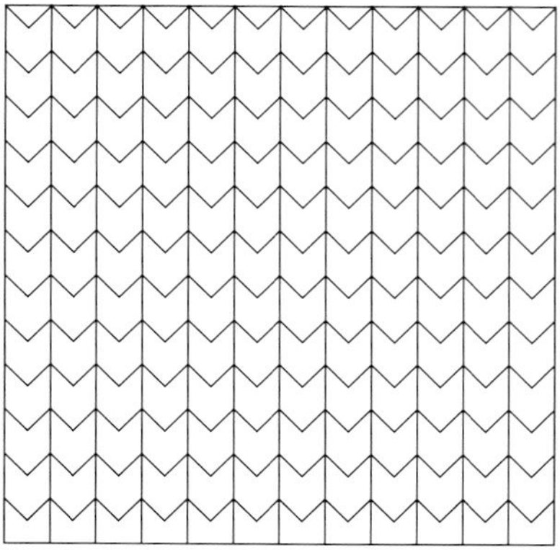

**700b**

(see **700a**) This pattern also works well without the vertical lines.

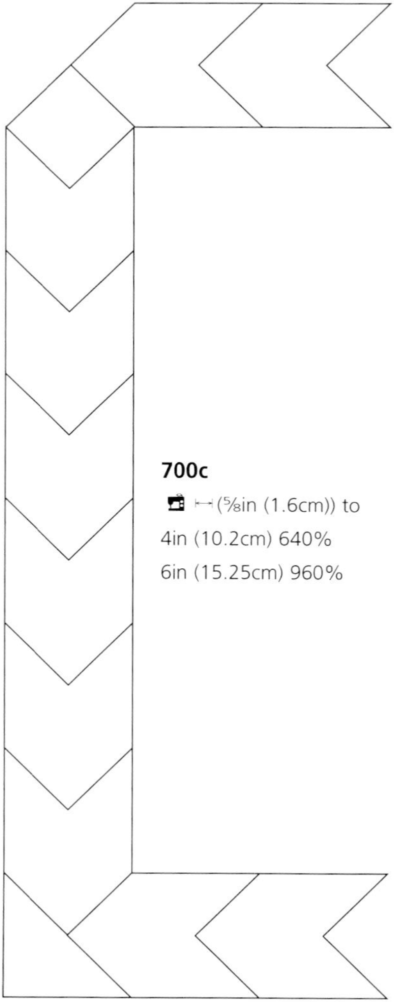

**700c**

(⅝in (1.6cm)) to
4in (10.2cm) 640%
6in (15.25cm) 960%

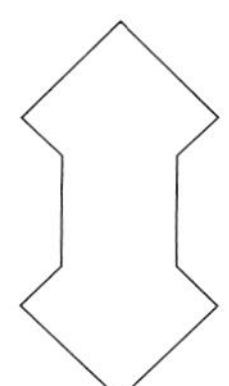

**701a**

This shape is made up of two squares on point with linking parallel lines.

(unit is 1in (2.5cm)) to
2in (5cm) 200%
4in (10.2cm) 400%
6in (15.25cm) 600%

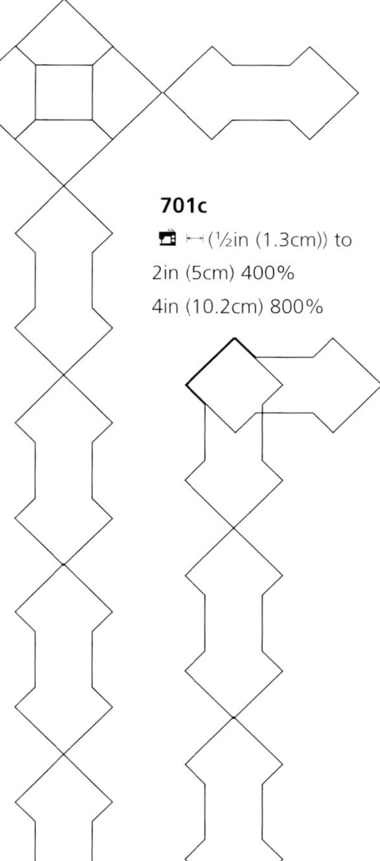

**701c**

↔(½in (1.3cm)) to
2in (5cm) 400%
4in (10.2cm) 800%

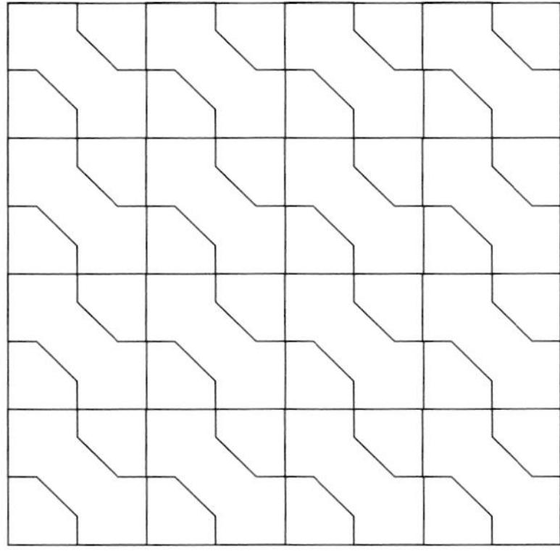

**701b**

(see **701a**) This pattern creates a secondary octagon (eight-sided) shape, that can be further embellished.

**701d**

↔(½in (1.3cm)) to
3in (7.6cm) 600%
5in (12.7cm) 1000%

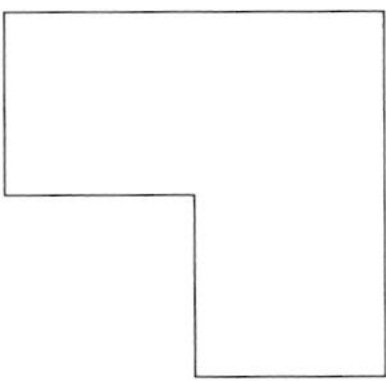

**702a**

This shape is made up of three squares and looks good when combined with other motifs.

(unit is 1in (2.5cm)) to
2in (5cm) 200%
4in (10.2cm) 400%
6in (15.25cm) 600%

**702b**

(see **702a**) This pattern may look complicated, but it has long lines of continuous stitching.

**702c**

(1in (2.5cm)) to
2in (5cm) 200%
4in (10.2cm) 400%

**702d**

(½in (1.3m)) to
2in (5cm) 400%
4in (10.2cm) 800%

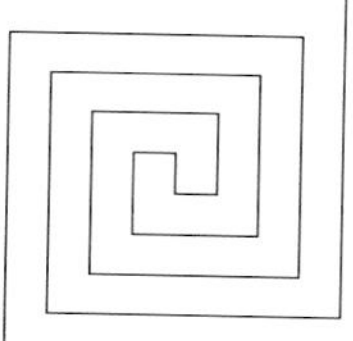

**703a**

This pattern may be made up of one continuous line, but it requires patience to stitch accurately.

(unit is 1in (2.5cm)) to
6in (15.25cm) 600%
8in (20.3cm) 800%

**703b**

(see **703a**) This filler pattern looks good stitched in stripes of contrasting thread.

**703c**

(1in (2.5cm)) to
2in (5cm) 200%
4in (10.2cm) 400%

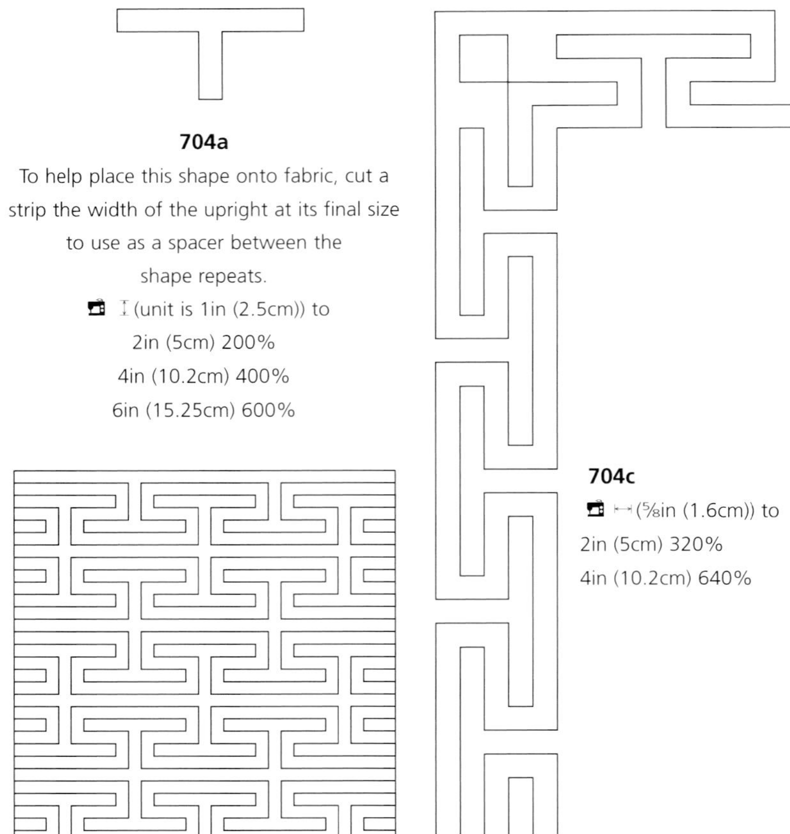

**704a**

To help place this shape onto fabric, cut a strip the width of the upright at its final size to use as a spacer between the shape repeats.

(unit is 1in (2.5cm)) to
2in (5cm) 200%
4in (10.2cm) 400%
6in (15.25cm) 600%

**704b**

(see **704a**) A feature pattern that will look good on plain fabrics.

**704c**

(⅝in (1.6cm)) to
2in (5cm) 320%
4in (10.2cm) 640%

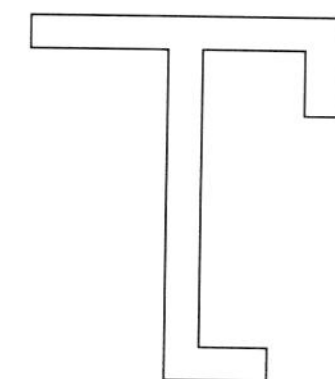

**705a**

This complex motif works best when it is the feature of the quilting and can be emphasized by either outlining or using embroidery thread.

(unit is 1in (2.5cm)) to
4in (10.2cm) 400%
6in (15.25cm) 600%

**705b**

(see **705a**) Highlight one chain of the motif to add a focal point.

**705c**

(1in (2.5cm)) to
2in (5cm) 200%
4in (10.2cm) 400%

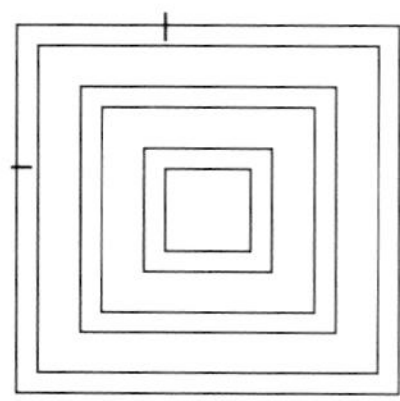

## 706a

This pattern can be used in a simple block repeat or to add overall structure to a design. The use of concentric outlines can be used on other shapes, too.

(unit is 1in (2.5cm)) to
4in (10.2cm) 400%
6in (15.25cm) 600%
8in (20.3cm) 800%

## 706b

(see **706a**) The motifs have been link by parallel lines to cre a pattern that could b repeated or used by it as the skeleton of an overall quilting design

**706c**

(see **706a**) This design can be made easier to draw by marking only one line and either using strips of masking tape to delineate the parallel lines or by stitching a second line using a distance guide on the sewing machine.

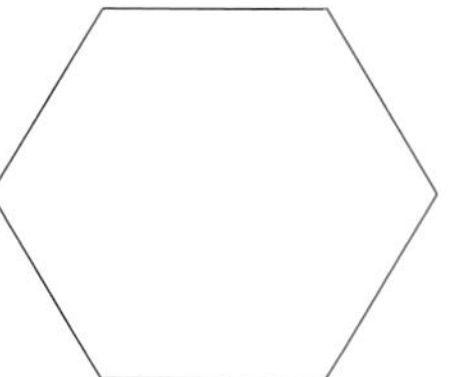

**707a**

The hexagon looks particularly good on a quilt top pieced with hexagons if the quilting is offset so that the point where three hexagons meet aligns with the center of the pieced block.

(unit is 1in (2.5cm)) to 2in (5cm) 200%

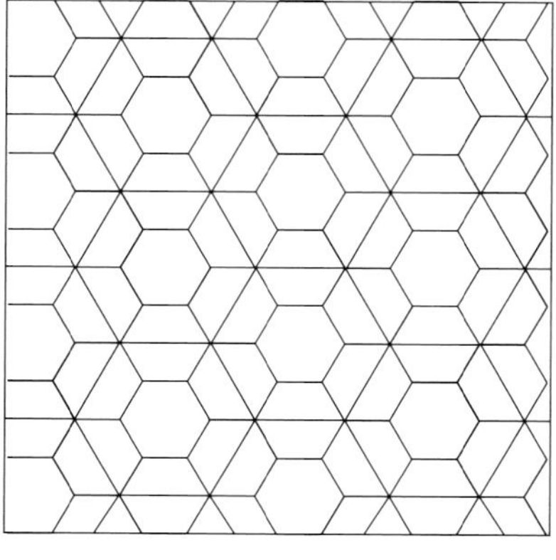

**707b**

(see **707a**) The bisecting lines can be extended to meet in the center of the middle hexagon.

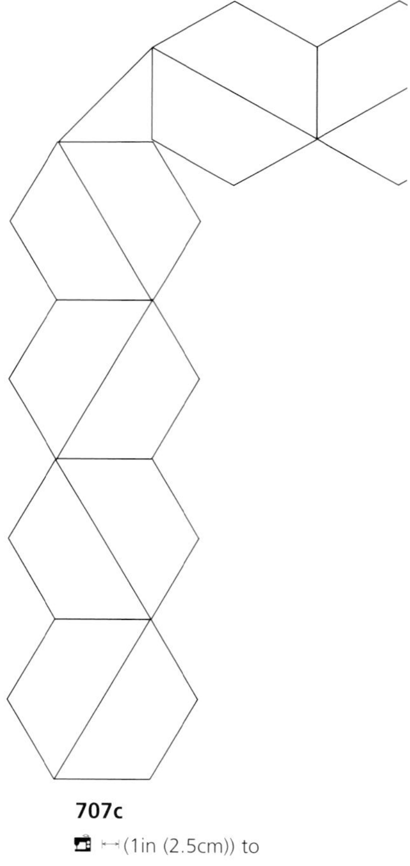

**707c**

(1in (2.5cm)) to
2in (5cm) 200%
4in (10.2cm) 400%

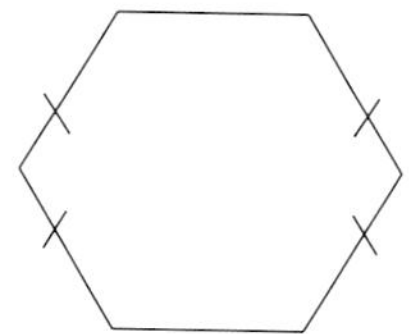

**708a**

This hexagon slightly overlaps the next to create a secondary pattern.

(unit is 1in (2.5cm)) to
2in (5cm) 200%
4in (10.2cm) 400%
6in (15.25cm) 600%

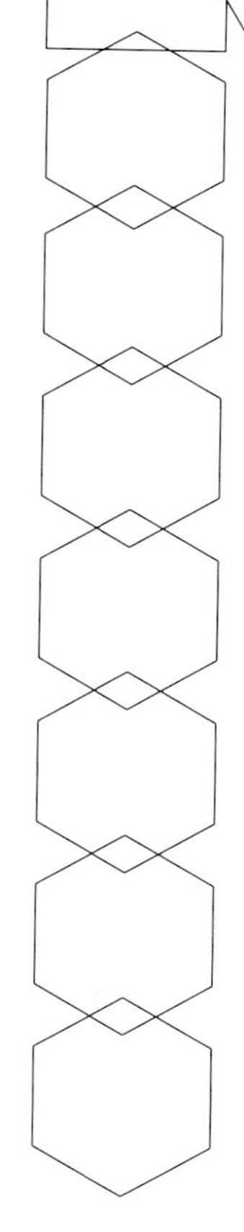

**708c**

(⅝in (1.6cm)) to
2in (5cm) 320%
4in (10.2cm) 640%

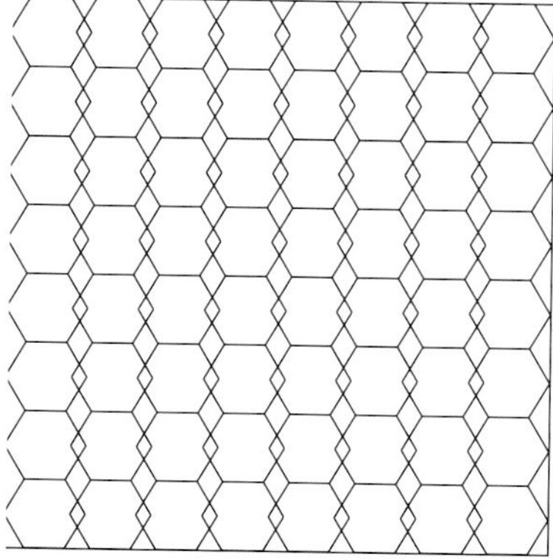

**708b**

(see **708a**) The negative shapes within this pattern can also be emphasized.

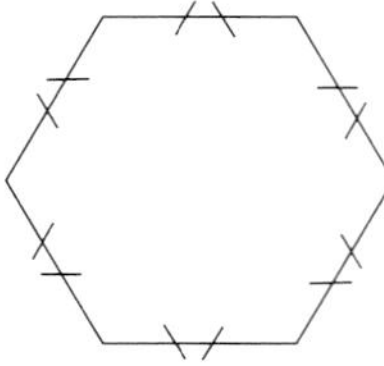

**709a**

This hexagon has alignment marks to facilitate an even overlap of the repeated shapes.

(unit is 1in (2.5cm)) to
2in (5cm) 200%
4in (10.2cm) 400%
6in (15.25cm) 600%

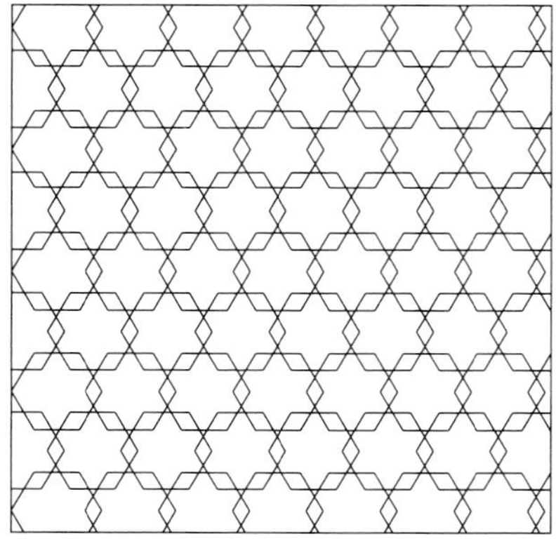

**709b**

(see **709a**) The negative shapes within this pattern form a star design.

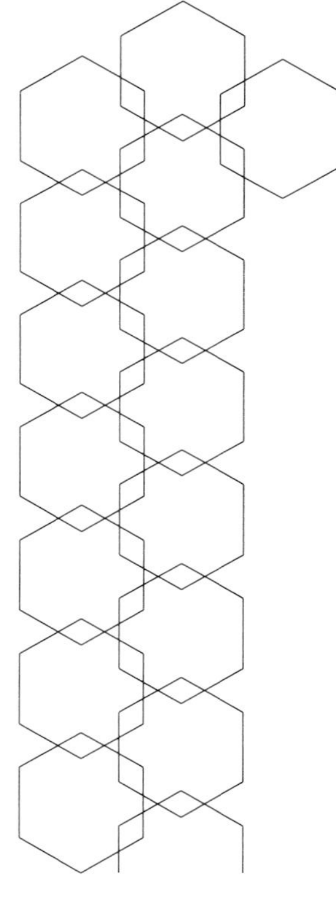

**709c**

(1in (2.5cm)) to
2in (5cm) 200%
4in (10.2cm) 400%

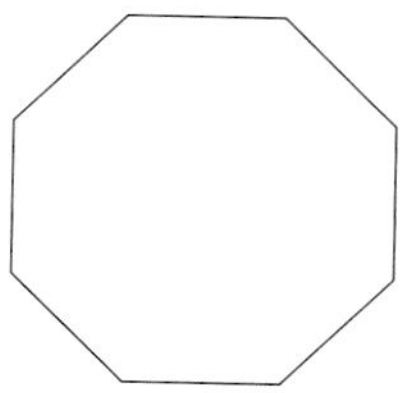

**710a**

This octagon may need another motif in its center to avoid sagging.

(unit is 1in (2.5cm)) to
2in (5cm) 200%
4in (10.2cm) 400%
6in (15.25cm) 600%

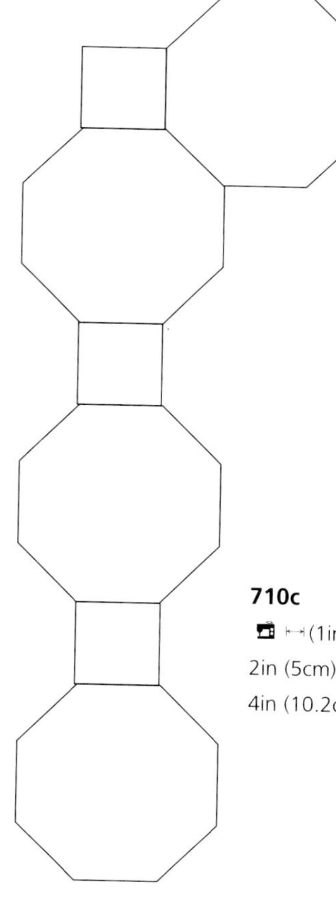

**710c**

(1in (2.5cm)) to
2in (5cm) 200%
4in (10.2cm) 400%

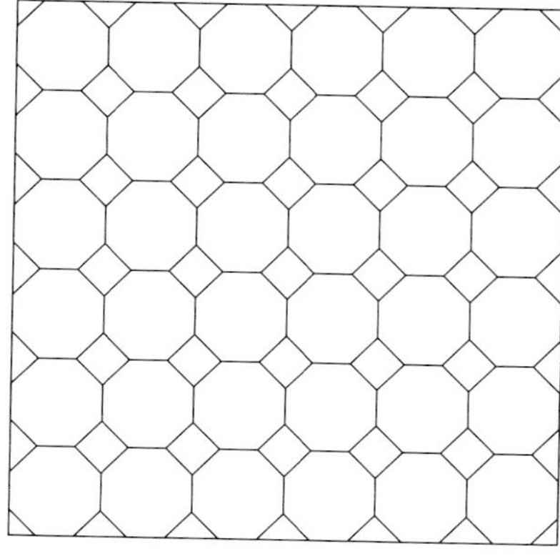

**710b**

(see **710a**) The square shapes created when the octagon is repeated can be stitched with additional motifs.

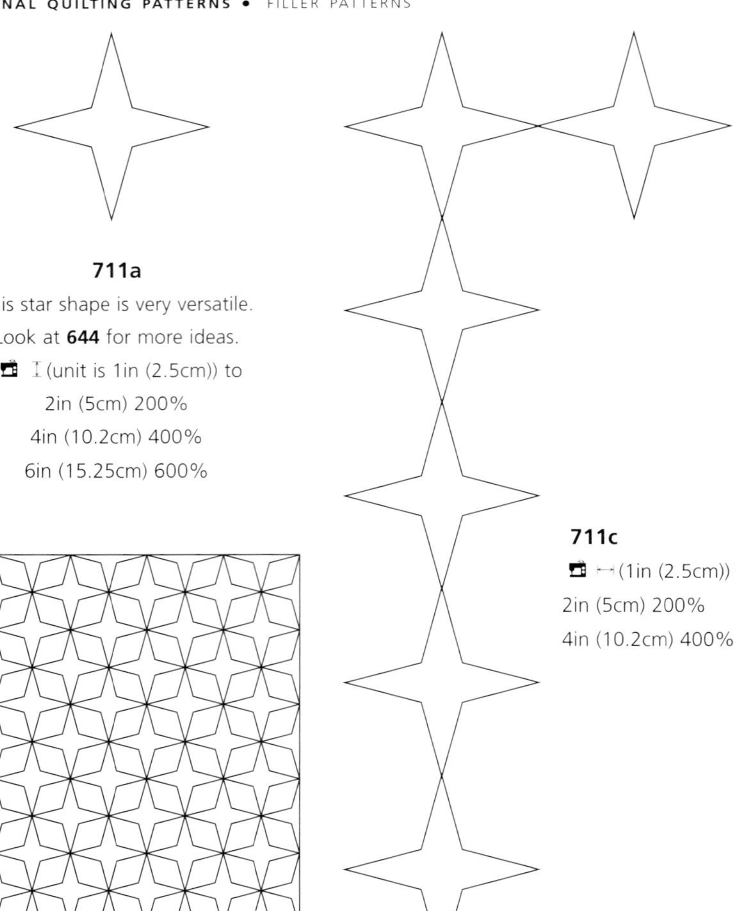

**711a**

This star shape is very versatile. Look at **644** for more ideas.

(unit is 1in (2.5cm)) to
2in (5cm) 200%
4in (10.2cm) 400%
6in (15.25cm) 600%

**711b**

(see **711a**) The negative diamond shape can also be made the focal point.

**711c**

(1in (2.5cm)) to
2in (5cm) 200%
4in (10.2cm) 400%

**712a**

This classic star shape can be used to highlight significant motifs such as signatures or personal individual additions to a quilt.

(unit is 1in (2.5cm)) to
2in (5cm) 200%
4in (10.2cm) 400%

**712b**

(see **712a**) This pattern does not look the same from all angles, so carefully consider its use before drawing it.

**712c**

(1in (2.5cm)) to
2in (5cm) 200%
4in (10.2cm) 400%

**713a**

The proportions of this basic star shape can be changed to suit any design by moving the inner and outer points to create spindly points or a more rounded star.

(unit is 1in (2.5cm)) to
4in (10.2cm) 400%
6in (15.25cm) 600%

**713c**

(see **713a**) The negative shapes in this filler are almost circular.

**713c**

(1in (2.5cm)) to
2in (5cm) 200%
4in (10.2cm) 400%

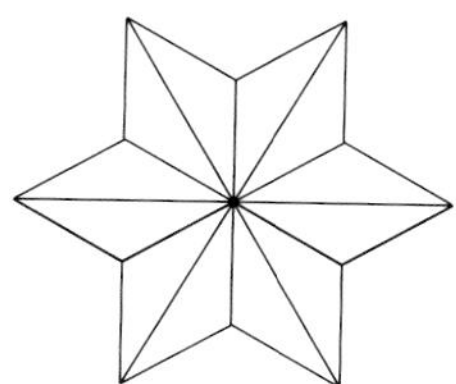

**714a**

This star is made up of diamonds that have been divided in two. This creates an interesting motif that can be enhanced by the use of colorful threads or simplified by removing some of the lines.

(unit is 1in (2.5cm)) to 6in (15.25cm) 600%

**714c**

(1in (2.5cm)) to
2in (5cm) 200%
4in (10.2cm) 400%

**714b**

(see **714a**) This design is a bit overwhelming and will work best where it can be the star of the quilt.

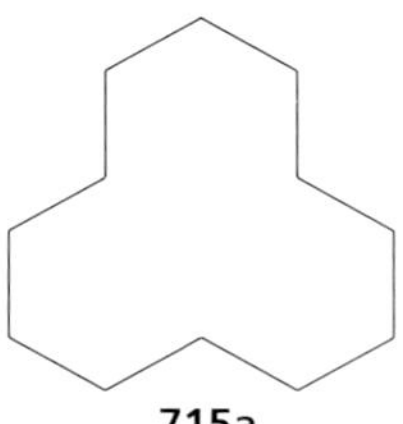

**715a**

This shape is created by placing three hexagons together. Try this pattern on a quilt pieced with hexagons, but offset, so the corners of the quilted hexagon fall in the center of the pieced hexagons.

(unit is 1in (2.5cm)) to
4in (10.2cm) 400%
6in (15.25cm) 600%

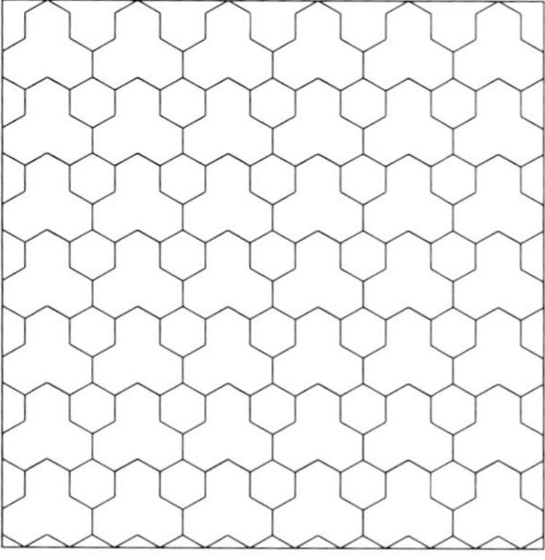

**715b**

(see **715a**) The negative shapes within this pattern are also hexagons.

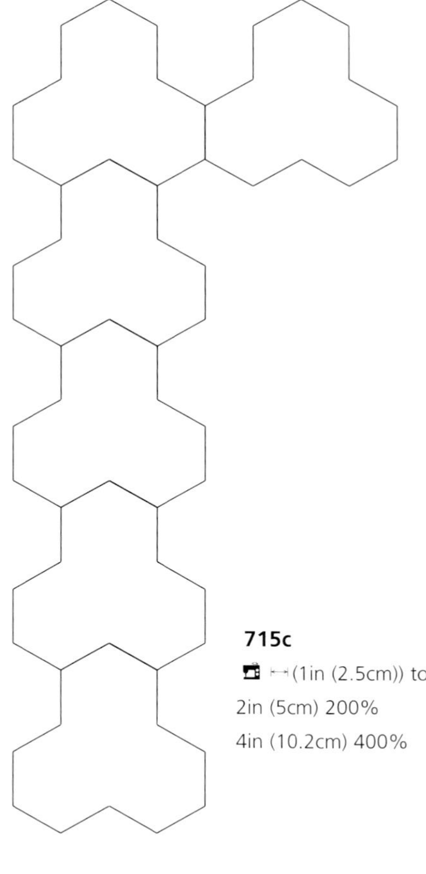

**715c**

(1in (2.5cm)) to
2in (5cm) 200%
4in (10.2cm) 400%

**715d**

(see **715a**) This pattern shows how the same shape can tessellate to create an even pattern where negative and positive shapes are the same.

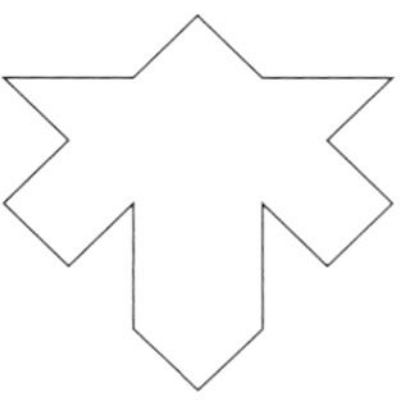

**716a**

This is a popular motif that can also be quilted to either echo a pieced motif or add a simple leaf motif to a themed quilt.

(unit is 1in (2.5cm)) to
2in (5cm) 200%
4in (10.2cm) 400%
6in (15.25cm) 600%

**716b**

(see **716a**) Selected leaf shapes can be picked out in a different color to give the impression of falling leaves.

**716c**

(1in (2.5cm)) to
2in (5cm) 200%
4in (10.2cm) 400%

**716d**

(¾in (1.9cm)) to
2in (5cm) 266%
4in (10.2cm) 533%

ALL PATTERNS ARE STANDARD 2IN (5CM) OR 4IN (10.2CM) UNLESS OTHERWISE STATED

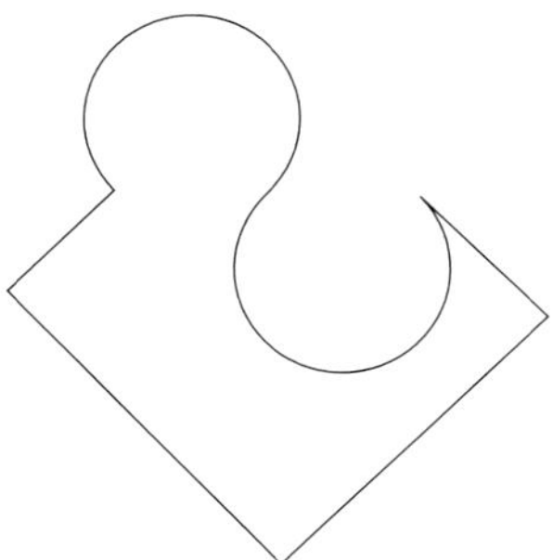

**717a**

This complicated template can be used to create a variety of interesting filler and border patterns.

↕ (unit is 1in (2.5cm)) to
4in (10.2cm) 400%
6in (15.25cm) 600%

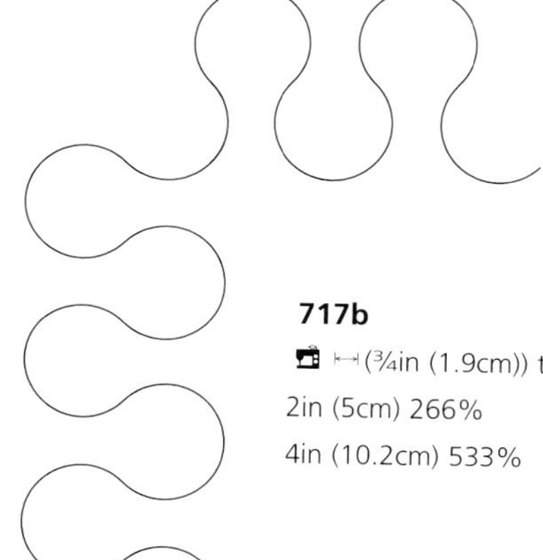

**717b**

↔ (¾in (1.9cm)) to
2in (5cm) 266%
4in (10.2cm) 533%

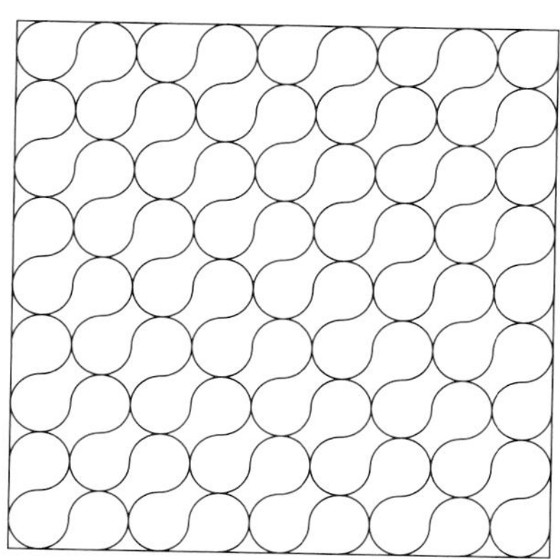

**717c**

↕ (see **717a**) Be aware that this pattern can be difficult to stitch well if using a sewing machine.

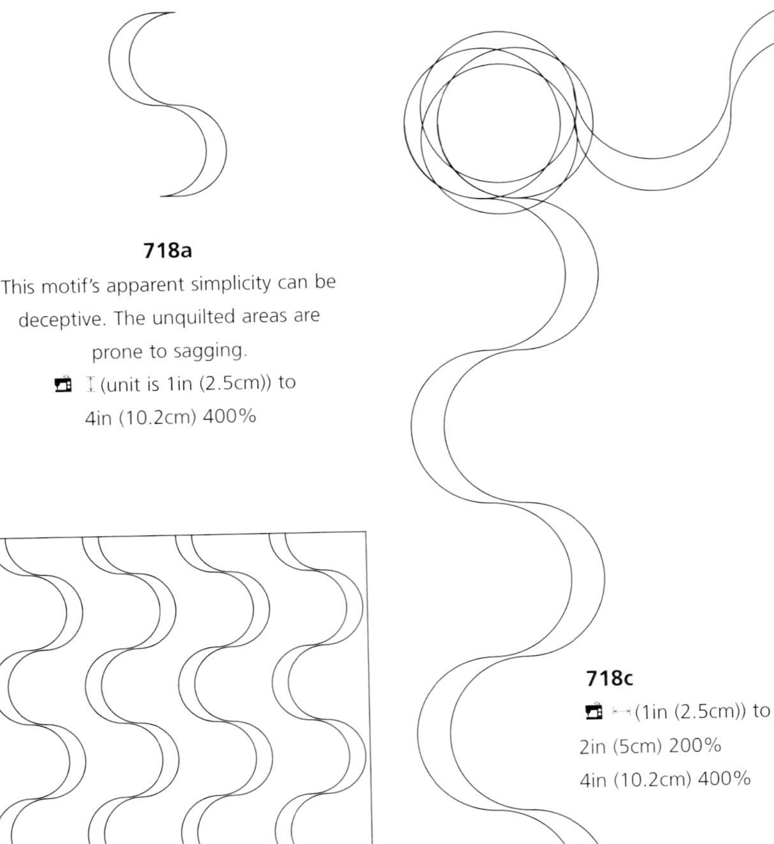

**718a**

This motif's apparent simplicity can be deceptive. The unquilted areas are prone to sagging.

(unit is 1in (2.5cm)) to 4in (10.2cm) 400%

**718c**

(1in (2.5cm)) to 2in (5cm) 200% 4in (10.2cm) 400%

**718b**

(see **718a**) The motif is repeated at this distance to create a circular negative shape for a second motif.

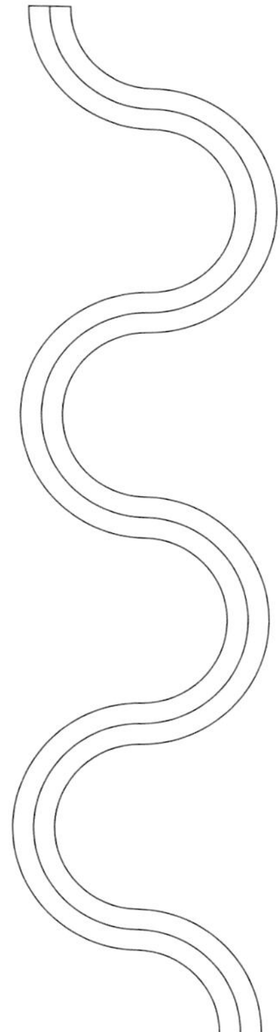

**719**

⟷(1in (2.5cm)) to
2in (5cm) 200%
4in (10.2cm) 400%
(see **592a** for corner)

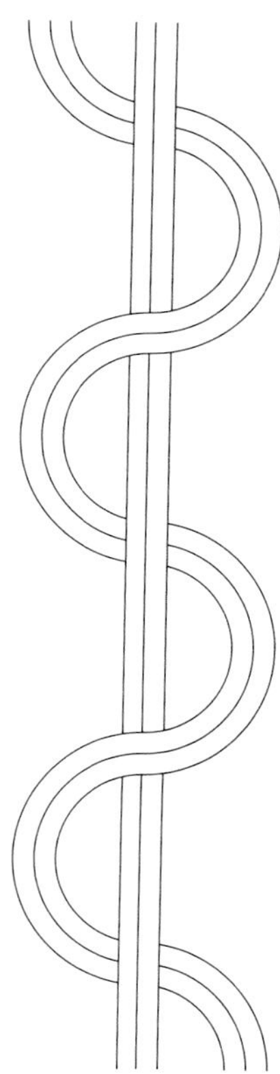

**720**

⟷(1in (2.5cm)) to
2in (5cm) 200%
4in (10.2cm) 400%
(see **592a** for corner)

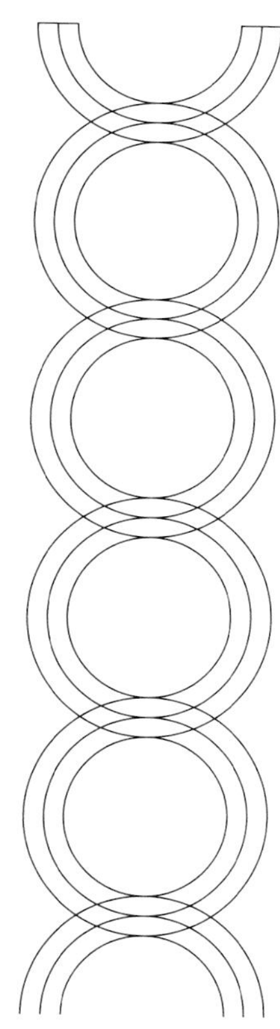

**721**

⟷(1in (2.5cm)) to
5in (12.7cm) 500%
6in (15.25cm) 600%
(see **592a** for corner)

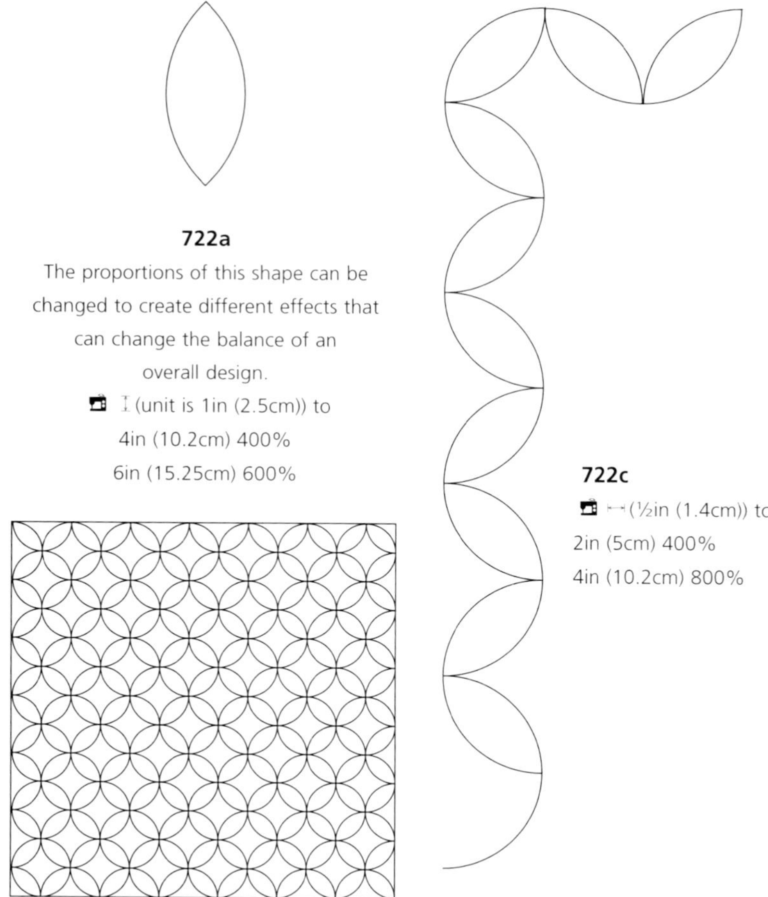

**722a**

The proportions of this shape can be changed to create different effects that can change the balance of an overall design.

(unit is 1in (2.5cm)) to
4in (10.2cm) 400%
6in (15.25cm) 600%

**722b**

(see **722a**) Used as it is, this shape creates an overlapping circle design.

**722c**

(½in (1.4cm)) to
2in (5cm) 400%
4in (10.2cm) 800%

**723a**

Rotating **722a** around one point four times creates this four-petal flower motif.

↕(unit is 1in (2.5cm)) to
4in (10.2cm) 400%
6in (15.25cm) 600%

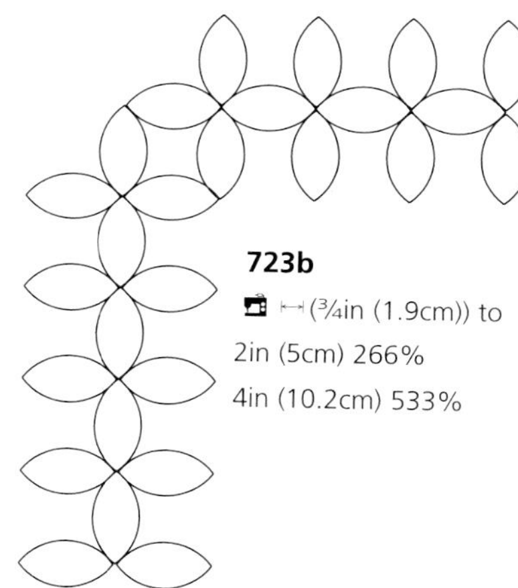

**723b**

↔(¾in (1.9cm)) to
2in (5cm) 266%
4in (10.2cm) 533%

**723c**

↕ (see **723a**) This design is very similar to **722b** but the pattern has a vertical bias.

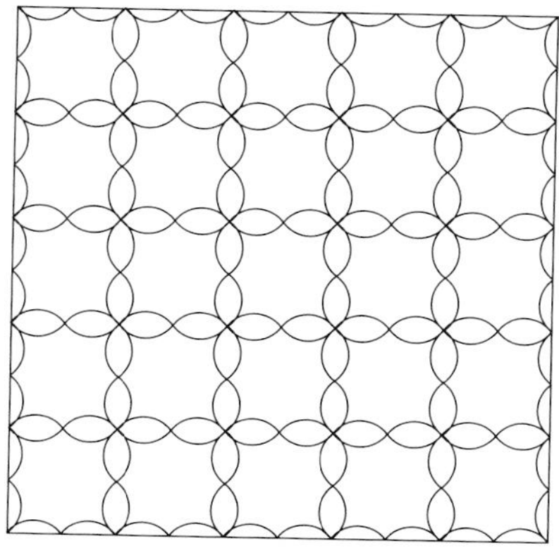

**723d**

↕ (see **723a**) This chain mail pattern may, on greater enlargements, need more quilting to prevent sagging.

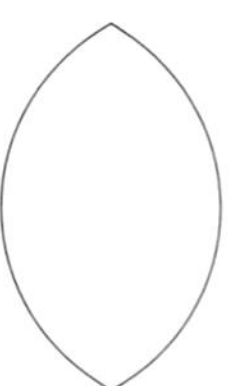

**724a**

For this motif, it is quicker to draw repeat patterns using a circle template marked where the circles overlap **(see 724c)**.

(unit is 1in (2.5cm)) to
4in (10.2cm) 400%
6in (15.25cm) 600%

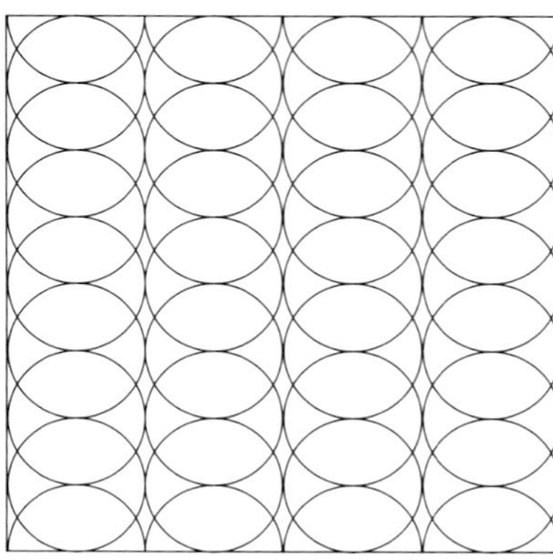

**724b**

(see **724a**) This design should be quilted as a series of adjacent half-circle motifs in a continuous line.

**724c**

(½in (1.4cm)) to
2in (5cm) 400%
4in (10.2cm) 800%

**724d**

(½in (1.4cm)) to
2in (5cm) 400%
4in (10.2cm) 800%

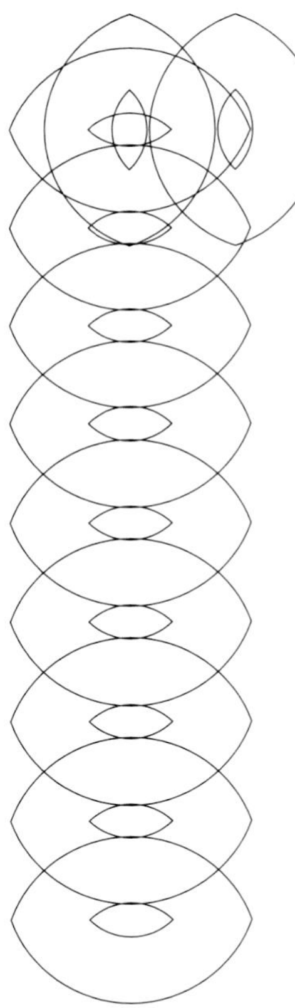

**725**

⟷(1in (2.5cm)) to
2in (5cm) 200%
4in (10.2cm) 200%

**726**

⟷(⅝in (1.6cm)) to
4in (10.2cm) 640%
6in (15.25cm) 960%
(see **722** for corner)

**727**

⟷(⅝in (1.6cm)) to
5in (12.7cm) 800%
6in (15.25cm) 960%
(see **722** for corner)

### 728a

To create this shape, rotate a circle six equal distances around a center point or photocopy the motif (right); the unit described is the bolder area.

(unit is 1in (2.5cm)) to
2in (5cm) 200%
4in (10.2cm) 400%
6in (15.25cm) 600%

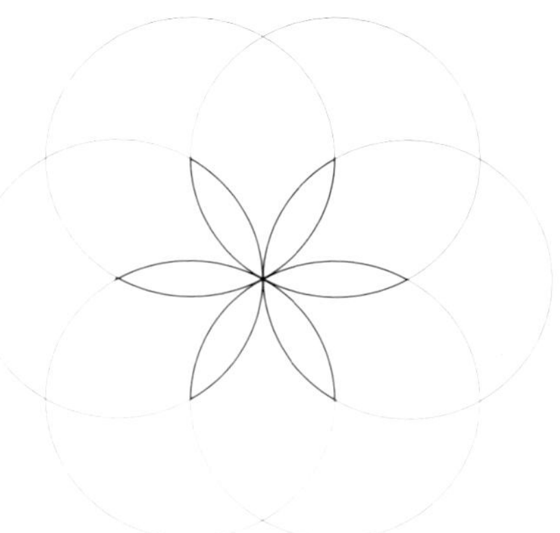

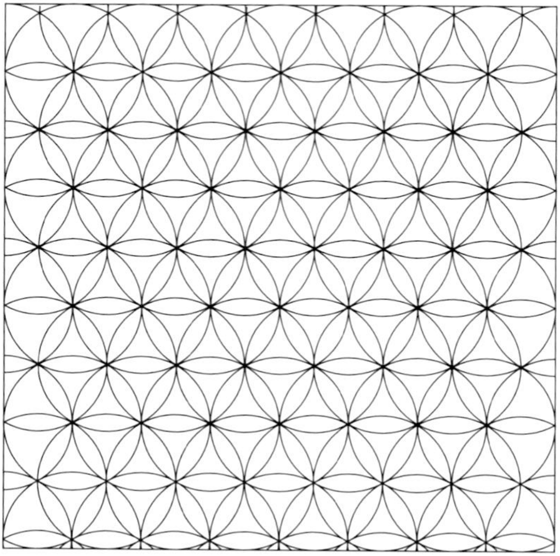

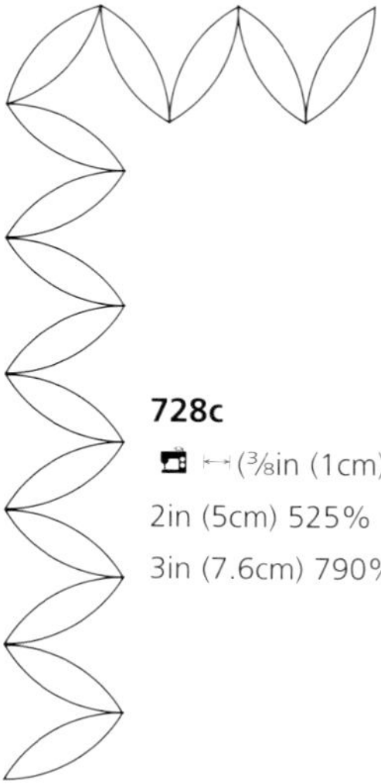

### 728c

(⅜in (1cm)) to
2in (5cm) 525%
3in (7.6cm) 790%

### 728b

(see **728a**) Use this pattern big and bold.

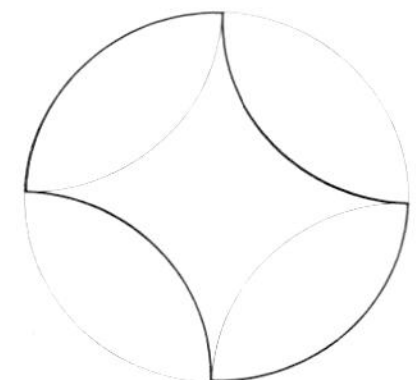

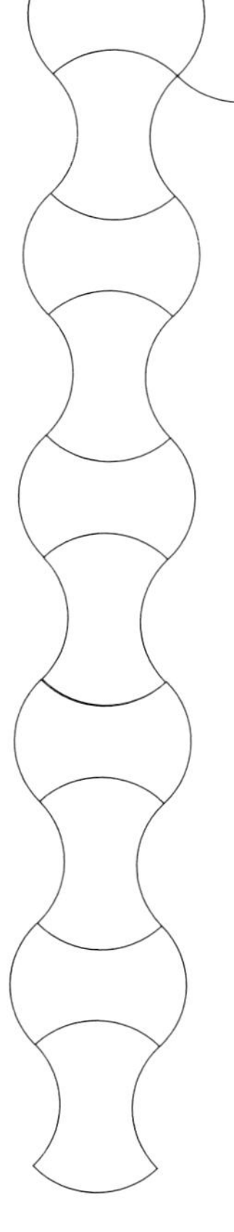

**729a**

A popular piecing pattern, this motif can be used to complement a piecing design or as part of another quilting scheme.

⌶ (unit is 1in (2.5cm)) to
2in (5cm) 200%
4in (10.2cm) 400%
6in (15.25cm) 600%

**729b**

⌶ (see **729a**) This pattern has an even texture that looks particularly good when contrasted with straight piecing patterns.

**729c**

↔ (⅝in (1.6cm)) to
2in (5cm) 320%
4in (10.2cm) 640%

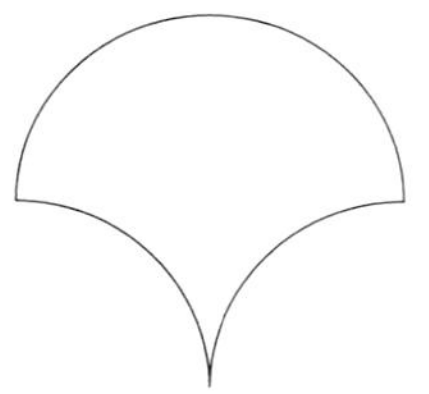

**730a**

This shape can be used as shown here or, if used larger, as an outline for feather designs.

(unit is 1in (2.5cm)) to
4in (10.2cm) 400%
6in (15.25cm) 600%
8in (20.3m) 800%

**730b**

(see **730a**) The other way up, this pattern resembles fish scales.

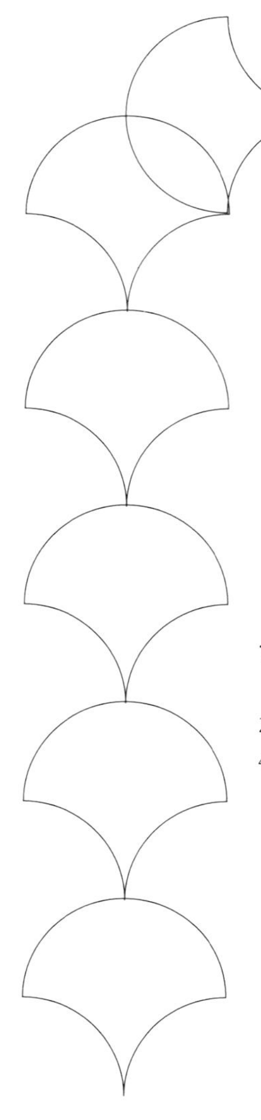

**730c**

(1in (2.5cm)) to
2in (5cm) 200%
4in (10.2cm) 200%

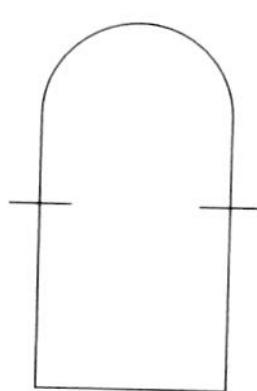

**731a**

A traditional sashiko design, this filler pattern works well as a focal pattern and stitches in bright threads.

(unit is 1in (2.5cm)) to
2in (5cm) 200%
4in (10.2cm) 400%
6in (15.25cm) 600%

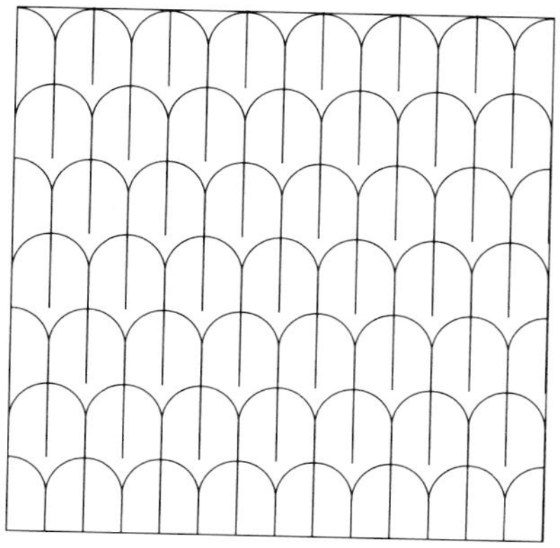

**731b**

(see **731a**) Try stitching every second row in a different color thread.

**731c**

(1in (2.5cm)) to
2in (5cm) 200%
4in (10.2cm) 200%

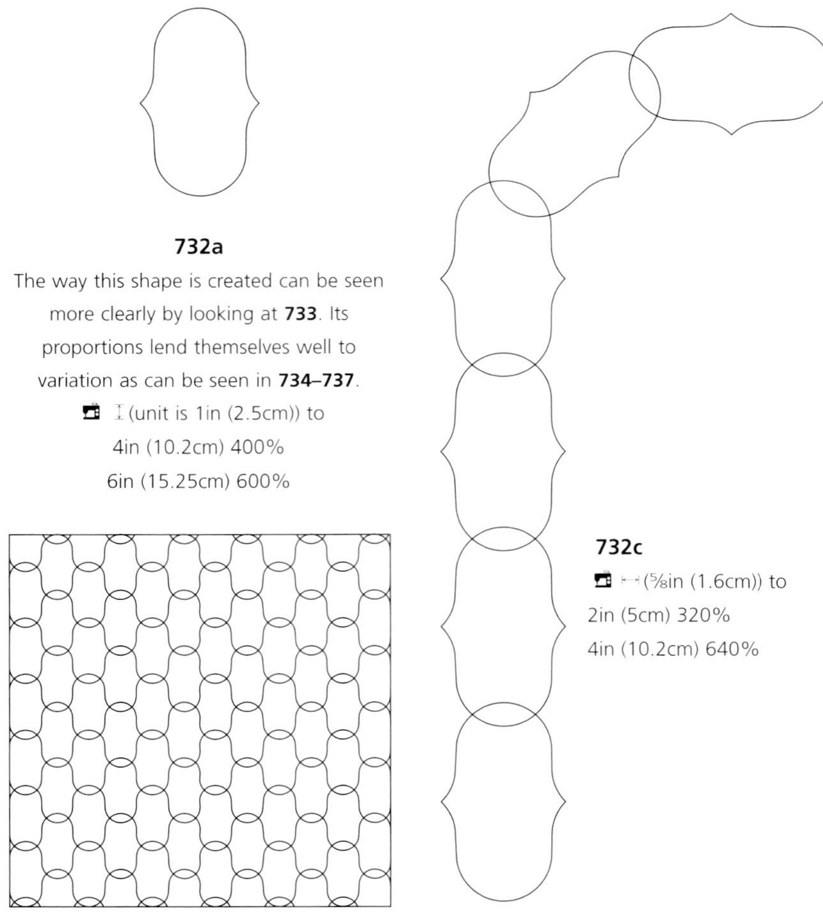

**732a**

The way this shape is created can be seen more clearly by looking at **733**. Its proportions lend themselves well to variation as can be seen in **734–737**.

(unit is 1in (2.5cm)) to
4in (10.2cm) 400%
6in (15.25cm) 600%

**732b**

(see **732a**) Mark on the edge of the template the position of the overlap to keep it constant.

**732c**

(⅝in (1.6cm)) to
2in (5cm) 320%
4in (10.2cm) 640%

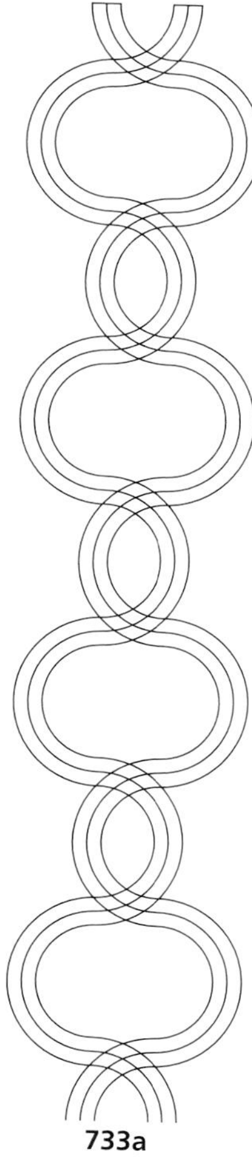

**733a**

⟷(1in (2.5cm)) to
2in (5cm) 200%
4in (10.2cm) 200%
(see **732c** for corner)

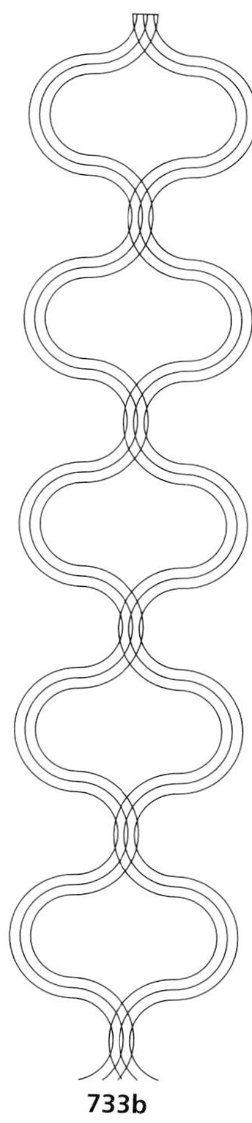

**733b**

⟷(1in (2.5cm)) to
5in (12.7cm) 500%
6in (15.25cm) 600%
(see **732c** for corner)

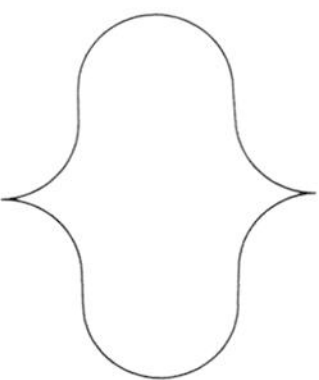

**734a**

This shape is very similar to **732** but has more elegant proportions.

(unit is 1in (2.5cm)) to

2in (5cm) 200%

4in (10.2cm) 400%

6in (15.25cm) 600%

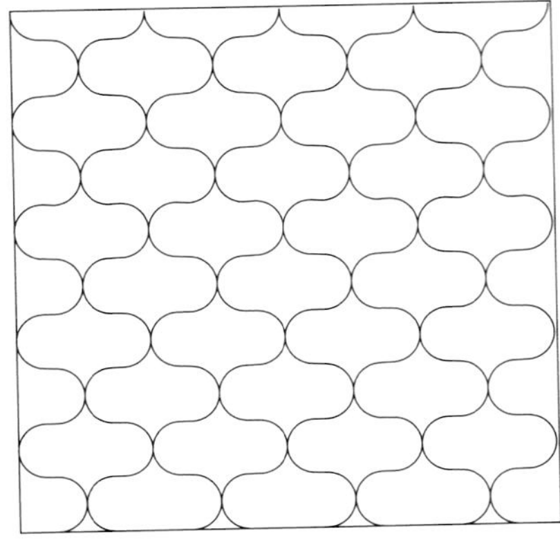

**734b**

(see **734a**) The motifs can also be overlapped **(see 732)**.

**734c**

(1in (2.5cm)) to

2in (5cm) 200%

4in (10.2cm) 200%

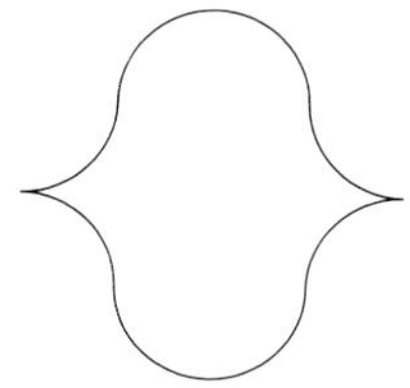

**735a**

This motif is a variation of the two previous ones. Look at their borders and patterns for more ideas on how to use them.

(unit is 1in (2.5cm)) to
6in (15.25cm) 600%
8in (20.3cm) 800%

**735c**

(1in (2.5cm)) to
2in (5cm) 200%
4in (10.2cm) 200%

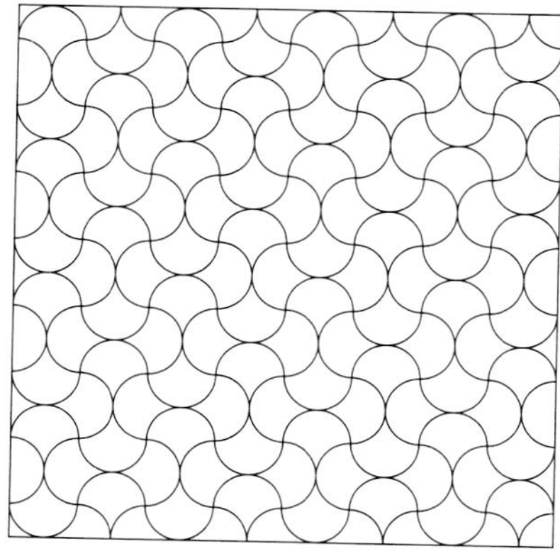

**735b**

(see **735a**) Complicated but fascinating, it looks good when stitched as large as the batting will allow.

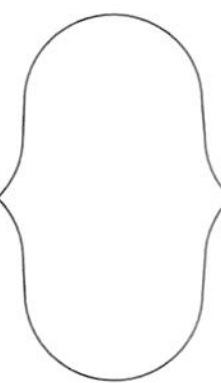

**736a**

This motif has different proportions from previous shapes. The corner of **736c** shows particularly well how it is created.

(unit is 1in (2.5cm)) to
4in (10.2cm) 400%
6in (15.25cm) 600%

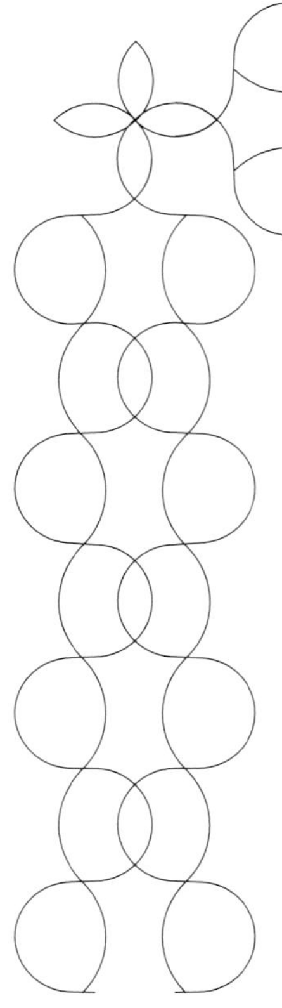

**736c**

(1in (2.5cm)) to
2in (5cm) 200%
4in (10.2cm) 200%

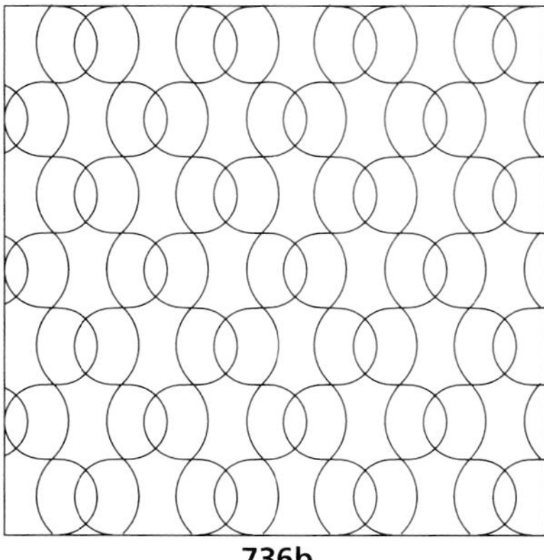

**736b**

(see **736a**) The motif has been combined with wavy vertical lines.

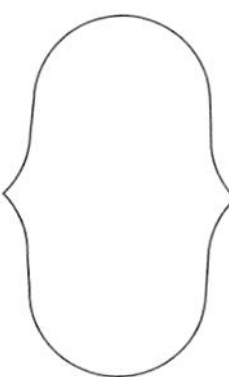

**737a**

For these patterns this motif has been used, but any of the previous similar shapes could be used to equal effect.

(unit is 1in (2.5cm)) to
4in (10.2cm) 400%
6in (15.25cm) 600%

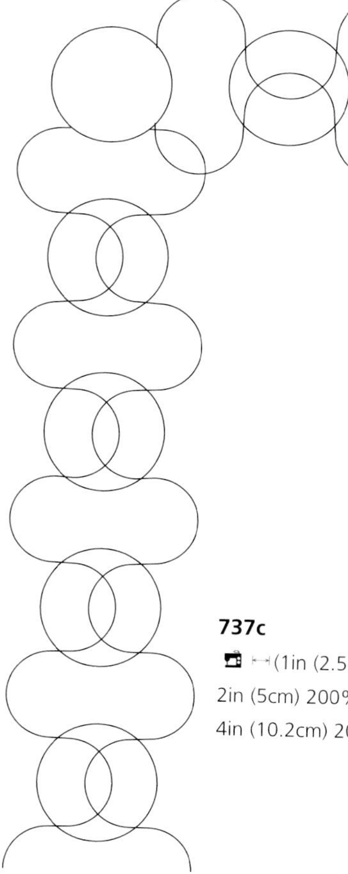

**737c**

(1in (2.5cm)) to
2in (5cm) 200%
4in (10.2cm) 200%

**737b**

(see **737a**) The motif has been combined with a repeat pattern of circles.

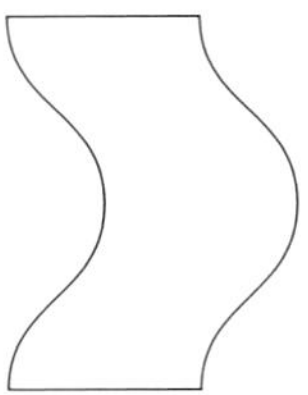

**738a**

This is a good motif to combine with others. Use other motifs such as flowing florals within its confines.

(unit is 1in (2.5cm)) to
2in (5cm) 200%
4in (10.2cm) 400%
6in (15.25cm) 600%

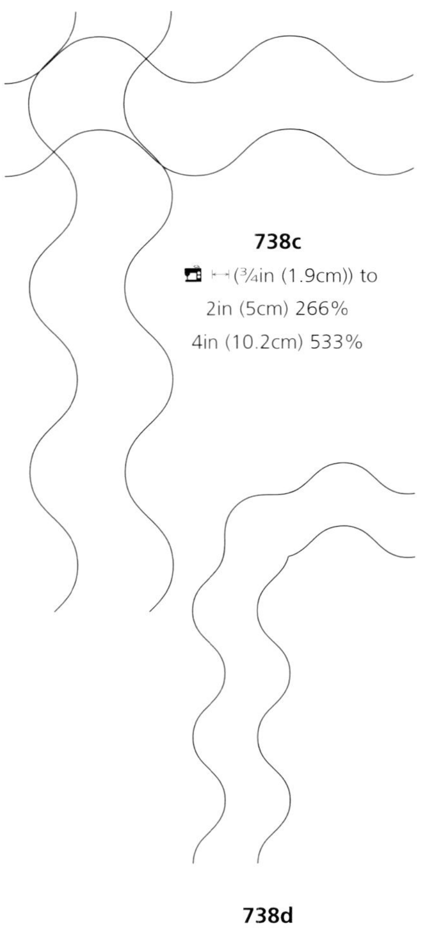

**738c**

(¾in (1.9cm)) to
2in (5cm) 266%
4in (10.2cm) 533%

**738b**

(see **738a**) This pattern is very simple but be particularly vigalant for sagging of the fabric.

**738d**

(½in (1.3cm)) to
2in (5cm) 400%
4in (10.2cm) 800%

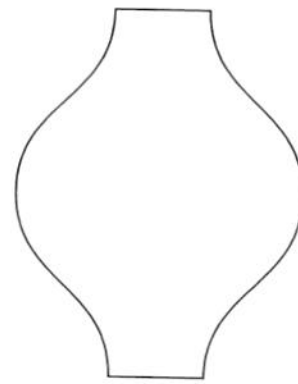

**739a**

This shape looks good by itself or with other motifs. It is also worth overlaying with a mesh of parallel lines.

(unit is 1in (2.5cm)) to
2in (5cm) 200%
4in (10.2cm) 400%
6in (15.25cm) 600%

**739b**

(see **739a**) This pattern can be used by itself if the lines are not too far apart but looks even better with a second motif.

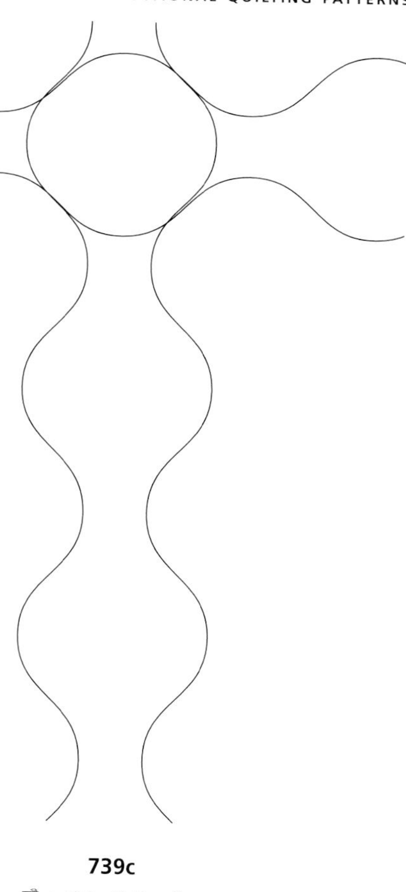

**739c**

(1in (2.5cm)) to
2in (5cm) 200%
4in (10.2cm) 200%

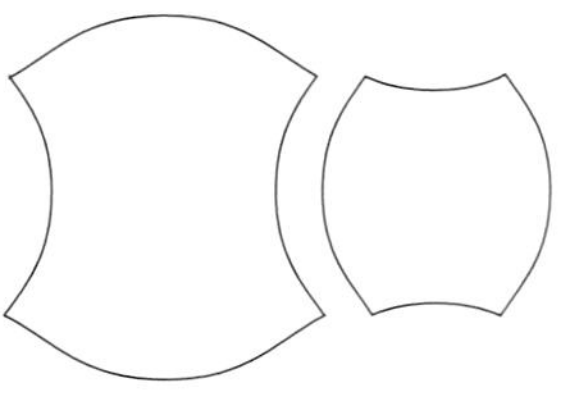

**740a**

This motif is based on a circle. The unit described refers to the larger shape.

(unit is 1in (2.5cm)) to
2in (5cm) 200%
4in (10.2cm) 400%
6in (15.25cm) 600%

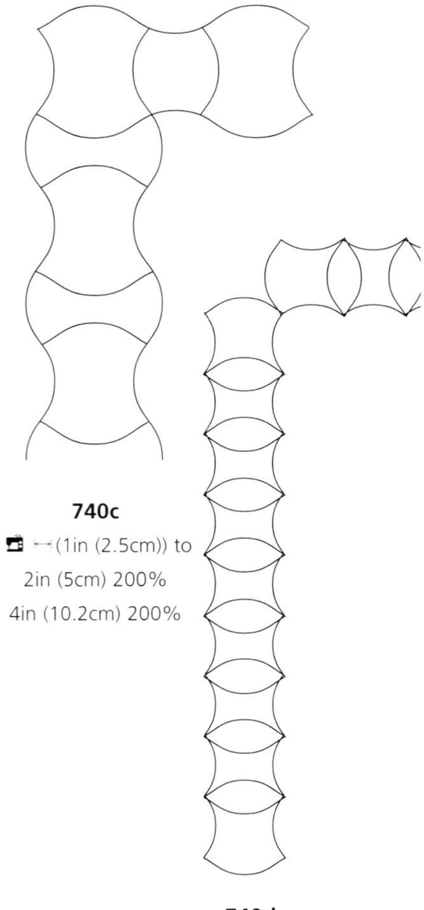

**740c**

(1in (2.5cm)) to
2in (5cm) 200%
4in (10.2cm) 200%

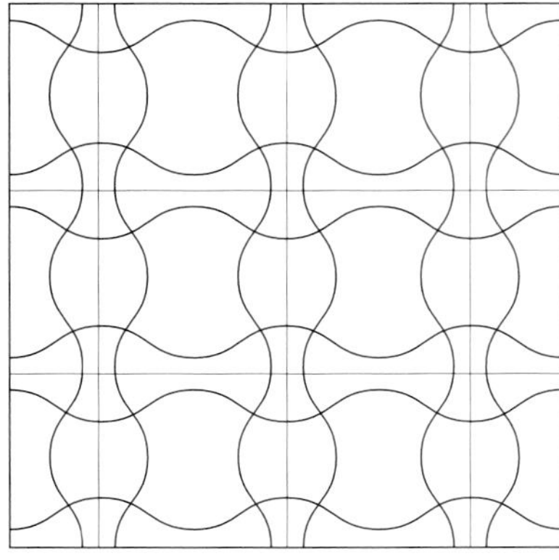

**740b**

(see **740a**) When this pattern is stitched, it has an uncontrived feel.

**740d**

(⅜in (1cm)) to
2in (5cm) 530%
3in (7.6cm) 800%

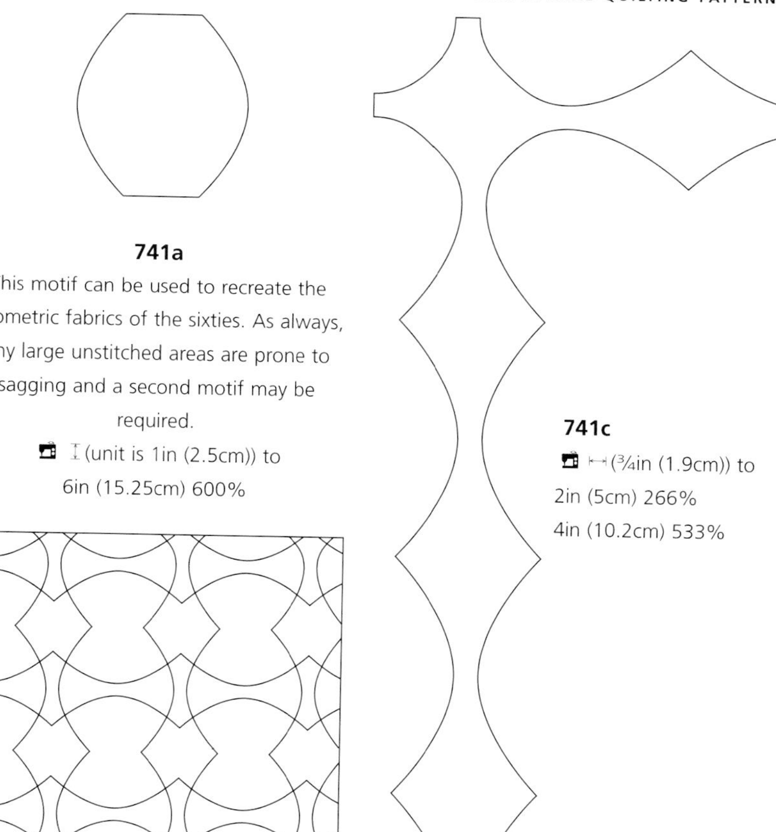

**741a**

This motif can be used to recreate the geometric fabrics of the sixties. As always, any large unstitched areas are prone to sagging and a second motif may be required.

(unit is 1in (2.5cm)) to 6in (15.25cm) 600%

**741c**

(¾in (1.9cm)) to
2in (5cm) 266%
4in (10.2cm) 533%

**741b**

(see **741a**) The negative shapes within this pattern are also worth emphasizing.

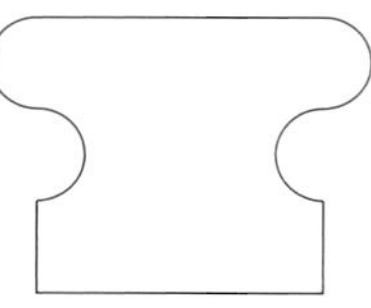

**742a**

This shape is slightly more difficult to stitch (see **704)** but it makes an excellent contrast to very angular piecing designs.

⟷(unit is 1in (2.5cm)) to
2in (5cm) 200%
4in (10.2cm) 400%
6in (15.25cm) 600%

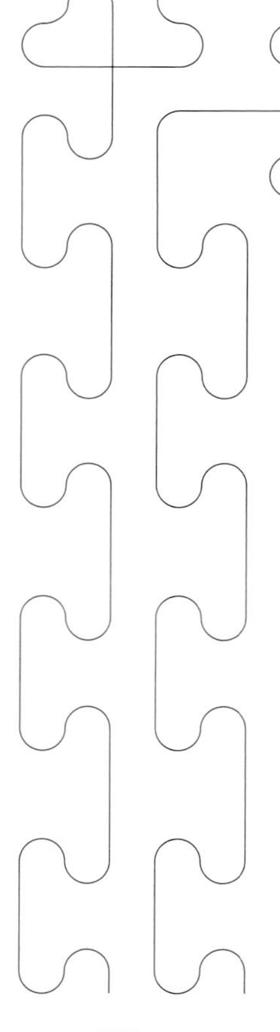

**742b**

⟷(see **742a**) Reminiscent of a pool of water, try varying the distances between the lines to accentuate the effect.

**742c**

⟷(1in (2.5cm)) to
2in (5cm) 200%
4in (10.2cm) 200%

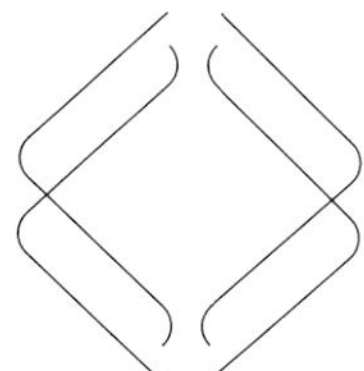

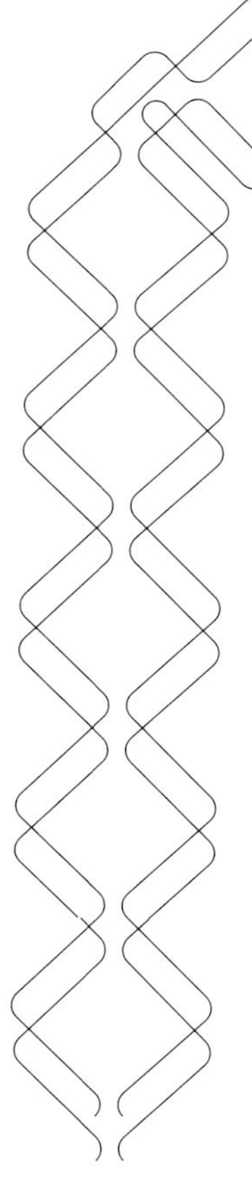

**743a**

The curves make this pattern more interesting than a standard square.

(unit is 1in (2.5cm)) to
4in (10.2cm) 400%
6in (15.25cm) 600%

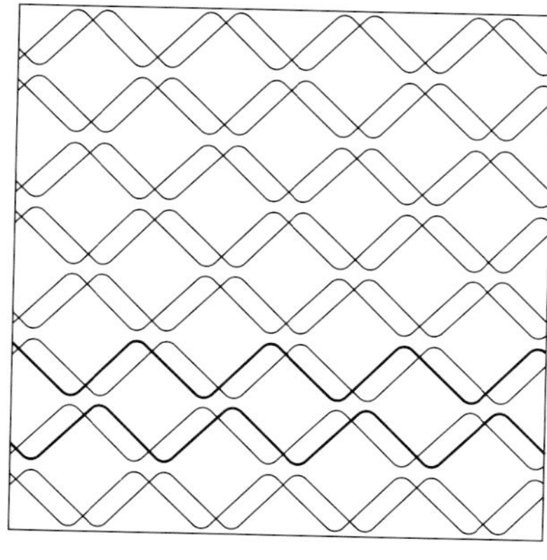

**743b**

(see **743a**) Try different thread combinations to vary the overall effect.

**743c**

(¾in (1.9cm)) to
2in (5cm) 266%
4in (10.2cm) 533%

**744a**

This shape can be used to create patterns that look like twirling ribbon. If the shape is elongated, the ribbon effect is reduced.

(unit is 1in (2.5cm)) to
2in (5cm) 200%
4in (10.2cm) 400%
6in (15.25cm) 600%

**744b**

(see **744a**) The negative shapes within this pattern can also be emphasized.

**744c**

(⅜in (1cm)) to
2in (5cm) 530%
3in (7.6cm) 790%

**744d**

(⅜in (1cm)) to
2in (5cm) 530%
3in (7.6cm) 790%

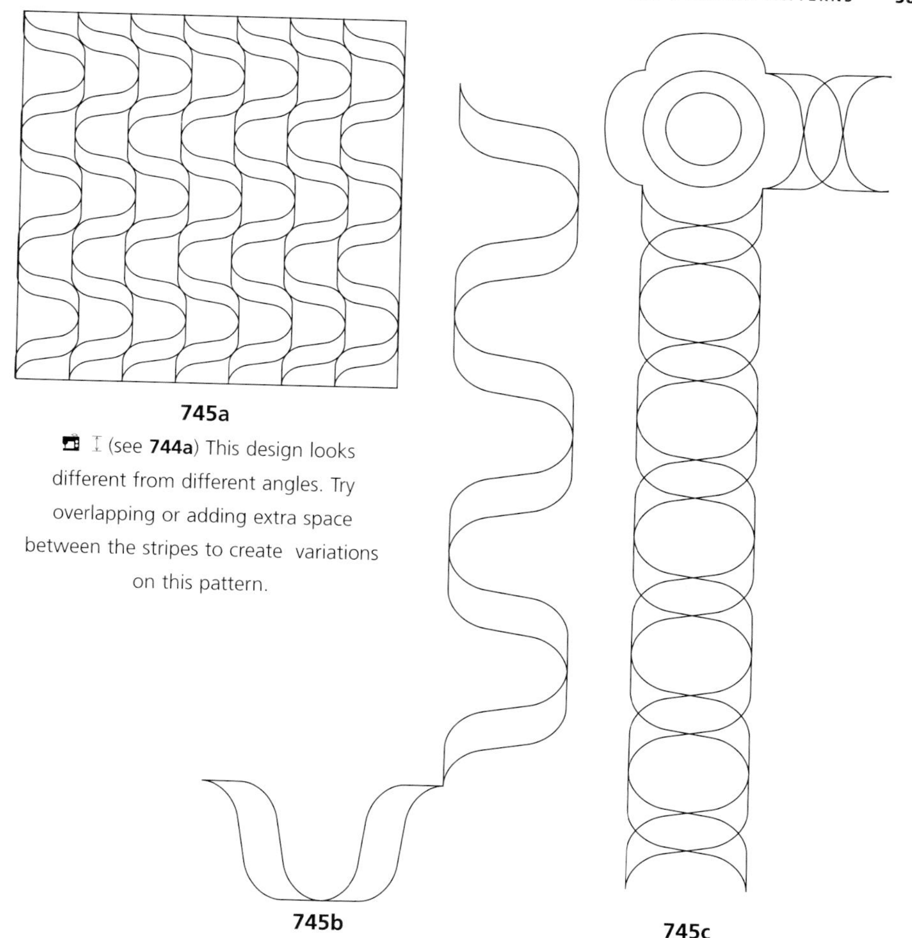

**745a**

(see **744a**) This design looks different from different angles. Try overlapping or adding extra space between the stripes to create variations on this pattern.

**745b**

(⅝in (1.6cm)) to
4in (10.2cm) 640%
6in (15.25cm) 960%

**745c**

(⅝in (1.6cm)) to
5in (12.7cm) 800%
6in (15.25cm) 960%

**746a**

(see **744a**) This design works well when the motif is large and bold in bright colors. This is a pattern that will not easily blend into the background.

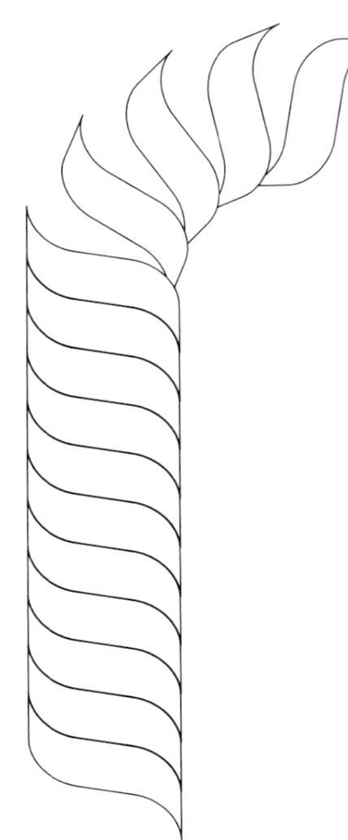

**746b**

(½in (1.3cm)) to
2in (5cm) 400%
4in (10.2cm) 800%

**747**

(⅝in (1.6cm)) to
5in (12.7cm) 800%
6in (15.25cm) 960%

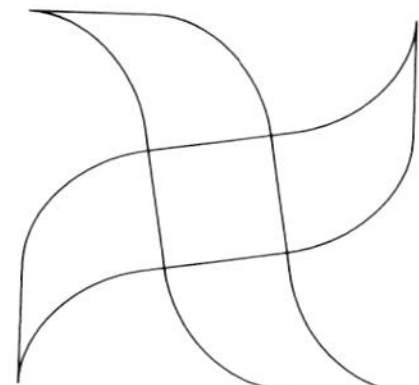

**748a**

For more ideas on how to use this pattern, look at pages 352–355 on star shapes.

(unit is 1in (2.5cm)) to
2in (5cm) 200%
4in (10.2cm) 400%
6in (15.25cm) 600%

**748b**

(see **748a**) The curved lines of this pattern can make it look as if it were sloping.

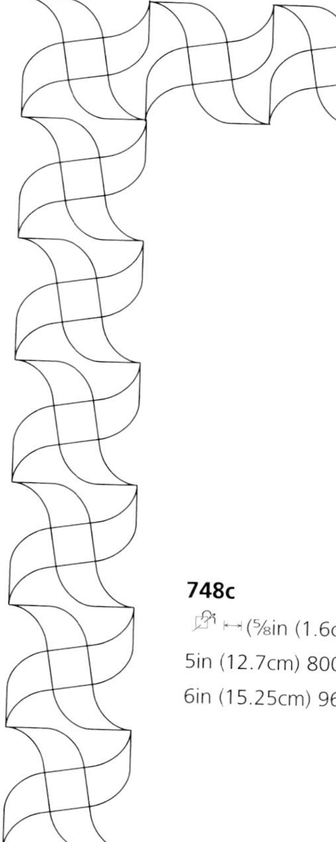

**748c**

(5/8in (1.6cm)) to
5in (12.7cm) 800%
6in (15.25cm) 960%

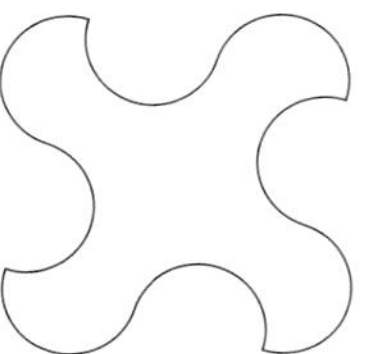

**749a**

This traditional Japanese design works well as a filler, but the center may need a second motif if it is used too large.

(unit is 1in (2.5cm)) to
2in (5cm) 200%
4in (10.2cm) 400%

**749b**

(see **749a**) This pattern would look good stitched in contrasting colors.

**749c**

(1in (2.5cm)) to
2in (5cm) 200%
4in (10.2cm) 200%

**750a**

This motif provides a subtle way to introduce a heart to a quilt design, but it also looks good when contrasted with striped piecing.

(unit is 1in (2.5cm)) to
2in (5cm) 200%
4in (10.2cm) 400%
6in (15.25cm) 600%

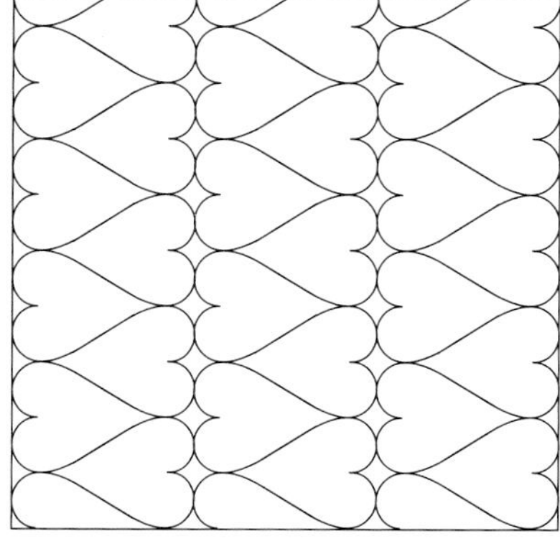

**750b**

(see **750a**) If the fabric is prone to sagging, add horizontal lines of stitching.

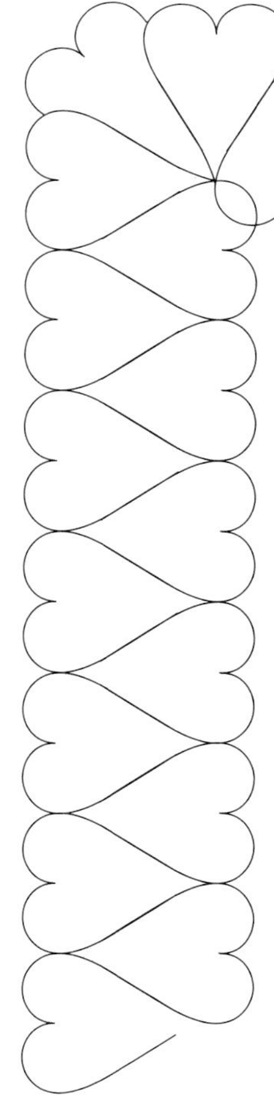

**750c**

(1in (2.5cm)) to
2in (5cm) 200%
4in (10.2cm) 400%

**751a**

This principles of this motif can be adapted to any heart shape.

(unit is 1in (2.5cm)) to
2in (5cm) 200%
4in (10.2cm) 400%
6in (15.25cm) 600%

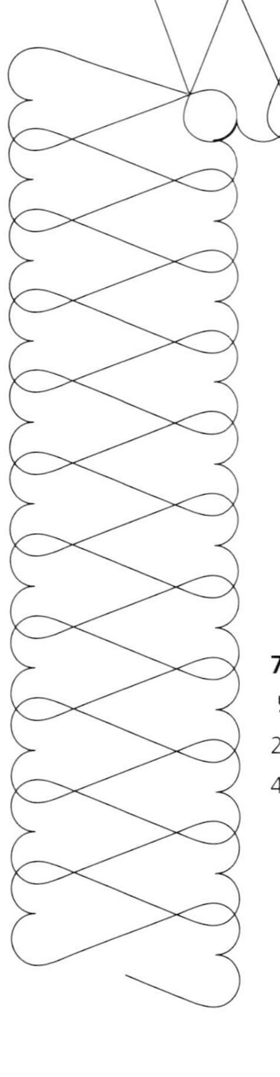

**751c**

(1in (2.5cm)) to
2in (5cm) 200%
4in (10.2cm) 400%

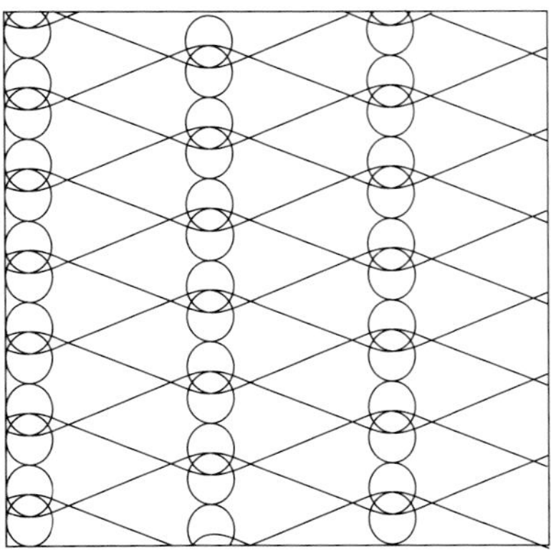

**751b**

(see **751a**) This pattern is made by overlapping design **751c**

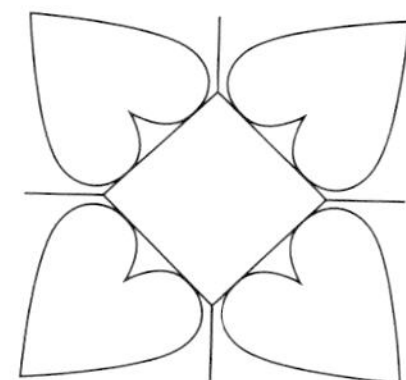

**752a**

This design demonstrates how most motifs can be used as a filler or border pattern if it fits into the overall scheme of a quilt.

(unit is 1in (2.5cm)) to
6in (15.25cm) 600%
10in (25.5cm) 1000%

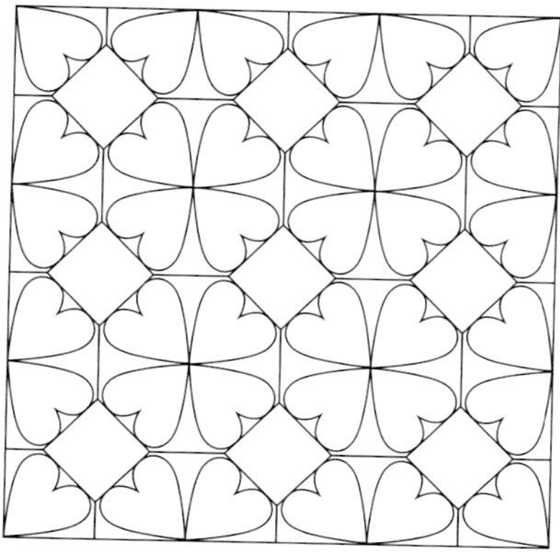

**752b**

(see **752a**) The shapes within this pattern make it a excellent structure for other motifs.

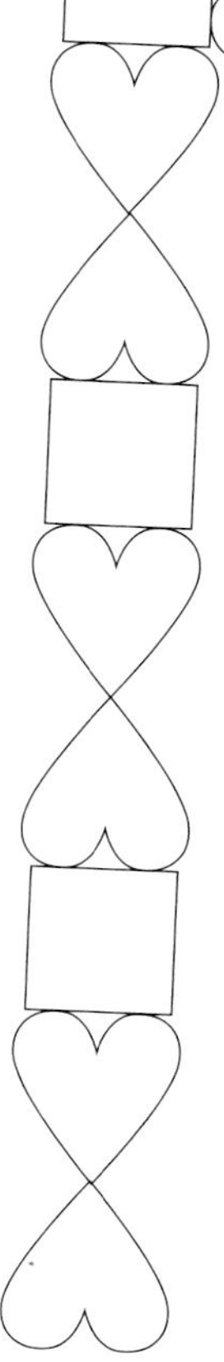

**752c**

(½in (1.3cm)) to
2in (5cm) 400%
4in (10.2cm) 800%

**753a**

This shape can be used with on-point quilts or for other patterns.

(unit is 1in (2.5cm)) to
4in (10.2cm) 400%
6in (15.25cm) 600%

**753b**

(see **753a**) The negative shapes as well as the squares may require additional stitching to avoid sagging.

**753c**

(1in (2.5cm)) to
2in (5cm) 200%
4in (10.2cm) 400%

**754a**

This pattern is particularly effective for use with a sewing machine because it can be stitched with long continuous lines.

(unit is 1in (2.5cm)) to
2in (5cm) 200%
4in (10.2cm) 400%
6in (15.25cm) 600%

**754b**

(see **754a**) This pattern looks good with a few flowers stitched in a different color.

**754c**

(1in (2.5cm)) to
2in (5cm) 200%
4in (10.2cm) 400%

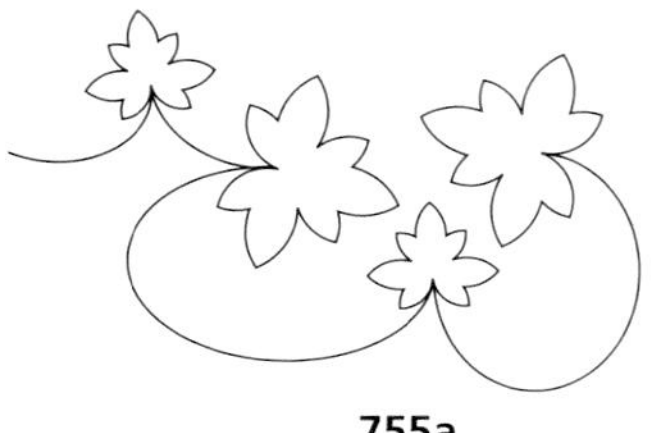

**755a**

Any pattern will link together if the start and end either vertically or horizontally as above.

(unit is 1in (2.5cm)) to
4in (10.2cm) 400%
6in (15.25cm) 600%

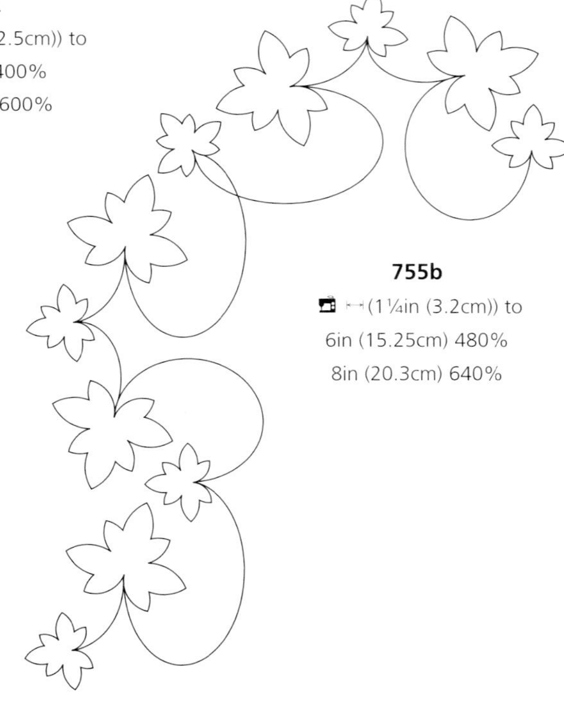

**755b**

(1¼in (3.2cm)) to
6in (15.25cm) 480%
8in (20.3cm) 640%

**755c**

(see **755a**) The motif in this pattern repeats from left to right and is then reflected horizontally to create the second row of the pattern. The edge motifs are then joined.

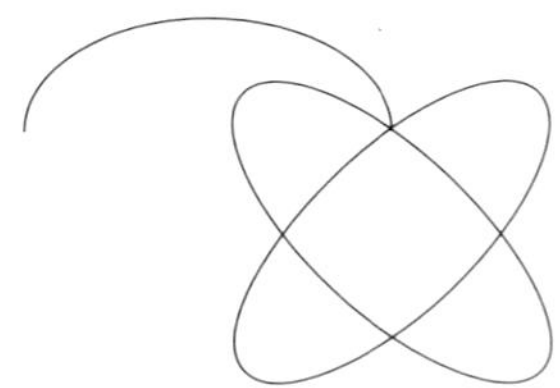

**756a**

Any motif that can be stitched in one continuous line can be linked to extend the line from one motif to another.

(unit is 1in (2.5cm)) to
2in (5cm) 200%
4in (10.2cm) 400%
6in (15.25cm) 600%

**756c**

(¾in (1.9cm)) to
2in (5cm) 266%
4in (10.2cm) 533%

**756b**

(see **756a**) Depending on the size chosen, the center of the motif may require additional stitching.

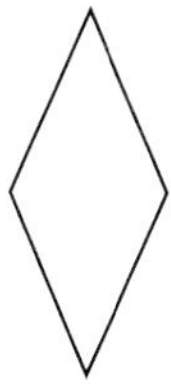

**757a**

Most of the designs in this chapter have linear repeats. This diamond shape is one of many shapes that were shown in radiating patterns in previous chapters.

(unit is 1in (2.5cm)) to
2in (5cm) 200%
4in (10.2cm) 400%
6in (15.25cm) 600%

**757b**

(see **757a**) A radiating design will create a focal point and is often a counter point to quilt tops with a strong horizontal or vertical visual bias.

# Patterns adapted for quilting

*This section features beautiful designs from around the world. Remember that all the designs can be enlarged to any of the sizes in the table on pages 504–506. The sizes beneath each design are given as suggestions only and show the range of enlargements that can be used.*

# Celtic designs

Celtic knots, swirls, curls, and spirals have always been an influence in traditional quilting patterns. Perhaps that's because the motifs ideally suit themselves to the seamless repetition that quilters often favor, and the knot motifs lend themselves perfectly to the corded quilting technique.

The designs also seem to add an air of mystery to a quilt. Whether or not that is because that period of history is often referred to as the Dark Ages is not clear. However, Celtic design is worthy of further investigation by quilters who are looking for something unusual to adorn their quilts.

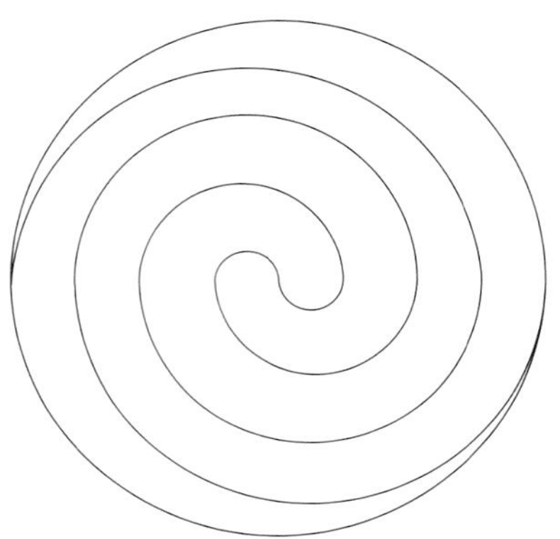

**758a**

↔ 4in (10.2cm) 200%

↔ 8in (20.3cm) 400%

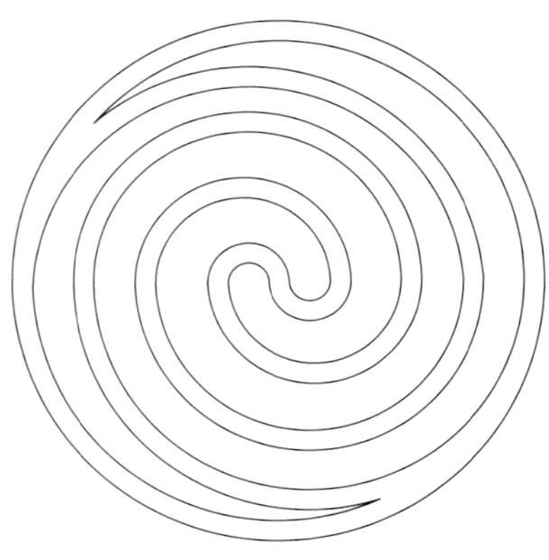

**758b**

↔ 6in (15.25cm) 300%

↔ 9in (22.9cm) 450%

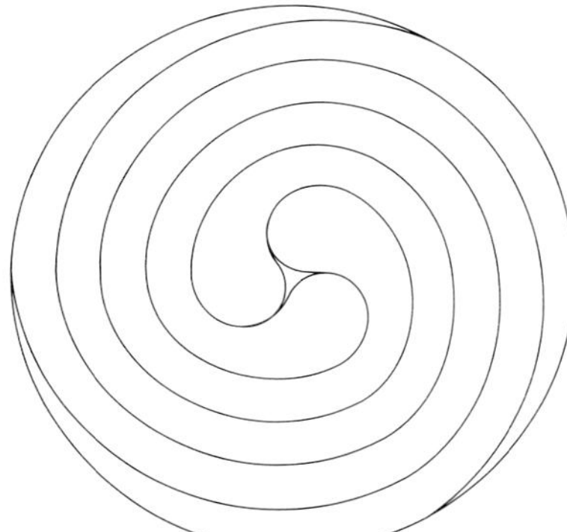

**759a**

6in (15.25cm) 300%

8in (20.3cm) 400%

**759b**

8in (20.3cm) 400%

12in (30.5cm) 600%

**760**

4in (10.2cm) 200%

9in (22.9cm) 450%

**761**

6in (15.25cm) 300%

10in (25.5cm) 500%

**762**

↔(1in (2.5cm)) to 5in (12.7cm) 500%

↔(1in (2.5cm)) to 9in (22.9cm) 900%

**763**

↔(1in (2.5cm)) to 6in (15.25cm) 600%

↔(1in (2.5cm)) to 8in (20.3cm) 800%

**765**

(1in (2.5cm)) to 4in (10.2cm) 400%

**764**

(⅞in (2.2cm)) to 4in (10.2cm) 457%

**766**

( 1½in (3.8cm)) to 6in (15.25cm) 400%

**767**

↦ 6in (15.25cm) 300%

↦ 8in (20.3cm) 400%

**768**

↦ 6in (15.25cm) 300%

↦ 8in (20.3cm) 400%

**769**

↦ 12in (30.5cm) 600%

↦ 16in (40.6cm) 800%

**770**

↦ 6in (15.25cm) 300%

↦ 8in (20.3cm) 400%

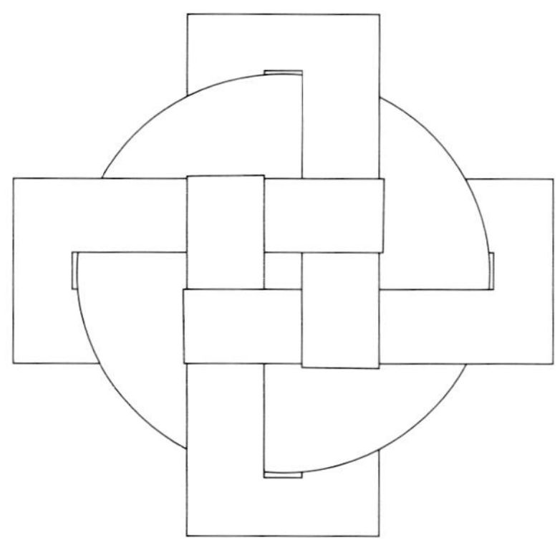

**771**

⟷ 6in (15.25cm) 300%

⟷ 8in (20.3cm) 400%

**772**

⟷ 10in (25.5cm) 500%

⟷ 16in (40.6cm) 800%

**773**

⟷ 5in (12.7cm) 250%

⟷ 8in (20.3cm) 400%

**774**

⟷ 6in (15.25cm) 300%

⟷ 8in (20.3cm) 400%

**775**

5in (12.7cm) 250%

9in (22.9cm) 450%

**776**

6in (15.25cm) 300%

8in (20.3cm) 400%

**777**

(1¾in (4.4cm)) 6in (15.25cm) 343%

(1¾in (4.4cm)) 8in (20.3cm) 457%

**778a**

5in (12.7cm) 250%

12in (30.5cm) 600%

**778b**

6in (15.25cm) 300%

8in (20.3cm) 400%

**779a**

6in (15.25cm) 300%

8in (20.3cm) 400%

**779b**

5in (12.7cm) 250%

12in (30.5cm) 600%

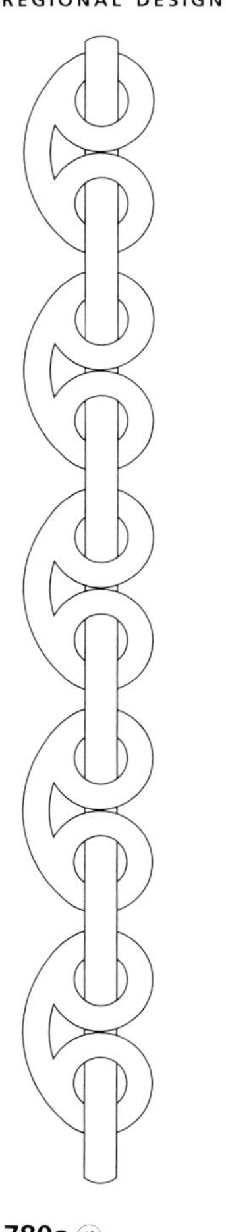

**780a**

(½in (1.3cm))
to 4in (10.2cm)
800%

**780b**

(½in (1.3cm))
to 4in (10.2cm)
800%

**781**

(⅝in (1.6cm))
to 4in (10.2cm)
640%

**782**

(⅝in (1.6cm))
to 5in (12.7cm)
800%

**783**
(1in (2.5cm)) to 6in (15.25cm) 600%

**784**
(½in (1.3cm)) to 5in (12.7cm) 800%

**785**
(⅞in (2.2cm)) to 6in (15.25cm) 685%

**786a**

6in (15.25cm) 300%

8in (20.3cm) 400%

**786b**

6in (15.25cm) 300%

8in (20.3cm) 400%

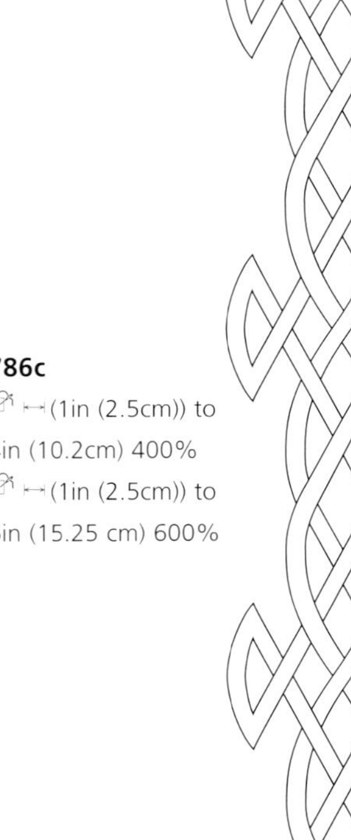

**786c**

(1in (2.5cm)) to 4in (10.2cm) 400%

(1in (2.5cm)) to 6in (15.25 cm) 600%

ALL PATTERNS ARE STANDARD 2IN (5CM) OR 4IN (10.2CM) UNLESS OTHERWISE STATED

**787a**

↦ 8in (20.3cm) 200%

↦ 16in (40.6cm) 400%

**787c**

↦ 6in (15.25cm) 300%

↦ 8in (20.3cm) 400%

**787b**

↦ 12in (30.5cm) 600%

↦ 18in (45.7cm) 900%

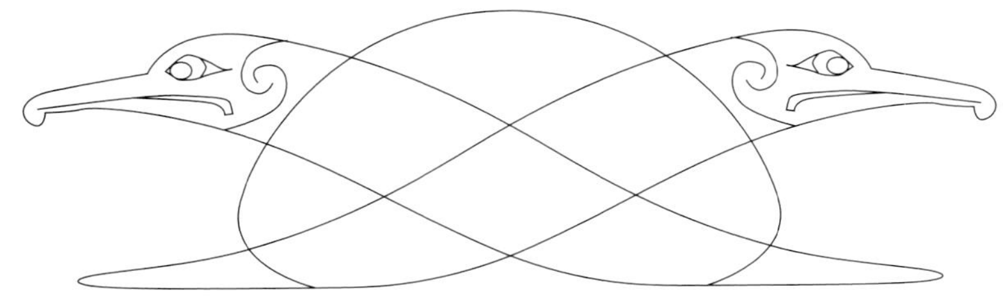

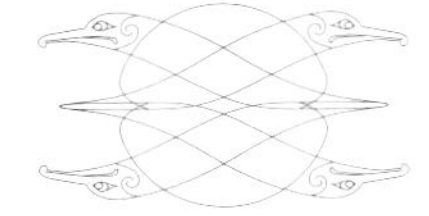

**788a**

⟷ 6in (15.25cm) 150%

⟷ 8in (20.3cm) 200%

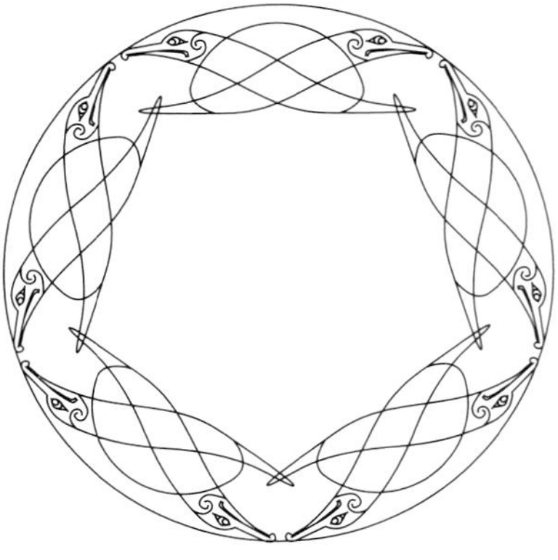

**788b**

⟷ 6in (15.25cm) 300%

⟷ 8in (20.3cm) 400%

**789**

⟷ 6in (15.25cm) 300%

⟷ 8in (20.3cm) 400%

**790**

⟷ 12in (30.5cm) 600%

⟷ 30in (76.2cm) 750%

**791**

⟷ 10in (25.5cm) 500%

⟷ 24in (61cm) 1200%

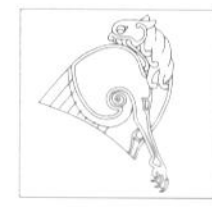

**NOTE:** *You may change the stance of the bird by changing the position of the legs.*

**792**

10in (25.5cm) 250%

18in (45.7cm) 450%

**793**

8in (20.3cm) 200%

24in (61cm) 600%

# Indian designs

The designs that follow are based on the henna patterns drawn on the hands and feet of brides in the Kasmir and Bangladesh regions of India. The henna is piped onto the skin using a piping bag similar to one you might use for icing. After drying, it leaves a flat, reddish brown, line on the skin. Sinuous lines and small filler repeat motifs are used to surround a central square or circular motif to create the illusion of fine lace gloves or socks.

Many of the designs are commonplace in the general Indian pattern vocabularly and can be seen on the fabrics that have been exported and copied for centuries. Their small spriglike designs or paisley motifs make them the perfect complement for any quilt.

**794**

⟷ 10in (25.4cm) 500%

⟷ 16in (40.6cm) 800%

**795**

⟷ 8in (20.3cm) 400%

⟷ 12in (30.5cm) 600%

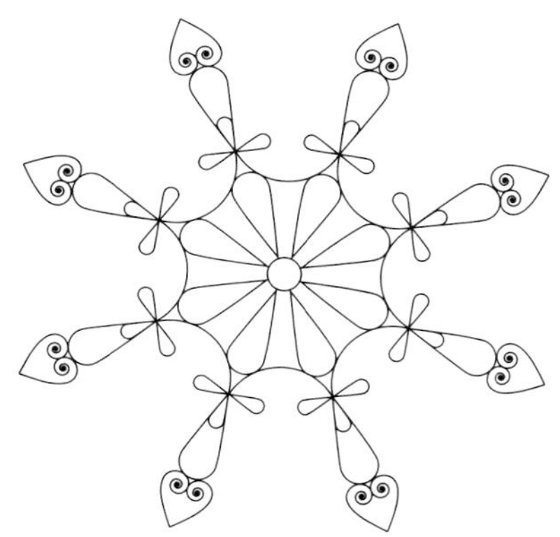

**796**

↦ 8in (20.3cm) 400%

↦ 12in (30.5cm) 600%

**797**

↦ 6in (15.25cm) 300%

↦ 8in (20.3cm) 400%

**798a**

↦ 6in (15.25cm) 300%

↦ 8in (20.3cm) 400%

**798b**

↦ 5in (12.7cm) 250%

↦ 12in (30.5cm) 600%

**799**

6in (15.25cm) 300%

**800**

6in (15.25cm) 300%

**801**

4in (10.2cm) 200%

**802**

6in (15.25cm) 300%

**803**

4in (10.2cm) 200%

6in (15.25cm) 300%

ALL PATTERNS ARE STANDARD 2IN (5CM) OR 4IN (10.2CM) UNLESS OTHERWISE STATED

**804**

8in (20.3cm) 200%

18in (45.7cm) 450%

**805**

8in (20.3cm) 200%

20in (50.8cm) 500%

**806**

12in (30.5cm) 300%

18in (45.7cm) 450%

**807**

8in (20.3cm) 200%

20in (50.8cm) 500%

**808**

⟼ (¾in (1.9cm)) to 5in (12.7cm) 667%

**809**

⟼ (½in (1.3cm)) to 4in (10.2cm) 800%

**810**

⟼ (⅝in (1.6cm)) to 5in (12.7cm) 800%

**811**

(¾in (1.9cm)) to 5in (12.7cm) 667%

**812**

(⅝in (1.6cm)) to 5in (12.7cm) 800%

**813**

(1¼in (3.2cm)) to 6in (15.25cm) 480%

**814**

↦ (⅞in (2.2cm))

to 6in (15.25cm) 680%

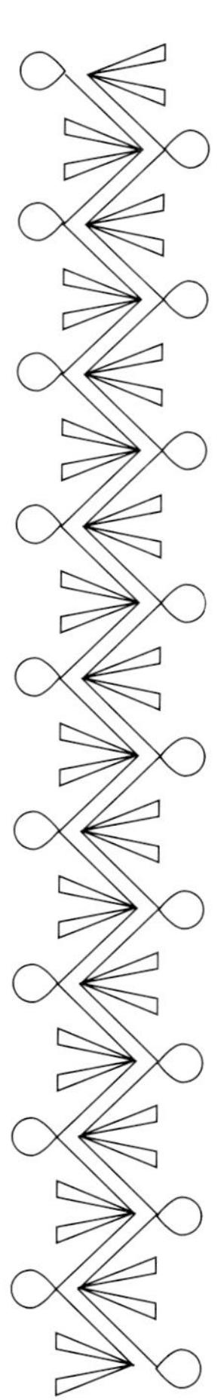

**815**

↦ (⅝in (1.6cm))

to 5in (12.7cm) 800%

**816**

↦ (¾in (1.9cm))

to 4in (10.2cm) 533%

**817**

(¾in (1.9cm))

to 6in (15.25cm)

800%

**818**

(⅝in (1.6cm))

to 6in (15.25cm)

960%

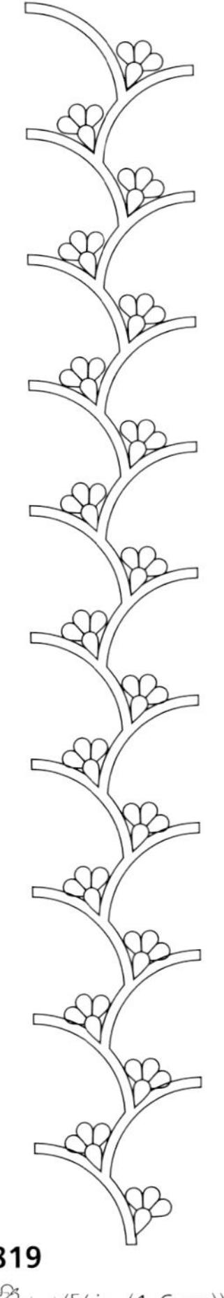

**819**

(⅝in (1.6cm))

to 4in (10.2cm)

640%

LEFT: *With a little bit of editing, the bird motif fits neatly into a circle.*

**820**

⟼ 6in (15.25cm) 300%

⟼ 8in (20.3cm) 400%

LEFT: *Select any pattern that can be divided in two for the tail design.*

**821**

12in (30.5cm) 300%

18in (45.7cm) 450%

**822**

(4½in (11.4cm)) to 12in (30.5cm) 266%

(4½in (11.4cm)) to 18in (45.7cm) 400%

# Chinese designs

The Chinese enjoy decorating their possessions with a wealth of large blossoms, sprigs of flowers, birds, and dragons, as well as complex mathematical patterns. And for centuries, the influence of Chinese artists has been exported to Europe and around the world through their ceramic designs, lacquer works, and silk fabrics.

Full of symmetry and movement, Chinese designs are perfect for adorning any quilt.

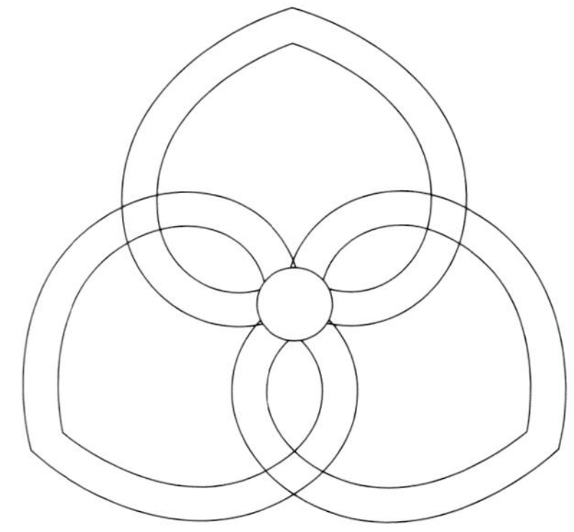

**823**

4in (10.2cm) 200%

6in (15.25cm) 300%

**824**

6in (15.25cm) 300%

8in (20.3cm) 400%

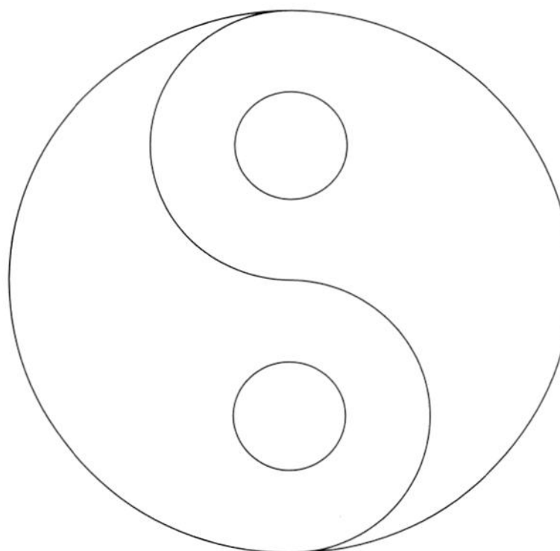

**825**

↦ 6in (15.25cm) 300%

↦ 8in (20.3cm) 400%

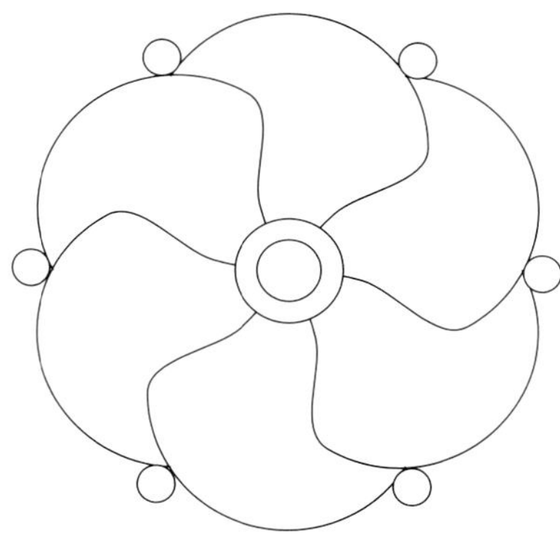

**826**

↦ 4in (10.2cm) 200%

↦ 6in (15.25cm) 300%

**827**

↦ 6in (15.25cm) 300%

↦ 10in (25.4cm) 500%

**828**

↦ 6in (15.25cm) 300%

↦ 8in (20.3cm) 400%

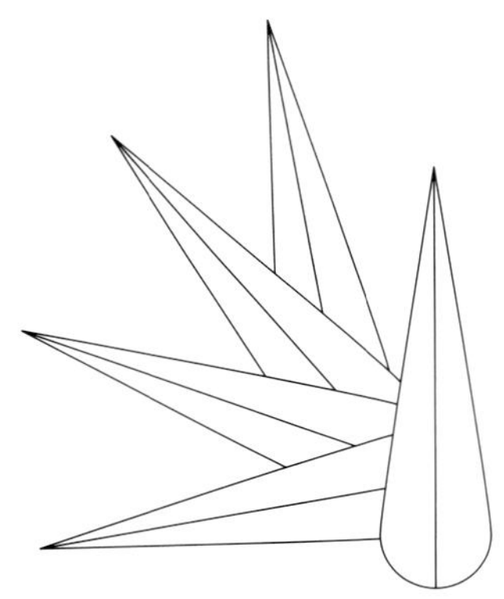

**829**
⟷ 4in (10.2cm) 200%
⟷ 6in (15.25cm) 300%

**830**
⟷ 6in (15.25cm) 300%
⟷ 8in (20.3cm) 400%

**831**
⟷ 8in (20.3cm) 400%
⟷ 12in (30.5cm) 600%

**832**
⟷ 6in (15.25cm) 300%
⟷ 8in (20.3cm) 400%

**833**

↦ 8in (20.3cm) 200%

↦ 12in (30.5cm) 300%

**834**

↦ 5in (12.7cm) 250%

↦ 8in (20.3cm) 400%

**835**

↦ 6in (15.25cm) 300%

↦ 8in (20.3cm) 400%

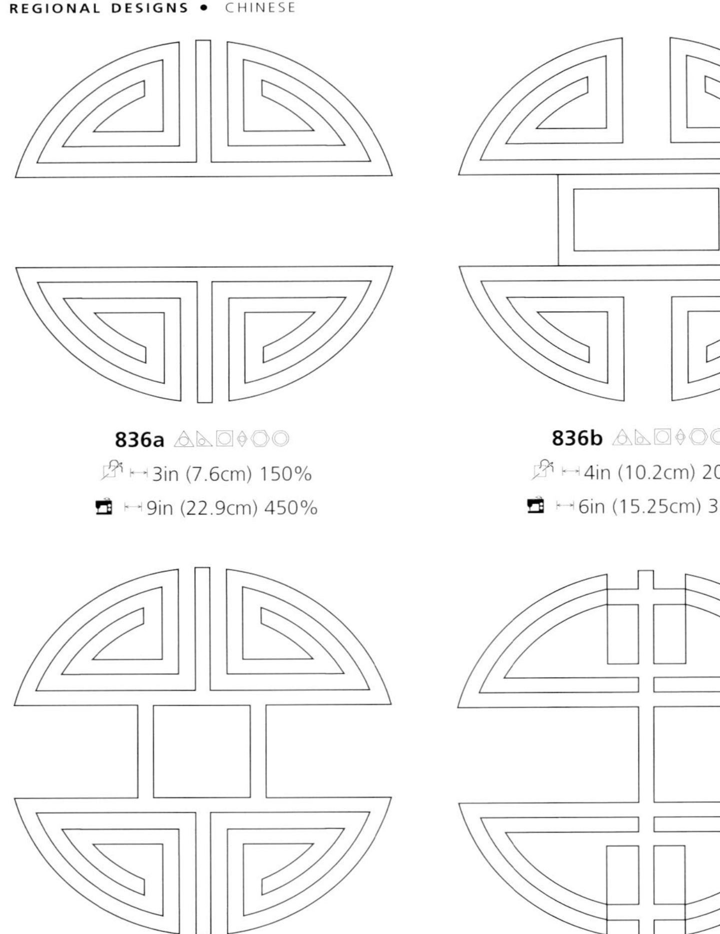

**836a**
⟷ 3in (7.6cm) 150%
⟷ 9in (22.9cm) 450%

**836b**
⟷ 4in (10.2cm) 200%
⟷ 6in (15.25cm) 300%

**836c**
⟷ 5in (12.7cm) 250%
⟷ 8in (20.3cm) 400%

**836d**
⟷ 4in (10.2cm) 200%
⟷ 6in (15.25cm) 300%

**837**

⟷ 10in (25.5cm) 250%

⟷ 16in (40.6cm) 400%

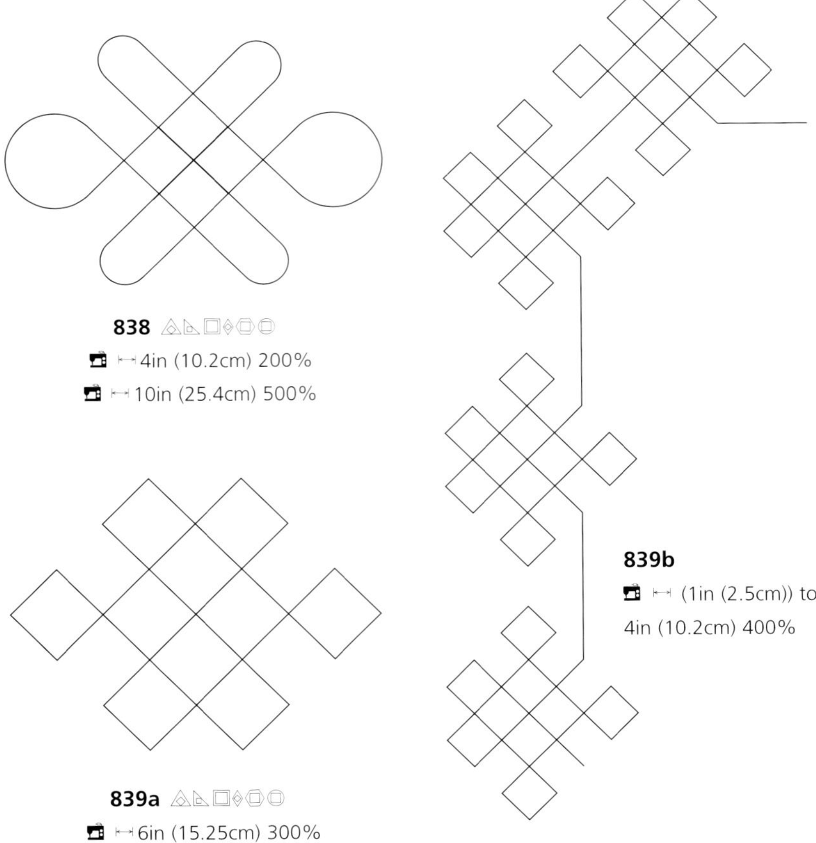

**838**

4in (10.2cm) 200%

10in (25.4cm) 500%

**839a**

6in (15.25cm) 300%

8in (20.3cm) 400%

**839b**

(1in (2.5cm)) to 4in (10.2cm) 400%

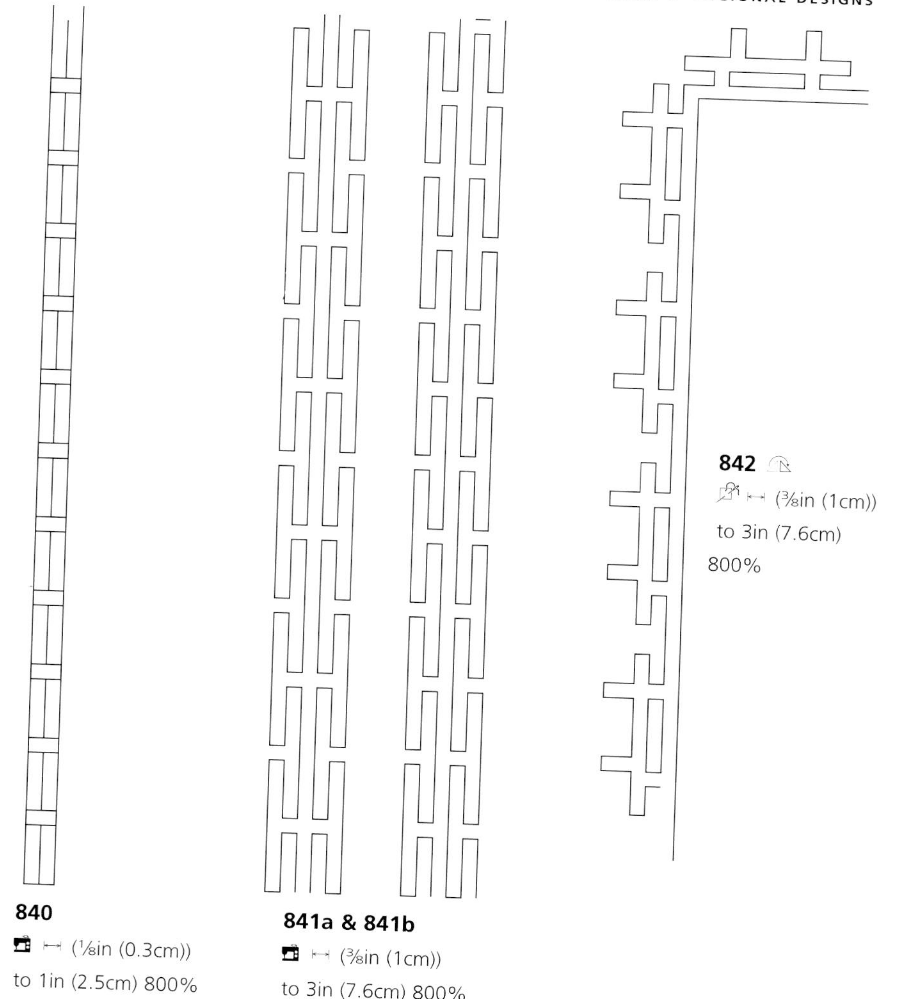

**842**

(⅜in (1cm)) to 3in (7.6cm) 800%

**840**

(⅛in (0.3cm)) to 1in (2.5cm) 800%

**841a & 841b**

(⅜in (1cm)) to 3in (7.6cm) 800%

**843**

6in (15.25cm) 300%

8in (20.3cm) 400%

**844**

6in (15.25cm) 300%

8in (20.3cm) 400%

**845**

4in (10.2cm) 200%

6in (15.25cm) 300%

**846**

6in (15.25cm) 300%

8in (20.3cm) 400%

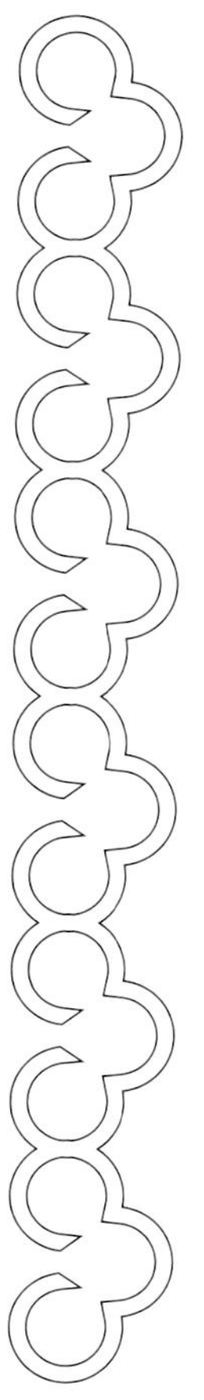

**847**

(½in (1.3cm)) to 2in (5cm) 400%

**848**

(1in (2.5cm)) to 6in (15.25cm) 600%

**849**

(1in (2.5cm)) to 6in (15.25cm) 600%

**850**

(1in (2.5cm)) to 8in (20.3cm) 800%

**851**

(1in (2.5cm)) to 6in (15.25cm) 600%

**852**

12in (30.5cm) 300%

18in (45.7cm) 450%

**853**

16in (40.6cm) 400%

24in (61cm) 600%

ALL PATTERNS ARE STANDARD 2IN (5CM) OR 4IN (10.2CM) UNLESS OTHERWISE STATED

**854**

12in (30.5cm) 300%

18in (45.7cm) 450%

**855** 

6in (15.25cm) 300%

8in (20.3cm) 400%

**856**

8in (20.3cm) 200%

18in (45.7cm) 450%

ALL PATTERNS ARE STANDARD 2IN (5CM) OR 4IN (10.2CM) UNLESS OTHERWISE STATED

**857**

12in (30.5cm) 300%

30in (76.2cm) 750%

# Polynesian designs

The area defined as Polynesia in the Pacific Rim has a huge diversity of cultures spread over hundreds of islands, which over the centuries have traded and exchanged ideas. Polynesian decoration has a rich, dense feel and appears on everything from household goods and possessions to markings on humans. The patterns are largely geometric in nature, removing areas from one shape to create another, as well as revealing a creative use of line and repetition. These principles create exciting, yet quick designs to carve or paint, and this simplicity makes a practical design source for quilters.

**858**

4in (10.2cm) 200%

6in (15.25cm) 300%

**859**

6in (15.25cm) 300%

8in (20.3cm) 400%

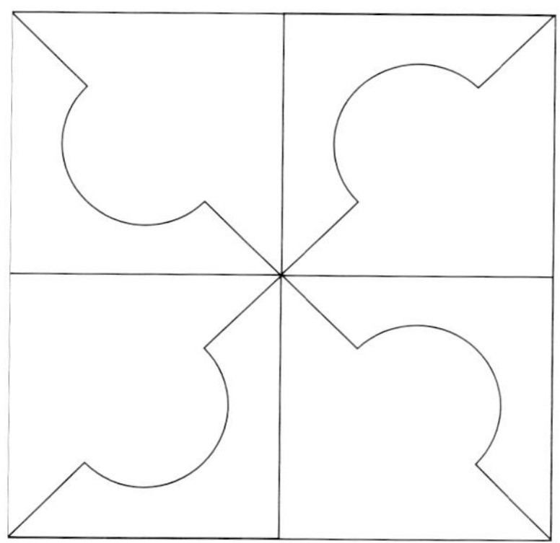

**860**

⟷ 4in (10.2cm) 200%

⟷ 6in (15.25cm) 300%

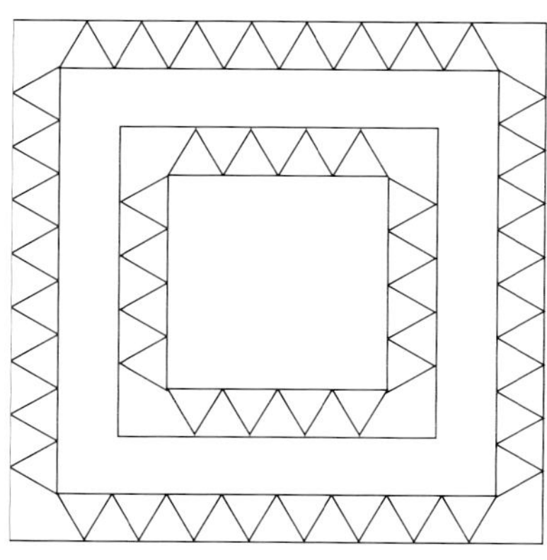

**861**

⟷ 6in (15.25cm) 300%

⟷ 8in (20.3cm) 400%

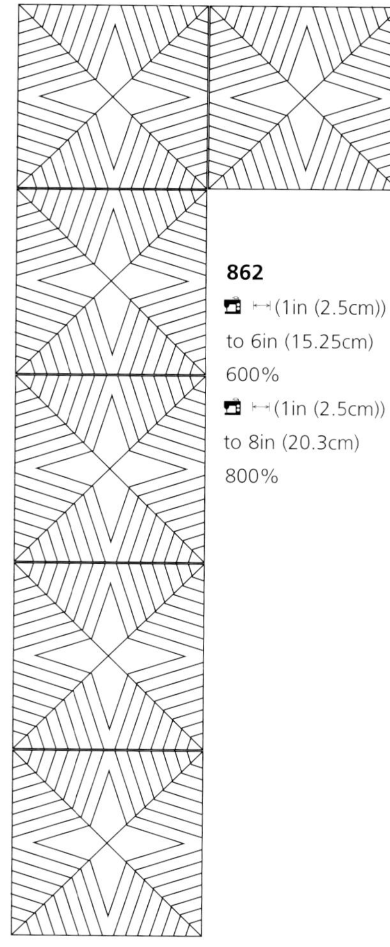

**862**

⟷ (1in (2.5cm)) to 6in (15.25cm) 600%

⟷ (1in (2.5cm)) to 8in (20.3cm) 800%

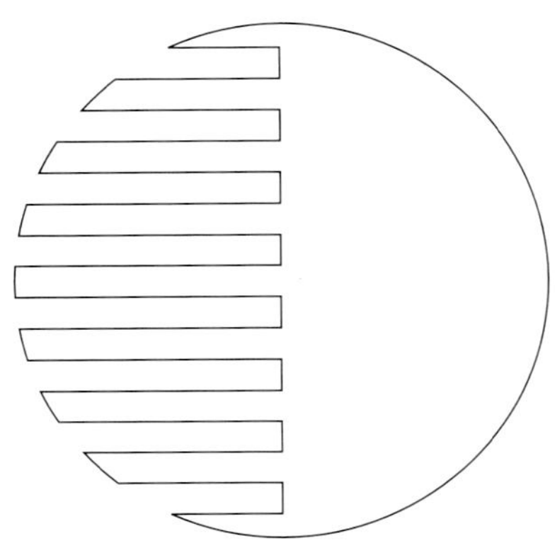

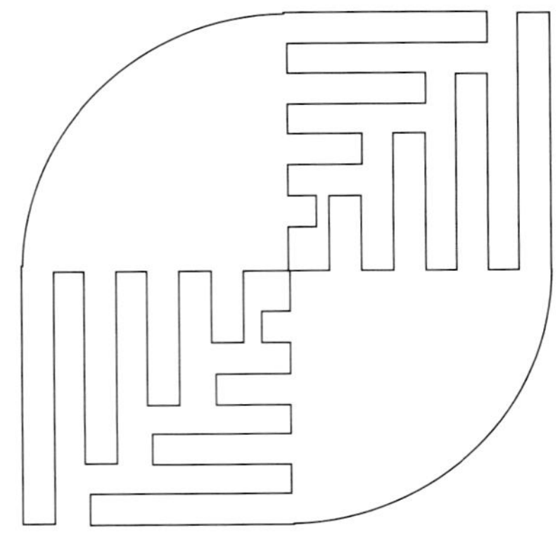

**863** 

6in (15.25cm) 300%

8in (20.3cm) 400%

**864**

6in (15.25cm) 300%

8in (20.3cm) 400%

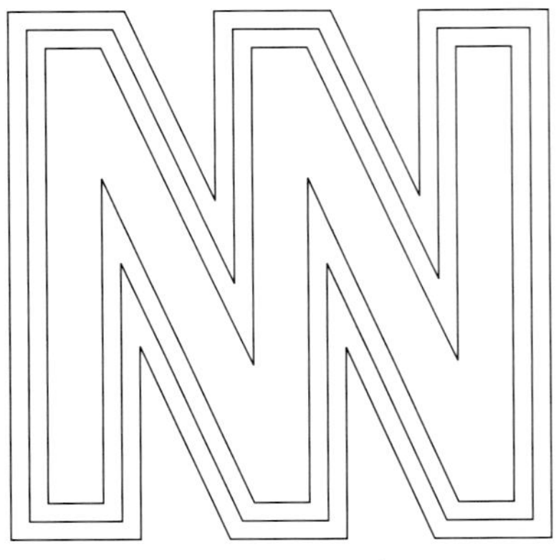

**865**

6in (15.25cm) 300%

8in (20.3cm) 400%

**866**

6in (15.25cm) 300%

8in (20.3cm) 400%

**867** 

(1in (2.5cm))

to 6in (15.25cm) 600%

**868**

(1⅛in (2.8cm))

to 6in (15.25cm) 533%

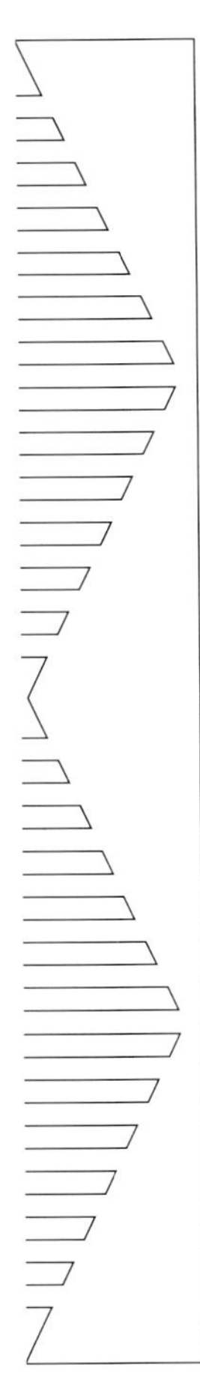

**869**

⟼ (⅝in (1.6cm) to 4in (10cm) 640%

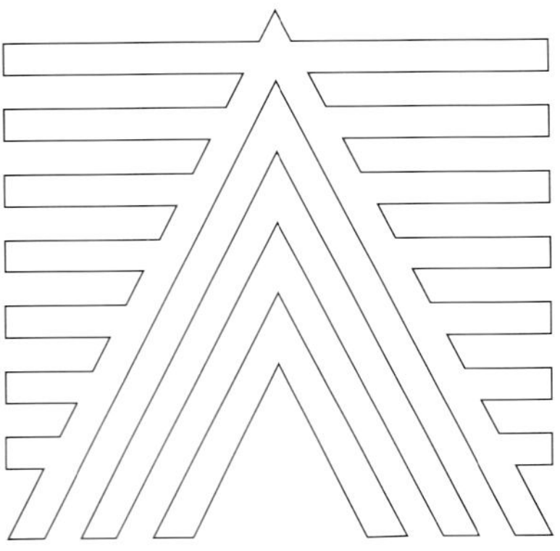

**870**

⟼ 6in (15.25cm) 300%

⟼ 8in (20.3cm) 400%

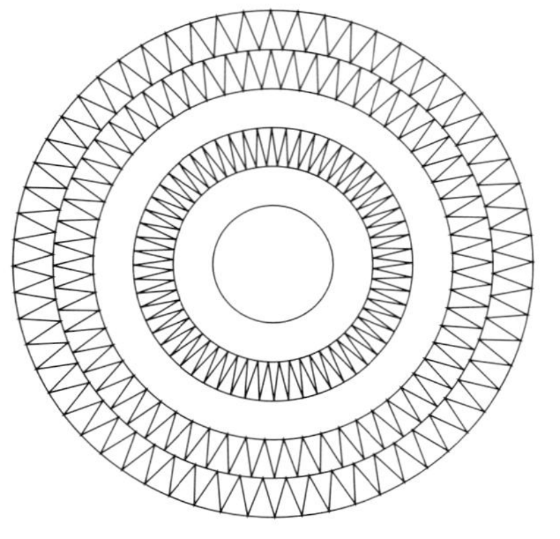

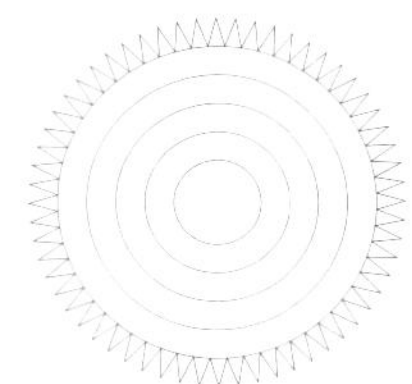

**871**

⟼ 6in (15.25cm) 300%

⟼ 12in (30.5cm) 600%

**872**

⟼ 12in (30.5cm) 300%

⟼ 20in (50.8cm) 500%

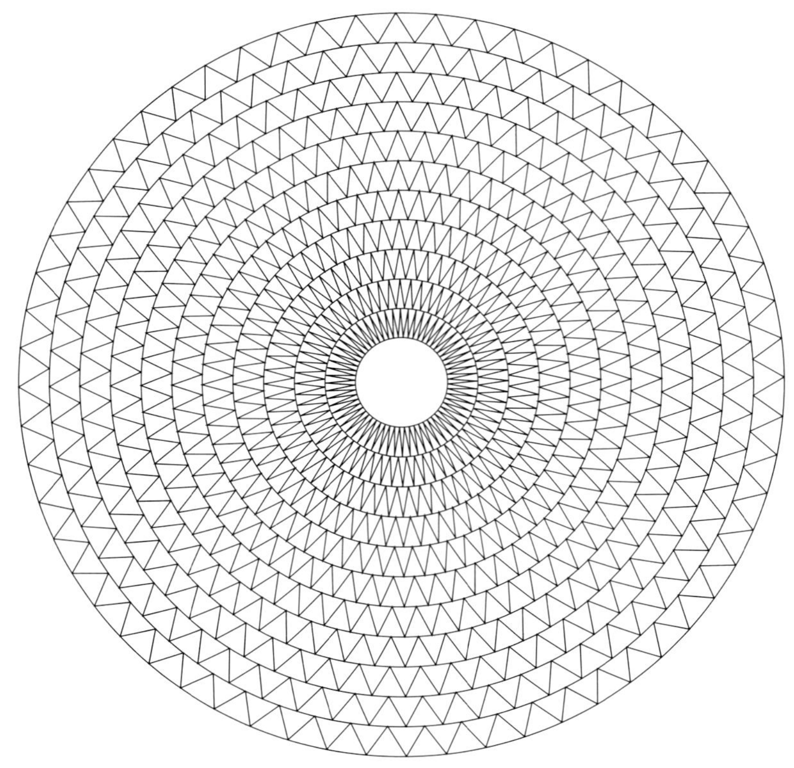

**873**

12in (30.5cm) 300%

20in (50.8cm) 500%

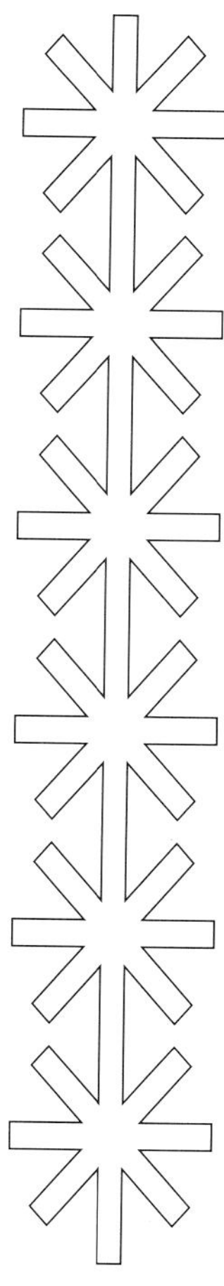

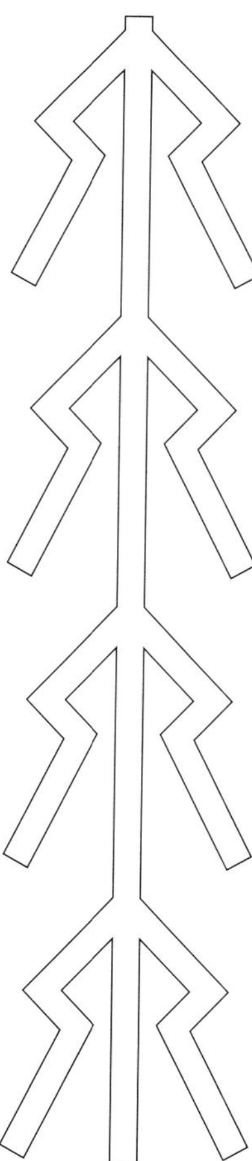

**874a**

 ⟼(¾in (1.9cm))
to 4in (10cm) 533%

**874b**

⟼(1in (2.5cm))
to 6in (15.25cm) 600%

**875**

⟼(1¼in (3.2cm))
to 6in (15.25cm) 480%

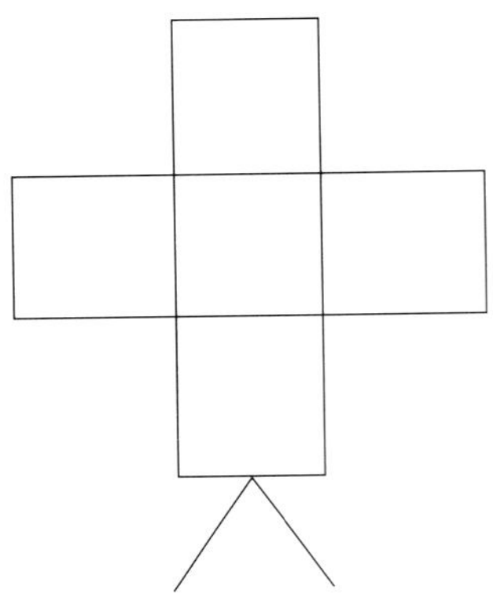

**876a**

4in (10cm) 200%

5in (12.7cm) 250%

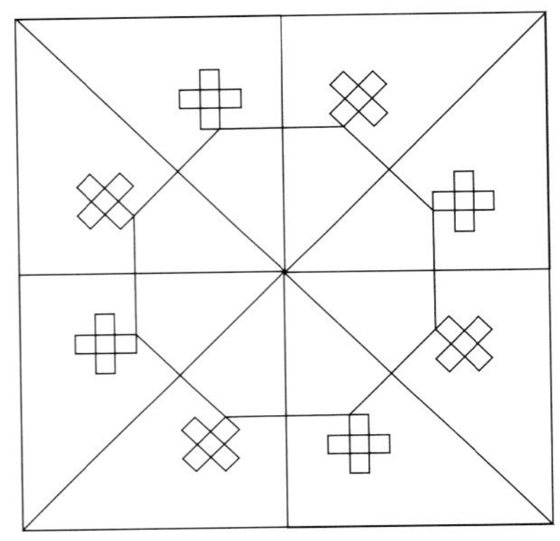

**876b**

6in (15.25cm) 300%

8in (20.3cm) 400%

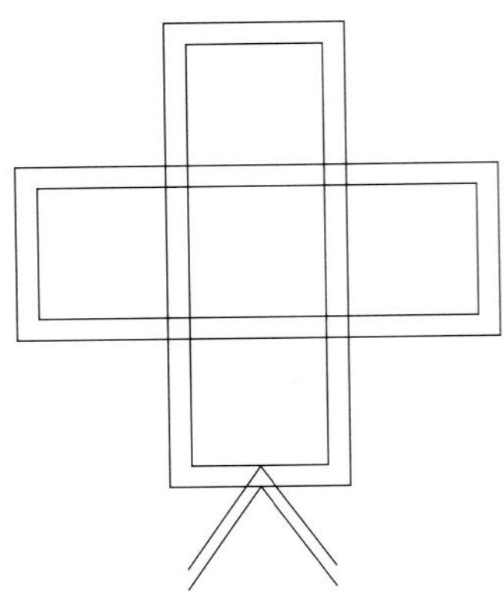

**877a**

6in (15.25cm) 300%

8in (20.3cm) 400%

**877b**

8in (20.3cm) 400%

12in (30.5cm) 600%

**878**

⟷ 8in (20.3cm) 200%

⟷ 18in (45.7cm) 450%

# Pueblo Indian designs

The following designs have been inspired by the Pueblo pottery of the Indians of the southwestern United States. Most of the geometric decorative motifs represent natural elements associated with fertility; the most recognizable is that of the rainbird. These motifs are often used in repetitive patterns in one or two colors and rely on their intriguing shapes for visual interest. Slightly more abstract than other designs in this book, it is these characteristics and the variation in line distances that make them interesting motifs for the modern quilter.

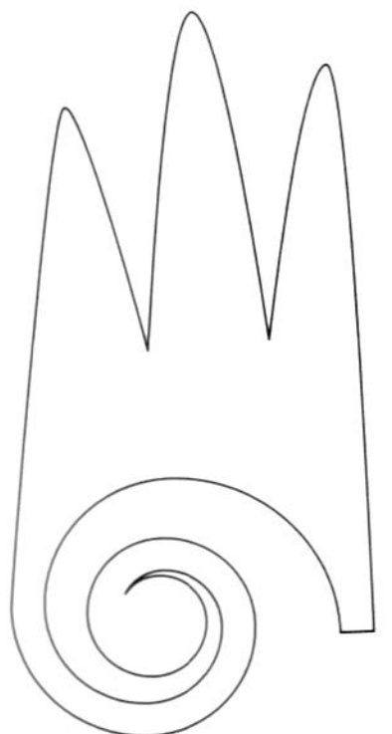

**879a**

6in (15.25cm) 300%

8in (20.3cm) 400%

**879b**

6in (15.25cm) 300%

8in (20.3cm) 400%

**879c**

(⅝in (1.6cm))

to 6in (15.25cm) 950%

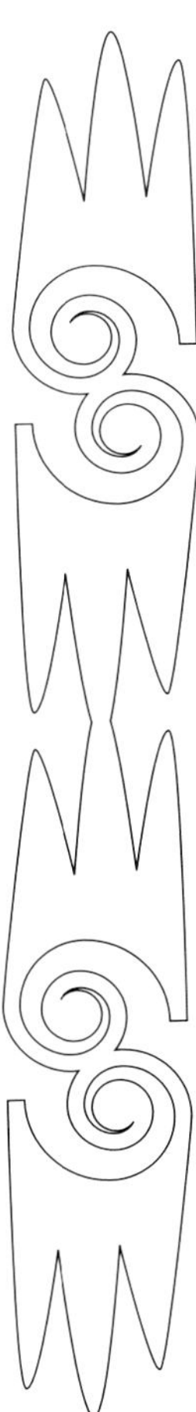

**879d**

(⅝in (1.6cm))

to 6in (15.25cm) 940%

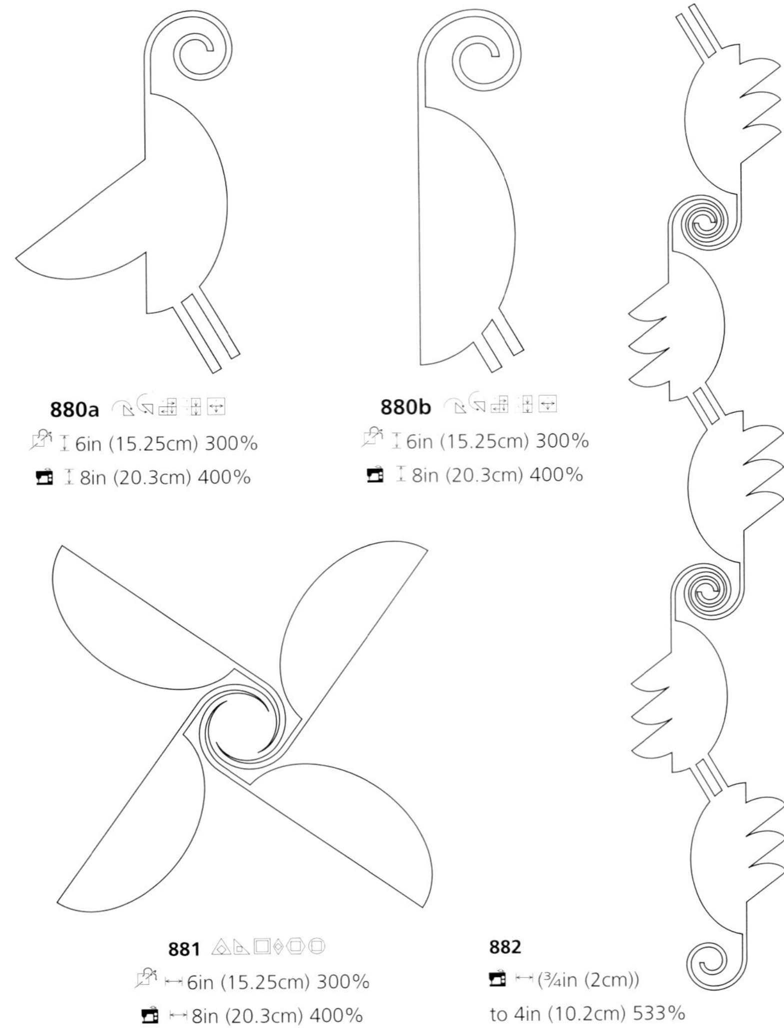

**880a**
6in (15.25cm) 300%
8in (20.3cm) 400%

**880b**
6in (15.25cm) 300%
8in (20.3cm) 400%

**881**
6in (15.25cm) 300%
8in (20.3cm) 400%

**882**
(¾in (2cm))
to 4in (10.2cm) 533%

ALL PATTERNS ARE STANDARD 2IN (5CM) OR 4IN (10.2CM) UNLESS OTHERWISE STATED

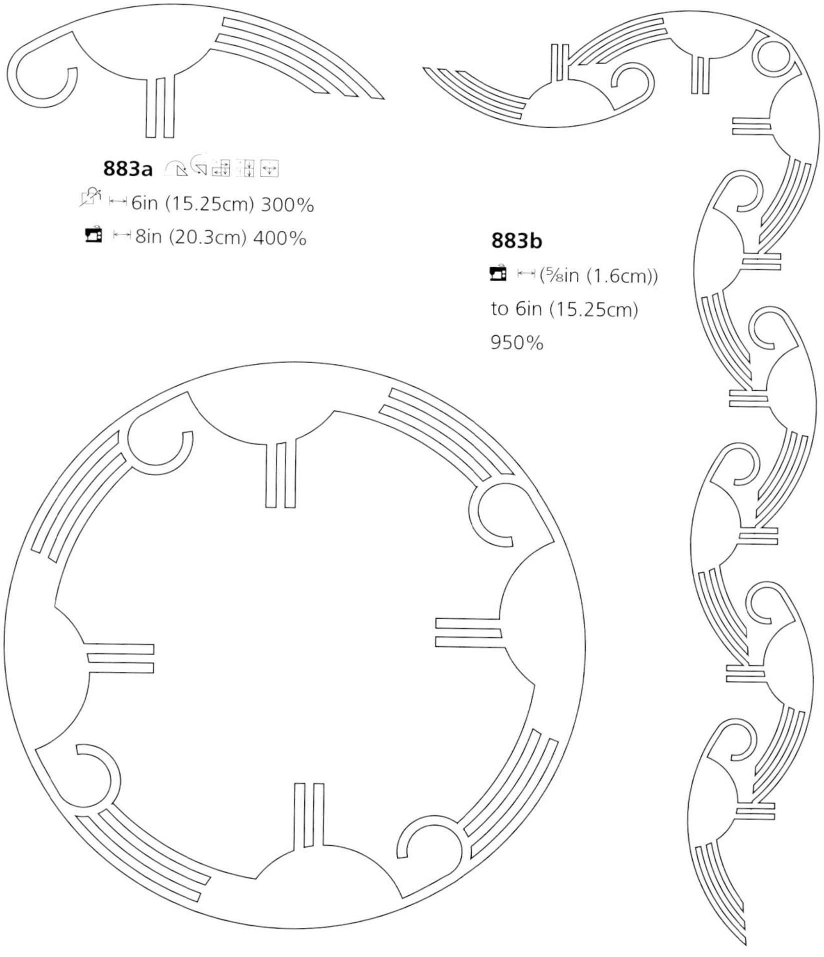

**883a**

↦ 6in (15.25cm) 300%

↦ 8in (20.3cm) 400%

**883b**

↦ (⅝in (1.6cm)) to 6in (15.25cm) 950%

**883c**

↦ (3in (7.6cm)) to 6in (15.25cm) 200%

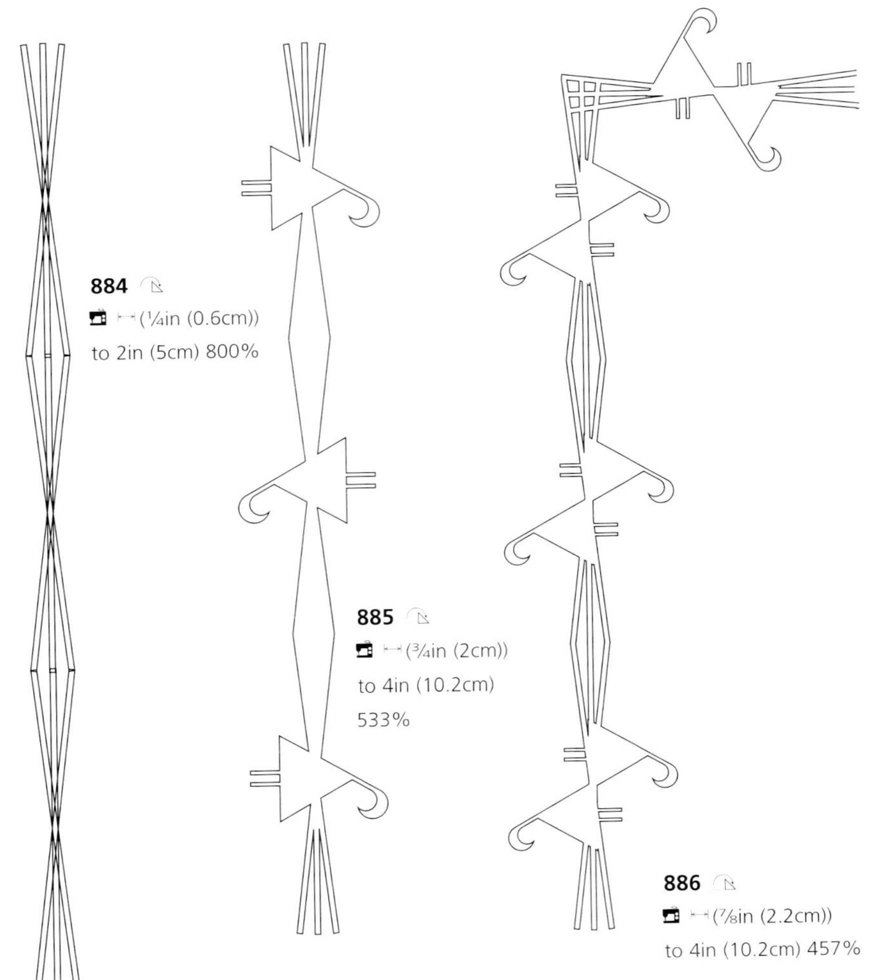

**884**
(¼in (0.6cm)) to 2in (5cm) 800%

**885**
(¾in (2cm)) to 4in (10.2cm) 533%

**886**
(⅞in (2.2cm)) to 4in (10.2cm) 457%

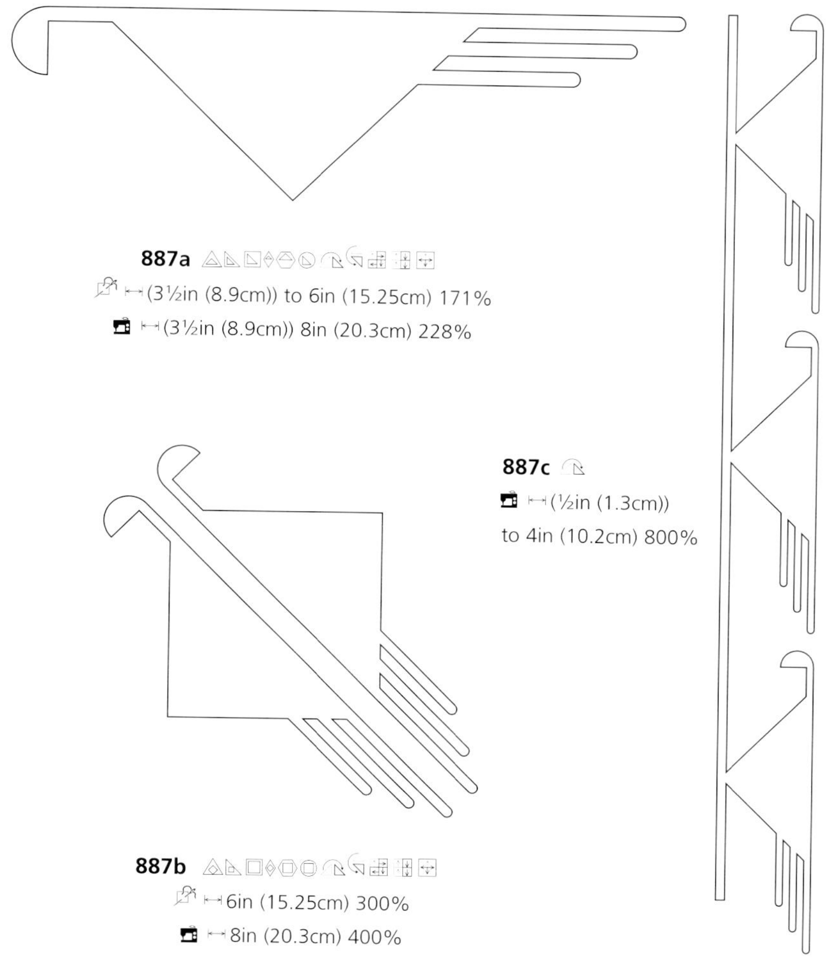

**887a**

(3½in (8.9cm)) to 6in (15.25cm) 171%

(3½in (8.9cm)) 8in (20.3cm) 228%

**887c**

(½in (1.3cm)) to 4in (10.2cm) 800%

**887b**

6in (15.25cm) 300%

8in (20.3cm) 400%

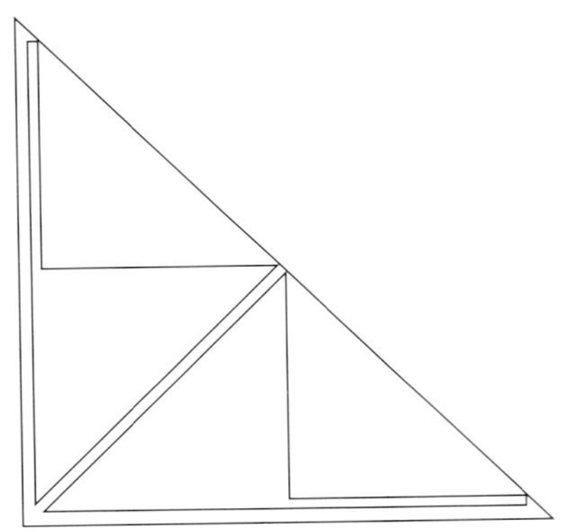

**888**

↦ 4in (10.2cm) 200%

↦ 6in (15.25cm) 300%

**889**

↦ 6in (15.25cm) 300%

↦ 8in (20.3cm) 400%

**890**

↦ (⅝in (1.6cm))

to 6in (15.25cm) 950%

**891a**

4in (10.2cm) 200%

6in (15.25cm) 300%

**891b**

6in (15.25cm) 300%

12in (30.5cm) 600%

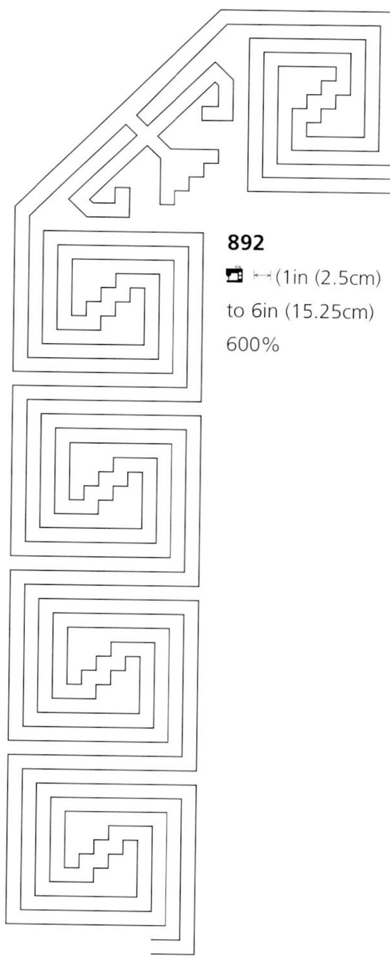

**892**

(1in (2.5cm) to 6in (15.25cm) 600%

**893**

↦ 6in (15.25cm) 300%

↦ 8in (20.3cm) 400%

**894**

↦ 6in (15.25cm) 300%

**895**

↦ (⅝in (1.6cm)) to 4in (10.2cm) 635%

**896**

↦ (⅝in (1.6cm)) to 4in (10.2cm) 635%

ALL PATTERNS ARE STANDARD 2IN (5CM) OR 4IN (10.2CM) UNLESS OTHERWISE STATED

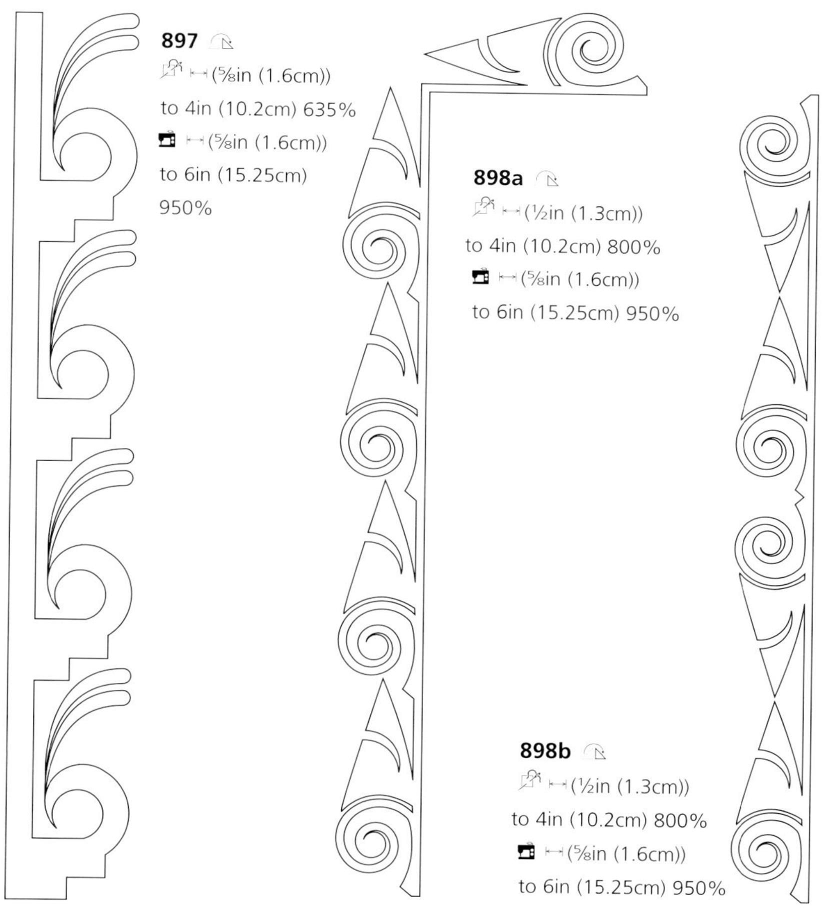

**897**

(⅝in (1.6cm)) to 4in (10.2cm) 635%

(⅝in (1.6cm)) to 6in (15.25cm) 950%

**898a**

(½in (1.3cm)) to 4in (10.2cm) 800%

(⅝in (1.6cm)) to 6in (15.25cm) 950%

**898b**

(½in (1.3cm)) to 4in (10.2cm) 800%

(⅝in (1.6cm)) to 6in (15.25cm) 950%

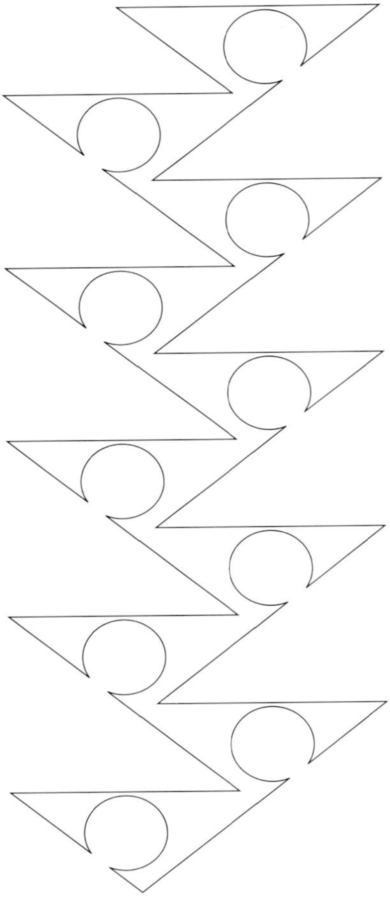

**899a**

⟼6in (15.25cm) 300%

⟼8in (20.3cm) 400%

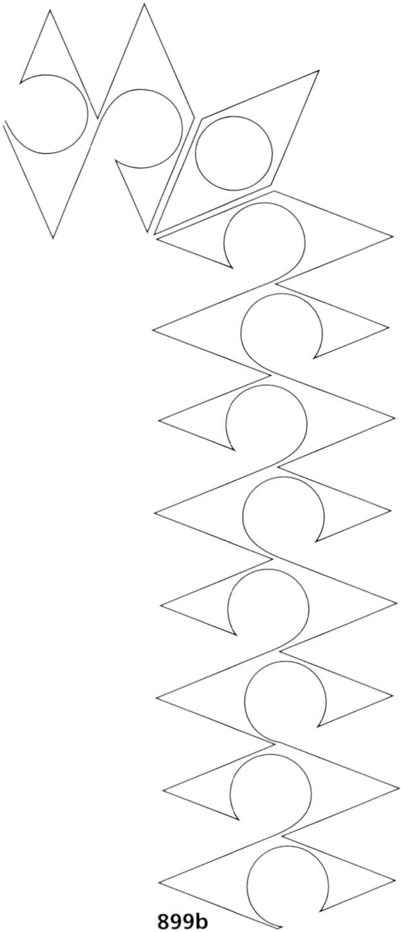

**899b**

⟼6in (15.25cm) 300%

⟼8in (20.3cm) 400%

**900a**

6in (15.25cm) 300%

8in (20.3cm) 400%

**900b**

8in (20.3cm) 400%

12in (30.5cm) 600%

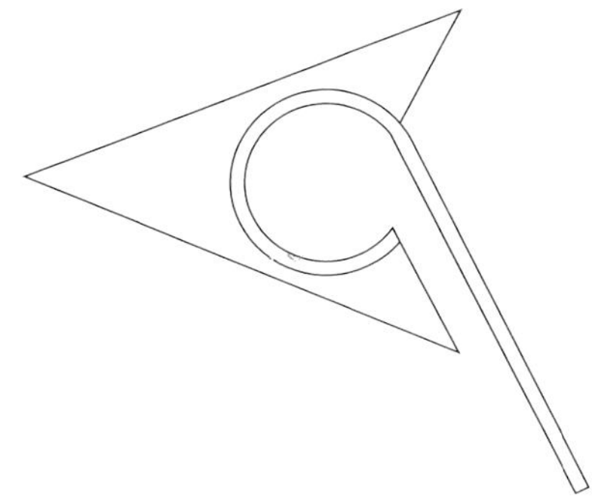

**901**

6in (15.25cm) 300%

8in (20.3cm) 400%

**902**

6in (15.25cm) 300%

8in (20.3cm) 400%

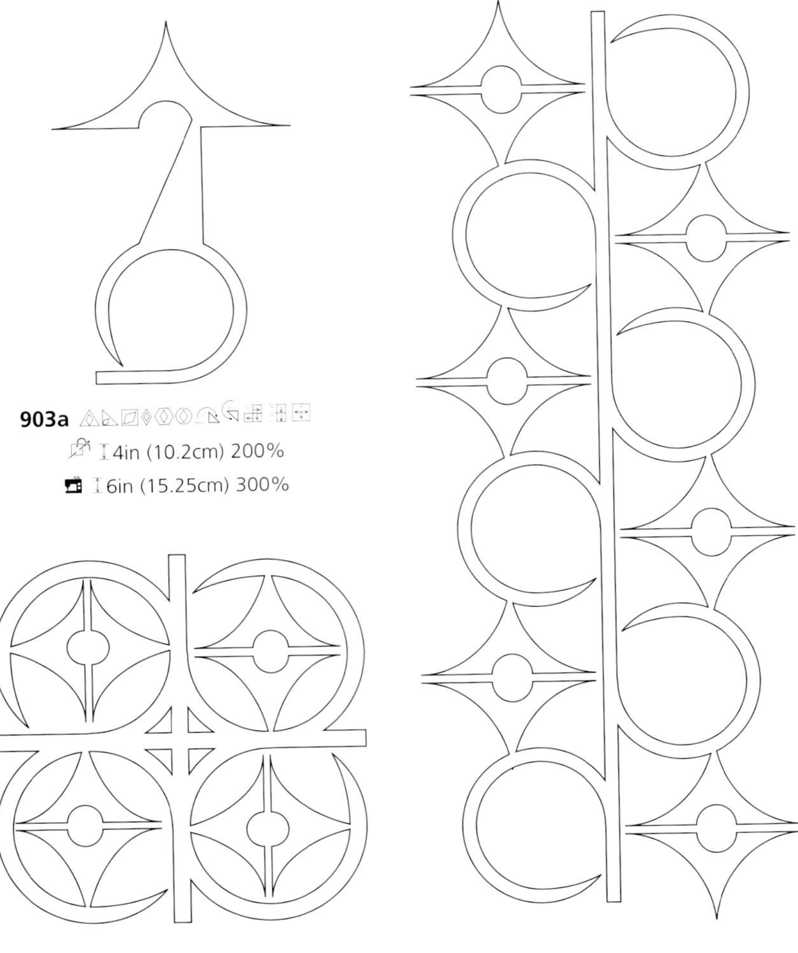

**903a**

4in (10.2cm) 200%

6in (15.25cm) 300%

**903b**

6in (15.25cm) 300%

**903c**

6in (15.25cm) 300%

ALL PATTERNS ARE STANDARD 2IN (5CM) OR 4IN (10.2CM) UNLESS OTHERWISE STATED

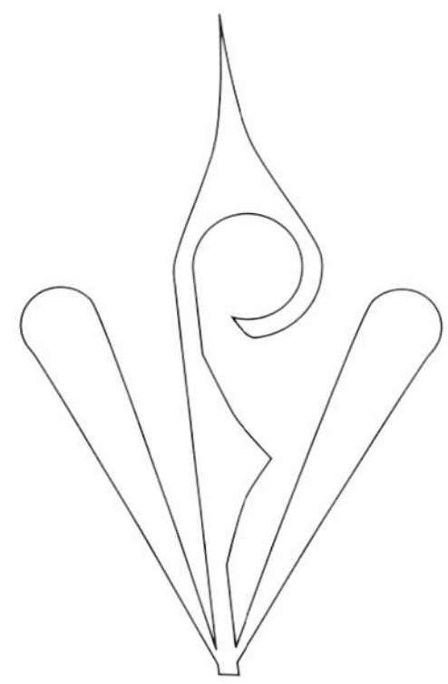

**904a**
4in (10.2cm) 200%
6in (15.25cm) 300%

**904b**
8in (20.3cm) 400%
12in (30.5cm) 600%

**904c**
8in (20.3cm) 400%
12in (30.5cm) 600%

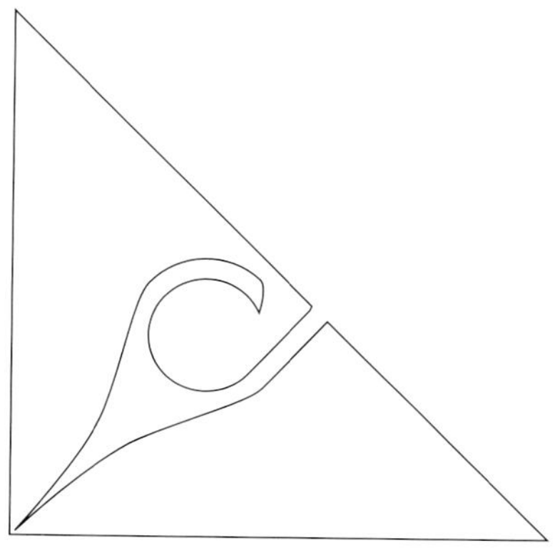

**905**
6in (15.25cm) 300%
8in (20.3cm) 400%

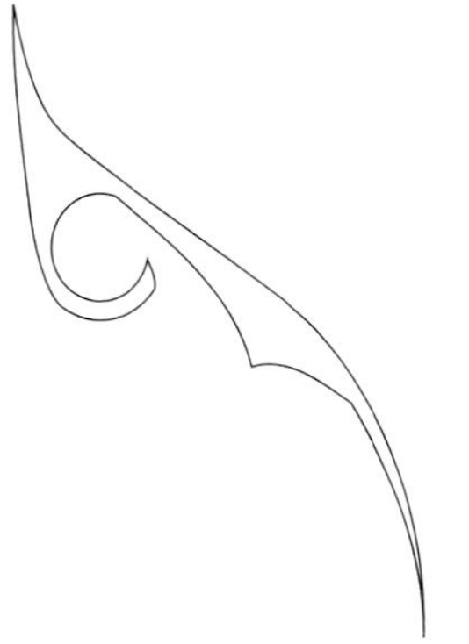

**906a**

4in (10.2cm) 200%

6in (15.25cm) 300%

**906b**

6in (15.25cm) 300%

**906c**

(1in (2.5cm) to 6in (15.25cm) 600%

**906d**

16in (40.6cm) 400%

24in (61cm) 600%

ALL PATTERNS ARE STANDARD 2IN (5CM) OR 4IN (10.2CM) UNLESS OTHERWISE STATED

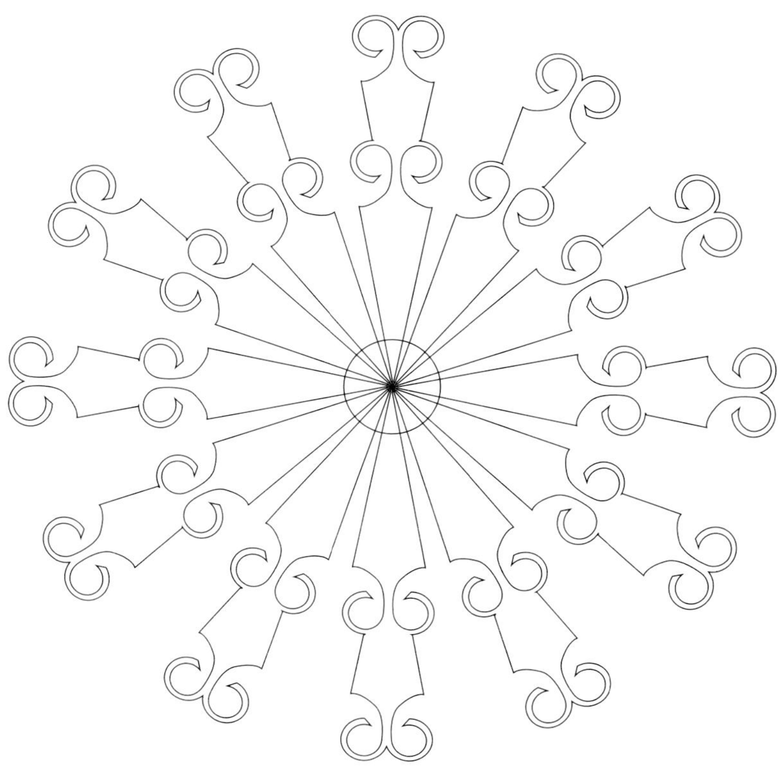

**908b**

8in (20.3cm) 200%

18in (45.7cm) 450%

# The finishing touch

The reasons for making a quilt are varied. They can be made to commemorate a special occasion, celebrate an event, or simply for the sheer tactile pleasure of drawing a needle through beautiful fabrics. It is still a delight, when looking at an old quilt to discover a signature or the reason for its making somewhere in the fabric. It doesn't even have to be as prominent as having a name and date placed in its center; it can even be a small scroll or banner incorporated into the quilt back or a discreetly placed symbolic motif.

If adding your name on the front doesn't seem appropiate for your quilt, then consider putting it on the back and stitching or presenting it as beautifully as the main quilting design. Stitch it on a separate piece of fabric and then attach it when the quilt is complete to avoid having the stitching show through on the front.

Here are some emblems and banners, along with alternative motifs that are easy to machine quilts. Also included are alphabet and zodiac signs.

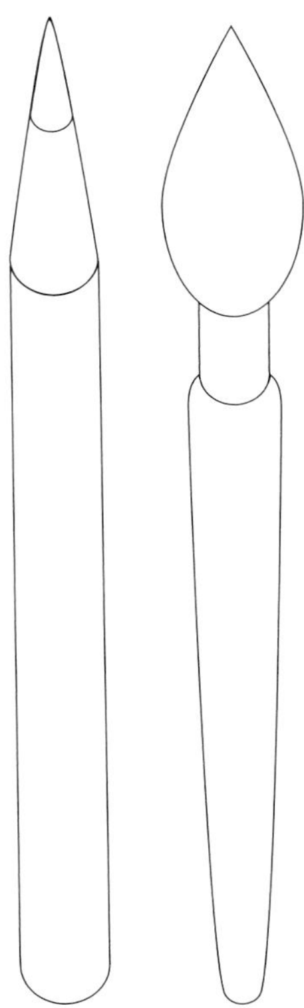

**909 & 910**

6in (15.25cm) 150%

8in (20.3cm) 200%

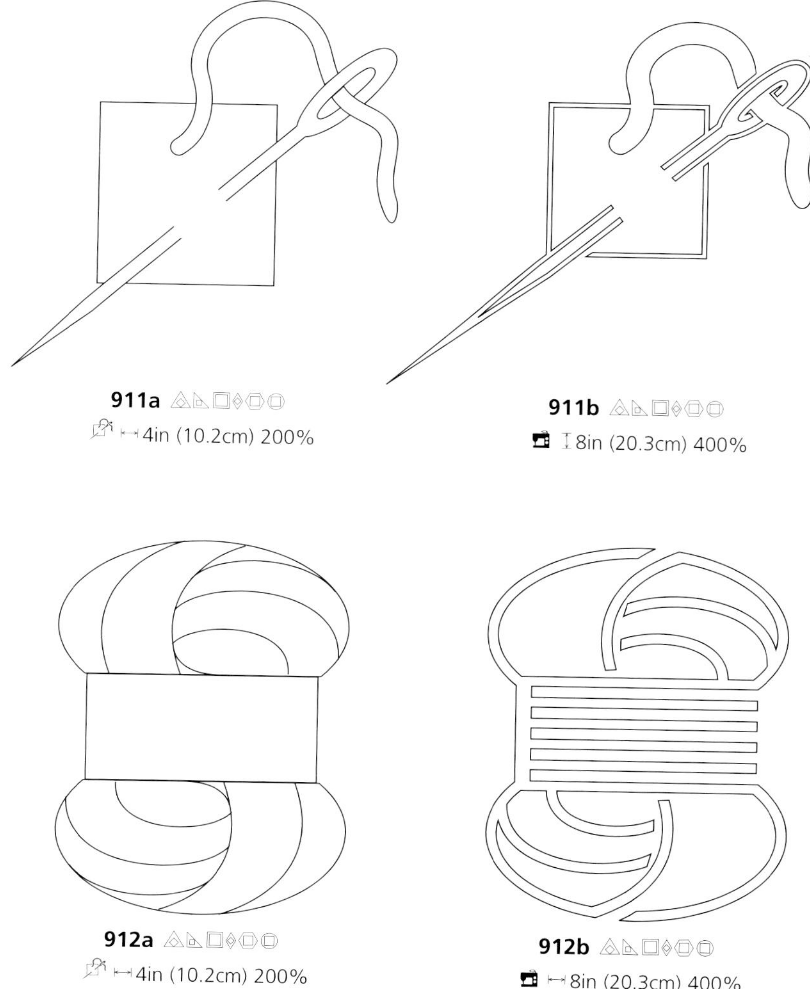

**911a**
4in (10.2cm) 200%

**911b**
8in (20.3cm) 400%

**912a**
4in (10.2cm) 200%

**912b**
8in (20.3cm) 400%

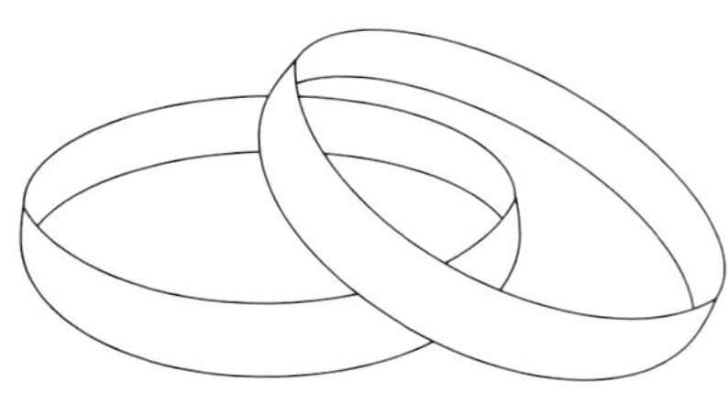

**913a**

4in (10.2cm) 200%

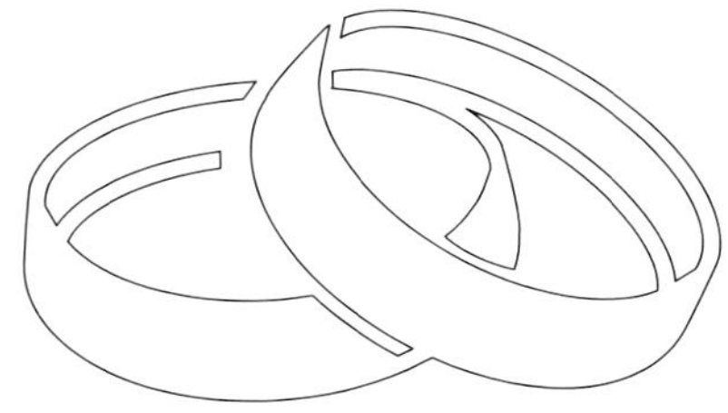

**913b**

6in (15.25cm) 300%

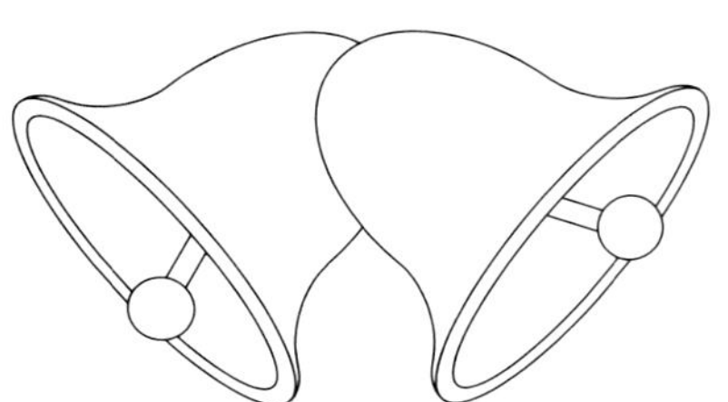

**914a**

4in (10.2cm) 200%

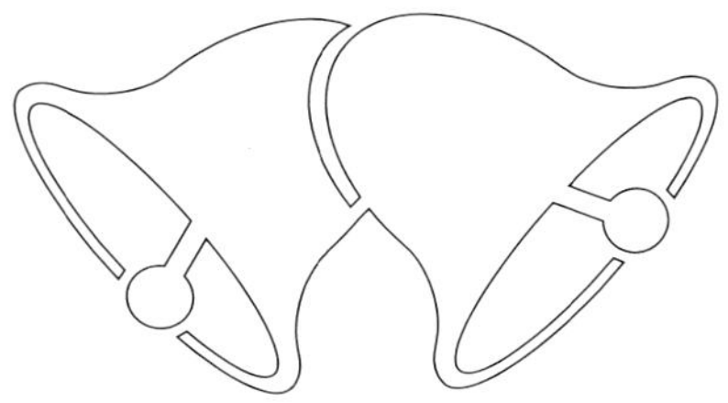

**914b**

8in (20.3cm) 400%

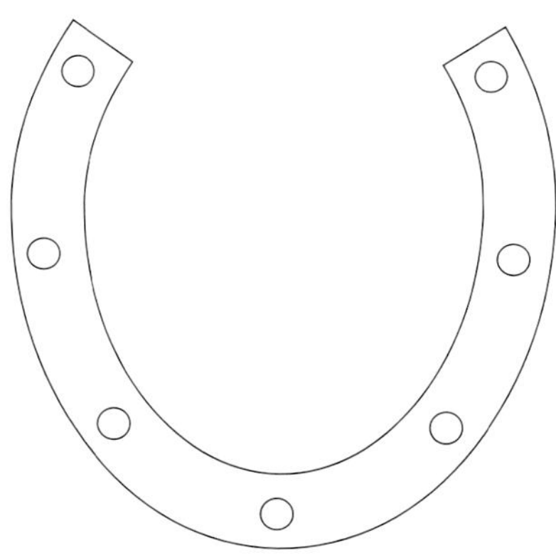

**915a**
4in (10.2cm) 200%

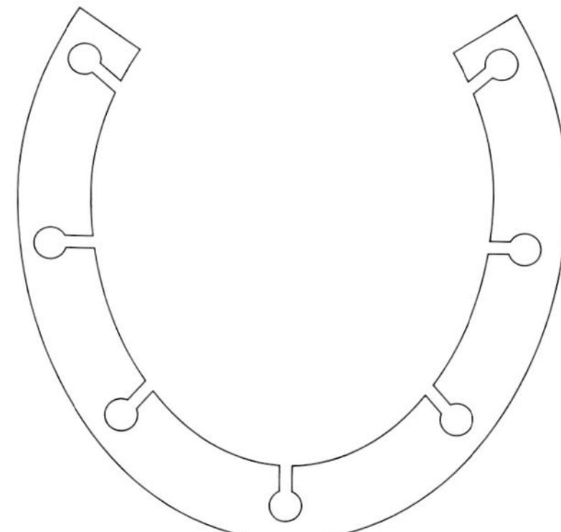

**915b**
8in (20.3cm) 400%

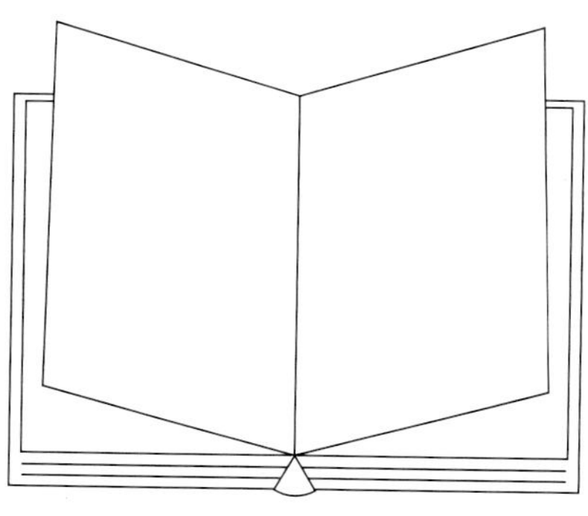

**916a**
6in (15.25cm) 300%

**916b**
8in (20.3cm) 400%

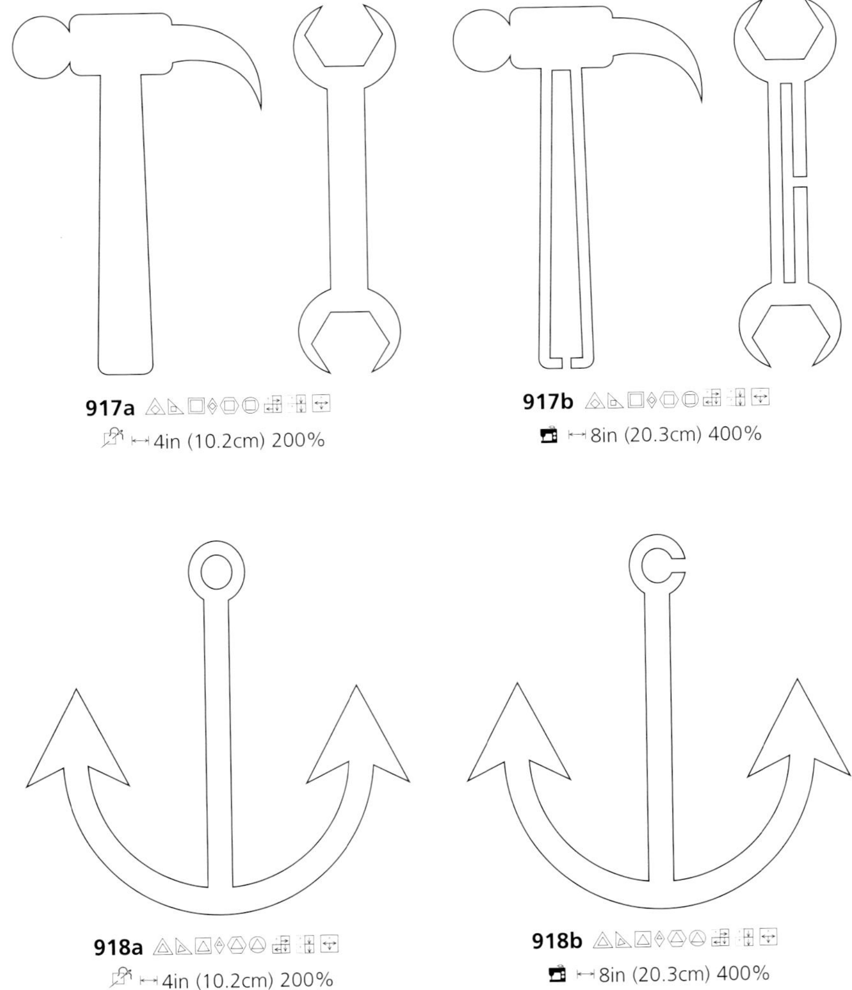

**917a**
4in (10.2cm) 200%

**917b**
8in (20.3cm) 400%

**918a**
4in (10.2cm) 200%

**918b**
8in (20.3cm) 400%

**919a**

↦ 6in (15.25cm) 300%

**919b**

↦ 8in (20.3cm) 400%

**920a**

↦ 6in (15.25cm) 300%

**920b**

↦ 8in (20.3cm) 400%

**921**

6in (15.25cm) 300%

**922**

8in (20.3cm) 400%

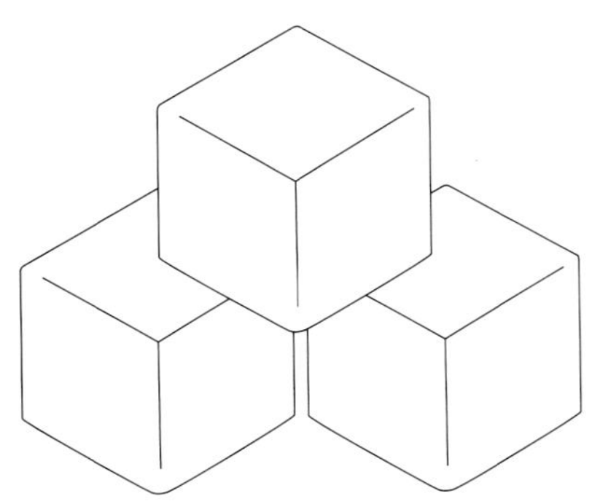

**923a**

4in (15.25cm) 200%

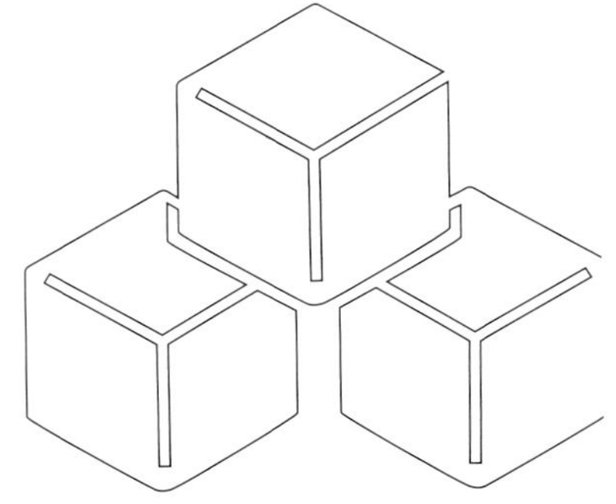

**923b**

8in (20.3cm) 400%

**924**

6in (15.25cm) 300%

8in (20.3cm) 400%

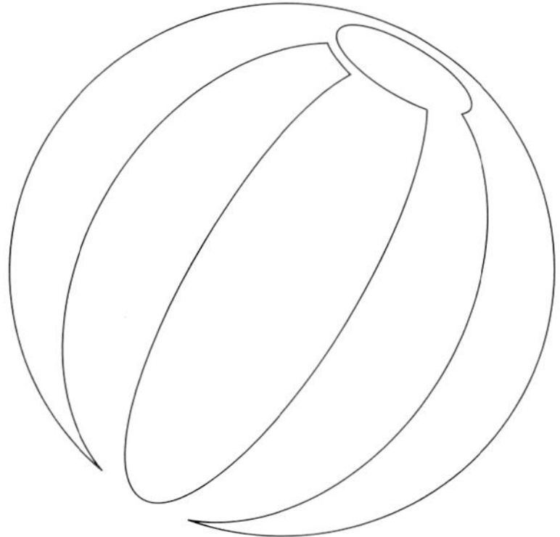

**925**

6in (15.25cm) 300%

8in (20.3cm) 400%

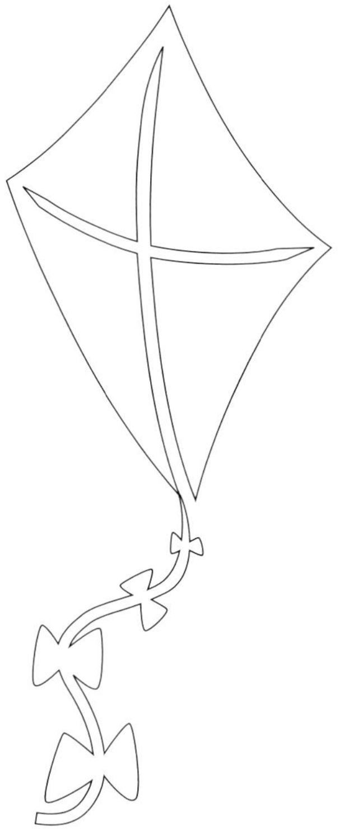

**926**

6in (15.25cm) 150%

8in (20.3cm) 200%

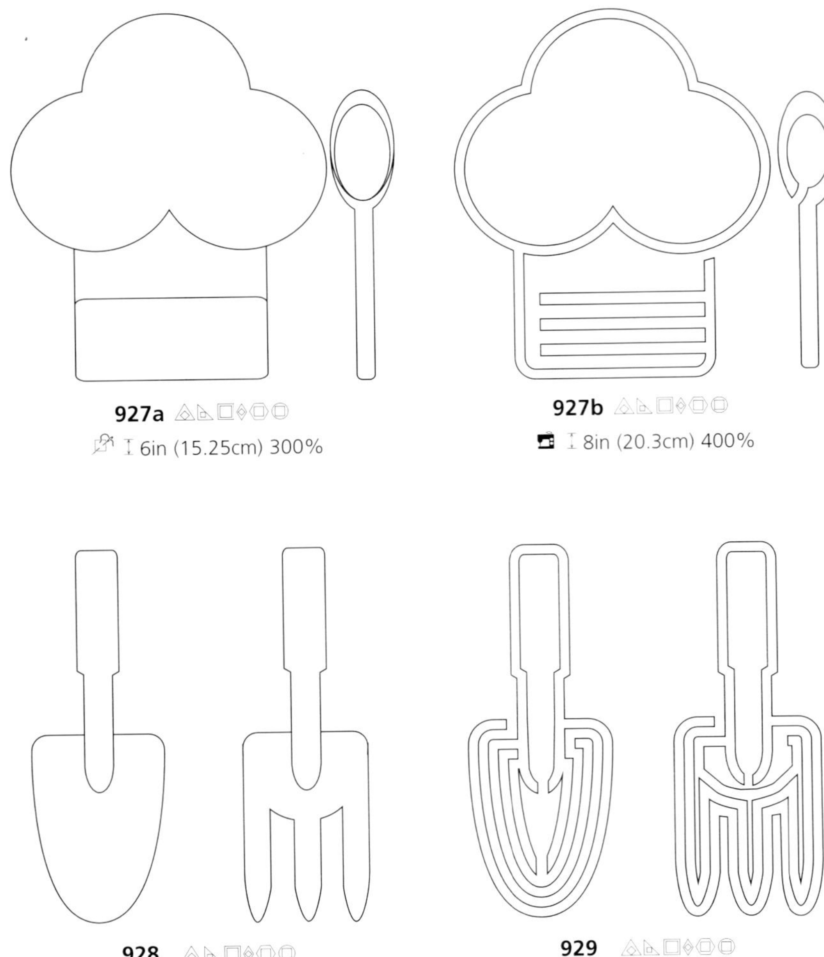

**927a**

6in (15.25cm) 300%

**927b**

8in (20.3cm) 400%

**928**

6in (15.25cm) 300%

**929**

8in (20.3cm) 400%

**930a**

6in (15.25cm) 300%

**930b**

8in (20.3cm) 400%

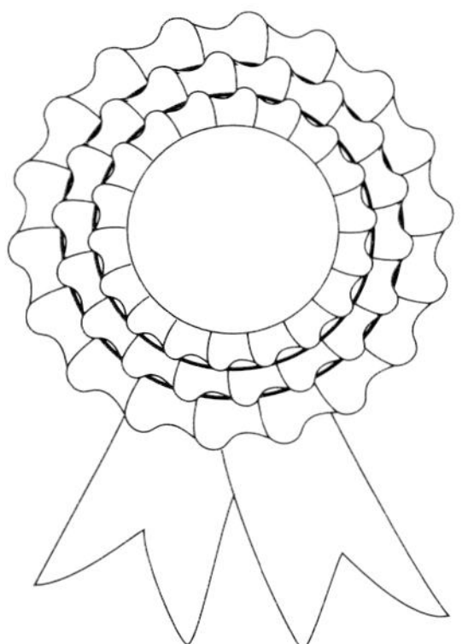

**931a**

6in (15.25cm) 300%

**931b**

8in (20.3cm) 400%

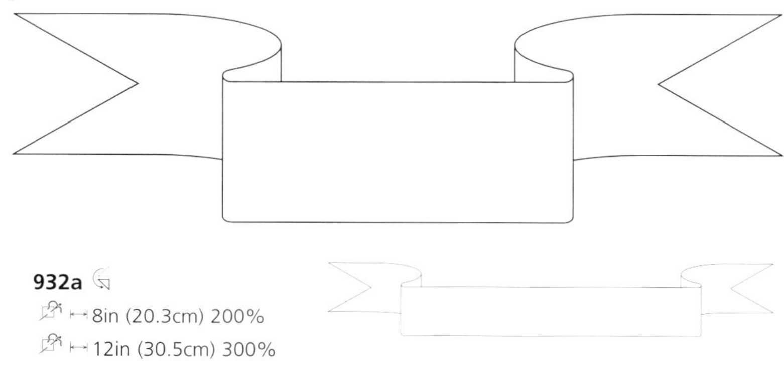

**932a**

8in (20.3cm) 200%

12in (30.5cm) 300%

NOTE: *This banner can look completely different if the middle straight section is extended.*

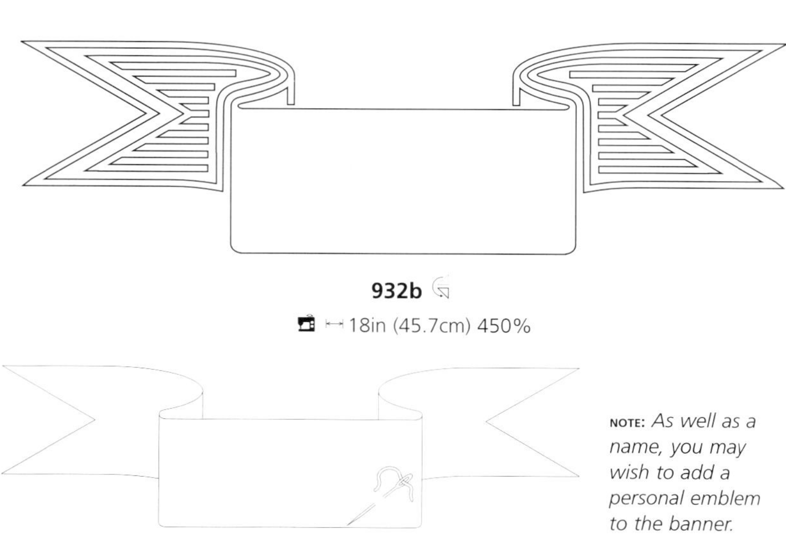

**932b**

18in (45.7cm) 450%

NOTE: *As well as a name, you may wish to add a personal emblem to the banner.*

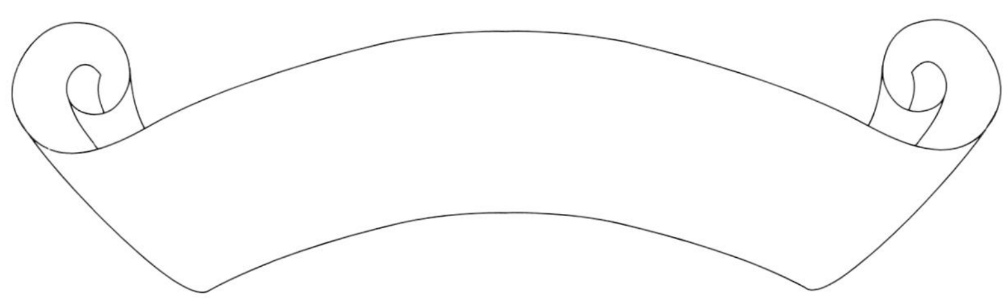

**933a**

↦ 8in (20.3cm) 200%

↦ 12in (30.5cm) 300%

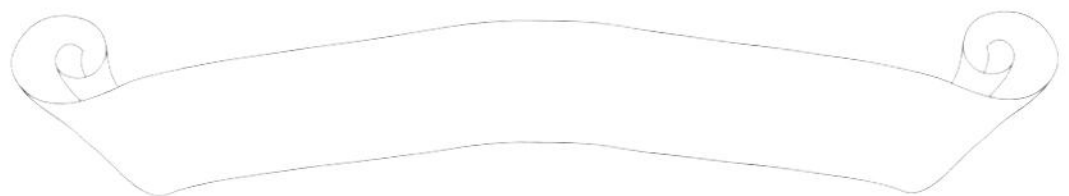

NOTE: *To create a different shape, in this case wider and narrower than the original, enlarge more horizontally than vertically.*

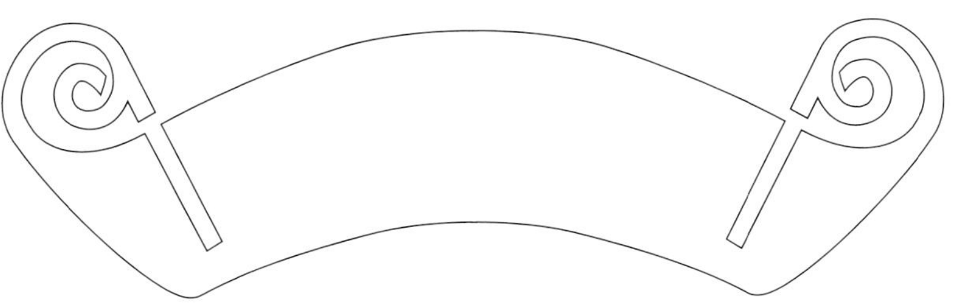

**933b**

↦ 18in (45.7cm) 450%

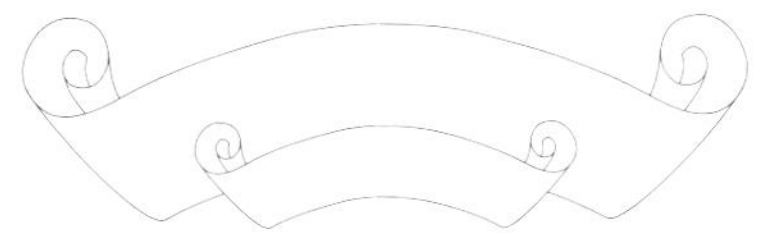

NOTE: *Put two banners together for different levels of text—a name and a date perhaps.*

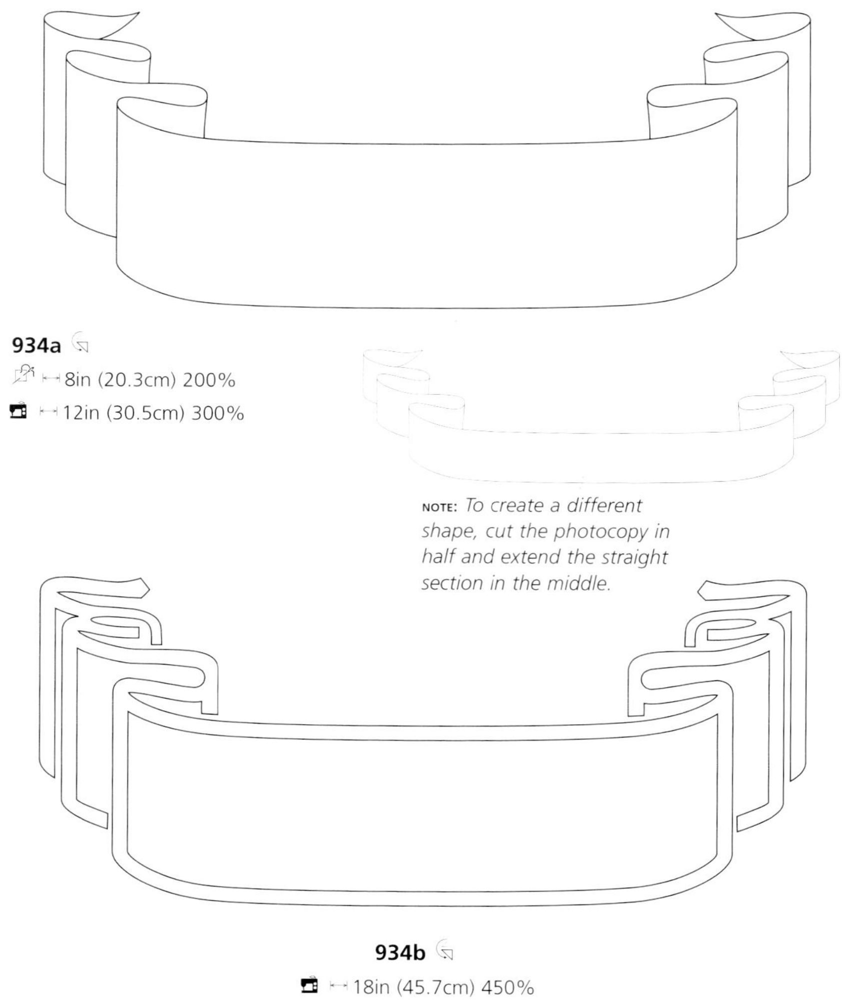

**934a**

8in (20.3cm) 200%

12in (30.5cm) 300%

NOTE: *To create a different shape, cut the photocopy in half and extend the straight section in the middle.*

**934b**

18in (45.7cm) 450%

ALL PATTERNS ARE STANDARD 2IN (5CM) OR 4IN (10.2CM) UNLESS OTHERWISE STATED

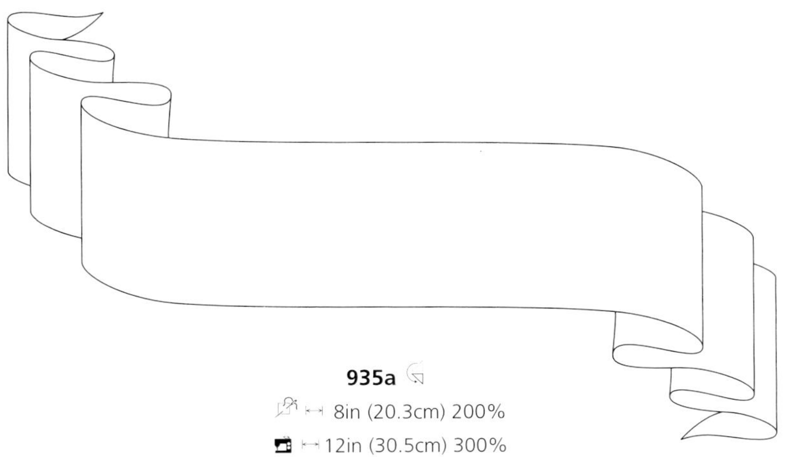

**935a**

8in (20.3cm) 200%

12in (30.5cm) 300%

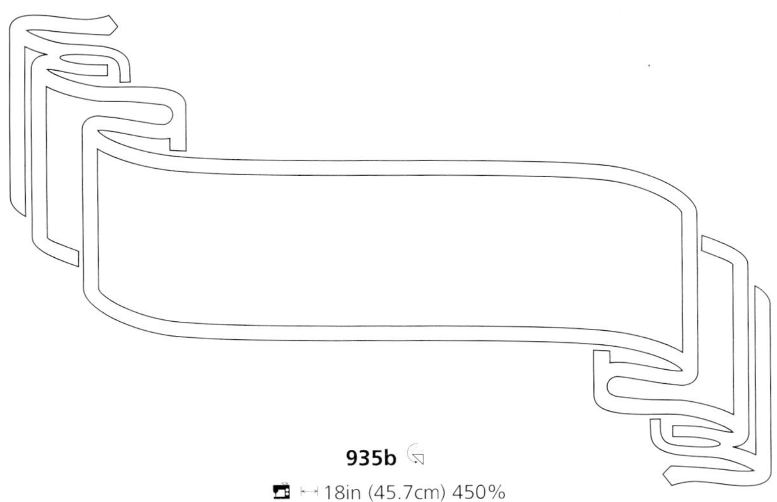

**935b**

18in (45.7cm) 450%

**936–941** height and width varies; for 4in (10.2cm) 150%.

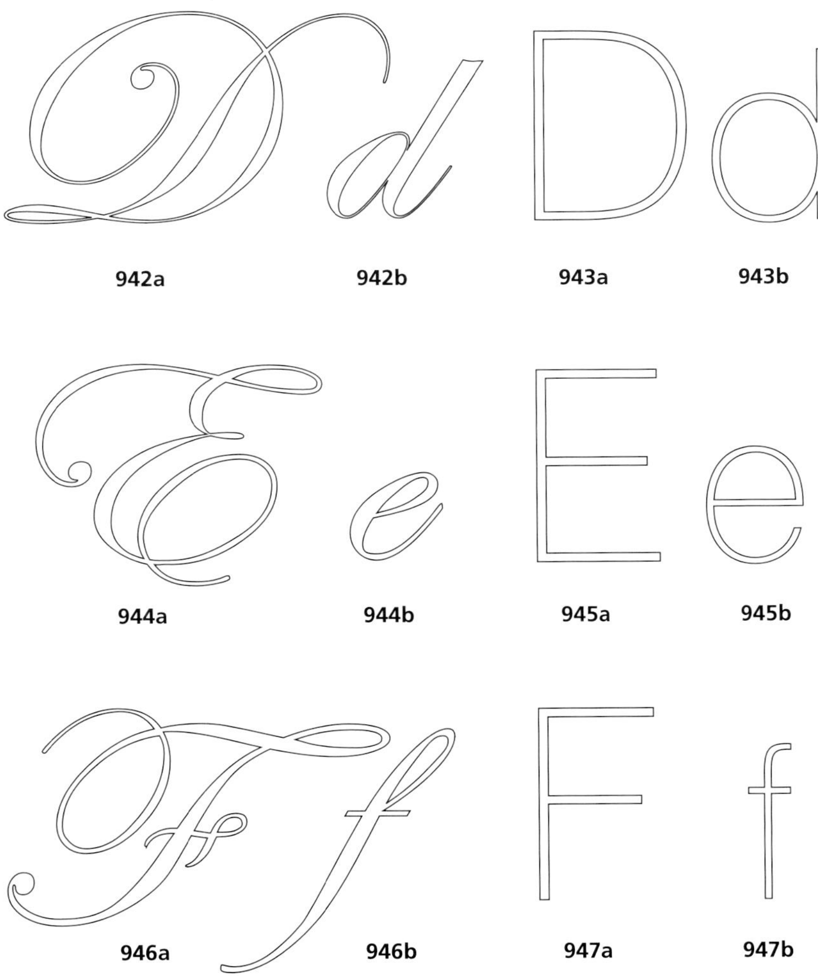


**942–947** height and width varies; for 4in (10.2cm) 150%.

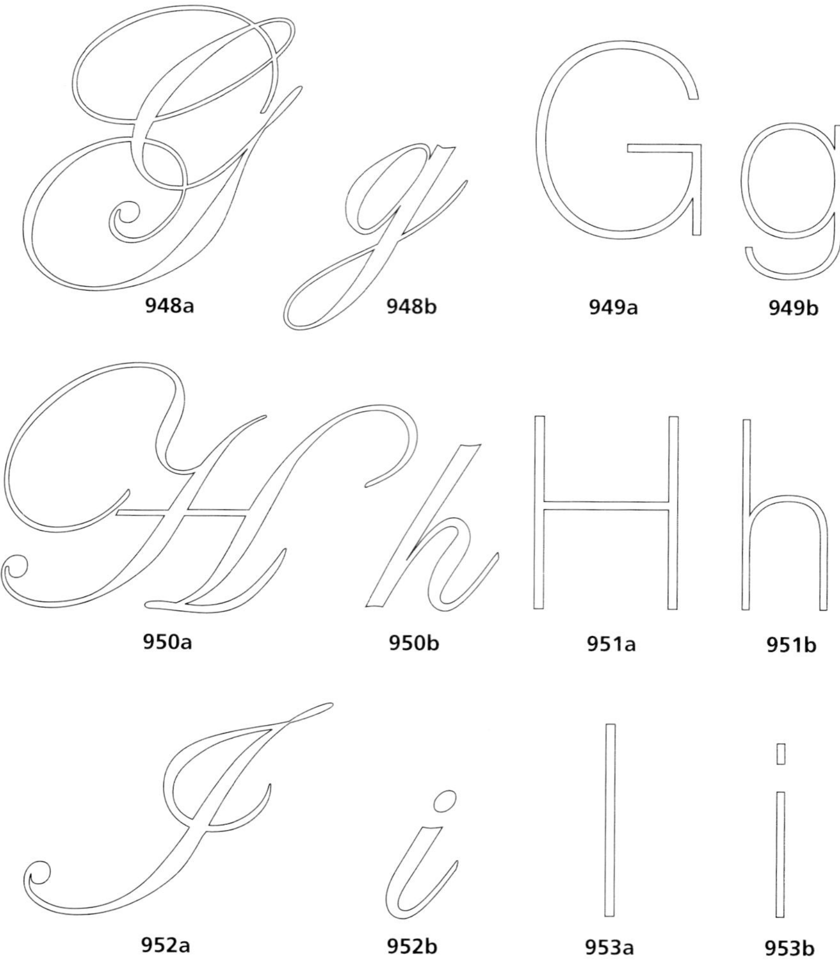

948a 948b 949a 949b

950a 950b 951a 951b

952a 952b 953a 953b

**948–953** height and width varies; for 4in (10.2cm) 150%.

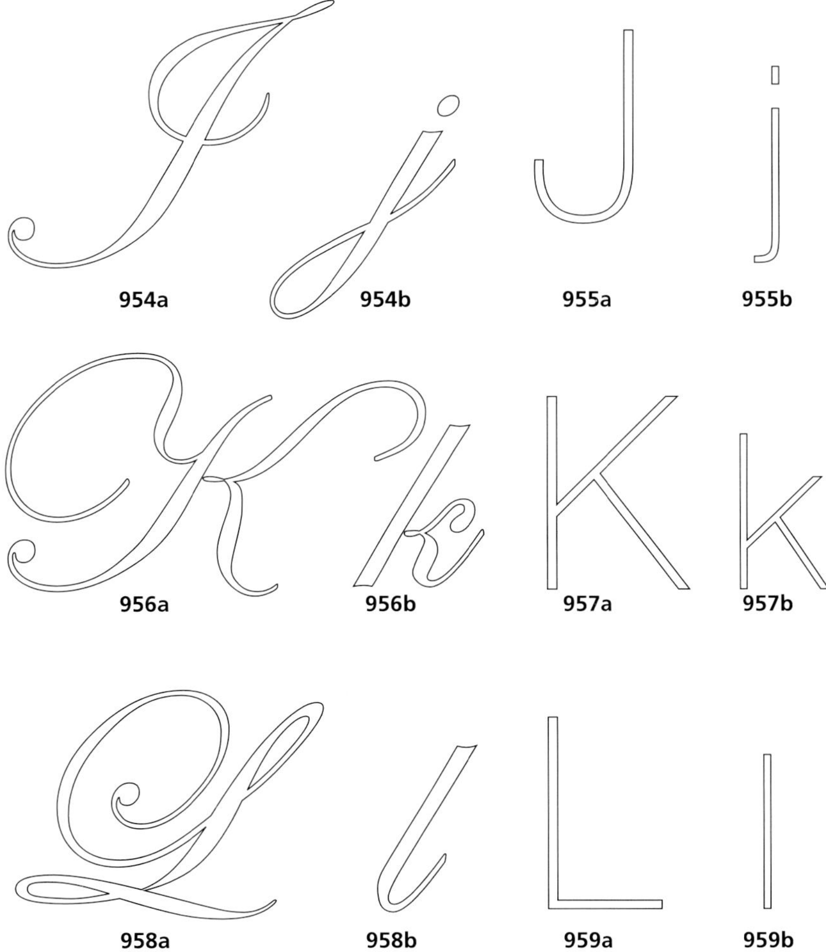


**954–959** height and width varies; for 4in (10.2cm) 150%.

**960a** **960b** **961a** **961b**

**962a** **962b** **963a** **963b**

**964a** **964b** **965a** **965b**

**960–965** height and width varies; for 4in (10.2cm) 150%.

ALL PATTERNS ARE STANDARD 2IN (5CM) OR 4IN (10.2CM) UNLESS OTHERWISE STATED

**966–972** height and width varies; for 4in (10.2cm) 150%.

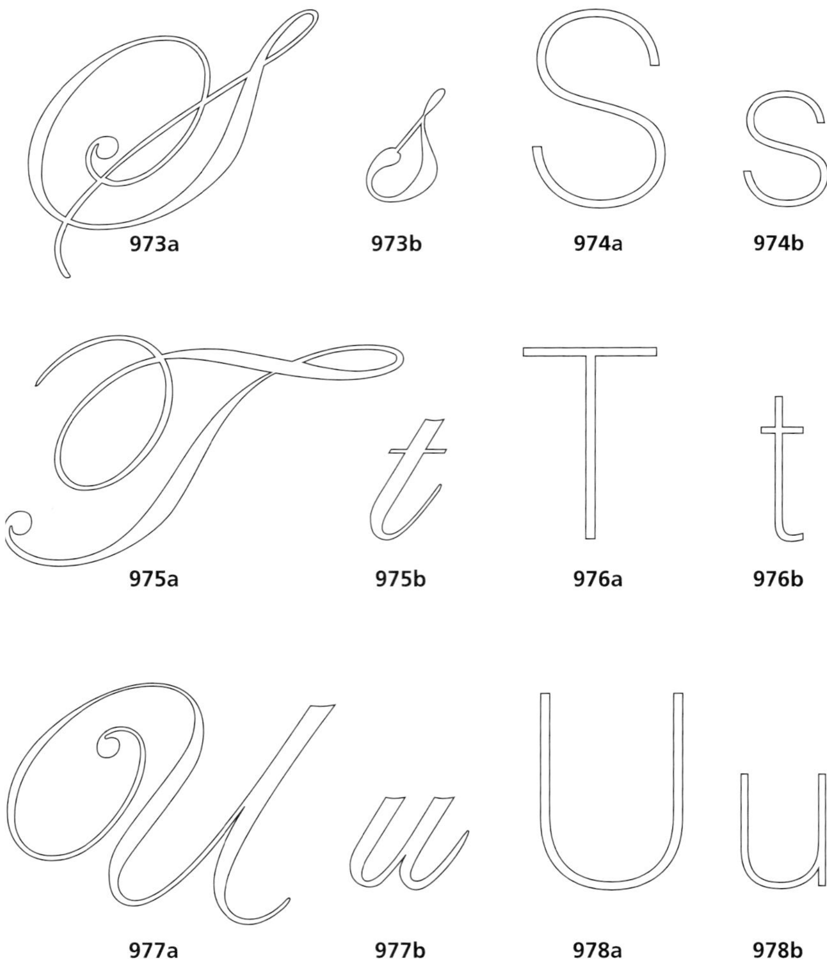

973a 973b 974a 974b

975a 975b 976a 976b

977a 977b 978a 978b

**973–978** height and width varies; for 4in (10.2cm) 150%.

**979–984** height and width varies; for 4in (10.2cm) 150%.

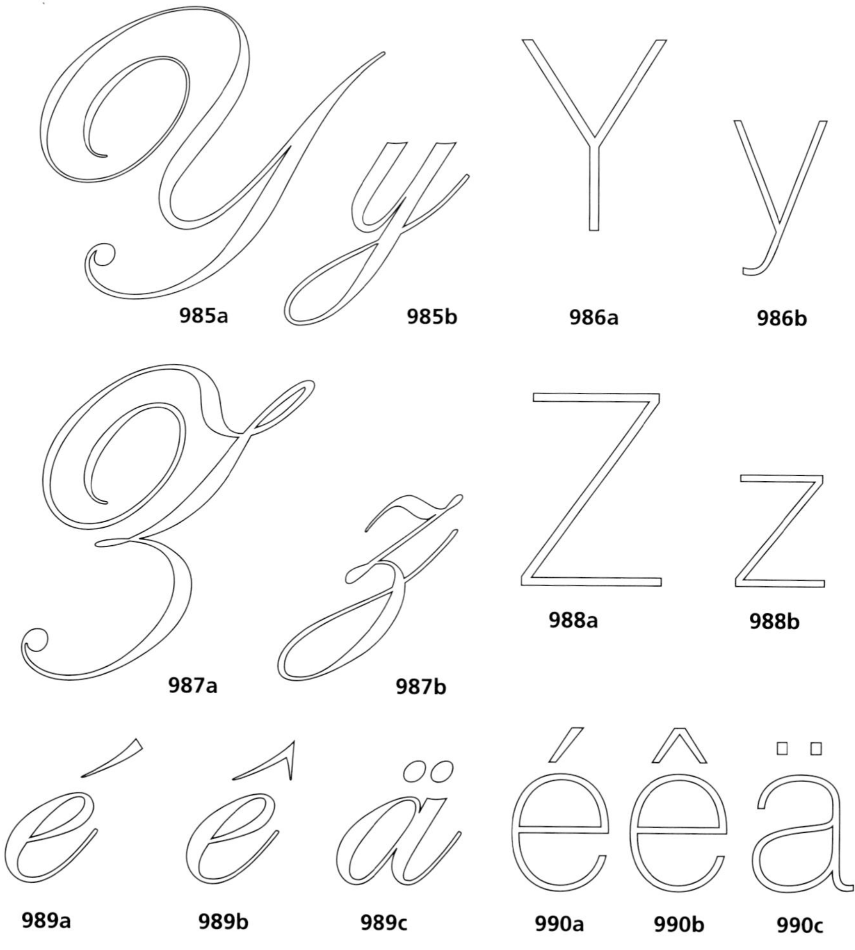


**985–990** height and width varies; for 4in (10.2cm) 150%.

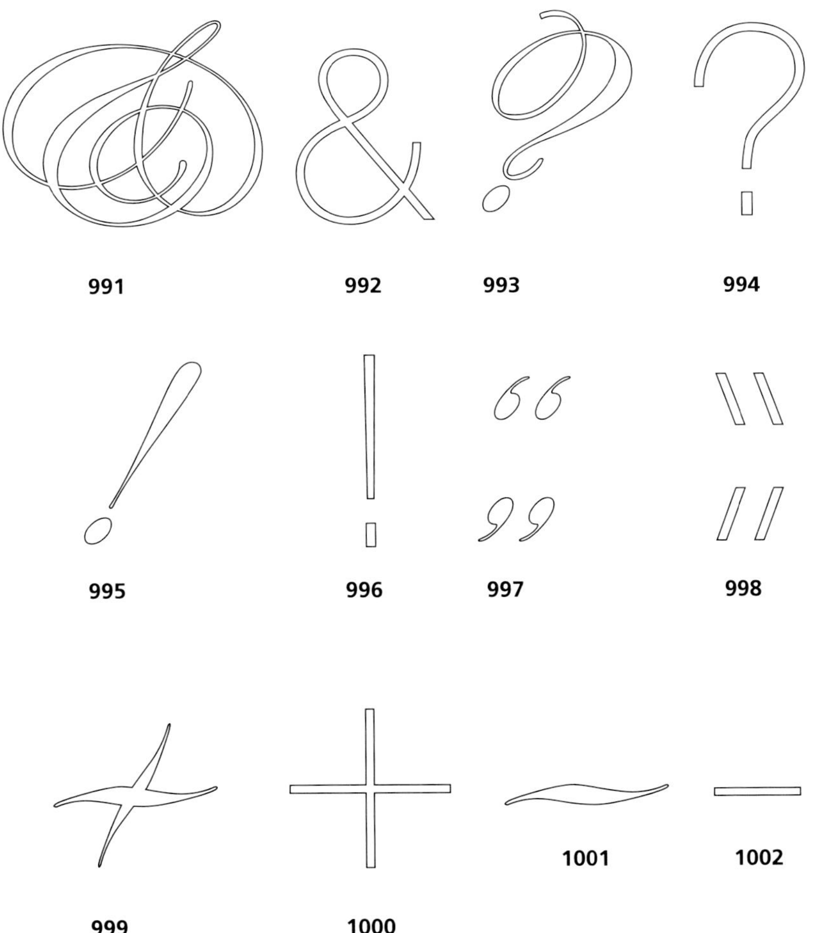


**991–1002** height and width varies; for 4in (10.2cm) 150%.

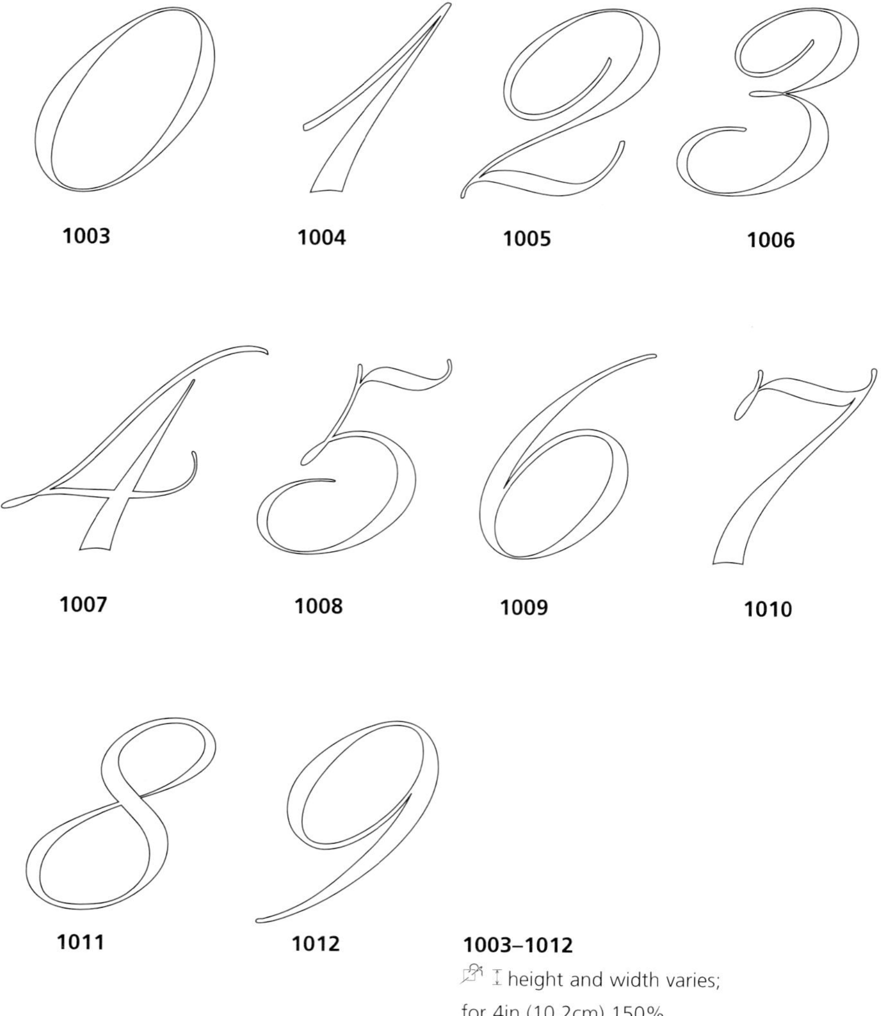

1003 1004 1005 1006

1007 1008 1009 1010

1011 1012

**1003–1012**

height and width varies;
for 4in (10.2cm) 150%.

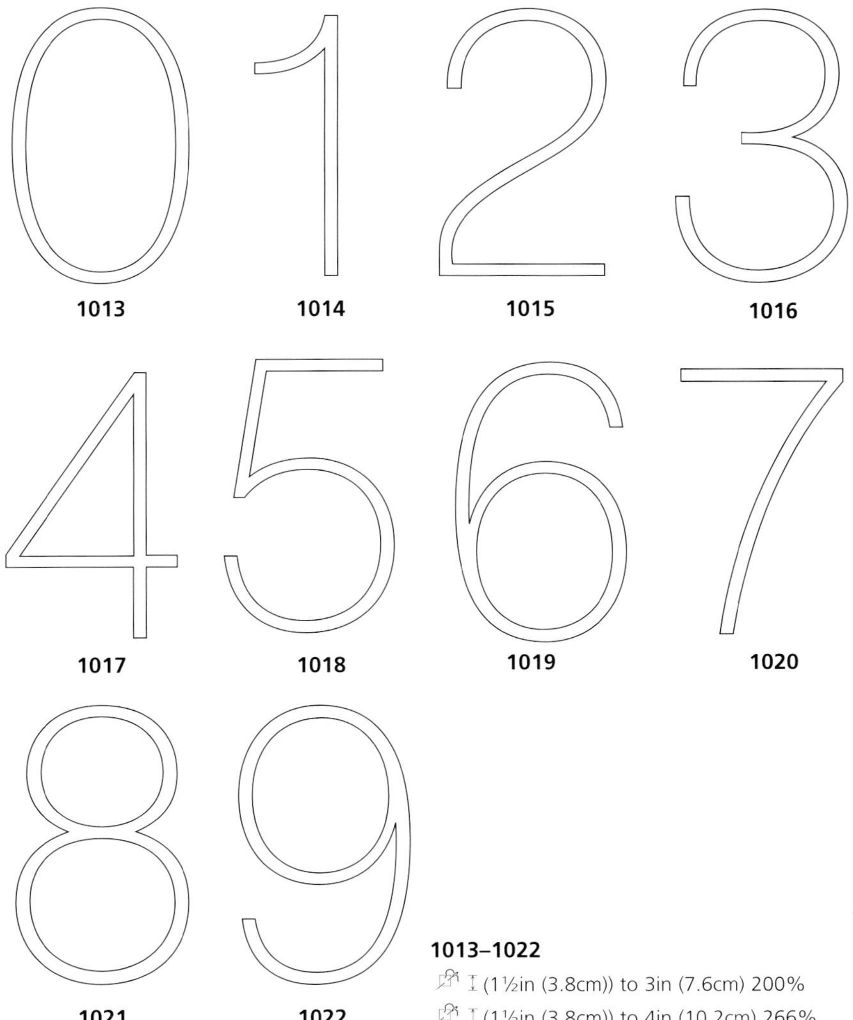


**1013–1022**

(1½in (3.8cm)) to 3in (7.6cm) 200%

(1½in (3.8cm)) to 4in (10.2cm) 266%

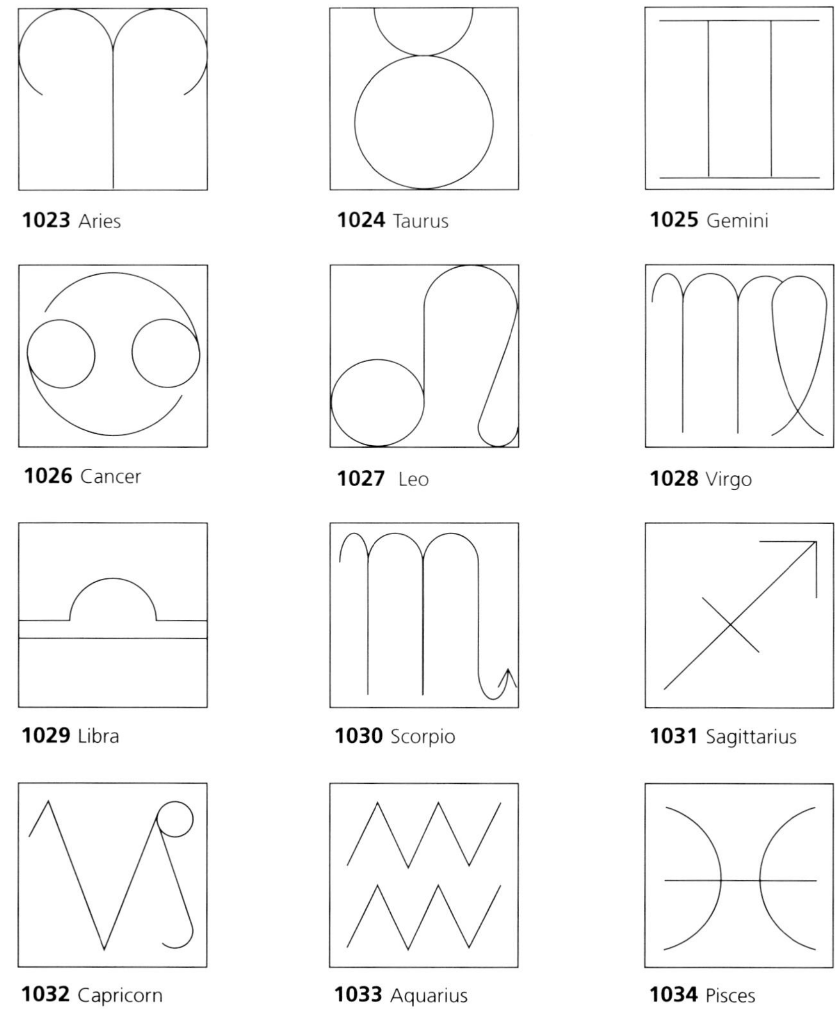

**1023** Aries

**1024** Taurus

**1025** Gemini

**1026** Cancer

**1027** Leo

**1028** Virgo

**1029** Libra

**1030** Scorpio

**1031** Sagittarius

**1032** Capricorn

**1033** Aquarius

**1034** Pisces

ALL PATTERNS ARE STANDARD 2IN (5CM) OR 4IN (10.2CM) UNLESS OTHERWISE STATED

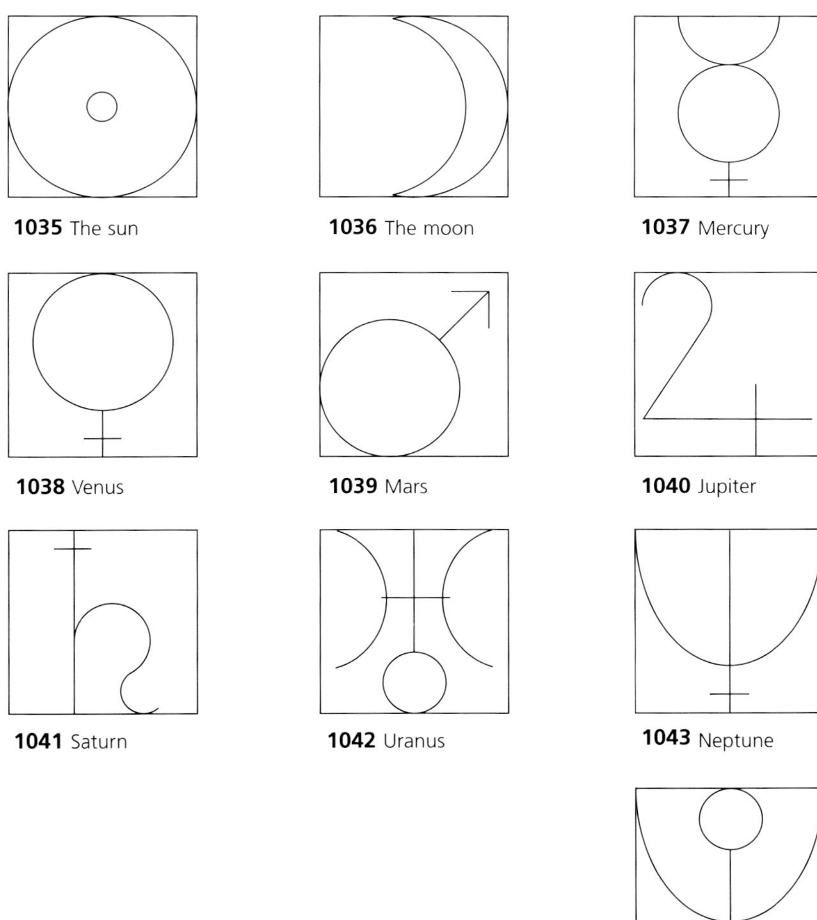

1035 The sun

1036 The moon

1037 Mercury

1038 Venus

1039 Mars

1040 Jupiter

1041 Saturn

1042 Uranus

1043 Neptune

1044 Pluto

**1023–1044**

↦(1in (2.5cm)) to 4in (10.2cm) 400%

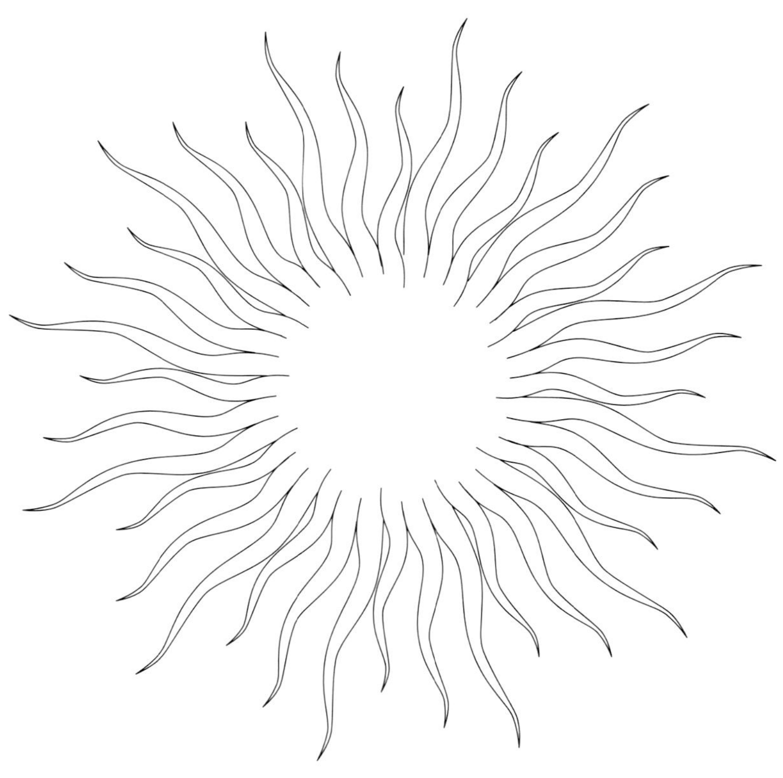

**1045**

6in (15.25cm) 150%

8in (20.3cm) 200%

ALL PATTERNS ARE STANDARD 2IN (5CM) OR 4IN (10.2CM) UNLESS OTHERWISE STATED

# Useful information

# Facts and figures

Most projects are planned and worked in round numbers, but there are always those odd measurements that it would be useful to know without having to resort to drawing or using a calculator. Here is a quick guide to some of those dimensions.

**NOTE:** The block measurements given are those most commonly used when working in inches or centimeters and are not conversions.

| Inches | | Centimeters | |
|---|---|---|---|
| **a** | **b** | **a** | **b** |
| 2in | 2 13/16in | 5cm | 7cm |
| 3in | 4 1/4in | 8cm | 11.3cm |
| 4in | 5 5/8in | 10cm | 14.1cm |
| 5in | 7 1/16in | 12cm | 17cm |
| 6in | 8 1/2in | 15cm | 21.2cm |
| 7in | 9 7/8in | 18cm | 25.4cm |
| 8in | 11 5/16in | 20cm | 28.3cm |
| 9in | 12 3/4in | 22cm | 31cm |
| 10in | 14 1/8in | 25cm | 35.4cm |
| 11in | 15 1/2in | 28cm | 39.6cm |
| 12in | 17in | 30cm | 42.4cm |
| 13in | 18 3/8in | 33cm | 46.7cm |
| 15in | 21 1/4in | 38cm | 53.7cm |

For block sizes not listed, look for a multiple of the required block and multiply or divide accordingly.

If **a** = 18in (or 44cm)
then **b** = (9in (or 22cm) block **b** measurement) × 2

## Geometry of a square

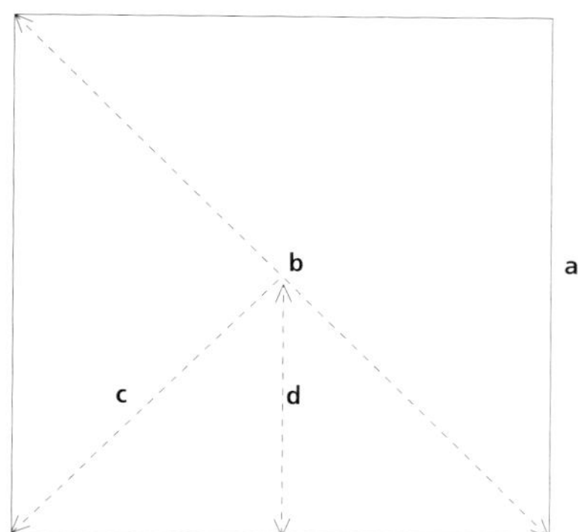


**The length of the diagonal**
**b** = $\sqrt{a^2 + a^2}$
($\sqrt{}$ is the symbol for square route)

Distances **c** and **d** are useful when creating on-point quilts.

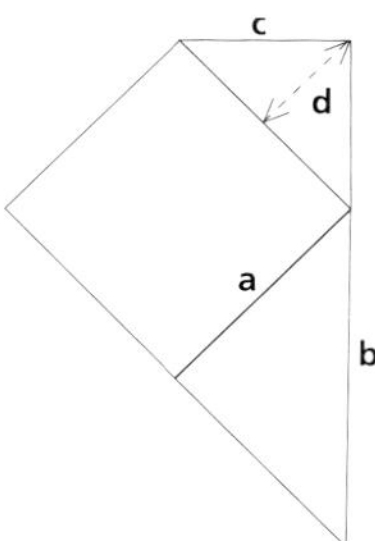


**c =** ½ b
**d =** ½ a

**The largest circle to fit within the square block**
**d** = the distance from the center of the circle to its outer edge (radius).

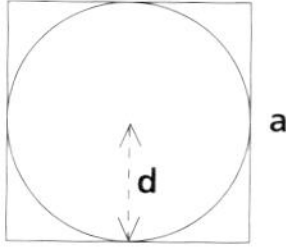

## Geometry of a circle

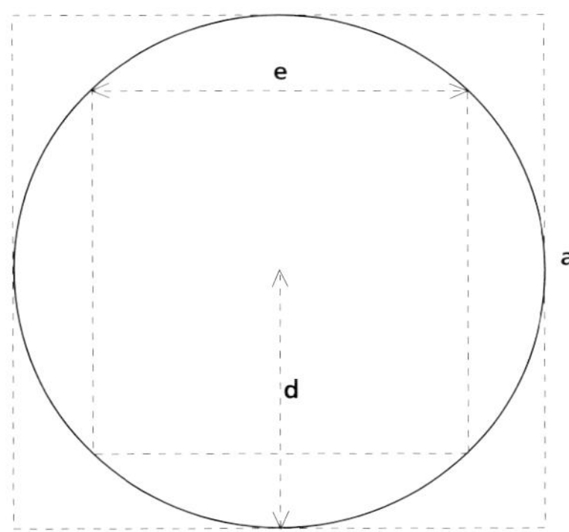


**The largest square that can fit inside a given circle**
with a diameter of the circle of **a**
**e** = $\sqrt{(a^2 \div 2)}$

**Inches**

| a | e |
|---|---|
| 2in | 1 7/16in |
| 3in | 2 1/8in |
| 4in | 2 7/8in |
| 5in | 3 1/2in |
| 6in | 4 1/4in |
| 7in | 5in |
| 8in | 5 5/8in |
| 9in | 6 3/8in |
| 10in | 7in |
| 11in | 7 3/4in |
| 12in | 8 1/2in |
| 13in | 9 3/6in |
| 15in | 10 5/8in |
| 18in | 12 3/4in |
| 20in | 14 1/8in |

**Centimeters**

| a | e |
|---|---|
| 5cm | 3.5cm |
| 8cm | 5.6cm |
| 10cm | 7cm |
| 12cm | 8.5cm |
| 15cm | 10.6cm |
| 18cm | 12.7cm |
| 20cm | 14cm |
| 22cm | 15.5cm |
| 25cm | 17.7cm |
| 28cm | 19.8cm |
| 30cm | 21.2cm |
| 33cm | 23.3cm |
| 38cm | 26.8cm |
| 45cm | 31.8cm |
| 50cm | 35.4cm |

**The largest equilateral triangle that can fit inside a given circle** with a diameter of the circle of **a** and 3 equal sides to an equilateral triangle,
**f** = a × 0.866

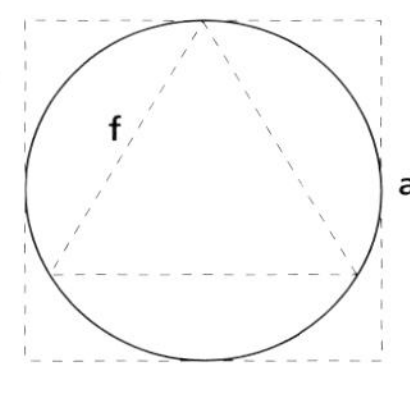


**Inches**

| a | f |
|---|---|
| 6in | 5 3/16in |
| 8in | 7in |
| 10in | 8 5/8in |
| 12in | 10 3/8in |
| 15in | 13in |

**Centimeters**

| a | f |
|---|---|
| 12cm | 10.4cm |
| 20cm | 17.3cm |
| 25cm | 21.6cm |
| 30cm | 26cm |
| 38cm | 33cm |

This formula can be adapted to calculate the width of any motif that appears at regular intervals around the circumference of a circle.
**f** = a × sine (180 ÷ no. of repeats or equal sides of a polygon)

For the following shapes sine values have been added and the formula simplified:

For a pentagon (five-sided shape):
**f** = a × 0.5878

For a hexagon (six-sided shape):
**f** = a × 0.5

For an octagon (eight-sided shape):
**f** = a × 0.39

For a 10-sided polygon:
**f** = a × 0.3090

# Enlargement tables

Use the following tables to calculate the percentage enlargements required for sizes not given with the patterns or for sizes that allow for spacing requirements and turnings.

① Select the correct table of percentages depending on the original pattern size; either 2in (5.08cm) or 4in (10.16cm).

② Read down the left-hand columns until the size required is found and read across to the right-hand column. The first bold figure is the overall percentage; the figures in the lighter typeface are the percentages required if more than photocopy enlargement is needed.

③ Using a photocopier, copy the original pattern design as stated.

If the size required is not shown, either estimate the correct percentage by looking at the sizes above and below, or use the following formula:

**size required ÷ actual size = percentage to enlarge**

This formula can also be used for the patterns that do not have a dimension of either 2in (5.08cm) or 4in (10.2cm) or if just a section of the pattern has been selected.

If the required size is larger than 16in or 40cm, then consider having the design photocopied professionally to avoid the inaccurate piecing of sheets of paper.

## % for 2in (5cm) patterns in inches

| size required | % | |
|---|---|---|
| 2in | **100%** | |
| 2¼in | **112%** | |
| 2½in | **125%** | |
| 2¾in | **137%** | |
| 3in | **150%** | |
| 3¼in | **162%** | |
| 3½in | **175%** | |
| 3¾in | **187%** | |
| 4in | **200%** | |
| 4¼in | **212%** • | 200% + 106% |
| 4½in | **225%** • | 200% + 112% |
| 4¾in | **237%** • | 200% + 119% |
| 5in | **250%** • | 200% + 125% |
| 5¼in | **262%** • | 200% + 131% |
| 5½in | **275%** • | 200% + 137% |
| 5¾in | **287%** • | 200% + 144% |
| 6in | **300%** • | 200% + 150% |
| 6¼in | **312%** • | 200% + 156% |
| 6½in | **325%** • | 200% + 162% |
| 6¾in | **337%** • | 200% + 169% |
| 7in | **350%** • | 200% + 175% |
| 7¼in | **362%** • | 200% + 181% |
| 7½in | **375%** • | 200% + 187% |
| 7¾in | **387%** • | 200% + 194% |
| 8in | **400%** • | 200% + 200% |
| 8¼in | **412%** • | 200% + 200% +103% |
| 8½in | **425%** • | 200% + 200% +106% |
| 8¾in | **437%** • | 200% + 200% +109% |
| 9in | **450%** • | 200% + 200% +113% |
| 9¼in | **462%** • | 200% + 200% +115% |
| 9½in | **475%** • | 200% + 200% +119% |
| 9¾in | **487%** • | 200% + 200% +122% |
| 10in | **500%** • | 200% + 200% +125% |
| 10¼in | **512%** • | 200% + 200% +128% |
| 10½in | **525%** • | 200% + 200% +131% |
| 10¾in | **537%** • | 200% + 200% +134% |

| size required | % | |
|---|---|---|
| 11in | **550%** | • 200% + 200% +137% |
| 11¼in | **562%** | • 200% + 200% +140% |
| 11½in | **575%** | • 200% + 200% +144% |
| 11¾in | **587%** | • 200% + 200% +147% |
| 12in | **600%** | • 200% + 200% +150% |
| 12¼in | **612%** | • 200% + 200% +153% |
| 12½in | **625%** | • 200% + 200% +156% |
| 12¾in | **637%** | • 200% + 200% +159% |
| 13in | **650%** | • 200% + 200% +162% |
| 13¼in | **662%** | • 200% + 200% +165% |
| 13½in | **675%** | • 200% + 200% +169% |
| 13¾in | **687%** | • 200% + 200% +172% |
| 14in | **700%** | • 200% + 200% +175% |
| 14¼in | **712%** | • 200% + 200% +178% |
| 14½in | **725%** | • 200% + 200% +181% |
| 14¾in | **737%** | • 200% + 200% +184% |
| 15in | **750%** | • 200% + 200% +187% |

## % for 4in (10cm) patterns in inches

| size required | % | |
|---|---|---|
| 4in | **100%** | |
| 4¼in | **106%** | |
| 4½in | **112%** | |
| 4¾in | **118%** | |
| 5in | **125%** | |
| 5¼in | **131%** | |
| 5½in | **137%** | |
| 5¾in | **144%** | |
| 6in | **150%** | |
| 6¼in | **156%** | |
| 6½in | **162%** | |
| 6¾in | **169%** | |
| 7in | **175%** | |
| 7¼in | **181%** | |
| 7½in | **187%** | |
| 7¾in | **194%** | |
| 8in | **200%** | |
| 8¼in | **206%** | • 200% + 103% |
| 8½in | **212%** | • 200% + 106% |
| 8¾in | **218%** | • 200% + 109% |
| 9in | **225%** | • 200% + 112% |
| 9¼in | **231%** | • 200% + 115% |
| 9½in | **237%** | • 200% + 119% |
| 9¾in | **243%** | • 200% + 122% |
| 10in | **250%** | • 200% + 125% |
| 10¼in | **256%** | • 200% + 128% |
| 10½in | **262%** | • 200% + 131% |
| 10¾in | **269%** | • 200% + 134% |
| 11in | **275%** | • 200% + 137% |
| 11¼in | **281%** | • 200% + 140% |
| 11½in | **287%** | • 200% + 144% |
| 11¾in | **293%** | • 200% + 147% |
| 12in | **300%** | • 200% + 150% |
| 12¼in | **306%** | • 200% + 153% |
| 12½in | **312%** | • 200% + 156% |
| 12¾in | **319%** | • 200% + 159% |
| 13in | **325%** | • 200% + 162% |
| 13¼in | **331%** | • 200% + 165% |
| 13½in | **337%** | • 200% + 169% |
| 13¾in | **347%** | • 200% + 172% |
| 14in | **350%** | • 200% + 175% |
| 14¼in | **356%** | • 200% + 178% |
| 14½in | **362%** | • 200% + 181% |
| 14¾in | **368%** | • 200% + 184% |
| 15in | **375%** | • 200% + 187% |
| 15¼in | **381%** | • 200% +190% |
| 15½in | **387%** | • 200% +193% |
| 15¾in | **393%** | • 200% +197% |
| 16in | **400%** | • 200% +200% |

## % for 5cm (2in) patterns in centimeters

| size required | % | |
|---|---|---|
| 5cm | **100%** | |
| 6cm | **120%** | |
| 7cm | **140%** | |
| 8cm | **160%** | |
| 9cm | **180%** | |
| 10cm | **200%** | |
| 11cm | **220%** | • 200% + 110% |
| 12cm | **240%** | • 200% + 120% |
| 13cm | **260%** | • 200% + 130% |
| 14cm | **280%** | • 200% + 140% |
| 15cm | **300%** | • 200% + 150% |
| 16cm | **320%** | • 200% + 160% |
| 17cm | **340%** | • 200% + 170% |
| 18cm | **360%** | • 200% + 180% |
| 19cm | **380%** | • 200% + 190% |
| 20cm | **400%** | • 200% + 200% |
| 21cm | **420%** | • 200% + 200% +105% |
| 22cm | **440%** | • 200% + 200% +110% |
| 23cm | **460%** | • 200% + 200% +115% |
| 24cm | **480%** | • 200% + 200% +120% |
| 25cm | **500%** | • 200% + 200% +125% |
| 26cm | **520%** | • 200% + 200% +130% |
| 27cm | **540%** | • 200% + 200% +135% |
| 28cm | **560%** | • 200% + 200% +140% |
| 29cm | **580%** | • 200% + 200% +145% |
| 30cm | **600%** | • 200% + 200% +150% |
| 31cm | **620%** | • 200% + 200% +155% |
| 32cm | **640%** | • 200% + 200% +160% |
| 33cm | **660%** | • 200% + 200% +165% |
| 34cm | **680%** | • 200% + 200% +170% |
| 35cm | **700%** | • 200% + 200% +175% |
| 36cm | **720%** | • 200% + 200% +180% |
| 37cm | **740%** | • 200% + 200% +185% |
| 38cm | **760%** | • 200% + 200% +190% |
| 39cm | **780%** | • 200% + 200% +195% |
| 40cm | **800%** | • 200% + 200% +200% |

## % for 10cm (4in) patterns in centimeters

| size required | % | |
|---|---|---|
| 10cm | **100%** | |
| 11cm | **110%** | |
| 12cm | **120%** | |
| 13cm | **130%** | |
| 14cm | **140%** | |
| 15cm | **150%** | |
| 16cm | **160%** | |
| 17cm | **170%** | |
| 18cm | **180%** | |
| 19cm | **190%** | |
| 20cm | **200%** | |
| 21cm | **210%** | •200% + 105% |
| 22cm | **220%** | •200% + 110% |
| 23cm | **230%** | •200% + 115% |
| 24cm | **240%** | •200% + 120% |
| 25cm | **250%** | •200% + 125% |
| 26cm | **260%** | •200% + 130% |
| 27cm | **270%** | •200% + 135% |
| 28cm | **280%** | •200% + 140% |
| 29cm | **290%** | •200% + 145% |
| 30cm | **300%** | •200% + 150% |
| 31cm | **310%** | •200% + 155% |
| 32cm | **320%** | •200% + 160% |
| 33cm | **330%** | •200% + 165% |
| 34cm | **340%** | •200% + 170% |
| 35cm | **350%** | •200% + 175% |
| 36cm | **360%** | •200% + 180% |
| 37cm | **370%** | •200% + 185% |
| 38cm | **380%** | •200% + 190% |
| 39cm | **390%** | •200% + 195% |
| 40cm | **400%** | •200% + 200% |

# Conversion table

It is always better to work in either inches or centimeters; not do mix the two.

**To convert inches into centimeters:**
inches × 2.54 = centimeters

**To convert centimeters into inches:**
centimeters ÷ 2.54 = inches

**To convert yards into meters:**
yards × 0.914 = meters

**To convert meters into yards:**
meters ÷ 0.914 = yards

| in | cm |
|---|---|
| 1/8 | 0.3 |
| 1/4 | 0.6 |
| 3/8 | 1 |
| 1/2 | 1.3 |
| 5/8 | 1.6 |
| 3/4 | 1.9 |
| 7/8 | 2.2 |
| 1 | 2.5 |
| 1 1/4 | 3.2 |
| 1 1/2 | 3.8 |
| 1 3/4 | 4.4 |
| 2 | 5.0 |
| 2 1/2 | 6.4 |
| 3 | 7.6 |
| 3 1/2 | 8.9 |
| 4 | 10.2 |
| 4 1/2 | 11.4 |
| 5 | 12.7 |
| 5 1/2 | 14 |
| 6 | 15.25 |
| 7 | 17.8 |
| 8 | 20.3 |
| 9 | 22.9 |
| 10 | 25.4 |
| 11 | 28 |
| 12 | 30.5 |
| 13 | 33 |
| 14 | 35.6 |
| 15 | 38.1 |
| 16 | 40.6 |
| 17 | 43.2 |
| 18 | 45.7 |
| 19 | 48.3 |
| 20 | 50.8 |

| in | cm |
|---|---|
| 21 | 53.3 |
| 22 | 55.9 |
| 23 | 58.4 |
| 24 | 61 |
| 25 | 63.5 |
| 26 | 66 |
| 27 | 68.6 |
| 28 | 71.1 |
| 29 | 73.7 |
| 30 | 76.2 |
| 31 | 78.7 |
| 32 | 81.3 |
| 33 | 83.8 |
| 34 | 86.4 |
| 35 | 88.9 |
| 36 | 91.4 |
| 37 | 94 |
| 38 | 96.5 |
| 39 | 99 |
| 40 | 101.6 |
| 41 | 104.1 |
| 42 | 106.7 |
| 43 | 109.2 |
| 44 | 111.8 |
| 45 | 114.3 |
| 46 | 116.8 |
| 47 | 119.4 |
| 48 | 121.9 |
| 49 | 124.5 |
| 50 | 127 |

# Index